T0367672

Hungary: Towards a Market Economy

Hungary: Towards a Market Economy offers the most recent and up-to-date assessment of the contemporary Hungarian economy, and follows its evolution in the immediate aftermath of the revolutions in Central and Eastern Europe. Part One describes the macroeconomy, the evolution of monetary policy, the link between the exchange rate and inflation, the inability of fiscal policy to come to terms with public debt and deficits, and the evolution of the underground economy. Part Two focuses on the microeconomy, the consolidation of the banking sector, the evolution of corporate governance and an analysis of the profitability of export-orientated firms. Part Three assesses the labour market and the system of welfare. *Hungary: Towards a Market Economy* is the latest in the successful sequence of volumes on major topics in international economics published under the auspices of the Centre for Economic Policy Research, of interest to both policy-makers and specialists.

László Halpern is Deputy Director at the Institute of Economics at the Hungarian Academy of Sciences in Budapest and a Research Fellow in CEPR's Transition Economics research programme. He has written widely on exchange rate theory, Central and East European exchange rate policy, macroeconomic stabilisation theory, enterprise behaviour, and international trade.

Charles Wyplosz is Professor of Economics at the Graduate Institute of International Studies, University of Geneva, and Research Fellow in CEPR's Transition Economics and International Macroeconomics research programmes. He is a founding Managing Editor of *Economic Policy* and serves on numerous editorial boards. He is also co-author, with Michael Burda, of *Microeconomics, A European Text*.

Centre for Economic Policy Research

The Centre for Economic Policy Research is a network of over 350 Research Fellows, based primarily in European universities. The Centre coordinates its Fellows' research activities and communicates their results to the public and private sectors. CEPR is an entrepreneur, developing research initiatives with the producers, consumers and sponsors of research. Established in 1983, CEPR is a European economics research organisation with uniquely wide-ranging scope and activities.

CEPR is a registered educational charity. Institutional (core) finance for the Centre is provided by major grants from the Economic and Social Research Council, under which an ESRC Resource Centre operates within CEPR; the Esmée Fairbairn Charitable Trust; the Bank of England; the European Monetary Institute and the Bank for International Settlements; 19 national central banks and 40 companies. None of these organisations gives prior review to the Centre's publications, nor do they necessarily endorse the views expressed therein.

The Centre is pluralist and non-partisan, bringing economic research to bear on the analysis of medium- and long-run policy questions. CEPR research may include views on policy, but the Executive Committee of the Centre does not give prior review to its publications, and the Centre takes no institutional policy positions. The opinions expressed in this volume are those of the authors and not those of the Centre for Economic Policy Research.

10 February 1998

Hungary: Towards a Market Economy

Edited by

LÁSZLÓ HALPERN

and

CHARLES WYPLOSZ

CAMBRIDGE
UNIVERSITY PRESS

CAMBRIDGE
UNIVERSITY PRESS

University Printing House, Cambridge CB2 8BS, United Kingdom

Cambridge University Press is part of the University of Cambridge.

It furthers the University's mission by disseminating knowledge in the pursuit of education, learning and research at the highest international levels of excellence.

www.cambridge.org
Information on this title: www.cambridge.org/9780521630689

Chapters 2, 3, 5, 6, 7, 9 and 11 are reproduced in revised form from papers presented at the October 1995 Budapest Conference on 'Hungary: Towards a Market Economy' which was organised by the Institute of Economics in the context of a European Commission PHARE/ACE Programme. Their content does not, however, express the Commission's official views. Responsibility for the information and views set out in the papers lies entirely with the editors and authors.

First published 1998

A catalogue record for this publication is available from the British Library

ISBN 978-0-521-63068-9 Hardback
ISBN 978-0-521-14270-0 Paperback

Cambridge University Press has no responsibility for the persistence or accuracy of URLs for external or third-party internet websites referred to in this publication, and does not guarantee that any content on such websites is, or will remain, accurate or appropriate.

Contents

PART TWO: INDUSTRIAL STRUCTURE

Figures

Tables

Foreword

The conference 'Hungary: Towards a Market Economy' was organised on 20–21 October 1995 in Budapest by the Institute of Economics, Hungarian Academy of Sciences, with the support of the Centre for Economic Policy Research (CEPR). It was intended to make an inventory of the Hungarian economic evolution since the early phase of transition.

The organisers built on the success of a first conference on Hungary, held in London on 7–8 February 1992. That conference and its proceedings – I. P. Székely and D. M. G. Newbery (eds), *Hungary: An Economy in Transition*, Cambridge University Press for CEPR, 1993 – had a powerful influence on policy and research. We are confident that this volume will keep up the tradition, and its title reflects the changes that have occurred.

At the time of this conference a number of major steps had been taken: the creation of the basic legal and institutional framework, the shift of economic agents' behaviour. The macroeconomy, however, was in bad shape. An austerity package had been adopted in March 1995, but its first effects were not yet visible. Inflation was high, and the debt crisis was not over. It was fashionable to label the Hungarian transition as a 'gradualist' one without closer scrutiny and to take a dim view of its achievements. This book should disprove both views.

The volume contains an up-to-date appraisal of the Hungarian economy. The papers combine in-depth analysis of the Hungarian economy with the use of modern tools and techniques. The target audience comprises all those interested in the process of economic transition: academic researchers, students, policy makers and analysts.

Financial support was provided by the European Commission under the PHARE/ACE programme (94–0483–0).

Special thanks go to Krisztina Bedő and Éva Kudor for organising the conference and to Barbara Docherty for particularly careful editorial assistance. During the long production process Kate Millward, helped by Sarah Northcott, has been travelling tirelessly through cyberspace, calling to order authors, editors and discussants. We are grateful to all of them.

Jenő Koltay   *February 1998*
Richard Portes

Acknowledgements

The editors acknowledge with thanks permission from the following to reproduce copyright material.

Southern Economic Journal, for data in table 5.2, from B.S. Frey and H. Weck, 'What produces a hidden economy?' (1983).

Springer Verlag, for data in table 5.2, from F. Schneider, 'Measuring the size and development of the shadow economy', in H. Brandstatter and W. Güth (eds.), *Essays on Economic Psychology* (1994).

International Economic Insights, for data in table 5.2, from M. Bordignon, 'Taxing lessons from Italy' (1993) and from B. Morris, 'Editorial statement' (1993).

Figyelő, for data in table 5.2, from J. Árvay and A. Vértes, 'Rejteni, ami rejthető' (1994).

Komercni Banka, for data in table 5.2, from V. Kadera, 'The importance and role of the shadow economy in the transformation period of the Czech republic' (1995).

Bankszemle, for data in table 8.1, from E. Marsi and J. Pap, 'A csődtörvény hatása a pénzintézetekre' (1993) and in tables 8.1 and 8.4, from R. Nyers and G. Lutz, 'A bankrendszer főbb jellemzői az 1987–1991 évi mérlegbeszámolók alapján' (1994).

Munkaügyi Szemle, for data in table 9.5, from I. G. Tóth, 'Bérmeghatározási rendszer' (1995).

TÁRKI, for data in table 10.1, from R. Andorka *et al.*, *The Hungarian Welfare State in Transition* (1994) and in table 10.4, from I.G. Tóth, 'Hungarian income inequalities in comparative perspective' (1996).

National Institute for Primary and Secondary Education, Budapest, for data in table 10.2, from G. Halász and J. Lannert (eds.), *Jelentés a magyar közoktatásról, 1995* (1996).

UNICEF, for data in tables 10.2, 10.7 and 10.8, from *Poverty, Children and Policy* (1995).

World Bank, for data in table 10.3, from *Hungary – Structural Reforms for Sustainable Growth* (1995).

International Center for Economic Growth, for data in table 10.5, from P. Bod, 'Formation of the Hungarian social insurance based pension system' (1995).

OECD, for data in tables 10.7 and 10.8, from *OECD Health Care Systems: Facts and Trends, 1960–1991* (1993) and *The Reform of Health Care: A Comparative Analysis of Fourteen OECD Countries* (1994).

Macmillan, for data in table 11.4, from W.H. Greene, *Econometric Analysis* (1993).

Chapman & Hall, for data in table 11.4, from R.D. Cook and S. Weisberg, *Residuals and Influence in Regression* (1982).

Biometrika, for data in table 11.4, from S.S. Shapiro and M.B. Wilk, 'An analysis for variance test for normality (complete samples)' (1965).

Journal of the Royal Statistical Society, for data in table 11.4, from J.B. Ramsey, 'Test for specification errors in classical linear least squares regression analysis' (1969).

List of conference participants

Árpád Ábrahám *Institute of Economics, Hungarian Academy of Sciences, Budapest*
Mária Augusztinovics *Institute of Economics, Hungarian Academy of Sciences, Budapest*
David Begg *Birkbeck College, London, and CEPR*
Michael Burda *Humbolt Universität zu Berlin and CEPR*
Ágnes Csermely *Kopint–Datorg Institute for Economic and Market Research and Informatics, Budapest*
Zsolt Darvas *National Bank of Hungary*
Imre Fertő *Institute of Economics, Hungarian Academy of Sciences, Budapest*
Pál Gáspár *Financial Research Ltd, Budapest*
László Halpern *Institute of Economics, Hungarian Academy of Sciences, Budapest, and CEPR*
István Hamecz *National Bank of Hungary*
Péter Kaderják *Budapest University of Economic Sciences*
Gábor Kertesi *Institute of Economics, Hungarian Academy of Sciences, Budapest*
Gábor Kézdi *Institute of Economics, Hungarian Academy of Sciences, Budapest*
Júlia Király *International Training Center for Bankers, Budapest*
János Köllő *Institute of Economics, Hungarian Academy of Sciences, Budapest*
Jenő Koltay *Institute of Economics, Hungarian Academy of Sciences, Budapest*
György Kopits *International Monetary Fund*
János Kornai *Collegium Budapest, and Harvard University*
Gábor Kőrösi *Institute of Economics, Hungarian Academy of Sciences, Budapest*
Álmos Kovács *National Bank of Hungary*

Mária Lackó *Institute of Economics, Hungarian Academy of Sciences,*
  Budapest
Michael Landesmann *Vienna Institute for Comparative Economic Studies*
Iván Major *Institute of Economics, Hungarian Academy of Sciences,*
  Budapest
Gyula Nagy *Budapest University of Economic Sciences*
Gábor Oblath *Kopint–Datorg Institute for Economic and Market*
  Research and Informatics, Budapest
Giancarlo Perasso *OECD*
Richard Portes *London Business School, and CEPR*
Gyula Pulay *Ministry of Labour, Budapest*
Attila Rátfai *Institute of Economics, Hungarian Academy of Sciences,*
  Budapest
Sándor Richter *Vienna Institute for Comparative Economic Studies*
Werner Riecke *National Bank of Hungary*
Gérard Roland *ECARE, Université Libre de Bruxelles, and CEPR*
Magdolna Sass *Institute for World Economics, Budapest*
Jérôme Sgard *Centre d'Etudes Prospectives et d'Informations*
  Internationales, Paris
Károly Attila Soós *Ministry of Industry and Trade, Budapest*
Jan Svejnar *University of Michigan, CERGE–EI, Prague, and CEPR*
Wim Swaan *Institute of Economics, Hungarian Academy of Sciences,*
  Budapest
László Szakadát *Budapest University of Economic Sciences*
Miklós Szanyi *Institute for World Economics, Budapest*
Ádám Török *Institute for Industrial Economics, Hungarian Academy of*
  Sciences, Budapest
Ákos Valentinyi *Kopint–Datorg Institute for Economic and Market*
  Research and Informatics, Budapest
Balázs Váradi *Institute of Economics, Hungarian Academy of Sciences,*
  Budapest
Éva Várhegyi *Financial Research Ltd, Budapest*
Balázs Világi *National Bank of Hungary*
János Vincze *National Bank of Hungary*
Sweder van Wijnbergen *University of Amsterdam and CEPR*
Charles Wyplosz *Graduate Institute of International Studies, Geneva, and*
  CEPR

1 The hidden Hungarian miracle

LÁSZLÓ HALPERN and CHARLES WYPLOSZ

1 Introduction

The papers brought together in this volume were initially presented at the conference 'Hungary: Towards a Market Economy', organised on 20–21 October 1995 in Budapest by the Institute of Economics, Hungarian Academy of Sciences, with the support of the Centre for Economic Policy Research (CEPR). This conference was designed as a follow-up to the highly successful and influential conference held in London nearly four years before.[1] Subsequently, we have invited three more contributions[2] to produce a reasonably complete account of the economic situation of Hungary six years into its transformation process. The rule was to ask Hungarian economists to write the papers and to invite 'Western' economists to criticise the original drafts and to comment on the final versions. The aim was to produce an evaluation of the situation by those who know best while striving for international standards of analysis.

Although Hungary prides itself on its gradualism, it is rapidly changing. It is not yet a full-blown market economy, but it is moving there. The evolution is often beset by setbacks, but in every one of them lies some silver lining. Macroeconomic mistakes often conceal significant microeconomic adjustment, to the point that it is often thought that Hungary leads in corporate restructuring among countries of the region. Improvement in the banking structure, in turn, sharpens choices regarding monetary and fiscal policies.

In early 1995, the Hungarian gradualist approach was perceived to be in serious crisis. Both external and internal balances were in a critical situation, privatisation was slowing down and international organisations and credit rating institutions classified Hungary as prone to follow Mexico into crisis. When the conference was being held, it was too early to detect unambiguously the effects of the policy package adopted in

March 1995. This package was a very classical macroeconomic stabilisation programme. It included a determined effort to curb budget expenditures to achieve a deficit which can be financed from the market without central bank financing, a commitment to contain nominal wages, and the adoption of a crawling peg following a strong devaluation.

Two years later, the Hungarian economy is at last growing. Its budget is improving and the external deficit is clearly sustainable. The economy has responded. Part of the response is vintage macroeconomics, but it now appears that another part is the consequence of deep microeconomic restructuring and institution-building which occurred during the period 1990–3. These achievements have long been obscured by macroeconomic imbalances and the image of gradualism cultivated by Hungarian policy makers themselves. In fact, restructuring has been a shock therapy: the very tough bankruptcy law adopted in 1991 has been vigorously implemented, resulting in the closing down of thousands of firms, with clear incentive effects on the surviving ones. No other transition economy has so quickly closed down so many firms, taking the risk of letting go potentially profitable companies rather than the opposite alternative of letting survive firms that eventually go bust. For this reason Hungary is probably furthest down the transition path. This impending success story may not be clear from the chapters which follow, but it is the thesis that we develop in this introductory chapter.

We start by providing a brief chronological overview. The following section focuses on the microeconomic reforms of the first part of the 1990s, including firm restructuring and a complete overhaul of the banking system with a unique openness to foreign operators. Section 4 presents the macroeconomic policies. Section 5 concludes with an upbeat revisionist view of Hungarian transition.

2   Overview of the years 1989–97

2.1   The hectic years, 1990–4

From the start, the large external debt inherited from the past imposed a severe restriction on policy choices. The authorities decided early on not to seek a debt restructuring. That decision has never been seriously challenged within Hungary, even though it has severely constrained the subsequent evolution. The intention was to build up the country's international credibility. This has been achieved, but there remains the question whether the price paid was justified.

The big shock in Hungary did not coincide, as elsewhere, with the sudden adoption of the market mechanism. By the end of 1989, the economy had for more than a decade been a mixed system of functioning markets and state ownership. Significant steps were made to liberalise trade and many prices and to cut general subsidies. The most important shock came later in 1991, when the CMEA collapsed.

Real GDP fell by almost 20 per cent between 1990 and 1992. Unemployment rose from a rate of zero in 1988 to 12 per cent by 1992. Enterprise profits turned negative in 1992 for the non-financial corporate sector and real wages were cut significantly. The budget worsened quite quickly as revenues dropped following the fall in output. However, public expenditures were not cut in an effort to deal with social tensions. The central bank financed the resulting deficits at preferential interest rates without limit. Inflation surged.

From 1991 to mid-1992, policy aimed at preventing further increases in the external debt. The current account exhibited slight surplus and foreign exchange reserves reached a secure level thanks to large foreign direct investments. By the end of 1992 Hungary's net debt had decreased by nearly USD 3 billion. The ratio of debt service to exports was reduced from 49 per cent in 1990 to 31 per cent in 1992, leading to better access to international capital markets.

Micro level adjustment started in 1990–1. A market oriented corporate sector did emerge, but the transition was costly and painful. The legal framework of the market economy was completed by new laws and institutional developments affecting financial institutions, the stock exchange, accounting and bankruptcy procedures and the central bank. Markets appeared slowly at first. For example, a spot (and later forward) exchange market opened in June 1992 within the Budapest Commodities Exchange, and institutional investors (investment funds, pension funds) entered the scene gradually. The supply-side reaction was muted until the Bankruptcy Law was implemented in 1992. Even then, it took time for a new competitive corporate sector to replace the non-competitive activities that were closed down.

In December 1991 the Central Bank Act passed by Parliament ruled out further access by the budget to preferential credit lines. The Act also set a limit on the direct finance of the budget deficit by the central bank. Macroeconomic policy was relaxed in 1993–4. As the current account was improving in 1992 the authorities thought the time had come to bring the decline in GDP to an end. Monetary policy aimed at lowering interest rates. This was achieved by not sterilising the inflows initially associated with the previously improving current account. When exports started to fall, exogenous and temporary factors were blamed. There was still a belief that investment would rise to meet increases in domestic demand. Interest rates declined further as the budget turned into a (temporary) surplus; maturing Treasury Bills were not rolled over and the monetary authorities abstained from mopping up the accompanying injection of liquidity. Finally, the central bank lowered the rate of mandatory reserves. Real yields on government securities with maturity less than one year and households' deposit rates turned negative in 1993. Household savings began to evaporate.

The macroeconomic policy targets were not achieved. GDP continued to fall throughout 1993. Domestic demand and imports grew strongly by 9.9 per cent and 18.6 per cent, respectively while exports declined by 10 per cent. The trade deficit quickly became the major problem. Part of the blame could be ascribed to unfavourable exogenous factors: a fall in external demand due to the wars in the former Yugoslavia and bad weather which hit agricultural production and exports. Improving profitability and performance in the new emerging sector did not counterbalance the lagging part of the economy. Fuelled by policy errors, inflationary and devaluation expectations developed. The public's confidence was shattered, directly affecting the credibility of the adjustable pegged exchange rate system. Speculation against the forint grew as the steadily deteriorating current account increased the probability of a devaluation. The external debt, already massive, started to grow again.

Eventually, the expansionary measures brought the GDP decline to a halt. In the election year of 1994, household consumption rose by nearly 2 per cent, investment by 20 per cent partly on account of the improved financial position of enterprises – both domestic and foreign – and partly due to support provided by the government to some large enterprises in the form of a state guarantee. Exports started to turn around but import demand continued to grow at a steep pace as domestic supply could not meet increasing domestic demand.

The interest rate decline directly improved debt service. Debt managers lengthened the average maturity of the outstanding debt by issuing longer maturity instruments (2–5 years) which resulted in temporarily lower debt service. The resulting improvement in the general government borrowing requirement (from 7.1 per cent of GDP in 1992 to 6.0 per cent in 1993) was misinterpreted as a positive development. In its medium-term economic programme, the new government elected in 1994 aimed at 'European standards' – a 3 per cent deficit and a 60 per cent debt.

As might have been expected, the declining trend of inflation stopped in 1994. It was further fuelled by rises in VAT and excise taxes which were implemented in an effort to limit the budget deficit. The currency was devalued by as much as 16 per cent in 1994, further pushing up prices and wages. Luckily, with foreign exchange reserves at approximately

USD 7bn, or 7 months of imports, the country remained creditworthy on international capital markets.

2.2   The stabilisation package, March 1995

By the end of 1994, the macroeconomic situation was clearly not sustainable. The 1994 growth rate of 2.9 per cent might have looked timid in comparison to Poland or Slovenia, but it was artificial. The budget deficit was approaching 9 per cent of GDP, with a current account deficit of similar size and growing rapidly. The usual debt measures (ratios of gross and net foreign debt to GDP) were increasing. In the wake of the Mexican crisis, yields on the Hungarian debt rose substantially, prompting action. The socialist–liberal government elected in May 1994 realised that electoral promises of easy-going policies could not be continued. In March 1995 – after a long and damaging hesitation – the government adopted the first comprehensive stabilisation package of Hungary's transition.

The package rested on three classical series of measures. First, to re-establish the budget public primary spending was cut by more than 15 per cent in real terms. Second, the currency was devalued by 9 per cent and its regime was changed from a fixed rate to a crawling peg, with a preannounced monthly rate of depreciation. A temporary import surcharge of 8 per cent amounted to a further devaluation. Finally, the government committed itself to containing nominal wage increases.

Fiscal adjustment was unavoidable. At about 55 per cent of GDP, tax pressure was clearly too high, more a legacy of the previous regime than a considered policy choice. The emergence of a private sector required that the public sector be rolled back. Additionally, Hungary had inherited a massive public debt. While budget deficits in the early phase of a transition can be justified on the basis of intertemporal consumption smoothing, the terms required from Hungary on international financial markets restricted borrowing to only highly profitable projects. The only reasonable way to finance deficits would have been to borrow domestically but this would have crowded out profitable private investment without providing for aggregate intertemporal smoothing.

The fixed exchange rate regime established in the early 1980s had been marked by recurrent and widely expected depreciations (a cumulated 81 per cent devaluation between January 1990 and December 1994, in 20 steps). The regime had no credibility left. It no longer restrained inflationary expectations and was hurting trade as depreciations lagged behind inflation. With inflation close to 20 per cent, the introduction of a crawling peg system, with preannounced rates of crawl, represented a step towards realism which helped to re-establish credibility and regain investors' confidence. The initial depreciation, complemented by an import tariff surcharge, re-established competitiveness in the tradable goods sector.

As a consequence of the reduction in spending, the public sector borrowing requirement substantially diminished and could be entirely financed from domestic sources. Along with other institutional developments – the establishment of a State Debt Management Agency and the creation of a primary dealers' network – the evolution of the budget made it possible to change the regulation affecting the central bank. Since the end of 1996 the NBH has adopted the EU standard which rules out direct financing of the budget deficit.

2.3   Growth path after 1995

The March 1995 measures had a rapid and lasting positive impact on the economy. The reduction in public expenditures led to significant improvements in internal and external imbalances. The ratio of general government deficit to GDP was reduced from peak 9.6 per cent in 1994 to 4.8 per cent in 1996, while the current account deficit declined by more than 5 percentage points from 9.4 in 1994 to 3.8 per cent in 1996. The current account deficit has been more than covered by FDI so that debt service indicators have improved significantly. The vicious circle of increasing interest rates leading to increasing borrowing requirement and worsening debt:GDP ratios turned into a virtuous circle of decreasing interest payments resulting in decreasing borrowing needs and costs leading to a declining debt:GDP ratio.

Over 1995, the trade balance improved by USD 1.2bn as exports increased at two-digit rates while imports stagnated. In 1996 exports remained buoyant and the trade imbalance deteriorated only because imports picked up, rising by 7.3 per cent. The net revenue from tourism was growing and almost doubled in 1996 while unrequited transfers originating mainly from households' remittances and unrecorded economic activities fluctuated around USD 1bn, with a peak in 1995.

The tough fiscal measures clearly poured cold water on growth. GDP growth slowed down and then stagnated over most of 1996, starting to improve only in 1997. The European Commission estimates a growth rate of 1.5 per cent for the year and a brighter 3 per cent for 1998 (see table 1.1), suggesting that the economy has finally turned around.

Inevitably, the exchange rate measures of March 1995 affected inflation. Among the successful reformers, Hungary is clearly under-performing in this respect, seeming to face a particularly strong inflation inertia. We

Table 1.1. Growth and inflation, 1994–8

	GDP growth					CPI inflation			
	1994	1995	1996	1997	1998	1995	1996	1997	1998
Hungary	2.9	1.5	0.5	1.5	3.0	26.3	23.0	18.0	13.0
Czech republic	2.6	4.8	4.4	4.6	5.0	9.1	8.8	8.5	8.4
Poland	5.2	6.9	6.1	6.5	7.0	28.7	19.9	15.0	12.0
Slovakia	4.9	6.8	6.8	5.9	5.4	9.7	5.8	6.0	5.5
Slovenia	4.9	3.9	3.5	4.2	4.8	14.3	9.7	8.2	9.2
CEC-8	4.1	5.0	4.5	5.0	5.6	22.6	16.9	13.0	10.7

Note: CEC-8 includes the countries listed and the Baltic States (Estonia, Latvia, Lithuania).
Source: European Economy, Supplement C, 2 (June 1997).

return to this issue in section 4.3 below, where we argue that the inflation effect of the 1995 devaluation has not triggered a new inflationary bandwagon; rather, we lay the blame on an inappropriate management of the new exchange rate regime.

While Hungary's growth rate is still low, and inflation still high in comparison with successful reformers, for the first time in a decade Hungary faces the prospect of a continuing growth path. In fact, Hungary may now have a comparative advantage. As elsewhere, the macroeconomy is finally stabilised even if inflation lingers; but most of the deep structural difficulties so visible (e.g. in the Czech republic or in the Polish banking sector) have been solved.

3   Early microeconomic adjustment

3.1   Restructuring and corporate governance

Pressure for restructuring came less from a sudden shift to market discipline than from the collapse of the CMEA. Judged from the data shown in table 1.2 Hungarian firms quickly managed to reorient trade towards the OECD area. However aggregates showing improving trade and current account balances conceal serious shortcomings. Indeed Halpern and Kőrösi (chapter 7) show that, unsurprisingly perhaps, small firms are faster to adapt than larger ones. This could be related to harder budget constraints if large firms are considered too big to fail. In fact, the evidence presented suggests that successfully reorienting firms tended to be less profitable during that process, as they were investing in reorientation. In fact, during the early period, the profitability of

Table 1.2. Country pattern of Hungarian foreign trade (per cent), 1989–95

	1989	1990	1991	1992	1993	1994	1995
Exports	100.0	100.0	100.0	100.0	100.0	100.0	100.0
Transition and non-market							
economies	47.3	37.7	23.6	23.3	26.4	23.3	24.9
East European countries	35.7	28.2	19.4	19.4	22.9	19.2	20.5
Market economies	52.7	62.3	76.4	76.6	73.6	76.7	75.1
developed countries	44.2	54.2	67.9	71.3	68.1	72.7	71.1
EU countries	24.8	32.2	45.7	49.8	46.8	51.5	64.3
Imports	100.0	100.0	100.0	100.0	100.0	100.0	100.0
Transition and non-market							
economies	44.3	36.9	24.4	25.5	29.8	24.2	24.0
East European countries	33.1	27.9	22.6	23.8	28.1	22.4	22.1
Market economies	55.7	63.1	75.6	74.5	70.2	75.8	76.0
developed countries	49.7	53.2	67.6	70.3	65.8	71.3	70.4
EU countries	29.0	31.0	41.7	43.1	40.5	45.8	61.5

Source: Own computation based on CSO data.

firms seriously deteriorated and non-performing loans accumulated, in spite of apparently and artificially good profitability at large commercial banks. This led to a series of policy actions which profoundly reshaped the microeconomy. Yet the resulting deep restructuring has been partly obscured by the fact that misguided macroeconomic policies allowed some firms and banks to delay adjustment to the new environment.

The Bankruptcy Law adopted in 1991 and taking effect on 1 January 1992 did not leave much room for delayed response. This Law required managers of firms with overdue arrears to file for bankruptcy or liquidation. The effects were dramatic. Table 1.3 shows that several thousand firms were taken into bankruptcy proceedings by their managers, and even more by their creditors.

Nearly one firm out of 10 filed for liquidation in both 1992 and 1993. The law was amended in September 1993 to remedy deficiencies and to ease the enormous pressure on the institutions dealing with bankruptcy and liquidation procedures. The amendments made filing by managers optional and reduced the threshold of the previously required 100 per cent approval of a reorganisation agreement. This explains why the number of filings for bankruptcy fell sharply thereafter. The number of liquidation announcements has remained stable, however. More than the numbers themselves, this procedure has left an essential enduring legacy. Inter-firm arrears, a frequent feature of transition, quickly disappeared in 1993. Simply put, Hungarian firms have met, and adjusted to, hard

Table 1.3. Bankruptcies and liquidations, 1992–5

	1992	1993	1994	1995
Bankruptcy				
Filings	4,169	987	189	145
Voluntary	1,016	137	136	139
Obligatory	3,153	850	53	6
Public announcements	2,500	887	79	28
Completed	1,260	740	351	175
Agreement	740	510	90	21
To be continued in liquidation	703	674	28	9
Liquidation				
Filings	9,891	7,242	5,711	6,316
Creditor	8,131	5,883	4,715	5,398
Debtor	1,760	1,359	996	918
Public announcements	2,227	2,593	2,484	2,799
Administrative completion	4,401	3,975	2,997	3,202
Full completion	562[a]	1,140	1,151	22,55
Number of economic corporations with legal entity	59,363	75,654	91,229	106,245

Note:
[a] Incomplete (data for 4 out of 19 departments are missing).
Sources: MoF; CSO.

budget constraints. This process is not yet complete in most other transition countries.

Another specific characteristic of Hungary has been its privatisation process. In contrast with mass privatisation schemes which privilege speed over sale value and ownership, Hungary has opted for a slow process of case by case sale. Furthermore, foreigners have not been discouraged – on the contrary, one of the avowed objectives of privatisation was to encourage transfer of technology and best business practice from abroad. One result is that Hungary has been by far the largest recipient of FDI in the region, which has helped enormously given the vulnerability of the external sector resulting from the inherited debt. Privatisation and tough bankruptcy laws have also shaped corporate governance. This link is analysed in chapter 6 by Ádám Török. Surveying in detail some 40 enterprises, he shows that Hungary has achieved a corporate structure that is stable and comparable to what exists in the major industrial countries. What has long been described as a frustratingly slow privatisation process and an excessively brutal bankruptcy procedure is presented as a key success story with a favourable and long-lasting impact on the management of Hungarian firms.

The introduction of prudential banking regulation and international standards has shed light on the poor quality of commercial bank portfolios. Bankruptcy rules forced banks to convert large amounts of inter-enterprise arrears into bad debt. The whole banking sector suddenly became a loss maker.[3] To date, Hungary has been alone in opening up its banking sector to foreign ownership. It has not been the preferred approach, to be sure. Between 1992 and 1994, Hungarian banks have undergone several rounds of costly restructuring – estimated at 10 per cent of GDP. This process of trial and (lots of expensive) errors is reported in chapter 8 by László Szakadát. Here again, gradualism has been the name of the game. This chapter shows that the result has been major errors and huge costs. These costs are sunk, now, and Hungary can rely on a solid banking sector.

3.2   Income distribution and labour markets

A standard feature of transition is growing income differences. This is not surprising given the initial situation. On one side, the increasing gap between poor and rich contributes to the creation of an entrepreneurial environment by richly rewarding successful entrepreneurs. On the other side, criminality and rent seeking boom. The result is less tolerance for, and faith in, the social justification of growing inequalities. Surprisingly, perhaps, the growing gap between the highest and lowest incomes has been accompanied by a narrowing of the gap between incomes of the middle class and those of the poor. The main reason behind this contrast is faster than average increase of welfare support programmes, mainly the minimum wage and pensions. The combination of this evolution and of a rapid increase of unemployment between 1991 and 1994, and more particularly the large share of long-term unemployment, raises the same kind of difficult questions faced in the much richer Western European countries: does the welfare system generate unemployment, and how can one deal with it?

In fact, real wages have displayed quite a lot of flexibility, as can be seen from table 1.4. This may explain why the rate of unemployment has not risen to levels seen elsewhere in the region. One reason is the fact that wage negotiations are essentially conducted at the plant level. This is known to be conducive to wage moderation as employees and employers better realise the impact of wages on employment and the firm's prospects. Yet, a different view is presented by Jenő Koltay in chapter 9. The minimum wage is the only wage which is set in formal, tripartite, negotiations. The main thesis of this chapter is that, in Hungary, the minimum wage fulfils a function quite different from its Western counterpart. Being indicative only, the minimum wage does not really set a floor.

Table 1.4. Main macroeconomic indicators, 1990–6

	1990	1991	1992	1993	1994	1995	1996[a]
Change in per cent							
Real GDP	−3.5	−11.9	−3.1	−0.6	2.9	1.5	~1
Domestic absorption	−3.1	−9.1	−3.6	9.9	2.2	−3.1	0.0
Private consumption	−2.7	−5.6	0.0	1.9	0.2	−6.1	−2.5
Gross fixed capital formation	−4.2	−10.4	−2.6	2.0	12.5	−4.3	−3.5
Exports		−13.9	2.1	−10.1	13.7	13.4	10.4
Imports		−6.1	0.2	18.6	8.8	−0.7	7.3
CPI	28.9	35.0	23.0	22.5	18.8	28.2	23.6
PPI	22.0	32.6	12.3	10.8	11.3	28.9	21.8
Nominal effective exchange rate	15.9	14.2	9.6	6.5	16.3	28.8	16.4
Gross wages	28.6	30.0	25.1	21.9	24.9	16.8	20.4
Net real wages	−3.7	−7.0	−1.4	−3.9	7.2	−12.2	−5.2
Unemployment rate	1.9	7.5	12.3	12.1	10.4	10.4	10.4
Savings ratio	6.7	15.1	10.4	4.7	7.7	8.4	10.2
Per cent of GDP							
General government balance budget	−2.9	−2.4	−7.0	−6.7	−9.6	−7.4	−4.8
General government balance primary	−1.0	−0.1	0.3	−2.4	−1.6	1.7	4.5
General government debt		75.2	79.2	90.0	87.6	87.7	75.4
Trade balance	1.0	0.6	−0.6	−8.4	−8.7	−5.6	−6.1
Current account	0.4	0.8	0.9	−9.0	−9.4	−5.4	−3.8
FDI	0.9	4.4	3.9	6.1	2.8	10.2	4.6
Gross external debt	64.3	67.8	57.6	63.7	68.4	71.5	62.4
Net external debt	48.2	43.6	35.0	38.7	45.4	38.0	32.2
Change in per cent							
M2 (annual average)	21.7	23.2	30.8	22.6	15.2	14.3	20.6
M3 (annual average)	26.1	27.3	36.4	19.4	14.3	15.3	22.9

Note: a Preliminary.
Source: NBH.

Many firms offer wages significantly below the official minimum. In fact, the median wage is considerably below the average wage. If the minimum wage does not provide an effective protection for the employees, should it be suppressed given the (recently challenged) presumption that it raises unemployment? Koltay defends what he calls the 'bargaining function' of the minimum wage. In a country where the social partners have not yet settled on how to bargain, the combination of both national and enterprise level negotiations is a source of fragmentation. Koltay argues that the national minimum wage has emerged as the only anchor for social cohesion, and should for that reason be maintained.

A special feature of Hungary is the presence of a large Gypsy population. Long discriminated against and with limited human capital, this population is arguably less prepared to deal effectively with massive economic changes, while subject to abuse when the political rules of the game suddenly become open to challenge and hardships mount. In chapter 11, Ábrahám and Kertesi study the situation of this group in different regions. They find that regional unemployment is related to the size of the local Gypsy population and to the average number of schooling years. These findings tend to confirm that Gypsies are more discriminated against on the labour market, and that they represent a larger proportion of the population in poorer regions.

3.3   Welfare

In chapter 10, Csaba and Semjén point at the unsustainability of the inherited welfare rules concentrating mainly around the budget. They show how early attempts aimed at reducing the increase of poverty and inequality eventually failed. In fact, the priority has shifted towards the transformation of the whole system.[4] Indeed, economic reforms have not percolated easily into the welfare system. Just as in the other transition countries, Hungary had to re-define the role of welfare while facing economic hardships and disadvantageous demographic conditions. For firms in a difficult situation, the sale of social assets was the easiest way to early adjustment. As a consequence, social services provided by firms to the employees were abruptly terminated, forcing the government to step in unprepared. Unemployment and growing income and regional inequalities further increased the demand for social benefits and services. On the supply side, conditions have also deteriorated due to budget tensions and price increases. The welfare sector remains the least reformed, and it is clear that its rehabilitation will be particularly challenging.

4   Macroeconomics

Hungary escaped the initial inflationary shock that affected most transition economies, largely because by 1989 the economy was already partially reformed. Yet, seven years down the road, the macroeconomic indicators are no better, and often worse, than elsewhere (tables 1.1 and 1.3). What has happened? In a nutshell, a combination of policy mistakes and the debilitating effect of a large external debt have prevented Hungary from reaping the benefits of its otherwise favourable position.

4.1   Fiscal policy

As table 1.4 shows, the budget steadily deteriorated until 1995. We have already discussed the misguided relaxation of 1993–4. The primary budget, however, warrants some comments. At 2.4 per cent of GDP, the peak deficit cannot be considered as reckless and the correction of some 6 per cent of GDP between 1994 and 1996 is spectacular. The fiscal conundrum itself is largely due to the combination of high inherited debt and the shift to deficit financing at market rates. Since a significant fraction of the debt is in foreign currency, the burden also depends on the real exchange rate. Table 1.5 reports a number of measures of the real exchange rate. For the present purpose, the relevant measures are those based on the CPI or on the GDP deflator. In both cases we observe a sizeable real appreciation until 1993 – hence a tendency for the debt burden to decline – followed by a depreciation at the time of the policy mistakes in 1993–4. The 10 per cent depreciation over 1993–5 explains about 4 out of the 6.7 percentage points increase in the debt:GDP ratio. Real appreciation after 1995 explains only a small fraction of the post-stabilisation improvement.

Fiscal policy has gone through three stages. The first, from 1989 to 1992 was one of caution. Facing declining incomes in the wake of the familiar transformational recession,[5] the authorities were able to maintain a nearly stable primary deficit. The actual deficit soared in 1992 when the debt burden rose due to higher interest rates and continuous devaluations. The second was when policy was mistakenly relaxed. Finally, since 1995 the budget has been brought under control. During the first two stages, deficits were partly financed by the NBH. This has now come to a halt.

In chapter 2, Pál Gáspár notes that the budgetary problem includes not only the issue of balancing the books, but also the size and role of the public sector and of the welfare system. Since January 1996, Hungary has set up a Treasury, hoping to alleviate the tensions within the public sector and to reduce the overall level of spending. Yet, we should not expect a quick fix. Important welfare-related measures of a fiscal stabilisation package were cancelled by the Constitutional Court. The social security and the pension budgets are in persistent disequilibrium. The transformation of these systems requires time (patience) and consensus among different groups (generations, experts, politicians). Both are in short supply. Still, total public spending (excluding interest payments) dropped from 53 per cent of GDP in 1994 to 40 per cent in 1997, most of the savings coming from a reduction of transfers.

Table 1.5. Real effective exchange rates[a] in manufacturing, 1990–6 (1989 = 100)

	1990	1991	1992	1993	1994	1995	1996
1 PPI-based real exchange rate	98.0	103.2	102.0	104.4	99.4	94.0	98.0
2 ULC-based real exchange rate	103.1	115.4	139.0	138.8	129.2	107.9	102.7
3 Profit-based real exchange rate (2/1)	105.2	111.8	136.3	133.0	130.0	114.8	104.8
4 GDP deflator-based real exchange rate	100.2	104.0	110.1	124.4	125.0	112.7	115.1
5 CPI-based real exchange rate	102.8	114.2	122.2	134.0	131.8	127.1	131.4
6 Export price-based real exchange rate	96.1	99.2	99.0	100.7	102.6	103.6	105.2

Note: *a* An increase means appreciation.
Sources: NBH; own computations.

4.2 Monetary policy

Two events have shaped the evolution of monetary policy. First, the 'divorce' between the government and the central bank in late 1992 and the absence of direct deficit finance in 1995 by the central bank, capped by a formal ban since 1996, have severed the link between the budget deficit and monetary policy. Second, the adoption of a preannounced crawling peg in March 1995 has provided the NBH with a clear target which can be monitored by the public at large and which serves as a benchmark of its commitment.

A few specific aspects of the post-March 1995 crawling peg deserve emphasis. First, the exchange rate is tied to a basket made up of DM for 70 per cent and of US dollars for 30 per cent (the DM replaced the ECU in January 1997). Second, it is accompanied by a band of fluctuation of ±2.25 per cent. This is the same width as the one in effect in the EMS until August 1993. Third, the NBH's policy is to intervene in support of the Forint only at the margin. Finally the monthly rate of crawl has been reduced from 1.9 per cent a month in early 1995 to 1.0 per cent in August 1997.

At the same time as it pursues a tight exchange rate target, the NBH publicly states its desire to monitor interest rates to encourage private savings. In doing so, the NBH seems motivated by recent experience. In 1993 household savings dropped dramatically to 4.7 per cent of GDP (down from 15.1 per cent in 1991). The result was a sharp deterioration of the current account as well as a fall in private investment, the sort of events that the central bank desires to avoid.

Of course, there cannot be many simultaneous objectives so the NBH is careful to recognise that the exchange rate target is preeminent in steering the interest rate. But what is the role of the interest rate? In chapter 3 Világi and Vincze attempt to determine what the transmission mechanism is. They find that the interest rate is extremely slow to respond to the central bank's actions, suggesting that monetary policy could not have been effective. One reason for this result could be the poor state of the banking system, leading to adverse selection and a lack of competition, which could have been a major factor in the past. The large banks have now gone through large-scale consolidation programmes and privatisation has begun. In addition, major steps have been taken to limit the quasi-fiscal activity of the central bank so that the public deficit is now financed at market conditions. Another interpretation is the prevalence of credit rationing. This is a highly plausible explanation, and credit rationing might continue to be present in the future, in which case concern with interest rate levels might be misguided.

This matters for monetary policy because of the latent conflict between the support of saving and the exchange rate target. Too high interest rates encourage capital inflows which in turn must be sterilised, leading to a standard policy dilemma. In the case of Hungary, the situation is made even more problematic by two features of the crawling peg. The margin of fluctuation is very narrow. For example, within the EMS, Italy, Spain and Portugal observed a margin of ± 6 per cent when their inflation rates were in the double-digit range, and even below. So did the UK during its brief fixed exchange rate period. Second, the stated policy of intervening only at the margin runs in complete contradiction with experience accumulated in the EMS. Restricting interventions to be conducted only at the margin means that, once the exchange rate is at the margin, the money supply is entirely market determined which may easily put the central bank in an extremely difficult position. Indeed speculation is encouraged by the fact that the central bank must make the market, the celebrated 'one-way bet'. It is precisely for that reason that, in 1987, the EMS countries agreed to intensify coordinated interventions inside the bands.

4.3 Inflation

Perhaps the biggest disappointment of Hungary's macroeconomic performance is the stubborn behaviour of inflation. The rate of price inflation has never been extremely high, peaking at 35 per cent in 1991, but it has never been reduced to single-digit levels either. As is always the case in such circumstances, it is tempting to rely on explanations which emphasise inertia in wage and price setting.

In chapter 4, Hamecz, Vincze and Zsoldos provide a thorough econometric analysis of the inflation process. They work with price indices for 160 goods, eliminate regulated prices to obtain a measure of 'core inflation' which is based on market mechanisms, and explore the links between prices, monetary aggregates and the exchange rate. They report few direct links between monetary aggregates and inflation and a limited impact of the nominal exchange rate, accepting some role for inertial inflation.

This kind of work is essential. Yet, it may be that their sample period is too short and marked by too many institutional changes (in both commercial and central banking) to allow the careful econometrician to find acceptable evidence. Our impression, however, is that inertial inflation has usually been used to justify monetary policies which fall shy of direct attacks on inflation and that there is no reason why, granted a changing relationship due to institutional transformation, inflation should not be driven by monetary policy.

Just looking at price and wage data, it is hard to detect strong nominal rigidities (table 1.4). The rate of crawl of the exchange rate must eventually, and rather quickly, drive inflation. The trend real appreciation observed since 1991 most likely ratifies productivity gains. In setting up modest declines in the rate of crawl the NBH is implicitly accepting that inflation recedes only slowly: central bank inertia rather than inflation inertia?

In fact, speeding up disinflation would require taking two risks if, as is likely, it takes time for inflation to adjust to a lower rate of crawl. The first is that the real exchange rate appreciation will be excessive and hurt competitiveness. With exports booming there is no evidence that the Forint is overvalued. Yet, in Hungary as everywhere else, producers constitute a powerful and highly vocal lobby in favour of a policy of undervaluation. The second is that if nominal interest rates react quickly to a lower rate of depreciation while inflation lags, real interest rates will decline, which could discourage savings. This is a possibility, but a very unlikely one. The effect is unlikely to be quantitatively large, to start with, as it is entirely based on inflation inertia. In the face of a visibly stronger exchange rate, inertia cannot be long-lasting. Moreover, a transitory decline in saving need not be a bad thing if, at the same time, lower real interest rates encourage investment. Second, an increase in consumption could help speed up growth. Finally, the current account deficit will indeed increase if domestic spending rises, but again this is a

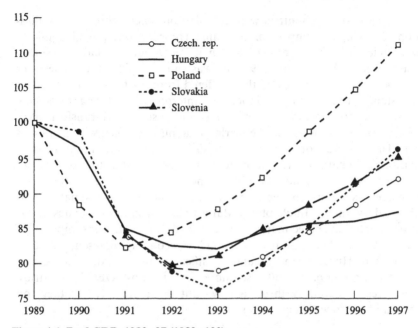

Figure 1.1 Real GDP, 1989–97 (1989=100)
Note: For Slovenia the index is set to be equal to the average of the other
   countries in 1991 since no data are available prior to that date.
Source: *European Economy*, Supplement C, No. 2, June 1997; IMF.

transitory effect. In addition, the current account effect can be avoided if
the budget deficit is further reduced.

Should the NBH take these risks? On one hand, these are small and
fairly inconsequential risks. On the other, there is little merit in
accelerating disinflation once it is stabilised at a moderate level. If there is
any trade off between growth and inflation – which, so far, has not been
established in Hungary – growth ought to come first after all these years
of misery.

4.4 Slow growth?

Figure 1.1 shows that, among the successful transformers Hungary,
which suffered the smallest transformation contraction, has had the
worst growth performance. One interpretation is that Hungary has paid
the price of its gradualist approach. Another interpretation is that
Hungary's growth has been stymied by its external debt. There is yet
another possibility, not necessarily incompatible with the previous ones.

While most other countries were focusing on macroeconomic stabilisation following the impact of big-bang, Hungary was pursuing microeconomic reforms, letting its macroeconomic situation slowly deteriorate. Thus, until 1995, it was not reaping the benefit of microeconomic reforms, and then suffered from the temporary effects of the stabilisation package. Under this interpretation, Hungary is now poised to grow fast and catch up with the other successful transformers.

Of course, as anywhere in the world, data must be taken with a grain of salt. This may be more the case in transition countries given that the state statistical apparatus has been refined over decades to monitor an economy which does not resemble the new one. Undoubtedly, there was a hidden economy in centrally planned systems, but its nature has changed overnight. In chapter 5 Mária Lackó proposes estimates of the size of the hidden economy derived from observed consumption of electricity. Her findings are that the hidden economy represents some 30 per cent in Hungary and Poland, significantly more than in the Czech and Slovak republics, and also more than in most OECD countries. These results certainly throw a new light on figure 1.1, but they too should be taken with a grain of salt.

5   Conclusion: revisionism and optimism

Conventional wisdom is that Hungary has made two major mistakes: it has opted for gradualism, allowing inherited distortions to drag on, and it has refused to negotiate a rescheduling of its very large inherited external debt. The result is comparatively slow growth and high inflation. We do not deny that these factors have played a role but we suggest that this interpretation is only part of the story, and possibly not the most important part.

Hungary has been unique in several respects. Its inherited external debt was huge and continues to constrain the authorities. Privatisation has been slower than in the other successful transforming countries, but more outward oriented. Most transition countries have decided that they would not 'sell to the foreigners'. The result has been mass privatisation and the distribution practically for free of state assets. Hungary's openness to foreign ownership has had a number of deep implications. Privatisation has been slow as it required the evaluation of asset values and negotiations with potential buyers, in a context of limited know-how. On the positive side, foreign ownership brings with it technology transfers and fresh capital. Indeed, foreign direct investments to Hungary have matched the sum of foreign direct investments in all other European transition countries for a long time. This in turn has led to the establishment of a deeper stock market. In addition, the resulting structure of corporate ownership is considerably better. This is particularly clear in the banking sector. After several expensive and ultimately failed attempts at rescuing the domestically-owned banking system that emerged from the early phase of transition, foreign banks have been allowed to come in, and have contributed to the establishment of what is arguably the most secure banking structure in the region.

Another Hungarian characteristic is associated with the bankruptcy procedure of 1992. In just a few months more than 10 per cent of firms went bankrupt. This may not have been optimal but, with hindsight, it may well turn out to be preferable to the kind of slow death which has been allowed, at high cost, in most transition countries. Similarly, Hungary may be the most advanced transition country in the restructuring of the welfare system, primarily health and pensions.

Why, then, have all of these positive developments failed to materialise in superior growth performance? To start with, microeconomic reforms are known to be slow to produce their effects. Second, good microeconomics work if the macroeconomy is in proper order: poor policy management in 1993–4, followed by a tough stabilisation programme in 1995, has stifled growth. Under that interpretation, the clean-up of the Hungarian economy is now complete: optimism becomes realistic.

NOTES

1 See Székely and Newbery (1993).
2 Chapters 10, 4 and 8, by Csaba and Semjén, Hamecz, Vincze and Zsoldos, and Szakadát, respectively, were not presented at the conference.
3 See details in Bonin and Schaffer (1995).
4 Detailed analysis and presentation of the reform for the old age pension system can be found in IBRD (1995).
5 See Kornai (1993).

REFERENCES

Bonin, J. and M.E. Schaffer (1995) 'Banks, bad debts and bankruptcy in Hungary, 1991–94', London School of Economics, *CEP Working Paper*, **657**, 84

IBRD (1995) *Hungary: Structural Reforms for Sustainable Growth*, Washington, DC: IBRD, 177

Kornai, J. (1993) 'Transformational recession: general phenomenon examined through the example of Hungary's development', *Economie Appliquée*, **46**, 181–27

Székely, I.P. and D.M.G. Newbery (eds.) (1993) *Hungary: An Economy in Transition*, Cambridge: Cambridge University Press

Part One
Macroeconomic policy

2 Fiscal difficulties in the transition: the case of Hungary between 1990 and 1995

PÁL GÁSPÁR

1 Introduction

With the exception of the Czech republic and Slovenia – which simultaneously had favourable shocks affecting their fiscal balances[1] and followed conservative fiscal policies – economic transition is associated in almost all economies with high fiscal deficits and increasing public debt. The reasons are manifold, including the common experience of output decline, a reduction in tax bases due to the privatisation of state-owned enterprises and growing tax evasion, a rise in social security and unemployment expenditures and increasing costs of deficit financing associated with the switch from money to domestic debt. Hungary is among those economies where the transition began with high public debt and – except in 1990 – relatively high fiscal deficits. These indicators worsened in the 1990s producing rapidly increasing public debt and permanent fiscal deficits, which have significantly impaired the success of both macroeconomic stabilisation and microeconomic adjustment policies.

This chapter analyses the major fiscal developments in Hungary between 1990 and 1995. It evaluates the factors leading to the simultaneous and closely related growth of fiscal deficit and public debt, the most pressing macroeconomic consequences of fiscal imbalances in the first years of transition. It analyses how sustainable these policies were and shows the initial outcomes of the comprehensive stabilisation policy of March 1995. The chapter is structured as follows. Section 2 presents some facts about the most important fiscal trends in Hungary between 1990 and 1995. Section 3 describes the major macroeconomic, structural and fiscal policy factors that determined this fiscal performance. Section 4 analyses the process of rapid accumulation of public debt, its special structure and the factors explaining both its dynamics and its macroeconomic consequences. Section 5 deals with the changes in the financing of the fiscal deficit and the most important macroeconomic consequences of growing fiscal deficit and public debt. Section 6 – based on the sustainability analysis – determines the required preconditions for the stabilisation of the debt:GDP and reduction of the deficit:GDP ratios. The chapter closes (section 7) with some conclusions and a summary of the Hungarian experience with fiscal policy that might be relevant for other economies in transition.

2   Fiscal trends in Hungary between 1990 and 1995

To analyse fiscal policies and their macroeconomic consequences, we initially present some facts on fiscal developments in Hungary. One of them is the relative stability in redistribution by the government, which remained above 50 per cent of GDP.[2] This level is high compared to developed as well as other transition and developing economies with a similar level of GDP *per capita* to Hungary.[3] This reflects the rigidity of certain government expenditures (especially social and administrative) and the emergence of new ones (unemployment, debt service), which have prevented any substantial decline of redistribution after the initial fall caused by the subsidy reduction associated with price liberalisation.[4] The high level of redistribution was, however, accompanied by strong structural changes on both the revenue and the expenditure side. On the revenue side (see table 2A.1, p. 47) this was related to the increasing substitution of direct revenues by indirect ones, due to several factors.

Similarly to other formerly centrally planned economies, the share of direct taxes in revenue before the transition was overwhelming due to the high taxation of enterprise profits, the absence of tax evasion and easy tax collection (Tanzi, 1992). This changed markedly as the output and profit of state-owned enterprises declined, while the emerging private sector was characterised by high tax evasion and the tax authorities were unable to monitor its income growth.

Direct taxes also declined because of the collapse of formerly important revenues from the banking sector. Its profitability was adversely affected by the rapid build-up of non-performing assets and associated profit losses, establishment of new accounting rules preventing the banks reporting non-realised revenues, and introduction of risk adjusted reserve requirements.[5] Finally, the Olivera–Tanzi effect influenced real direct tax revenues more than indirect ones: moreover, the decline of consumption and turnover was much less than that of output and incomes. While the share of direct tax revenues declined, personal income taxes increasingly replaced corporate profit taxes within them.[6] After the initial decline associated with import liberalisation, the share of tariffs and import duties also increased, reflecting the growth of import demand and the reintroduction of certain protectionist measures. Finally, the share of social security contributions increased – although simultaneously with growing payment arrears – as the financing requirements of welfare systems failed to decline.

On the expenditure side, the most important change was the growth of debt service expenditures (see table 2A.2, p. 47), reflecting the rapid increase of total and especially domestic public debt. Between 1990 and 1995 the share of debt service expenditures more than doubled, reaching levels similar to those prevailing in highly indebted developed market economies such as Belgium, Greece and Italy.

The growth of debt service expenditures is primarily the outcome of a high and increasing central government borrowing requirement. It also shows the switch in the financing of the fiscal deficit from the earlier cheap central bank loans and foreign public debt to the very costly domestic public debt. Since this shift was very rapid and was accompanied by high inflation, growing nominal interest rates and very volatile savings ratios, it resulted in an explosion of domestic interest expenditures. Unlike the developed economies, where public debt and interest expenditures mostly reflect earlier accumulated fiscal deficits, these interest expenditures were partly the outcome of the build-up of public debt unrelated to the PSBR, but associated with the assumption by the government of several microeconomic costs of transition (especially the cleaning of accumulated non-performing loans from the public banks' balance sheets, see chapter 8). The share of debt associated with this structural adjustment in the increase of the total consolidated domestic public debt is about 35 per cent.

The growing debt service expenditures also reflected the increase of amortisation expenditures (principal repayments) and the high real interest rate level at which the domestic public debt was rolled-over. The growth of amortisation expenditures is caused by rapidly increasing financing requirements and by an initially short-term maturity of domestic public debt. While in developed market economies principal expenditures are stable and do not put an additional pressure on the capital markets and governments, their growth had strong macroeconomic implications in Hungary as capital markets were initially closed and illiquid.

Besides interest expenditures there were two other areas which showed strong inertia. Administrative expenditures could not decline as public employment increased and nominal wages were not controlled, and social expenditures increased, reflecting the social costs of output decline and growing unemployment and a too generous social security provision.

The share of subsidies declined significantly as the majority of prices were liberalised. Some fiscal indicators (especially the current deficit), however, also reflect the fact that the share of public investments and capital expenditures declined even more. Therefore public capital investments – vital for the support of recovery of private investments[7] – were missing and the structure of fiscal expenditures shifted from the capital towards the current account, with a negative impact on the available capital stock.

The structural changes on the expenditure and revenue sides were accompanied by an increasing fiscal deficit. This growth had certain special features compared to other economies in transition, which can be revealed by looking at selected indicators of the fiscal balance. They differ from each other by the weight they attach to certain expenditure items (interest expenditures, principal repayment, capital expenditures).[8] The biggest increase occurred in the PSBR, which was simultaneously driven by the growth of the primary deficit and amortisation and interest expenditures. Its growth was followed by a smaller worsening of the GFS balance, which excludes amortisation payments. In order to determine the factors responsible for the growth of the fiscal deficit, we have to decompose it into the primary balance and interest expenditures (table 2.1). Principal repayment is indicated separately, to show what should be covered by the central government's high borrowing requirement.

The figures in table 2.1 reveal that the primary balance, which was in substantial surplus in 1990, worsened afterwards and stabilised at relatively modest levels. A small improvement was recorded in 1994 and a much more significant one in 1995 as a result of fiscal adjustment measures.

While the primary balance has gradually improved, both the interest and principal expenditures increased throughout the whole period. The growth of interest expenditures after the strong fiscal adjustment in 1995 was caused by their much greater increase due to high inflation and associated nominal interest rates and further growth of public debt, which outweighed the shift in the primary balance. Amortisation expenditures started to grow rapidly in 1993 due to the principal role of short-term government debt instruments in financing domestic public debt.[9]

Since after the initial corrective price explosion in 1991 inflation remained in a moderate range between 18 and 28 per cent, it had a significant impact on the fiscal balance and stance of fiscal policy. In order to see how the fiscal balance would have developed in the absence of inflation we use an operational deficit including the primary balance and real interest expenditures. The difference between the operational

Table 2.1. Changes in the different indicators of balance of central government, 1991–5 (percentage of GDP)

	1991	1992	1993	1994	1995
Revenues	**28.9**	**27.5**	**29.7**	**26.6**	**28.8**
Expenditures	**32.8**	**33.5**	**34.7**	**32.5**	**31.3**
Domestic repayment	0.6	0.7	0.7	1.6	2.5
Foreign repayment	0.2	0.2	0.1	0.4	0.4
Principal repayment	0.8	0.9	0.8	2.0	2.9
Interest payment	**3.8**	**5.9**	**4.6**	**6.9**	**8.6**
GFS balance	−3.8	−5.9	−4.9	−5.9	−2.5
PSBR	−4.6	−6.8	−5.7	−7.9	−5.4
Primary balance	−0.6	−0.03	−0.3	0.9	3.2
Current balance	−1.6	−3.6	−3.1	−4.2	−4.6
Operational balance		−4.2	−3.9	−2.6	1.3

Source: Own calculations.

balance and the PSBR shows the inflationary element of fiscal deficit. Table 2.1 shows that the impact of inflation on fiscal performance was substantial as the difference between the GFS and operational balance reflects the inflationary part of the nominal interest expenditures. But since the operational deficit itself is over 3 per cent of GDP, it shows that the fiscal stance was only partly determined by inflation and the high interest rate level.

Finally it is important to notice again the worsening of the current balance, which reflects the fiscal balance without investment expenditures. This shows that the share of investment expenditures declined and the increase of the fiscal imbalances was associated with the shift from investment towards consumption expenditures.

3   Factors affecting fiscal developments

After looking at the changes in the fiscal indicators, the factors contributing to this performance are analysed. Among them were some structural ones partly exogenous to fiscal policy related to the fiscal aspect of transition, such as the increase of the tax evading private sector, weakening of a tax compliance typical of planned economies and the growth of a 'black' economy accompanying privatisation. These factors were partly unavoidable, but they negatively affected government revenues and required simultaneous adjustment on the expenditure side.

Besides these structural changes, fiscal balances were initially influenced by the unfavourable macroeconomic developments related to the collapse of external markets and associated terms of trade losses, and rapid price and import liberalisation. This resulted in the sharp decline and slow recovery of recorded output and incomes, high corrective inflation followed by very strong inflation persistence and rigidity and increasing and high real interest rate levels. These factors, combined with the lack of fiscal adjustment, initially (1991–2) worsened the primary balance, and then (1993–5) contributed to the increase in interest expenditures. Fiscal developments were also heavily influenced by the heritage from the centrally planned period, mostly by the high foreign debt and the associated debt service payments.

Looking at the evolution of balances over time, transition brought in Hungary – as in other economies – an initial improvement in fiscal balances. This was associated with the collection of inflationary revenues due to the corrective inflation, with the temporary growth in enterprise profits due to the price liberalisation and with the regulations forcing the banking sector to show interest revenues due as actual income.[10]

After this temporary improvement in 1990, the years 1991–6 can be divided into three different periods. In 1992–3 there was a worsening primary balance accompanied by growing nominal interest expenditures, which produced a significant increase in the government's borrowing requirement. In 1993 and 1994 the primary balance turned from a slight deficit into a small surplus, while interest expenditures continued to increase, further weakening the adjustment achieved. Finally, unsustainable macroeconomic policies led in early 1995 to a sharp fiscal adjustment, which significantly increased the primary surplus and led to the improvement of all fiscal indicators.

The reasons for the worsening primary balance between 1990 and 1992 were partly related to factors prevailing in other transition economies. The liberalisation of prices and imports, the reduction of existing monetary overhang and the opening of the economy produced a rapid contraction of GDP. This initial revenue shock was deepened in 1991 by the collapse of the CMEA and its spillover effects and in 1992 by the introduction of bankruptcy regulations aimed at strengthening the financial discipline of the enterprise sector (see chapter 6). The corrective and later the persistent moderate inflation led to the Olivera–Tanzi effect on real tax revenues, which was only partly offset by the growing indirect revenues and the impact of fiscal drag. These and other factors also contributed to an increase in the 'black' economy (which produced in 1994–5 about 30 per cent of GDP on average, see chapter 5), which reduced the efficiency and equity of tax collection and created serious revenue losses.

Declining revenues were also associated with increasing primary expenditures, reflecting the impact of transition on unemployment, pension outlays and demand for other social expenditures. The increase of 'transition' expenditures was not offset by the adjustment of the inherited welfare and administrative costs and the rapid increase of both real expenditures and expenditure/GDP was accepted and financed by the growing public debt. Simultaneously with these factors increasing the primary deficit, its financing switched from direct monetary measures in the form of central bank credits to domestic debt measures, leading to increasing debt service expenditures.

From 1993 the primary deficit gradually began to improve and the slight deficit turned to a moderate surplus in 1994: this shift was caused by improving macroeconomic conditions without any fiscal adjustment. The economy started to recover from the post-stabilisation recession after mid-1993, led by the recovery of both industrial exports and public and private consumption. The recovery was also supported by soft macroeconomic policies, forcing down interest rates, leading to highly negative real returns in 1993, and allowing a 7 per cent increase in real incomes in 1994. The recovery lowered unemployment-related and other social expenditures, increased tax revenues (especially indirect ones as consumption increased rapidly), whereas the associated growth in import demand increased tariff revenues. Some of these changes favourable for the fiscal balance produced serious macroeconomic difficulties (increasing the current account deficit or lowering the savings ratios due to the forced reduction of domestic interest rates in 1993 and increasing consumption in 1994) and gradually started to highlight the unsustainability of domestic macroeconomic policy.

The improvement in the primary balance was accompanied by growing interest expenditures which more than offset the improvement. The growth of interest expenditures was partly caused by the shift in deficit financing: while the central bank at first financed the deficit with low-interest credits, after 1992 it was obliged to buy a predetermined and decreasing-term share of government bonds if the markets were unwilling to absorb their supply[11] and the PSBR was exclusively financed by interest-bearing domestic debt. This shift increased central bank independence, but led to increasing interest expenditures due to high borrowing requirements and a growing interest rate level.

After 1993 interest expenditures also increased due to the two-stage implementation of consolidation measures in the banking sector (see chapter 8). In the first stage the non-performing loans among the banks' assets were replaced by consolidation bonds, while in the second the banks were recapitalised by similar bonds in order to reach an 8 per cent capital:asset ratio (CAR). As the interest payments on these bonds were linked to market rates, this produced a significant increase in interest expenditures between 1993 and 1995 – almost 3 per cent of GDP.

While the factors described were the decisive ones in the accumulation of public debt and the growth of a fiscal deficit, the inconsistent fiscal measures and the lack of fiscal reforms also contributed to the worsening balance. In order to stabilise the deficit at a given level in the light of growing interest expenditures a more significant improvement in the primary balance would have been needed. The longer this adjustment was postponed, the bigger the inevitable change in the primary balance became. Another factor causing increasing fiscal problems was the repeated postponement of a public sector reform which should have resulted in the reduction of fiscal redistribution, rationalisation of welfare expenditures and reform of the administrative system. The lack of any public sector reform maintained the rigidity of the expenditure structure and brought an almost proportional increase in most expenditures.

The sustainability problems after the Mexican crisis led to the adoption of corrective measures in early 1995, requiring a huge shift in the fiscal balance. A stabilisation package aimed at correcting the deficit and reversing the accelerating inflation was introduced. The stabilisation programme included, after a substantial devaluation and the introduction of a temporary import surcharge, a switch from an adjustable peg to the preannounced crawling peg regime with the monthly rate of the crawl decreasing in 1995 and 1996. Tough incomes policies were also announced, leading to significant real wage decreases, and strict monetary and fiscal measures were introduced.

The fiscal stabilisation included both revenue- and expenditure-related measures. Among the revenue measures, a temporary import surcharge was introduced, some indirect taxes were adjusted and privatisation revenues were increasingly used to finance current expenditures. On the expenditure side several social security and welfare outlays were reduced and the rules governing access to them were adjusted, while the nominal expenditures of the central government were fixed, resulting in a more than 10 per cent real decline. These corrective measures increased the primary surplus by almost 2.5 per cent of GDP, and the GFS balance, which includes the privatisation revenues as current ones, declined from 5.6 per cent of GDP in 1994 to 2.9 per cent in 1995. If the privatisation revenues are excluded the correction was less, from 6.4 per cent of GDP in 1994 to 5.6 per cent of GDP in 1995. While also based on temporary factors, this correction signalled a reversal in fiscal policies, which was further strengthened a year later with more sizeable improvements in the fiscal balance.

4   The growth of public debt

Closely associated with the growing fiscal deficit there was a rapid accumulation of public debt leading to very high levels by international comparison. The increase of public debt simultaneously reflected the impact of fiscal imbalances, the initial lack of efficient debt management policies to deal with the increasing PSBR, the strong distortions on the market for government securities and the costly refinancing of the existing debt due to the generally high real interest rates. The growth of public debt was also stimulated by structural factors related to central government's assumption of the microeconomic costs of transition, while it was mitigated by privatisation revenues used to reduce accumulated debt. [12]

Since foreign public debt was issued by the central bank and re-lent to the central government, whereas domestic public debt was issued by the central government, the best available gross figure of public debt is the consolidated one which excludes the (non-market, basically interest-free) debt of the central government to the central bank. The structure of the growing consolidated public debt reveals some of the most important factors determining its more recent growth (see table 2.2).

While the government's gross debt increased by more than 20 percentage points of GDP, this was exclusively due to the growth of domestic public debt. The gross foreign debt of both the central bank and of the government did not change significantly between 1990 and 1995, although there were some fluctuations between individual years. While the foreign public debt increased only slightly, the domestic public debt grew with increasing speed from 3.6 per cent of GDP in 1990 to 24.5 per cent in 1995. This important structural change was related to the shift in financing the fiscal deficit from foreign to domestic public debt, as the country had by 1991 almost reached its external financing constraint. One could also observe changes in the structure of foreign public borrowing, as the share of the central government increased while that of the central bank declined.

Several factors explain these dynamics of debt accumulation. The first is related to the high PSBR, which put an increasing pressure on domestic capital markets, resulting in the rapid increase of interest-bearing domestic public debt. Another factor was the changing structure of deficit financing. Monetary financing and seigniorage revenues (amounting to 2.5–4 per cent of GDP in 1990–2) were the main source of deficit financing at the beginning of the transition.[13] Later this fell as its inflationary tax component declined with the reduction of inflation and

Table 2.2. The changes in consolidated public debt, 1990–5, HUF bn and percentage of GDP

	1990	1991	1992	1993	1994	1995
Gross consolidated public debt HUF bn	1,260.2	1,675.6	1,919.5	2,959.6	3,607.4	4,757.3
per cent of GDP	60.3	67.6	66.5	83.7	83.7	86.5
–Domestic public debt HUF bn	74.4	137.9	355.4	822.8	1,026.3	1,349.0
per cent of GDP	3.6	5.6	12.3	23.3	23.8	24.5
–Foreign public debt HUF bn	1,185.8	1,537.7	1,564.1	2,136.8	2,581.1	3,408.3
per cent of GDP	56.8	62.0	54.2	60.4	59.9	62.0
Gross debt of general government HUF bn	1,411.9	1,878.8	2,331.1	3,192.3	3,826.3	4,821.7
per cent of GDP	67.6	75.9	80.7	90.2	88.8	87.7
Gross foreign debt of NBH HUF bn	1,148.4	1,418.9	1,430.2	1,934.1	2,339.4	3,088.4
per cent of GDP	55.0	57.3	49.6	54.7	54.3	56.2

Source: NBH Yearly Report (1995).

gradual increase in money demand and legal constraints put a ceiling on direct financing of public debt by the central bank.

The main source of seigniorage revenues before transition was the accumulation of foreign liabilities by the central bank which was no longer a viable option in the 1990s. Therefore both the external financing constraint and the establishment of central bank independence forced the government to change deficit financing from monetary to domestic public debt measures. But this shift occurred just when nominal and real interest rate levels were high (although very volatile), domestic savings were low due to the weak savings propensity and strong currency substitution, and capital markets were distorted and under-developed, requiring the holders of public debt to pay a significant premium. It was not recognised by policy makers how rapidly the accumulation of public debt and the growth of interest expenditures could produce a snowball effect in interest expenditures.

Besides increasing the PSBR the growth of public debt was also stimulated by the financing of structural deficits associated with the economic transition by issuing domestic public debt. The government thus assumed some of the microeconomic costs of transition, the most important of which was the increase of bad loans in the commercial banks' portfolio, sharply worsening their flow and stock position.[14] The support given in the banking consolidation programmes amounted to almost 10 per cent of GDP and was an indirect subsidy given to the enterprise and banking sectors, appearing in the increase of public debt and associated interest expenditures instead of the primary balance. Both solutions were aimed at reducing current government expenditures and placing the burden of recapitalisation on future generations. While initially it seemed a cheap solution, it proved to be very costly due to the amounts involved, the high interest rate levels and the dependence of interest payments on these bonds on short-term interest rate developments as their returns were linked to returns on short-term Treasury bills. The high nominal interest rate levels in general and the inverted yield curve (leading to much higher returns on short-term securities) led to a rapid increase of interest expenditures related to consolidation efforts (table 2A.3, p. 47) equal to 2.5–3.5 per cent of GDP.

The growth of public debt was also stimulated by the under-developed nature of domestic capital markets, dominated by short-term savings due to high inflation and uncertainty, the risk aversion of domestic households and the lack of institutional investors with a long-term investment horizon. As liability and asset structures should match each other, this implied that short-term government securities dominated the market. Within domestic debt financing more than 50 per cent of financing in

1994 was done with Treasury bills and within them the market was also skewed towards shorter-term (one- and three-month) bonds.[15] This clearly increased interest and principal expenditures after the accumulated government debt.

A similar reflection of market imperfections was the yield structure of different debt instruments and the inappropriate risk:yield relation. There were two serious and costly distortions on the capital markets for public debt management. Unlike economies with developed capital markets, there was a reverse relationship between returns and risks: the almost riskless government securities had the highest yields.[16] Risk considerations were outweighed by financing requirements, while the market for private debt was very under-developed. The reverse relationship held between returns and risks: the yield curve was inverted because of high uncertainty, unfavourable expectations and the risk averse behaviour of savers prevented the emergence of a market for long-term government bonds, while on the short-term edge the financing requirements and the real returns in domestic currency determined the minimal interest rate level.

The accumulation of high public debt was also due to high interest rate levels. Real interest rates on domestic interest-bearing public debt were very volatile between 1990 and 1995, but in general they were highly positive.[17] In general the yields on government securities determined the market interest rates, which in turn influenced the costs of financing the PSBR.

Besides fiscal imbalances there were other partly exogenous fiscal policy factors contributing to high interest rate levels. One of them was the inability of economic policy to reduce inflation below 20 per cent for several years. This moderate inflation had strong inertial and expectational elements, its reduction was costly and strongly influenced nominal interest rate levels. Moderate inflation and inflation uncertainty contributed to currency substitution which was also influenced by the expected and unexpected depreciation of the currency. Currency substitution determined the minimal level of deposit interest rates which had grown considerably between 1992 and 1994 as exchange rate policy switched from nominal to real depreciation.

Apart from its impact through currency substitution the adjustable peg regime and the inconsistencies between macroeconomic policies and exchange rate developments led between mid-1993 and early 1995 to frequent speculative attacks against the domestic currency. These speculative attacks were associated with rapid increases in interest rates which were not followed with symmetric declines after the speculation ceased. This reflected attempts by the Central Bank to restrain the growth of money supply to avoid new attacks against the domestic currency, and the remaining lack of credibility of exchange rate policy. The exchange rate uncertainties and the increased risk premia were important factors affecting interest developments after 1993.

The switch from the adjustable peg to the preannounced crawling peg in early 1995 also had profound implications for interest rate developments. The forward-looking crawling peg regime established a lower threshold for interest rate levels determined by the international interest rate level, predetermined devaluation of the currency and the risk premium. But as domestic inflation and the monthly devaluation of the currency was still significant (although declining), a long time was needed to re-establish the credibility of macroeconomic policy, and this position did not change with the 1995 interest rate developments. In accordance with the experiences of exchange rate-based stabilisation domestic interest rates have converged only very slowly to a level consistent with arbitrage parities.

The final important factor influencing the interest rate level was the intention of the Central Bank again to follow a more restrictive policy from 1994. But as the capital account had been partly liberalised, the private sector tried to offset the decline in domestic credits by increasing its foreign borrowing which led to the growth of foreign liabilities of the private (both enterprise and banking) sector. While the capital inflows from mid-1994 did not require sterilisation measures of the amount observable in other transition economies (notably the Czech republic, Slovenia and Poland), the central bank had to reduce the liquidity of the banking system by increasing reserve requirements, reducing its active open market operations and increasing sales of government securities. These sterilisation measures increased both deposit and lending rates, which in turn influenced the interest rates on government debt.

It can be concluded that the growth of public debt was the result of several macroeconomic, institutional and structural factors. If we look at the sustainability equation relating the change in public debt to the primary balance, the difference between real economic growth and real interest rates and the seigniorage revenues, it may be concluded that all these factors contributed to its increase. Unlike the fiscal balances public debt increased further in 1995 and began to be stabilised only a year later. The main reason was that interest expenditure in 1995 partially offset the correction in the primary balance, which reduced the speed of debt correction. Several partly exogenous fiscal correction factors in 1995 increased both domestic and foreign public debt.

The growth of the public debt had very serious macroeconomic implications. It contributed to the increase in interest expenditures of the central government, putting strong pressure on the PSBR and creating a snowball effect in both the interest rate level and interest expenditures. Although high public debt did not bring the creditworthiness of the public sector into question and did not create the expectation of a possible default, it led to increasing interest premia. Whereas there are other countries with much higher public debt, and different levels of public debt may be sustainable depending on long-term growth prospects, both the level and especially the dynamics of debt accumulation brought the long-term sustainability of the fiscal policy into question.

Another problem of the growing public debt was that with unchanged fiscal policies it could be sustained only by increasing seigniorage revenues with a strong inflationary impact. As the difference between real economic growth and real interest rates remained significant and negative in the absence of adjustment in the primary balance, the debt burden could be reduced only by renewed resort to inflationary finance. This occurred partly in Hungary in 1995 when the debt:GDP rate was stabilised as much by the reversal in the primary balance as by the higher inflation and nominal GDP growth.

Finally the real burden of high public debt was deepened by the decline of the public sector's assets as a result of privatisation. While privatisation revenues could be used only to retire part of the existing debt, the depletion of public assets led to the worsening of the net worth indicator, which indicates that asset sales would no longer be a viable solution to stabilise the debt:GDP ratio.

5   Macroeconomic impact of the growing fiscal deficit

There have been widespread disputes regarding the macroeconomic consequences of increased fiscal deficits. Some (Kornai, 1995; Erdős, 1995) argued that the growth of fiscal deficits was responsible for the persistence of inflation, increase in the current account deficit and net foreign debt and inconsistent monetary and fiscal policies. Others (Oblath, 1995; Mellár, 1995) said that the increase of fiscal deficits had been due to exogenous, inherited factors, and that the macroeconomic problems were not the consequences but the causes of current fiscal issues.[18] This reversed causation was said to occur because of the structural features of the deficit analysed above: interest expenditures increased while the primary balance was in surplus.

This chapter now tries to clarify some of the more contradictory consequences of fiscal deficit and increasing public debt. Fiscal policies and the growing deficit have strongly influenced price developments. The initial worsening of the primary balance was associated with corrective inflation caused by a subsidy reduction which was smaller in Hungary than in other transition economies due to earlier price and import liberalisation. Deficit financing also had inflationary consequences. While the bulk of financing was through domestic debt, monetary financing also remained significant due to the Central Bank's obligation to purchase a predetermined but gradually declining amount of the domestic public debt issued. This monetary financing made the effective regulation of money supply very uncertain and produced inflationary outcomes.[19] Moreover the rather soft stance of monetary policy between 1990 and 1993 allowed the banking sector (through the increase of net lending from the Central Bank to the commercial banks) to accumulate government bonds and therefore the Central Bank could indirectly contribute further to the financing of the PSBR.

There were two other inflationary impacts of the increasing fiscal deficit. The growth of primary expenditures was partly financed by tax increases which – especially in the case of rapidly growing indirect taxes – had a strong impact on inflation. Fiscal expenditures predominantly fall on the non-tradables sector, which leads to real exchange rate appreciation due to the excess demand created. The real exchange rate was already appreciating due to equilibrium changes (Halpern and Wyplosz, 1995) and exchange rate adjustments did not compensate for international and domestic price differences (Oblath and Csermely, 1995). The growing fiscal deficit strengthened this impact which was then reversed in 1994 by severe devaluation, with a strong impact on inflation. Simultaneously with their inflationary impact, fiscal deficits widened the already existing gap between consumer and producer price indices. Besides factors exogenous to fiscal policy,[20] this gap was influenced by the increase of indirect taxes. On the other hand fiscal expenditures fell mainly on the non-tradables sector where the increase in demand led to relatively high price increases compared with the tradables sector. As the CPI reflects price developments in the non-tradable sector (since it includes service products as well), while the PPI that in tradables, this contributed to the widening gap between them.[21]

A controversial impact of the fiscal deficit was related to its effect on domestic aggregate demand and the external balance. In an inflationary environment the direct demand impact of fiscal policy is captured by the operational deficit which takes into consideration the primary balance and the government's real interest expenditures. It excludes from the demand impact the inflationary component of interest payments which simply offset capital losses due to inflation and do not affect aggregate demand if there is no money illusion. Due to the particular structure of foreign debt accumulation and current foreign public debt service by the central bank, this direct demand impact in Hungary is captured by the primary balance and interest payments paid by the government to domestic government debt holders outside the NBH. This measure also assumes that there is no money illusion and that in an inflationary environment only real interest expenditures matter.

Measured in these terms, the contribution of the fiscal deficit to the growth of domestic demand and trade deficit gradually declined after 1991. This was due to the improving primary balance, while real interest expenditures did not significantly affect the change in this modified operational deficit measure. The demand impact according to this measure was modest except in 1991 and 1992. But in determining the precise amount of the demand impact one should also look more closely at the structure of domestic public debt. The accumulation of public debt was only partly related to financing the fiscal deficit with domestic interest-bearing debt, and partly also reflected the issue of domestic debt to cover the costs of banking consolidation. This was a subsidy provided to the banking sector and the recipients of consolidation bonds were not saving from their disposable incomes.

Interest incomes thus did not compensate past savings efforts, but provided new revenues and thus interest revenues contributed not only to a significant part of domestic demand but – depending on the savings propensity of holders of consolidation bonds – also to nominal interest revenues covering capital losses due to inflation. Since the savings propensity of holders of consolidation bonds was low (considering their public ownership, moral hazard issues, short-term planning horizons, etc.), the contribution of interest revenues to this part of the public debt was closer to its nominal than its real value. Therefore the actual contribution of the fiscal deficit to domestic demand was above the levels indicated by conventional measures and reached 2–3 per cent of GDP in the years before the fiscal correction. This demand impact can be regarded as significant.

One may therefore find a much closer link between fiscal imbalances and inflation, exchange rate and interest developments, and changes in the current account and trade balances, although other factors exogenous to fiscal policy also contributed to these macroeconomic developments.

Another disputed impact of the growing fiscal deficit is related to its impact on the crowding-out of private investments. Some (Oblath, 1995; Mellár, 1995) argued that the growth of the fiscal deficit did not lead to the crowding-out of private investments since investment propensity was low and the high nominal and real interest rates had been more the outcome of macroeconomic developments and policy changes exogenous to fiscal policy. The growth of the fiscal deficit was also (Mellár, 1995) said to have resulted in an increase of domestic savings which were financing the increased demand for loanable funds from the government.

But the possible crowding-out impact of the fiscal deficit was more complex. In the period between 1990 and 1992 there was no significant crowding-out of private investments. The increase in the fiscal deficit was associated with the rapid growth of domestic savings which fully matched the demand for loanable funds from the central government and the rapidly declining demand of the enterprise sectors. Besides that, interest rates were driven more by the changes in the portfolio of commercial banks, the increasing gap between lending and deposit interest rates and the impact of underlying and expected inflation. Finally the interest sensitivity of private investments was low, since they were determined more by output and profitability collapse and less by interest rate changes.

But the impact of the fiscal deficit on private investments changed significantly after 1993, and a strong crowding-out impact could be observed. All of the factors mentioned changed the other way. After the surprising increase in domestic savings, savings ratios declined rapidly after 1992 and reached values more characteristic of the 1980s. The supply of domestic savings was far less than the growing public sector financing requirement while the demand for loanable funds from the enterprise sector started to grow very rapidly after 1993, reflecting the recovery of private investments.

On the other hand increasing fiscal deficits started to exert a strong impact on interest rates. Both the level and especially the variation of interest rates were heavily influenced by the government's financing requirements. These high financing requirements widened further the gap – already existing due to the increased reserve requirements of the banks against their worsening portfolio and the central bank's heavy implicit taxation of financial intermediation – between the deposit and lending interest rates, both in nominal and in real terms. This simultaneously weakened savings propensities and led to higher lending rates.

The government's high financing requirements resulted both in growing domestic interest rates and in the use of domestic loanable funds. Looking at the composition of banking sector credits, it can be seen that the commercial banks almost exclusively financed the fiscal deficit. The share of credits extended to the central government more than doubled between 1990 and 1994 while those to the enterprise sector increased by less than 30 per cent, creating a very significant real decline.

The strong crowding-out impact of government financing needs led to the increase of foreign borrowing by the enterprise and commercial banking sector. In 1991 and 1992 the growth of savings was sufficient to cover the central government's and the private sector's domestic borrowing requirements, but from 1993 onwards savings were insufficient to meet the increased demand. This resulted in growing external borrowing which increased significantly in 1993 and 1994 and was responsible for the growth of gross foreign debt. The result of substituting monetary and external debt financing by domestic debt financing was a changing composition of external debt as foreign private debt increased while public debt declined. The private sector was forced to accumulate external liabilities even if domestic terms were not worse than external ones, since it was almost completely crowded-out by the financing requirements of the central government.

Besides declining savings propensities and the strengthening impact of the fiscal deficit on interest rates, the interest sensitivity of private investments significantly increased. This may be seen from the changing composition of domestic and foreign loans in investment financing, explained primarily by interest differences. These changes in savings propensities, the interest sensitivity of private investments and changes in the impact of deficits on interest rates show that the crowding-out impact of the growing fiscal deficit became very significant after 1993. The growing fiscal deficit had an adverse impact on the efficiency and credibility of the monetary policy pursued. The high financing requirements of the central government were not met on the domestic market and this resulted in a significant – and, contrary to initial assumptions, not declining – resort to financing from the Central Banks. The obligation of the Central Bank to purchase a given amount of government bonds reduced its independence and created difficulties for liquidity management.

The Central Bank had to follow a restrictive monetary policy to reduce the high and unsustainable current account deficit and inflation. In order to achieve this goal in the light of high government financing it had to reduce the liquidity of the domestic banking sector, primarily by reducing the refinancing facilities and repurchase agreements provided by the Central Bank to commercial banks. At the same time the Central Bank increased reserve ratios and kept the interest paid after domestic and foreign currency denominated deposits far below the market average. This produced significant revenues for the central bank, reflected in an increasing contribution of its profits to the budget.

While the increase of implicit taxation of the commercial banks proved to be more efficient in reducing domestic liquidity than other measures,[22] it also produced unexpected and unfavourable outcomes. It maintained the high spread between deposits and lending rates since this high implicit taxation increased the costs of intermediation for the banks. Moreover the associated increase of domestic interest rates stimulated foreign borrowing by both domestic commercial banks and enterprises. But when this borrowing reached a significant amount due to both strong crowding-out and implicit taxation of the banking sector, it weakened the efficiency of monetary policy, since inflows of foreign capital offset the decline of the domestic component of money supply. The efficiency of monetary policy was weakened not only by direct financing of the deficit but also because of implicit taxation of the commercial banks.

One positive impact of the growing public debt on monetary policy was the development of liquid markets in government securities which made it relatively easy for the Central Bank to implement its open market operations.

6   The reduction of the fiscal deficit and stabilisation of public debt

Due to the high share of interest expenditures in the fiscal balance the stabilisation of public debt and the reduction of the fiscal deficit were closely related issues. As interest expenditures were partially exogenously determined, the reduction of fiscal deficit and the stabilisation of the debt:GDP ratio required immediate changes in the primary balance. Based on the sustainability equation of the public debt, there were four options which could be used if the government was to stabilise the debt:GDP ratio in a non-inflationary way:

(1) the primary balance had to be improved
(2) the real interest rate level had to be reduced
(3) the rate of real economic growth had to be increased
(4) public debt had to be retired by the sale of public assets.

The increase of seigniorage revenues was less readily available to stabilise the debt:GDP ratio. The Act on the National Bank was planned to be modified and the purchase of government bonds by the Central Bank on the primary market was to be disallowed, it being authorised to purchase these papers only through its open market operations.

The second source of seigniorage revenues – the increase of tax on financial intermediation – was also less readily available due to its already considerable extent and its unfavourable macroeconomic consequences (the growth of net foreign debt, increasing inflation and domestic interest rate level, etc.). Therefore, the Central Bank started to refrain from increasing this tax, which was reflected in the significant increase of interest rates paid on the compulsory reserves of banks and later in the gradual decline of reserve requirements. The stabilisation of public debt therefore required adjustment in the primary balance and reduction of the gap between real economic growth and high real interest rates. Besides that, further financing of structural costs of the transition by issuing public debt had be stopped and additional revenues realised to retire a portion of the public debt.

There was a sequence of measures that would produce the required improvement as stabilisation of the debt:GDP ratio should begin with the improvement of the primary balance. This was due to the relatively slow convergence of real economic growth and real interest rate levels in the short run. The growth of real GDP was restrained by supply-side factors such as high public expenditures, the distortions and disincentives produced by the tax system and high inflation and unfavourable expectations, and the significant gap between real returns on investments and domestic government securities.

Meanwhile the real interest rates were to decline only gradually even if disinflation had continued and the newly introduced crawling peg regime had proved to be credible and successful in reducing the built-in country risk element. This was due to the restrictive stance of monetary policy to improve the current account and sterilise the impact of growing foreign borrowings, to the slow convergence of domestic interest rates to levels consistent with parity conditions because of market distortions, a gradually declining PSBR, slow improvements in the credibility of the exchange rate regime and volatile savings rates.

All these factors predicted a slow decline in the gap between real economic growth and real interest rates. This was to produce an increasing debt service burden and put most of the required fiscal adjustment on the primary balance. In the light of the accumulated debt and predicted real interest rate developments a primary surplus of the government equal to 3–3.5 per cent of GDP was required to begin the stabilisation of the public debt:GDP ratio. This target was partly met in 1995 and almost fully a year later when the government recorded a primary surplus of 4 per cent of GDP.

The adjustment in the primary balance greatly contributed to the reduction of the PSBR, mitigated the pressures on interest rates and the crowding-out impact of deficit financing. Another important element of fiscal adjustment and debt stabilisation was the use of the huge privatisation revenues for the retirement of existing foreign public debt. These privatisation revenues were realised at the end of 1995 and were used for debt reduction in 1996. The inflow of privatisation revenues did not therefore affect the debt and balance figures for 1995, but was reflected a year later in the sizeable decline of both external net and gross public debt. Moreover the use of privatisation proceeds for debt reduction reduced the interest expenditures and had a long-term beneficial effect on public finances.

The other two elements of debt consolidation were not favourable in 1995 as a strong fiscal adjustment had been associated with the weakening of output recovery observed in 1994. This weakening was not very significant, however, which is consistent with international experience (Calvo and Végh, 1993) with exchange rate-based stabilisation programmes which were associated with rather good output performance. On the other hand, interest developments were even worse in 1995 than predicted, as in the second half of 1995 they stabilised at very high levels and did decline until early 1996 when the renewed commitment to the crawling peg regime and the inflow of privatisation revenues increased the chance of a more positive outcome. The slow convergence of domestic interest rates to the levels consistent with parity conditions was due to the low initial credibility of stabilisation policy, a huge PSBR associated with only gradually increasing private savings, the restrictive stance of monetary policy and the very high degree of sterilisation of foreign capital inflows.

The adjustment in the primary balance established the preconditions for the stabilisation of the debt:GDP ratio. Simultaneously with the improvement in the primary balance other measures were required to reduce the gap between real GDP growth and real interest rate levels. There was some scope for economic policy to reduce the high real interest rate levels in general, and the interest rates paid after public debt in particular.

A crucial factor in interest rate developments was the behaviour of the exchange rate and the credibility of the anti-inflationary policy pursued. If the crawling peg regime is consistent with the changes in inflation and succeeds in reducing expectations, then it supports the decline of nominal and real interest rate levels. If the expected devaluation does not cover the inflationary differentials then the risk premium will remain high and, as in the adjustable peg regime, speculation may emerge to produce interest premia.

Some other measures reduced the interest rates on public debt as the market imperfections were addressed by matching the risks and returns on different securities more closely and eliminating the inverted yield curve. This was achieved by the gradual increase of maturities of government bonds, more direct reliance on household and institutional investors, and much closer integration of domestic capital markets with international ones.

While initially the burden of fiscal correction fell on the primary balance, in the long run the recovery of GDP and the decline of both nominal and real interest rate levels should help to stabilise the debt:GDP ratio. At the same time it seems inevitable that, at least for a couple of years, a high primary surplus will be required in order to maintain the credibility of fiscal and monetary policies and to avoid any future increased reliance on domestic debt growth.

7   Conclusions

This chapter has analysed the causes and consequences of the rapid increase in both public debt and fiscal deficit in Hungary in the course of the transition to a market economy. The main findings of the chapter and the policy lessons from Hungarian fiscal policy are as follows:

(1) Hungary inherited a very unfavourable fiscal situation from the centrally planned system. The main element was the high external foreign debt, which put a significant burden on fiscal policy in the form of debt service expenditures. To meet this requirement the well known double transfer of resources had to be carried out. At the same time, Hungary had already started to reform its tax system and reduce subsidies in the course of the price liberalisation before transition. Therefore less room remained for an initial rapid adjustment of the primary balance in the course of transition through the reduction of subsidies and introduction of a tax system more characteristic of market economies.[23] The reduction of subsidies and the introduction of new taxes in the late 1980s was not used to produce fiscal adjustment but to finance inefficient welfare systems and other public expenditures.

(2) The macroeconomic and microeconomic consequences of economic transition produced very unfavourable fiscal outcomes. The rapid decline of GDP, the increase of unemployment and the 'black' economy associated with privatisation and the spread of the private sector, the inability to monitor that sector's income growth and the rigid, moderate inflation put an increasing burden on fiscal policies. Since these macroeconomic trends coincided with the assumption of the microeconomic costs of transition, they had strong and long-term fiscal implications.

(3) These fiscal difficulties were aggravated by the rapid shift from monetary and external financing of the fiscal deficit to domestic debt financing. While this produced positive macroeconomic results and was inevitable to increase the independence of the Central Bank, this shift occurred when the macroeconomic conditions for debt financing were not very favourable. The shift from monetary to domestic debt financing was therefore accompanied by growing

nominal and real interest rates and strong crowding-out of private investments.

Moreover, the rapid switch from money to domestic debt financing produced developments similar to Sargent–Wallace's arithmetic, as the increasing interest expenditures of the central government prevented the central bank from reducing direct monetary financing. The rapid increase of interest expenditures following the switch from money to domestic debt financing maintained direct monetary financing above the levels targeted and prescribed by law, and increased indirect financing by soft monetary policies and credit growth passed from the Central Bank to the domestic banks to enable them to finance domestic public debt growth. Domestic debt financing also created serious distortions on the capital markets. The financing requirements were so high that the accumulation of foreign debt continued, but by the private sector crowded-out from domestic markets.

(4) These factors were responsible for the increased fiscal burden, but fiscal problems were deepened by the lack of fiscal adjustment. Fiscal policies were not directed at adjusting to the new burdens but remained passive and allowed the rapid build-up of fiscal deficit and public debt. The longer the fiscal adjustment was postponed, the bigger the adjustment required in the primary and the full balance. Between 1990 and 1994 Hungary was an example of repeated inconsistent and failed attempts at fiscal adjustment, which did not bring a solution but only increased the resistance to ultimately inevitable measures.

(5) Another important development was the accumulation of public debt which was only partly related to the fiscal imbalances and difficulties of deficit financing already mentioned. It grew as the government assumed certain microeconomic costs of the transition by issuing government bonds. Contrary to initial expectations these measures proved to be very costly and created a continuous financing requirement for the government. The absence of fiscal adjustment then resulted in an unsustainably rapid growth of public debt. This Hungarian experience shows the dynamics of debt accumulation if the main elements of the sustainability equation lead to debt growth, and the appropriate dampening policies are missing.

(6) The macroeconomic consequences of an increasing fiscal deficit are similar to those prevailing in other economies having problems with their budget. High fiscal deficits and public debt contributed to increasing and high nominal interest rates and interest rate spreads and inflation persistence after 1993, the crowding-out of domestic

private investments and an increasing foreign indebtedness of the private sector. Fiscal problems also weakened the efficiency and credibility of monetary policy and contributed to the collapse of the adjustable peg regime. On the other hand these macroeconomic problems strengthened the snowball effect of growth in interest expenditures.

(7) The stabilisation of the public debt:GDP ratio and the improvement of the fiscal balance was closely related to and required measures affecting both the primary balance and interest expenditures. In the short term the burden of adjustment fell on the primary balance as the gap between real economic growth and real interest rates declined only gradually, and no more seigniorage revenues were available for deficit financing. Interest developments moreover hindered the reduction of the PSBR as they increased considerably after the implementation of fiscal adjustment and declined only gradually thereafter. Moreover, fiscal adjustment was hampered by the by-product of stabilisation success: increased inflows of foreign capital, creating renewed inflation pressures and high fiscal and quasi-fiscal costs of sterilisation policies.

(8) The experience of Hungary shows that excessive deficits and rapid public debt accumulation should be avoided in transition economies. These developments may result in very unfavourable macroeconomic imbalances and may seriously reduce the credibility of economic policies and policy makers: these outcomes can be observed in developed market economies, but they are magnified in a typical transition economy where the capital markets are under-developed, the planning horizon of economic agents is very short-term and the openness of economies is still rather restricted.

While fiscal policies are also influenced by political economic assumptions, the costs of postponing fiscal adjustments are higher than those of allowing the deficit to mount. All these considerations underline the importance of following balanced and prudent fiscal policies in transition economies.

Appendix 2.1: structural financial data, 1990–5

Table 2A.1. Changes in the structure of revenues of the central government, 1990–5 (per cent)

	1990	1991	1992	1993	1994	1995
Corporate sector tax and tariff payments	40.2	27.8	24.2	22.0	22.0	24.1
Tax on financial institutions	7.6	6.2	0.2	1.1	3.1	1.0
Consumption-related taxes (consumption and VAT)	39.8	4 0.0	43.2	44.1	42.0	39.2
Household taxes	9.7	18.6	20.2	24.1	22.0	19.7
Revenues related to debt service	–	4.5	6.7	6.1	8.1	12.9

Source: MoF (1995).

Table 2A.2. Changes in the structure of expenditures of central government, 1990–5 (per cent of total expenditures)

	1990	1991	1992	1993	1994	1995
Enterprise subsidies	10.9	6.8	5.5	5.0	7.1	5.6
Consumer subsidies	5.7	5.1	1.9	2.1	2.1	1.9
Investment expenditures	8.6	6.6	6.8	5.2	5.0	6.3
Support to social security funds	-	11.6	11.5	11.1	13.1	11.8
Support of central government institutions	29.3	24.5	24.4	23.1	26.1	21.7
Support of local government	17.6	23.0	22.6	23.2	20.1	18.5
Debt service	11.0	16.6	19.2	16.3	24.5	29.1

Source: MoF (1995).

Table 2A.3. Interest expenditures of the central government, 1990–5 (per cent of GDP)

	1990	1991	1992	1993	1994	1995
Deficit financing	**1.7**	**2.2**	**3.1**	**3.1**	**3.9**	**5.0**
NBH credit	1.5	1.9	1.8	1.3	1.1	0.9
Treasury bills	0.1	0.2	0.9	0.9	1.3	1.9
Bonds	1.0	0.1	0.4	0.8	1.5	2.2
Other obligations	**1.0**	**1.4**	**2.2**	**1.4**	**2.7**	**3.6**
NBH credits	0.9	1.3	1.1	0.7	0.6	0.5
Bonds	0	0	1.1	0.6	2.0	3.1
Gross interest expenditure	**2.7**	**3.6**	**5.3**	**4.4**	**6.6**	**8.6**

Source: NBH (1995).

NOTES

1 These favourable shocks were mostly associated with the separation of these two economies from the former federal states of Czechoslovakia and Yugoslavia, where they were both net contributors to the federal budgets with the yearly amounts reaching several per cent of GDP.

2 In 1995 and 1996 the rapid decline in redistribution was due to the fiscal correction as fiscal expenditures remained constant in nominal terms when consumer prices increased by 29.0 and 24.5 per cent, respectively, and to the rapid increase of nominal GDP.

3 The share of the government in GDP in 1994 in Poland and the Czech republic was 49.5 per cent, in Slovenia 47.3 per cent, in Portugal 52.2 per cent and in Spain 44.6 per cent of their respective GDP, while the OECD average was 41 per cent.

4 The high redistribution:GDP ratio was also due to the 20 per cent loss of GDP between 1990 and 1993. Unlike the expenditure side, redistribution declined rapidly on the revenue side and stabilised at a much lower level, creating a huge gap between revenues and the level of expenditure.

5 While direct tax revenues declined sharply, the indirect taxation of commercial banks in the form of high reserve requirements – remunerated below the market returns – remained very significant.

6 This reflected high marginal personal income tax rates, strong reliance on fiscal drag (due to the missing indexation of tax brackets) and reduction of loopholes in the tax system.

7 The close relation between private and public capital formation and the crowding-in impact of certain public investments (infrastructure, services) on private ones is analysed in Solimano and Serven (1993) and Easterly *et al.* (1994).

8 A detailed breakdown of fiscal indicators can be found in Blejer and Cheasty (1993).

9 Amortisation expenditures increased in 1995 to 3.1 per cent of GDP and more than fourfold between 1993 and 1995. In 1995 all debt service expenditures reached 12 per cent of GDP.

10 The taxation of non-realised banking incomes later became an especially serious problem since their growth coincided with the increasing amount of non-performing loans in the banking sector's portfolio. The banks had to pay increasing taxes instead of building reserves against their non-performing loans, which would have mitigated the sharp impact of bankruptcy regulations introduced in 1992 on the banks' flow and stock position.

11 The amount of central bank financing was linked to the revenues of central government. According to the Act on National Banks the amount of domestic debt that could initially be purchased by the central bank was 5 per cent of revenues, declining gradually to 3 per cent in 1994. The actual amount was much higher in 1994 (by almost 50 per cent) than allowed by the law, as the central government financing requirement far exceeded the supply of loanable funds from domestic savings.

12 The growth of public debt in a simple sustainability analysis (Blanchard *et al.*, 1990; Buiter, 1985) depends on the current primary deficit adjusted for seigniorage revenues and public debt accumulated in the past. The current debt:GDP ratio is then:

$$B1 = (r - n)B0 + (Pd - S) \tag{1}$$

where

B = public debt:GDP
Pd = primary balance in GDP
S = seigniorage revenues in GDP
r = real interest rate level
n = real rate of economic growth

Applying this equation to Hungary it should be modified to include the impact of debt accumulation not related to fiscal deficit but to other obligations (microeconomic costs of transition) assumed by the government and the privatisation revenues used for the amortisation of public debt. The equation then changes to

$$B1 = (r - n)B0 + (Pd - S) + Ndd - Pr \qquad (2)$$

where

Ndd = share of public debt not related to fiscal deficit in GDP
Pr = privatisation revenues used for debt reduction

13 The role of seigniorage revenues in formerly centrally planned economies and the first years of transition was extensively discussed in Hanousek and Tuma (1994) and Oblath and Valentinyi (1993).

14 This increase in non-performing loans had profound fiscal implications as well, since important tax revenues from the banking sector were not realised.

15 While Treasury bills are used in developed economies to offset seasonal differences between expenditures and revenues, they participated very actively in Hungary in the financing of the government's borrowing requirement.

16 These high nominal returns were associated in 1993 and 1994 with even higher after-tax returns as tax concessions were granted after savings in government debt instruments.

17 There were exceptions to this general behaviour in some periods, such as between mid-1992 and the first quarter of 1993 when the NBH tried artificially to reduce the interest rate level, leading to negative real returns on both deposits and government securities. But the gap between the government's financing requirements and the supply of loanable funds produced a very strong counter movement in real interest rates from mid-1993.

18 For example, the high current account deficit reflecting significant interest payments on the accumulated foreign debt led to increasing interest expenditures of the central government, the high inflation was responsible for the increase of nominal interest rates and thus debt service expenditures, and the slow recovery widened the gap between primary revenues and government expenditures.

19 This was not always the case, since in 1992 and 1993 one could observe a significant increase in the money demand which partly neutralised the inflationary consequences of relaxed monetary policies.

20 There were several factors that explain the relatively significant gap between producer and consumer prices in almost all transition economies. The most important are the rapid increase of the service sector, the introduction of current account convertibility and import liberalisation which restricted price increases in the tradables but not in the non-tradables sector, and the productivity differences in these two sectors.

21 The gap between the two indices was significant between 1990 and 1994 but practically disappeared in 1994 and 1995 as producer prices grew rapidly, reflecting supply-side price shocks.

22 In 1994 the liquidity regulation was not in accordance with initial goals because while open market operations reduced liquidity, foreign exchange swaps resulted in a higher than expected increase in domestic liquidity.
23 In this respect it is important to note that the introduction of value added taxes in both the Czech republic and Poland contributed to the improvement of the fiscal balance.

REFERENCES

Barbone, L. and N. Marchetti (1995) 'Economic transformation and the fiscal crisis', Washington, DC: World Bank

Blanchard, O., J.-C. Chouraqui, R.P. Hagemann and N. Sartor (1990) 'The sustainability of fiscal policy: new answers to an old question', *OECD Economic Studies*, **15** (Autumn)

Blejer, M. and A. Cheasty (1993) 'How to measure the fiscal deficit', Washington, DC: International Monetary Fund

Buiter, W. (1985) 'A guide to public sector debt and deficit', *Economic Policy* (November)

Calvo, G.A. and C. Végh (1993) 'Exchange rate based stabilization under imperfect credibility', in H. Frosch and A. Wörgötter (eds.), *Open-economy Macroeconomics*, London: Macmillan

Dedák, I. (1995) 'Seigniorage or debt or money financing of fiscal deficit?', Institute of Economics, Budapest (August), mimeo

Dornbusch, R. (1991) 'Policies to move from stabilisation to growth', in Proceedings of the World Bank Annual Conference on Development Economics, Washington, DC

Easterly, W., C. Rodriguez and K. Schmidt-Hebbel (1994) *Public Sector Deficits and Macroeconomc Performance*, Oxford: Oxford University Press

Erdős, T. (1995) 'A tartós gazdasági növekedés realitásai és akadályai' (The reality and constraints of long-term economic growth), *Közgazdasági Szemle*, **1995/7**

Halpern, L. and C. Wyplosz (1995) 'Equilibrium exchange rates in transition economies', *IMF Staff Papers*, **44(4)** 430–60

Hanousek, M. and Z. Tuma (1994) 'Seigniorage revenues in transition economies', *CERGE Working Paper*, Prague

Kornai, J. (1995) 'A magyar gazdaságpolitika dilemmái' (Dilemmas of Hungary's economic policy), *Közgazdasági Szemle*, **1995/7–8**

Mellár, T. (1995) 'A költségvetési deficit és az államadósság felhalmozódása' (The accumulation of fiscal deficit and public debt), *Bankszemle*, **1995/10**

Oblath, G. (1995) 'A költségvetési deficit makrogazdasági hatásai Magyarországon' (Macroeconomic impact of fiscal deficits in Hungary), *Külgazdaság*, **1995/7–8**.

Oblath, G. and A. Csermely (1995) 'Exchange rate policy and exchange rate regimes in selected economies in transition', Budapest, mimeo.

Oblath, G. and Á. Valentinyi (1993) 'Seigniorage és inflációs adó – néhány makroökonómiai összefügés magyarországi alkalmazása' (Seigniorage and inflation tax – Hungarian application of certain macroeconomic relationships), *Közgazdasági Szemle*, **1993/10**, 11

Solimano, A. and L. Serven (1993) 'Striving for growth after adjustment', Washington, DC: World Bank

Tanzi, V. (1992) 'Fiscal policies in economies in transition', Washington, DC: International Monetary Fund

Discussion

DAVID BEGG

Chapter 2 is a nice contribution to an important topic. I agree with its three central premises, namely that fiscal difficulties are prevalent in transition; that they are not only significant in their own right but also the source of many problems in other aspects of transition; and that these difficulties were manifested acutely in Hungary, whose experience is of interest both in particular and in general.

The first section of the chapter catalogues the period of fiscal deterioration during 1990–5. It is a familiar cocktail with a few Hungarian twists. The familiar components are reluctance to abandon generous welfare spending, erosion of tax revenues through a lower tax base and problems of compliance, learning how to depend less on seigniorage and the inflation tax, fiscal liabilities incurred through accumulation of bad debts in the bank, subsequently written off by government, and unnecessary delay in acknowledging the fiscal deterioration of the public finances and the need for fiscal adjustment.

What are the Hungarian twists? First, the high level of inherited government debt which, being denominated in foreign currency, could not simply be inflated away. Gáspár demonstrates clearly the continuing burden that this imposed. The early exhaustion of the capacity to borrow abroad then forced the government to borrow at home, in a limited pool of saving and with a large risk premium, compounding the fiscal problem.

The appropriate measure of the differential burden of borrowing at home and abroad is not of course the interest differential but rather the deviation from uncovered interest parity. Since the Forint was being steadily devalued during this period, simple interest differentials vastly over-state the true excess cost of borrowing at home. Although it is true that, properly measured, Hungary did indeed face a larger cost *ex post* in borrowing at home rather than abroad, two points should be made. First, some *ex ante* risk premium may have been appropriate. Second, Hungary's deviation from interest parity was in fact smaller than that in many other transition economies. The burden on the debt therefore owes more to the inability to inflate away the initial debt, and refusal to enter negotiations with international creditors to reduce the burden of this foreign debt, than it does to the interest rates subsequently paid.

A second Hungarian twist was the recurring sequence of banking clean-

ups, each new round being undertaken despite the failure of banks to
meet assurances, even conditions, associated with the previous round.
Gáspár tells us that the cumulative fiscal cost of bailing out the banks
was around 10 per cent of GDP. Perhaps it is unkind to single out
Hungary: country after country has experienced recalcitrant problems
associated with bad debts and poor corporate governance. Since
Hungary simultaneously had tough, even draconian, bankruptcy legislation, this may also have contributed to the problem; if so, it shows yet
again that brave steps in a single dimension rarely succeed if the rest of
the policy package is less sound.

A third element of the Hungarian twist, and here there can be little
disagreement, is the softly, softly policy that characterised the pace of
early reform. A government treading gingerly on structural adjustment,
overtly fearful of unemployment, and with the avowed policy of frequent
devaluation to prevent significant changes in the real exchange rate is one
unlikely to achieve either monetary and fiscal discipline or significant
supply-side improvement via productivity growth. And all this despite
remaining the number one European transition economy in receipt of
private FDI. The evolution Gáspár documents does nothing to elucidate
the benefits of gradualism.

The nettle was grasped finally in March 1995; Gáspár seems to imply
that the recent example of crisis in Mexico may have confirmed
Hungarian resolve. Certainly, since that date Hungary has been a
country transformed. The twin deficits were tackled by what had become
increasingly conventional medicine: sharp fiscal adjustment, initial
devaluation immediately reinforced by adoption of a crawling exchange
rate band with a predetermined rate of change, gradually to be reduced
as the new stabilisation package took hold, and renewed emphasis on
Central Bank independence. To date, the policy is working. Growth has
been resumed and the rate of crawl has been steadily reduced. Capital
inflows in 1995, associated in part with privatisation, provided the
revenues in 1996 to retire some of the external government debt, thereby
beginning to tackle one of the fiscal fundamentals with which I began.

The challenge now for Hungary is twofold. To make much more rapid
progress with structural adjustment, on which the fate of all transition
programmes ultimately depends. There are optimistic signs, not least in
banking where foreign ownership has been allowed. This is a bold step,
one that many countries are too fearful to take. Given the prevalence of
banking problems, and the key role of banks as terminators within the
market economy – it is banks not shareholders who enforce budget
constraints and decide whether or not companies will close – the twin
steps of admitting more managerial expertise to the banking industry and

recognising that careful and informed regulation of banks is no luxury but an essential underpinning of transition now offers the prospect of greater microeconomic efficiency and productivity growth.

Against such hopes, the main task of macroeconomics is not to get in the way. Getting in the way can mean unnecessarily lax monetary and fiscal policies, thereby promoting the resumption of inflation and the return of old doubts about the true resolve of policy; it can also mean an inappropriate exchange rate policy, either *per se* or induced by an injudicious monetary fiscal mix, that leads to serious misalignment and frustration of the export growth that is so helpful to the rest of transition.

Given the current fashion for exchange rate bands, which in many ways appear attractive as a resolution of the conflicting objectives of providing a transparent nominal anchor whilst allowing a margin of short-term flexibility, let me in conclusion make three points. First, where bands are too narrow, any downturn in confidence quickly provokes an exchange rate crisis, whilst any upturn in confidence induces a capital inflow on a sizeable scale. Attempting to sterilise this has usually been both futile and expensive – as Gáspár has reminded us, interest parity doesn't hold and borrowing at home to build up foreign exchange assets is a further fiscal burden. From this I conclude that greater exchange rate flexibility is desirable. Bands should be wider rather than narrower.

Second, it is impossible simultaneously to assert that the *ancien régime* was deeply wasteful and that the new regime offers little scope for rapid productivity growth. Sooner or later, transition economies should display rapid real growth; we have already seen glimpses in Poland and elsewhere. When this happens, it is appropriate that the real exchange rate appreciates, and desirable that as much of this as possible is achieved through nominal appreciation rather than domestic inflation.

Finally, as we continue to monitor fiscal developments, we should be aware that there is nothing sacred about the budget balance. It is not difficult to imagine circumstances in which only a fiscal surplus will be appropriate. Substantial confidence in transition may unleash renewed access to foreign credit even for the purposes of immediate consumption – think of the UK in 1988, newly united Germany in 1990–1, or the Czech republic in 1996–7 – in which case the policy choices are (1) allow overheating and an upturn in inflation, (2) tighten interest rates to stave off inflation but at the price of a dramatic real appreciation, or (3) tighten fiscal policy even if this means a substantial surplus. My vote unhesitatingly would be for (3) should this (happy) situation arise.

3 The interest rate transmission mechanism in Hungary, 1991–1995

BALÁZS VILÁGI AND JÁNOS VINCZE

1 Introduction: Hungarian monetary policy, 1991–5

Hungarian monetary policy has had two principal goals since 1990: ensuring the country's international solvency, and keeping the rate of inflation within bounds. To achieve these goals was not trivial in either case: the country started the transition in precarious external balance, while the transitional shocks had increased inflation to about 30 per cent per annum by 1991. Uncertainty concerning economic behaviour discouraged the National Bank of Hungary (NBH) from targeting money aggregates, and compelled it to use interest rates as the intermediate target on the strong conviction that it was a powerful instrument for improving external balance and for lessening inflationary pressures. On the other hand the NBH had to experiment with monetary policy procedures due to the underdeveloped and changing nature of the banking sector and capital markets.[1]

Until 1993 refinancing credits provided the main vehicle for supplying central bank funds to the banking system. There existed quantitative limits to the supply of funds, and costs were either set by the NBH, or determined at auctions. Another important channel of monetary policy during this period was the use of the foreign exchange swap and kindred facilities. These facilities were provided by the NBH in order to insure banks against foreign exchange risk, an insurance possibility thought to be absent from domestic private markets. Through 1991 and 1992, when the NBH gradually reduced the amount of refinancing credits, swaps became the only (practically) unlimited funding source for many banks. This time, the cost of these funds was closely related to short-term government securities yields. Auctioning government securities started in the late 1980s in Hungary, but the government paper market and, in general, interest rate setting has been liberalised only since 1991. Primary auction yields, however, have never been allowed to move outside of a

54

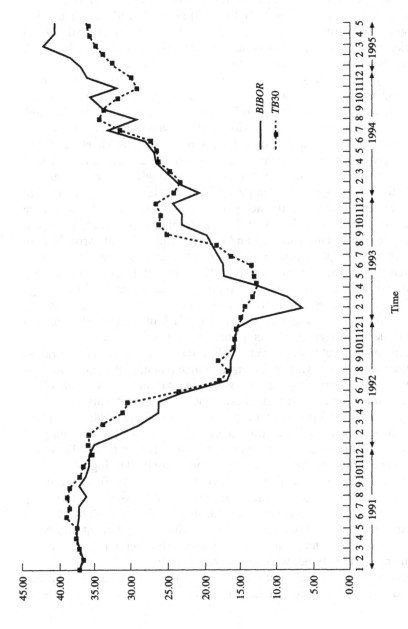

Figure 3.1 Interbank rates and 30-day T-bill rates, 1991:1–1995:5

limited range, set by the government on the advice of the NBH. Active, organised secondary markets for government securities have not been in existence, thus one has to turn also to the interbank market as a source of information concerning market yields. This market became a really free, not NBH intermediated, market only in 1991. Comparison of interbank rates with Treasury Bill (T-bill) auction yields (see figure 3.1) suggests that auction yields deviated sometimes substantially from market rates, indicating that T-bill auctions were too much administered, i.e. without paying due attention to market developments.

January 1993 marked a significant change in NBH procedures. Repurchase agreements (repos) were introduced as a distress lending facility, with the repo rate set well above current market rates. Though not a monetary policy action in itself, at the same time the government initiated the consolidation of the banking sector, which should have influenced bank behaviour and the transmission mechanism. In several waves substantial amounts of bad debt were bought by the government, with the overall goal of cleaning up banks' balance sheets in order to enable them to meet capital adequacy ratios. Through 1993 there were spells of speculation for large Forint devaluations, which prompted banks to buy foreign currency and convert it into Forint through swap operations. Simply borrowing in Forint and escaping into foreign currency was not a viable option as the prudential regulation of open positions would have made it illegal on a large scale. (Net foreign exchange liability of banks was limited to 30 per cent of bank capital.) On the other hand capital controls and the lack of convertibility made it infeasible for foreigners to attempt this on their own account.

Beginning in September 1993 the NBH, responding to the deterioration of the balance of payments, changed course again, and decided to raise interest rates. Perceiving that Hungarian capital markets were unable to raise liquid funds within a short time, it achieved this goal in a roundabout way. First, repo rates were set below the yields realised on government paper of identical maturity, implying the possibility of interest rate arbitrage for domestic banks. In this way the NBH pushed up interest rates without reducing money supply. During this period repos became a substantial source of commercial banks' funds, contrary to the original plan. Later, when higher rates stabilised, the maturities of central bank lending were so changed, in several stages, that arbitrage became impossible. Still, repos have remained a significant source of commercial bank financing, which implies that repo rates were not permanently at variance with money market rates.

During 1994 the philosophy of NBH procedures remained basically unchanged. There were changes in certain details, however. The NBH altered maturities and other conditions of swaps and repos in order to exclude arbitrage or near-arbitrage possibilities whenever it was necessary. After September 1994 the term structure was forced to take a positive slope in the short end, when changes on auctions were instituted that led to a drop in the yields on 30-day T-bills *vis-à-vis* the yields on 90-day T-Bills. Due to periodically strengthening devaluation expectations swaplike facilities were repeatedly utilised, while repos, by and large, maintained their role in commercial bank financing.

The next important change in monetary policy was the introduction of a crawling peg, with symmetric bands of 2.25 per cent, following a larger devaluation in March 1995. Such a change should, in principle, restrict the scope of monetary policy according to the received wisdom about the relationship between interest rates and fixed exchange rates. Since during 1995 there were further measures of liberalisation with respect to foreign exchange transactions (e.g. enterprises could keep foreign currency denominated deposits) this measure might have led to the loss of independence in domestic interest rate policy. However, two caveats are in order here. First, the relatively generous band width provided cause for concern for speculators in the very short-term, making betting on Forint assets somewhat risky. Secondly, it took time to build up credibility as other countries' experiences have shown that realignments in similar situations have not been uncommon. In fact, it was only in January 1996 that the first signs of a market-led drop in interest rates could be discerned, in accordance with the uncovered interest rate parity hypothesis.

Thus during 1991–5 the process through which monetary authorities controlled the short-term money market rate underwent significant changes. This makes it practically impossible to pick out any one monetary instrument for a statistical analysis. Open markets were rather shallow, except for short-term markets involving banks. The opportunities for firms to borrow at costs close to short-term market rates, or the possibilities for households to invest in securities, of comparable risk, at yields substantially different from those provided by the banking sector, were rare. As more and more firms have been able to borrow from abroad, and as the relative weight of government securities in household portfolios has increased, this statement has been becoming invalid. We do not know, however, how much foreign borrowing is 'real', and not just a form of capital transfer to the domestic government paper market. It is also possible that, due to transactions costs, the yields households earned on short-term securities were closer to the deposit rates offered by banks than the short-term yield earned by the banks themselves. Thus, for most of our period, it seems to be a tenable assumption that domestic short-term rates determined the marginal (opportunity) costs of banks and banks, in their turn, set their own offers that most private lenders and borrowers had to face on this basis.

This chapter addresses problems concerning the interest rate transmission mechanism in Hungary during the early 1990s. We were particularly interested in the behaviour of the banking sector, but we also wished to lay some foundation for an informed assessment of policy effectiveness. As the previous discussion suggests, the independence of monetary policy may be an issue in Hungary, a small open economy. It is also problematic how different interest rate series characterise monetary policy. Section 2 takes up these problems. In section 3 the general theoretical issue of the monetary transmission mechanism is first discussed, then a simple model of commercial banks is set up and analysed. This model serves as a benchmark, by indicating the general form of equations to be estimated, and by helping to interpret parameter estimates. Section 4 reports transmission equations and interprets our findings, while section 5 summarises and draws conclusions concerning policy effectiveness.

2   Characterising monetary policy

A necessary condition for policy effectiveness is its independence. As is well known monetary policy in small open economies with fixed exchange rates (such as Hungary) loses degrees of freedom. However, real economies may not satisfy the exact conditions responsible for the policy impotence proposition. Hungary has had capital controls, its foreign debt has not been regarded as a perfectly safe investment, and double-digit and volatile inflation has made any sort of exchange rate commitment less than fully credible. Indeed, the Hungarian exchange rate system was sometimes called a 'dirty peg' system. There occurred frequent devaluations of the Forint, but in a rather irregular fashion. The size of individual realignments was normally small but, at least in five cases, they could be called major. The system was managed jointly by the government and the NBH leaving scope for the interplay of conflicting interests. For several years the semi-announced goal was to maintain some level of the real exchange rate, calculated on the basis of the domestic PPI, while also using the nominal exchange rate as a brake on inflation. The result was a regime where realignment expectations frequently ran high. In such a situation, money cannot flow very easily across borders, and domestic monetary policy presumably had a certain freedom.

In what follows, we look at several interest rate series, examine their time series properties, including their relationship with the exchange rate, and provide evidence for the independence of monetary policy.

A main assumption of our analysis in section 4 will be that money market rates represent 'operative or intermediate targets' of monetary policy.[2] In this section we seek statistical justification for this assumption. We examined three rates: the overnight interbank rate (*BIBOR*), the average auction yield on 30-day T-bills (*TB30*), and that on 90-day T-bills (*TB90*). All interest rate series are those published in the Monthly Bulletins of the NBH. For comparability all interest rate series were transformed to annual yields, applying guesstimates for average maturity whenever necessary. Each of these has its own problems which makes a choice between them difficult. The interbank rate is volatile, and reflects very short-term, unintended, fluctuations in liquidity, including those caused by reserve requirement regulation which was itself not stable during the period. These objections notwithstanding, it may express the liquidity regulating aspect of monetary policy better than the T-bill rates. There were periods when T-bill rates were kept artificially low, despite there being almost no demand at auction, and in other periods T-bill auction yields did not fall, though significant excess demand existed. Also the regulation of auction participation changed over time, and sometimes certain types of non-market players (such as governmental agencies) had an all too important influence on yields.

How can we support the hypothesis that any of the short-term rates served as a valid intermediate target for monetary policy, i.e. that the monetary authorities could indeed control these rates? One possible approach would consist in investigating the uncovered interest rate parity hypothesis. In the circumstances described with respect to the exchange rate regime, the quantitative modelling of exchange rate expectations must be a knotty problem, which we cannot even hope to address here. We are not aware of any sophisticated attempt to address this issue for the Hungarian case, thus the adoption of the assumption of perfect foresight seems to be the easiest, and not totally unacceptable, solution.

Darvas (1995) took this approach, and studied the uncovered interest rate parity hypothesis for 1990–5, by using traditional methods (i.e. jointly assuming rational expectations, risk neutrality, perfect mobility and substitutability of capital), and found that the evidence was against it. He also compared simple investment strategies, such as investing always in Forint versus in a portfolio of other currencies. He found that the excess yield on Forint assets was variable across both currencies and subperiods. It was significantly positive until 1993, and since then it has been close to zero, but slightly positive. Darvas' interpretation of these results is that the authorities could implement relatively independent exchange rate and interest rate policies, though very wide deviations were corrected via some policy reaction function. In our opinion there probably was a substantial premium on the Forint for any sophisticated investor who could predict realignment timing well, and for whom transactions costs were not too high.[3] To create such profit opportunities is a common practice of indebted countries that want to attract foreign capital, but also wish to discourage investors who are too naive or unreliable.

We can search for other evidence bearing on the issues at hand. We derived dynamic equations for Hungarian T-bill yields and interbank rates with the average foreign T-bill yields as the explanatory variable. Applying the Bardsen transformation to an ADL model with one lag (see Bardsen, 1989) we calculated long-run coefficients describing the 'eventual' dependence of money market rates on foreign yields. (*FATB* is the *ex post* foreign yield as calculated by Darvas. For details of construction see Darvas, 1995.) The long-run coefficient was 0.84 for both *TB30* and *TB90*, whereas it turned out to be exactly 1 for the interbank rate. This suggests some long-term coherence in domestic exchange rate and interest rate policies, but also that they are far from being completely interdependent. Reinforcing this conclusion, Granger-causality-tests show that foreign yields do not provide additional predicting power for domestic rates, and reverse causality can also be rejected at conventional significance levels (see table 3.1).

The relative roles of money market rates can be assessed by univariate analyses, too. As the three domestic interest rate series are first-order integrated according to Augmented Dickey–Fuller tests (see table 3.2), we estimated ARIMA models for *BIBOR*, *TB30* and *TB90*, and then looked at the residuals of these equations, and of the ADL equations. For the T-bill yields there were a few dates that showed the same large outlying residual, whether an ARIMA or a regression involving the foreign yields were used. These dates are 92:6 and 93:9 for *TB30*, and 92:7 and 93:9 for *TB90*, when interest rate policy took a downward and an upward turn, respectively. These interventions did not have much to do with exchange rate developments. The interbank rate outliers are quite different from the T-bill rate outliers, indicating that interest rate policy was not always in accordance with the liquidity of the banking sector.

To sum up, our conclusion is that we can meaningfully speak of an interest rate policy by the NBH, and that it is best reflected by T-bill yields, but interbank rates might contain additional information concerning monetary policy, making them worthy of further consideration.

Table 3.1. Granger-causality-tests between interest rate series

	FATB	TB30	TB90	BIBOR	C1Y	D1Y
FATB		0.818	1.297	1.436	6.933	0.578
		(0.521)	(0.286)	(0.238)	(0.287)	(0.680)
TB30	0.354		1.547	0.629	8.288	4.028
	(0.840)		(0.205)	(0.644)	(0.000)	(0.007)
TB90	0.049	2.065		1.030	7.023	1.533
	(0.995)	(0.102)		(0.402)	(0.000)	(0.209)
BIBOR	1.289	2.544	3.938		6.933	3.763
	(0.289)	(0.053)	(0.008)		(0.000)	(0.012)
C1Y	0.445	1.051	1.883	2.386		2.424
	(0.776)	(0.392)	(0.130)	(0.066)		(0.062)
D1Y	0.425	2.700	3.232	1.152	6.617	
	(0.790)	(0.043)	(0.021)	(0.345)	(0.000)	

Null hypothesis: variable in row does not Granger-cause variable in column
Sample: 1991:01–1995:09, lags:4. Cells contain F-statistics with associated probability values in parentheses. $C1Y$ and $D1Y$ represent corporate borrowing and deposit rates, respectively

Table 3.2. Augmented Dickey–Fuller-tests for the stationarity of interest rate series

	Levels	First differences
TB30	−0.5052	−4.4312 **
TB90	−0.5911	−4.7937 **
BIBOR	−0.6266	−6.5375 **
C1Y	−0.4393	−2.6873 **
D1Y	−0.7179	−1.9815 *

Null hypothesis: existence of a unit root. Cells contain the t-statistics. * (**) indicate significance at the 5(1) per cent level, respectively. Lag length in test regressions was determined by t-tests in the test equations, which contained neither intercept nor trend. Sample: 1991:1–1995:9.

3   Theoretical background

In this section we first discuss the monetary transmission mechanism in general, and then proceed to set up a model of commercial banks that will serve as the theoretical basis for the econometric analysis reported in section 4.

3.1   The monetary transmission mechanism

The monetary transmission mechanism is a central problem in macro-economics, both theoretical and empirical. Many different transmission stories have been developed, and their relevance has been tested to an increasing extent. Some researchers have emphasised the role of bank liabilities (the money view), others the importance of bank credit (the credit view), while monetarists usually take a portfolio choice approach. Recently the old debt–deflation story of Irving Fisher has been gaining substantial currency, together with variants that focus on the effect of monetary policy on asset values. (For an overview of transmission mechanisms see Mishkin, 1995.)

Though in theoretical discussions monetary policy is usually defined as the control of the money supply, one could just as well frame a transmission scenario using some interest rate as the principal monetary policy instrument or intermediate target. Indeed, in most countries policy can directly affect short-term rates, and can influence some monetary target only via this channel. These rates are usually lending rates of the Central Bank (e.g. discount rate, refinancing rate, repo rate), but in countries where government debt is sold through the bank, it may also happen that the Central Bank sets the primary market yield on such debt. Whatever the particular instrument the bank ends up using, it is generally safe to assume that it has significant control over short-term market rates, too. On the other hand, it is not at all clear whether short-term market rates determine fully the formation of other interest rates (long-term bond rates, business loan rates, deposit rates, mortgage rates, etc.). For instance the early 1990s witnessed episodes in industrial countries when monetary authorities were, predictably, successful at changing short-term rates, while the response of other rates was sluggish, to say the least. (See, for instance, BIS, 1994; Cottarelli and Kourelis, 1994.)

A partial account (with a Keynesian flavour) of the monetary transmission mechanism would look like this. The Central Bank alters the short-term rate (the instrument), which engenders a change in open market risk-free rates (operative or intermediate targets). This leads to further changes in other open market rates (bond rates, commercial chapter rates, etc.), and also, through influencing bank balance sheets and bank's marginal opportunity costs, to changes in commercial bank lending and deposit rates. If one assumes that financial markets clear, then these interest rates determine the costs (yields) of funds for non-financial agents in the economy, and through these, their decisions as to how much to consume, save or invest.[4] The belief in the relevance of this mechanism entails two more basic beliefs: that there is short-run price rigidity allowing real interest rates to covary with nominal rates, and that there is a strong impact of interest rates on agents' decisions. (See Taylor, 1995, for a fuller exposition.)

Within this general framework different stories can be set up, depending on how one models the securities and banking markets, and basically equivalent ideas can be expressed in different forms according to the particular market framework one posits. If one adopts the assumption of market clearing then the dependence of bank determined rates on money market (risk-free) rates (interest rate transmission) would serve as a very important structural relationship. Quick and full adjustment of bank determined rates would imply, *ceteris paribus*, powerful transmission of monetary policy impulses. On the other hand, if one subscribes to a credit rationing view, interest rate transmission relationships would not be quite sufficient to evaluate the effectiveness of monetary policy, and quantity channels would have to be analysed, too. Also, it is possible to define the credit view by reference to policy induced changes in the loan supply curve. (For macroeconomic models with non-trivial bank intermediation see Bernanke and Blinder, 1988, without, and Stiglitz and Weiss, 1992, with credit rationing.)

In open economies there exists another channel for monetary policy transmission, the effect of interest rates on the exchange rate. Raising domestic interest rates results in the appreciation of the home currency if the exchange rate is floating and capital movements are not restricted, since it becomes more attractive to investors, either foreign or domestic. Thus monetary policy is able to adjust the relative supply of the country's currency and, thereby, to control the exchange rate. In addition, with some rigidity in commodity prices, it has effects on real output. However, as is well known, monetary policy in open economies with a truly fixed exchange rate loses its independence if, besides capital mobility, there is no difference in default risk across countries. In reality, for many countries with substantial external debt default, risk is not negligible which is one reason why pure interest rate arbitrage involving government bonds might not exist. However, this would not necessarily invalidate the proposition, if allowance is made for a risk premium, but it would make it rest on a less secure basis. A better reason for believing in the effectiveness of domestic monetary policy would be the existence of capital controls that, in effect, make the marginal cost of transferring capital increase. In addition to these, it is also the case that a truly fixed (fully credible) exchange rate regime is rather rare in practice, especially in economies with double-digit inflation.

Obviously a full account of the monetary transmission mechanism may be forbiddingly complex. No wonder that empirical investigators have applied shortcuts. Many researchers sidestepped both interest rate transmission and the details of the mechanism, and estimated reduced form equations linking some measure of policy to an indicator of economic activity. (A partial list of references includes King, 1986; Romer and Romer, 1990; Bernanke and Blinder, 1992; Gertler and Gilchrist, 1993.) In these works monetary policy is first defined (for instance, by some money or credit aggregate, central bank rate or short-term market interest rate, or even through an event analysis), and then some time series technique (including regressions, Granger-causality-tests, variance decompositions, and structural VARs) is employed in order to make inferences about the existence and strength of the effects of the selected policy indicator on variables representing economic activity.

Another simplification occurs if one analyses the interest rate transmission mechanism in isolation. Two multicountry projects have made attempts at its quantification and its relation to structural features of the financial sector. The Bank for International Settlements organised a conference on the subject in the context of 14 OECD countries (see BIS, 1994), whereas Cottarelli and Kourelis (1994) carried out a comparative study focusing on a group of industrial and developing countries. The approach involved the estimation of equations relating short-term money market rates or policy rates to various commercial bank and open market rates. Both formal and informal discussions were offered regarding the influence of financial market structure on the transmission mechanism. Authors usually found that better developed, more competitive markets were conducive to faster adjustment, and *a fortiori*, to more effective policy.

3.2   A model of commercial banks

The simplest model of the banking firm assumes risk neutrality, neglects reserve management and treats banks as purely financial entities by suppressing labour and real capital inputs. (For a class of similar, and more general models see Klein, 1971.) Also, banks' own capital is taken as zero. (In our model the alternative specification of exogenously given capital would not change the analysis.) Thus, a bank can be represented by its balance sheet, containing only deposits (D) on the liability side. Deposits finance three kinds of assets: risky loans to the public (L), mandatory reserves (R) held with the Central Bank, and riskless government securities (B). The latter variable can take on positive and negative values as well, since we cannot exclude the possibility that a bank is a net borrower from the consolidated (central bank *plus*

Treasury) government. (1) is an accounting identity, describing the balance sheet of a bank

$$L + R + B = D \tag{1}$$

The required reserve ratio is α, set by the monetary authorities. We leave no room for any need to hold additional reserves, thus R can be written as

$$R = \alpha D \tag{2}$$

The model is a single period one where decisions are made at the beginning of the period, and profits are realised at the end. The objective of a bank is to maximise expected end-of-period profits. The expected profit function has four ingredients, like the balance sheet identity. (1) Deposits are costly, and we write as $EC(D)$ the expected cost of deposits of size D. (2) Mandatory reserves yield interest at rate ι, set by the central bank.[5] (3) The interest on risk-free market securities (i) is exogenous to banks, thus the component of profits derived from it is simply iB. (4) Risky loans of size L yield expected revenue $EP(L)$, which is the difference between interest income and losses caused by default

$$E\Pi = EP(L) + \iota R + iB - EC(D) \tag{3}$$

The behavioural assumption of expected profit maximisation dispenses with the consideration of risk taking, whereas risk averse behaviour is a distinct possibility for the banking firm (see Stiglitz, 1992). Risk neutrality is important for getting the dichotomy result (see below) which simplifies the analysis. An important source of risk aversion would be bankruptcy costs. However, in Hungary the scene has been dominated by relatively large and state-owned banks, whose failure was very improbable. In the following we will assume that the short-term risk-free rate is exogenous. This assumption is quite general in the literature, and must be fulfilled if money markets are reasonably competitive. In fact this assumption was not necessarily valid in Hungary. As the National Savings Bank (OTP) has been an overwhelming participant in the household deposit and in the interbank market, it has always been a substantial player in the government securities market, too. However, this bank had only a small share on the enterprise credit and deposit markets, the ones that are central to our empirical analysis (see section 4). Thus even if the Savings Bank had had significant power in short-term markets, it would have remained true that banks dealing with the corporate sector would have had to take their marginal costs as given.

In our model non-financial costs do not exist, and financial costs or revenues derived from financial services are also omitted. The former can be a tenable assumption considering the short span of our data. The latter, however, will leave a few serious questions unanswered. Our sample contains months when average lending rates were below money market rates, and months when average enterprise deposit rates were higher than money market rates. One can reasonably assume that the presence of upfront and other fees made lending both on average, and on the margin, *ex ante* profitable. Whether the contribution of fees to income was relatively constant is a problem. On the deposit side, treating deposit rate setting as a part of pricing related products (deposits and payment services), would be theoretically attractive. Lack of data prevents us from doing such an exercise, and we could only hope that the bias is not significant.

The model set out in this general form can be solved easily, and the solution can be characterised by two equations. The interpretation of these is obvious. First, the expected marginal revenue of lending must be equal to the risk-free market rate ((4)), and the expected marginal cost of deposit taking should be equal to the effective marginal revenue from deposits ((5)), which is an average of the interest rate paid on mandatory reserves and the money market rate, where the weight of the former is equal to the required reserve ratio.

$$EP'(L) = i \tag{4}$$

$$EC'(D) = \alpha\iota + (1 - \alpha)i = i' \tag{5}$$

This is just elementary microeconomics. Note that the risk neutrality assumption enabled us to get a nicely dichotomised system, where the deposit and credit side decisions are separable in the sense that the only link between them is the risk-free rate that determines their marginal revenue and cost, respectively.[6] Reserve regulation affects only the lending side, which is a non-trivial restriction imposed by the model.

The next step is to further specify those two functions that should reflect the essential features of financial markets, i.e. the expected loan revenue and the expected deposit cost functions.

3.2.1 Lending rates

Let us assume that p, the revenue derived from a unit loan, is a continuous random variable, with density function f which depends on the lending rate. Furthermore each density in this family parameterised by r has support $[0,r]$, and $f(r;r) = 0$. Then in the competitive case $EP(L)$ takes the form

$$EP(L) = L \int_0^r pf(p;r)dp \qquad (6)$$

Thus (4) can be written as

$$EP'(L) = \int_0^r pf(p;r)dp = i \qquad (4.1)$$

Also, we assume that, as suggested by the adverse selection hypothesis,[7] the density depends on r in such a way that the expected revenue per unit loan is increasing and strictly concave in r. These assumptions have strong implications. Linearising the left-hand side we get

$$a + br \cong i \qquad (7)$$

where $a>0$, and $b<1$. After inverting to express the lending rate as a function of the money market rate one gets a relationship with the slope exceeding 1, and a negative intercept.

If we suppose that banks have market power and recognise both the impact of interest rates on the size of lending, and their effect on default, the expected revenue function becomes

$$EP(L) = L \int_0^{r(L)} pf(p;r(L))dp \qquad (6.1)$$

and (4.2) gives the relevant optimality condition

$$EP'(L) = \int_0^{r(L)} pf(p;r(L))dp + Lr'(L) \int_0^{r(L)} pf_r(p;r(L))dp = i \quad (4.2)$$

Here the straightforward interpretation is that $r(L)$ is the inverse of the demand function for loans. However, we can find another meaning for a relationship between the average lending rate and the size of lending, which implies a positive relationship between these two variables.

For a start, let us consider the simplest model of credit rationing where there is one group of (indistinguishable) borrowers, and raising the interest rate results in adverse (self-)selection. If there exists a rate at which the expected revenue is maximised, and this rate is smaller than the one at which demand would match supply, then the group is rationed, i.e. some of the identical (from the point of view of the bank) potential borrowers could, and some of them could not, borrow. If this theory is valid the lending rate is a constant, that does not vary in response to changes in marginal cost. In the more plausible case of redlining (see for example Jaffee and Stiglitz, 1990) there exist several groups whose specialised rates of interest differ, demand is satisfied for inframarginal groups while the marginal group is rationed, and the worse than marginal groups are completely excluded from the market. If one makes the additional assumption that the group-specific rates are higher for groups that are of worse quality, it follows that the average rate moves in the same direction as the total amount of loans granted. Thus this function resembles a traditional loan supply function defined for price taking banks. Though with price setting banks the notion of a supply curve has no meaning, we may call it a pseudo-supply curve. It describes a relationship between the size of lending and interest charged, an outcome of simultaneously optimising two different components of credit contracts. In this case the first stage of decision making involves the determination of the pseudo-supply curve, then the bank's final decision consists in finding a point on the pseudo-supply curve that maximises expected profits.[8]

It is an unambiguous consequence of (4.2) that the amount of loans is a decreasing function of the marginal (opportunity) cost, whenever the first-order condition determines the true optimum. Thus the marginal cost and the average lending rate move together if $r(L)$ is a decreasing, and in opposite directions if $r(L)$ is an increasing function. The latter seems to be a strange conclusion that makes the credit rationing hypothesis in this form lacking in credibility. Additional assumptions can be made to save it. We can notice that it is possible that the pseudo-supply curve depends on the money market rate. If increasing money market rates shift the pseudo-supply curve leftwards, then marginal cost and lending rates may move in the same direction. As the pseudo-supply relation contains elements of credit demand and expected revenue, such a shift might have different sources. For instance, if increasing money market rates are signals of tighter monetary policy, and policy has effects on future demand, then it is plausible to assume that demand at given rates would decrease, while the perceived riskiness of loans would increase. Both effects would lead to a leftward shift in the pseudo-supply curve.

Then in principle we should deal with three problems on the credit side: (1) whether there is any adverse selection effect, (2) the nature of competition, and (3) whether contracts are on the demand or on the pseudo-supply curve. It is reasonable to assume that structural relations are influenced by other variables (prices, wages, income, etc.) that probably affect different structural relations simultaneously. Thus, when searching for an econometric specification, we expect to find a reduced form relationship such as

$$r = ai + bW \tag{8}$$

where W is a vector of relevant (possibly deterministic) explanatory variables, including lagged terms in i or r, and it may also contain higher-order and cross-terms in r, representing non-linearity in the underlying relationships. As we have seen, the existence of default risk together with perfect competition can be associated with a tendency of over-reaction to security rate changes (a long-run coefficient on i larger than 1). The adverse selection effect would reinforce the deviation from unity, while it would drive the intercept to become negative. On the other hand a regime of supply determined credit, which also presupposes the adverse selection effect, would tend to produce negative or small positive long-run slope coefficients.

3.2.2 Deposit rates

The general form of the expected deposit cost function under our assumptions is

$$EC(D) = d(D)D \qquad (9)$$

where $d(D)$ is the inverse of the deposit supply function, which can depend on other variables as well.

First, let us assume that the deposit market exhibits perfect competition. In our context this amounts to the proposition that each individual bank is a price taker, and faces a deposit rate d, exogenous to it. Then (5) becomes a market equilibrium condition rewritten as

$$d = i' \qquad (5.1)$$

If there is imperfect competition, a wedge exists between price and marginal revenue which, we can assume, is a function of the semi-elasticity of deposit supply. Different assumptions concerning the deposit supply function imply different semi-elasticities. For instance, in the case of a constant elasticity (in deposit rate) function one can derive that the semi-elasticity is linear in deposit rates, the coefficient being the inverse of the constant elasticity times λ, where λ is the coefficient that 'measures' market power, and can assume values between 0 and 1 (it is 0 for perfect competition, and 1 for a pure monopoly)

$$d + \lambda(\frac{1}{\epsilon_D})d = i' \qquad (5.2)$$

Rearranging (5.2) to express d as a function of i' yields a slope below 1, and an intercept of 0.

On the other hand a linear supply function gives an expression that is also linear, but depends on other variables entering the deposit supply function, too

$$d + \lambda(d + \kappa Z) = i' \tag{5.3}$$

(Here Z contains all the other relevant variables.) Rearrangement now yields a coefficient between 0.5 and 1 on i', whereas other variables, and possibly a non-zero intercept, are also present.

As we do not want to assume anything *a priori* about the form of the demand curve, and will not attempt to identify λ, we adopt a generic specification that corresponds to (5.3).

$$d = ai' + bZ \tag{10}$$

The deposit side raises one interesting issue with respect to the specification of the set of Z variables, namely the possibility that money market rates influence supply (semi-)elasticities as well as the marginal revenue of banks. This may happen whenever the supply function is not of the constant elasticity type. Intuitively, the stronger competitors money market instruments to bank deposits are, the closer bank deposit rates to short-term market yields must be. As a limiting case an alternative model for deposit rate determination would be obtained by supposing that there is a competitive fringe of financial intermediaries that could offer their services at the current money market rate, and that the transactions services of bank deposits are not very interesting for depositors. (This situation is more likely to exist for very short-term, within-month deposits, and seems less plausible for somewhat longer maturities.) In terms of our model it would mean that banks are price takers on the deposit market, and deposit rates must not be lower than i. Thus deposit rates would react to the money market rate, rather than to the adjusted money market rate, i'.

Again we can only expect to get suggestions from estimates of deposit rate transmission equations. For instance, if we had a 'best' equation for the deposit rate which contains only the effective money market rate as explanatory variable, with a long-run slope of approximately 1, and an intercept of 0, then we can say that evidence would not be disfavourable to the competitive market hypothesis. Any clear deviation from these parameters would imply the presence of some market imperfection.

4   Econometric analysis

Our final goal is to estimate interest rate transmission equations, and interpret the estimates in the light of the discussion offered in section 3. Ideally we should formulate a system of four equations, including the two first-order conditions, as well as loan demand and deposit supply functions, as in other studies of the banking industry (see Schaffer, 1993).

Then we can, in principle, identify structural parameters and test appropriate cross-equation restrictions. Our discussion of the loan and deposit markets indicated that this would be a formidable task in any case. On the other hand we did not find satisfactory data for the detailed analysis of banking markets. The monthly frequency seems to be inappropriate for demand (supply) function estimation as we do not have monthly income figures to give us a chance to identify the adverse selection effect, and only stock data for loans and deposits are available. In addition to these problems, all the quantity data series have been revised several times, and fully comparable series have not been published. Also loan data probably contain a large volume of rolled-over bad loans in 1991–2, whose time decomposition is impossible. Thus data problems restrict us to proceeding on single equation lines.

Though our estimates must only be suggestive for market structure analysis, they may be meaningful for studying interest rate stickiness. Price rigidity has been the subject of several papers dealing with the retail deposit market, where rates are administered, and the cost of price adjustments is an obvious candidate for being the cause of price rigidity (see Hannan and Berger, 1991). In the literature there exist explanations that deliver rigidity from explicit models of the banking industry and intertemporal utility maximisation by households (an example is Hutchison, 1995).

4.1   Preliminary data analysis

Our focus will be on the corporate loan and deposit rates, as these provide the best data for statistical analysis.[9] We selected two series representing commercial bank rates. Lending rates (ClY) are within-year corporate (Forint) rates charged on new loans (see figure 3.2), enterprise deposit rates (DlY) (see figure 3.3) refer to rates offered to non-financial corporations for time deposits with a maturity exceeding a month but less than a year. These series are published in the *Monthly Bulletins* of the NBH. For comparability they were transformed to annual yields, by applying guesstimates for average maturity (two and three months for deposits and loans, respectively).

First we established the degree of integration of our series. Augmented Dickey–Fuller tests showed that both commercial bank rate series are I(1) (see table 3.2).

Next we carried out Granger-causality-tests. F-tests reported in table 3.1 indicate that money market rates are in general Granger-causally prior to commercial bank rates, and that we can reject the hypothesis that the enterprise deposit rate series did not Granger-cause $TB90$ at the

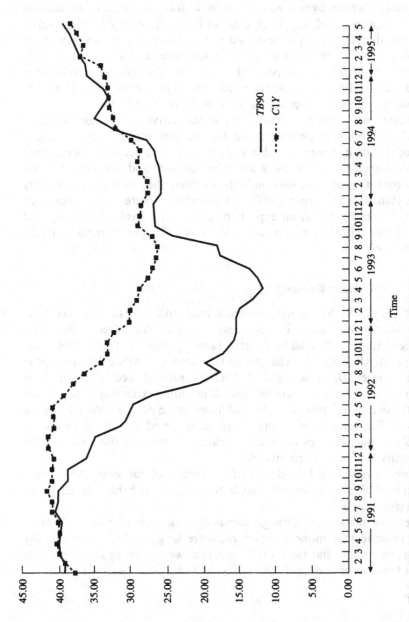

Figure 3.2 90-day T-bill rates and lending rates, 1991:1–1995:5

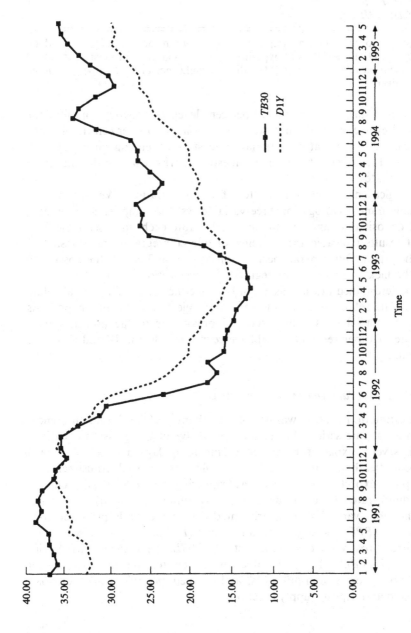

Figure 3.3 30-day T-bill rates and enterprise deposit rates, 1991:1–1995:5

Table 3.3. Johansen-tests for cointegration

Series	No cointegration	At most 1 CE	At most 2 CEs
CI Y,DI Y,TB30	**		
CI Y,DI Y,TB90	**		
CI Y,DI Y,BIBOR	*		

Lags: 1 to 2. Test assumption: No deterministic trend in the data. Sample: 1991:1–1995:9. Null hypotheses: no cointegration, at most 1, at most 2 cointegration relationships. * (**) indicate significance at the 5(1) per cent level, respectively.

5 per cent, and *TB30* at the 10 per cent level, respectively. In all of the other 'reverse' cases the null was accepted at the 10 per cent level. Thus we can conclude that conditional forecasting of lending rates may be a meaningful exercise, but we have question marks regading the enterprise deposit rate.

A logical next step was to test for cointegration. We applied the Johansen methodology for three-variable systems comprising the lending and deposit rate, and one money market rate each time (see table 3.3). Test results indicated the existence of one cointegration relationship in each system. Our general specification of section 3 entails the possibility of the lack of pairwise cointegration between money market rates and bank determined rates. This might be due either to the short (in absolute time) data set, or to the bias towards non-rejection of the null hypothesis of a unit root caused by structural breaks, or to the non-stationary nature of other relevant variables incorporated in the W and Z sets of variables.

4.2   Interest rate transmission equations

Our estimation strategy was flexible, involving both levels and differences of interest rate series. We set up general dynamic regression equations with several explanatory variables, including lagged ones. (A lagged deposit (lending) rate variable may allow for partial adjustment, or adaptive expectations, as well as capturing any effects past deposit (lending) rates have on deposit (loan) supply (demand).) As other explanatory variables we experimented with the monthly producer price inflation (*PPI*), the log of broad money (*LM2*), the log of seasonally adjusted gross wage costs in industry (*WAGES*), and the *ex post* Forint yields (*FATB*).[10] These variables were selected on the grounds of availability on a monthly basis, and of their possible impact on loan demand and deposit supply functions.

Table 3.4. Wald-tests for the exclusion of exogenous variables in the lending rate equations

	C1 with TB30	C1 with TB90	D1 with TB30	D1 with TB30E
FATB	0.551	0.883	0.801	0.843
	(0.582)	(0.423)	(0.455)	(0.439)
PPI	1.435	1.216	0.041	0.082
	(0.252)	(0.309)	(0.956)	(0.921)
WAGES	0.122	0.237	0.348	0.335
	(0.886)	(0.790)	(0.709)	(0.712)
LM2	0.350	0.208	2.386	1.286
	(0.708)	(0.813)	(0.303)	(0.290)

Cells contain F-statistics with associated probability values.

4.2.1 Lending rate equations

For the level series we used Wald (F and X^2)-tests to establish lag lengths. In each case only the first lag proved to be significant. Then the relevance of explanatory variables was checked by the same Wald-tests (see table 3.4). Testing resulted in excluding all of the explanatory variables, except for the money market rates.

Exclusion of non-interest rate variables may be a consequence of poor data quality, so we should not necessarily interpret it as confirmation of the competitive market hypothesis. Next we looked at the individual t-statistics in the remaining equations, and found that in none of them was the lagged money market rate significant at the 5 per cent level. Though dropping the lagged exogenous variable is usually not advocated for statistical reasons there was another motive that compelled us to exclude it from the final estimates. Recursive coefficient estimates showed visible instability when a lagged money market rate was included in any equation. Thus we obtained models that can be interpreted as partial adjustment models, where the desired value of the commercial bank rate depends on the money market rate, but banks adjust their rates only slowly.

We considered the possibility of having structural breaks in parameters. We used the Chow forecast test to check the hypothesis of a structural break in 1993:1 (the beginning of bank consolidation that might have affected bank behaviour, see section 3), and 1995:1 to check the influence of the new exchange rate regime. Parameter constancy broke down in 1993:1, thus we put in a step dummy, allowing for a change in the intercept.[11] After re-estimating the equation we carried out the Chow forecast-test for 1995:1. The F-statistic was 3.606, while the (X^2)-value was 21.608. In both cases rejection of parameter constancy occurs at the

Table 3.5. Lending rate equations

	Levels	Levels	First differences	First differences
$Cl(-1)$	0.80 (17.39)	0.80 (16.53)	0.35 (3.04)	0.32 (2.79)
$TB30$	0.11 (8.36)		0.16 (3.28)	
$TB90$		0.10 (7.72)		0.17 (3.28)
$CONSTANT$	4.35 (2.76)	4.35 (2.62)		
$DUMMY$	−0.95 (−2.18)	−0.96 (−2.08)	−1.75 (−2.53)	−0.96 (−2.74)
LRS	0.54	0.50	0.24	0.25
R^2	0.99	0.99	0.45	0.45
SC	−0.85	−0.76	−0.57	−0.57
JB	0.47 (0.79)	0.40 (0.92)	0.005 (0.99)	1.49 (0.48)
$BG\ F$	1.59 (0.22)	0.95 (0.40)	1.14 (0.33)	0.88 (0.42)
χ^2	3.38 (0.18)	2.08 (0.35)	2.34 (0.31)	1.76 (0.42)
$ARCH\ F$	0.17 (0.69)	0.31 (0.58)	0.10 (0.75)	0.03 (0.86)
χ^2	0.17 (0.68)	0.32 (0.57)	0.11 (0.74)	0.03 (0.86)
$WH\ F$	0.93 (0.51)	0.84 (0.58)	0.68 (0.67)	1.74 (0.14)
χ^2	7.67 (0.47)	7.05 (0.53)	4.33 (0.63)	9.73 (0.14)
$CH\ F$	1.59 (0.14)	1.36 (0.23)	1.27 (0.28)	1.03 (0.46)
LR	31.26 (0.01)	27.86 (0.03)	25.89 (0.06)	21.89 (0.15)
$RESET\ F$	0.12 (0.88)	0.19 (0.82)	0.29 (0.75)	0.31 (0.73)
LR	0.28 (0.87)	0.44 (0.80)	0.66 (0.72)	0.70 (0.70)

Individual t-statistics are shown after coefficient estimates. LRS is the long-run slope coefficient on the money market rate variable, and R^2 is the coefficient of determination. Other (diagnostic) statistics include:

SC: *Schwarz Criterion*, $SC = \ln(\hat{\sigma}^2) + k\ln(T)/T$ where: $\hat{\sigma}^2 = [T/(T-k)]\hat{\sigma}^2$

and $\hat{\sigma}$ is the estimate of the standard error of the regression, k is the number of independent variables and T is the sample size (smaller SC means better regression).

BG: *Breusch–Godfrey (BG) residual autocorrelation LM-test,* testing the null of a white noise error process. The test-statistic has an F- and a χ^2 form.

JB: *Jarque–Bera-test for normality,* under the null of normal disturbances the statistic has a χ^2 distribution with two degrees of freedom.

WH: White's-test *for heteroscedasticity with cross-terms,* the null hypothesis is unconditional homoscedasticity, and the alternative is that the variance of the error process depends on the regressors, and other second-order terms. It has an F- and a χ^2-form.

$ARCH$: LM-test *for autoregressive conditional heteroscedasticity,* it has an F- and a χ^2-form, too.

CH: *Chow's forecast-test,* it tests for parameter constancy after a prespecified date (93:09 in this case). There is a χ^2- and an LR-statistic with associated probability values.

$RESET$: *Ramsey's general misspecification-test,* it has an F- and an LR-form.
Equations reported in tables 3.5 and 3.6 were all estimated by OLS.

1 per cent level. Accordingly in the final versions reported in table 3.5 we selected 1991:1–1994:12 as the estimation period. Table 3.5 presents lending rate equations in both levels and differences, with *TB30* and *TB90* as the money market rates. (We did not include the equations with *BIBOR*, since these were similar to the others, but had much worse quality in terms of fit and diagnostics.)

Our results suggest that lending rates are quite sticky in the short-term, and stickiness appears to be significant in the long run, too.[12] Indeed, the long-run slope coefficient is incredibly low in the differenced form equations. Both types of equations perform quite well, according to the diagnostics, though the differenced ones have a better score in terms of predictive performance. The significance of the dummy indicates that bank consolidation initiated around the beginning of 1993 influenced the level of lending rates, in a downward direction. The constant term is definitely positive in all of the level equations which, together with the below-unity long-run slopes, seems to refute the competitive market hypothesis. The redlining argument in its pure form cannot be substantiated by our results, since money market and lending rates have tended to be positively correlated. However, it may be the case that the low rate of long-run adjustment reflects partly the negative lending rate effect of redlining.

4.2.2 Deposit rate equations

In line with our discussion in section 3, we supposed that deposit rates were influenced by the effective marginal revenue of deposits (i'). However, we wanted to leave open the possibility of strong interbank competition in the deposit market, as represented by the unadjusted money market rate as an alternative yield for short-term corporate investments. As the *TB90* series seemed not to Granger-cause the deposit rate, we dropped this variable, and used the effective variants for the other two money market rates, and the unadjusted one for the 30-day T-bill.

We carried out the same testing procedures for establishing lag length, and for the exclusion of variables as in the case of the lending rate. Results were similar to those obtained in the previous case. We selected a single lag, and dropped all the non-interest rate variables. (For exclusion tests, see table 3.4.)

Though the lagged money market rate was also insignificant in this case, we did not drop it, as it did not seem to influence parameter stability. When testing for parameter constancy Chow forecast tests did not indicate structural breaks either for 1993:1 or for 1995:1. However, all equations exhibited very large residuals for 1992:7, and several diagnostic

Table 3.6. Deposit rate equations

	Levels	Levels	First difference	First difference
CONSTANT	−0.20 (−0.61)	−0.33 (0.99)		
D1(−1)	0.86 (33.12)	0.87 (34.04)	0.38 (2.86)	0.40 (2.96)
TB30E	0.24 (4.32)		0.22 (2.99)	
TB30		0.21 (4.41)		0.19 (2.94)
DUMMY	−3.01 (−4.45)	−2.95 (−4.28)	−1.86 (−2.91)	−1.86 (−2.88)
TB30E(−1)	−0.09 (−1.42)		0.12 (1.41)	
TB30(−1)		−0.08 (−1.45)		0.10 (1.30)
LRS	1.07	1.00	0.55	0.48
R^2	0.99	0.99	0.62	0.61
SC	−0.67	−0.65	−0.19	−0.17
JB	7.39 (0.02)	7.92 (0.02)	2.31 (0.31)	2.12 (0.35)
BG F	0.68 (0.51)	0.56 (0.58)	3.57 (0.04)	4.05 (0.02)
χ^2	1.54 (0.46)	1.28 (0.53)	6.91 (0.03)	7.70 (0.02)
ARCH F	0.03 (0.86)	0.07 (0.80)	2.26 (0.14)	2.76 (0.10)
χ^2	0.03 (0.86)	0.07 (0.79)	2.24 (0.13)	2.71 (0.10)
WH F	0.59 (0.81)	0.52 (0.86)	0.33 (0.97)	0.33 (80.97)
χ^2	6.58 (0.76)	5.95 (0.82)	4.49 (0.95)	4.39 (0.96)
CH F	0.36 (0.99)	0.43 (0.57)	0.48 (0.95)	0.50 (0.94)
LR	8.45 (0.78)	21.43 (0.61)	22.72 (0.54)	23.43 (0.49)
RESET F	0.68 (0.51)	0.67 (0.52)	2.26 (0.12)	2.33 (0.11)
LR	1.56 (0.46)	1.55 (0.46)	4.93 (0.08)	5.07 (0.08)

Variables: *C1*: lending rate, *D1*: deposit rate, *TB30*: 30-day T-bill yield, *TB90*: 90-day T-bill rate, *TB30E*: effective 30-day T-bill yield, *TD931* step dummy after 1993:1, *B927*: impulse dummy for 1992:7.
In the differenced equations first differences of the corresponding variables are taken.

tests indicated specification failure. The easiest solution was an impulse dummy for this date, which made most of the diagnostical failures disappear. Final versions were estimated for 1991:1–1995:6, and results are reported in table 3.6. (Again we do not report equations with *BIBOR*, since point estimates were similar, but fits significantly worse than in the other cases.)

The differenced form equations show very significant autocorrelations in the residuals, indicating that this model is misspecified, and the true relationship is, in fact, between levels. The level equations suffer from non-normality, putting test results into doubt. On the whole the insignificance of the intercept, and long-run slopes close to unity are broadly in favour of the competitive market hypothesis. The slowness of adjustment resembles that in the case of lending rate transmission.

Table 3.7. Weak exogeneity tests

	t-statistics (probability values)
Cl Y with *TB30*	0.05 (0.95)
Cl Y with *TB90*	0.91 (0.37)
Dl Y with *TB30E*	0.005 (0.003)
Dl Y with *TB30*	0.002 (0.14)

To improve our estimates we made the additional hypothesis that bank behaviour is in some sense conditioned on the uncertainty of money markets. This might be expressed as a residual variance that increases with the uncertainty (variance) of money market rates. Thus we re-estimated some of the equations with weighted least squares, i.e. consistently with this postulated form of heteroscedasticity, where we used as weights squared residuals from money market rate regressions and ARIMAs. This change was only partly successful as the re-estimated equations showed a substantially better fit than the original ones, while non-normality did not disappear, and other diagnostical failures emerged, too.[13]

4.3 Exogeneity

The banking model of subsection 3.1 implies that money market rates (or certain functions thereof) represent marginal opportunity cost for banks. Whatever view we take of their nature as policy variables they must satisfy weak exogeneity for our statistical inferences to be valid. We conducted simple tests for weak exogeneity of money market rates, following the procedure proposed by Engle (Engle, 1984). We tested for the inclusion of the estimated money market innovation processes in lending and deposit rate equations, and found that weak exogeneity is not rejected in any of the cases (see table 3.7). These results, together with the Granger-causality-tests reported in table 3.1, indicate that money market rates are strongly exogenous with respect to the lending rate but, in view of reverse Granger-causality, they are not with respect to the deposit rate.

At this stage we cannot carry out a formal test for super-exogeneity. Structural breaks in the lending rate transmission process attest that structural invariance was not satisfied with respect to this rate, and despite the apparent strong exogeneity of money market rates, monetary policy makers cannot be certain whether qualitative changes would not alter the transmission mechanism in the future. Indeed, it seems that the crawling peg system, coupled with further liberalisation of the capital account, might already have caused such a change, as estimating long-run coefficients from the data set including the first three-quarters of 1995 gave estimates close to unity. Though the deposit rate transmission seems to be untouched by recent developments, deposit rate estimates appear to be fragile, and responsive to monetary policy changes to some extent.

5   Summary

Our analysis suggests substantial short-run rigidity in both deposit and lending rates.[14] This finding can be interpreted in several ways. One straightforward interpretation is to take the partial adjustment model literally, and conclude that banks, because of organisational reasons, perhaps, react very slowly to changes in their environment. Alternatively, one may guess that banks form their expectations through very slow adaptation which, in the light of the substantial predictability of money market rate series, is just another form of institutional irrationality. One objection to this is that Cottarelli and Kourelis (1994) found that adjustment is generally slower in countries where money market (i.e. marginal cost) uncertainty is higher. We found that money market series contain differential information, which may signal that the true marginal cost may be more uncertain than any series we experimented with. On the other hand other explanations can be devised, too. For instance long-run (customer) relationships between banks and corporations could imply such a low slope coefficient, by reflecting interest rate smoothing provided by banks, where a positive intercept would represent an insurance premium.[15] This hypothesis may be tested in the future by looking at individual, rather than aggregate, data.

The lending rate transmission is burdened with substantial stickiness, even in the long run. It turned out that allowing for a change in the intercept, in order to take into account policy interventions, was crucial for this conclusion as, without it, the estimate of the long-run adjustment coefficient would have been much higher.[16] We tentatively attribute this to imperfect competition and redlining, though it must be clear that the results from single equations can only be regarded as the refutation of the simple competitive market hypothesis. To test the redlining hypothesis one should have access to individual enterprise data. If we had time series data on the cross-sectional distribution of lending rates, the redlining hypothesis would be supported by the finding that higher money market rates compress the cross-sectional distribution.

According to our estimates enterprise deposit rates adjusted practically fully in the long run, indicating a more or less competitive market for enterprise deposits. However, our mixed findings concerning cointegration raise doubts with respect to this conclusion. Also, it appears that money market developments had some effect on the deposit market, though probably in a more complicated manner than could be captured with the simple correction for heteroscedasticity we attempted to make. The good performance of the unadjusted T-bill rate can be suggestive of the irrelevance of reserve regulation, at least for the enterprise deposit market. Of course, reserve regulation may be important for household deposit rates or, possibly, for money market rates.

Though super-exogeneity of monetary policy was disproved, we can ask what our analysis can tell us about the effectiveness of monetary policy in the past. In a simple *IS–LM* model, augmented with a banking sector where banks are the only intermediaries, it is easy to prove that slow interest rate transmission makes both the *IS* and the *LM* curves more vertical, leading to a situation where monetary policy can cause large swings in government paper yields without affecting the real side too much. However, if we are right in insisting, on the basis of our results, that at least some type of credit rationing has been present in Hungary, then interest rate transmission equations are not very informative about policy effectiveness. Thus we are faced with a difficult interpretation problem. If we believe that the slow adjustment coefficients can be explained without credit rationing, then we should infer from slow adjustment the ineffectiveness of monetary policy. If, however, these coefficients are so small that they suggest the existence of a pseudo-supply curve of loans, then policy effectiveness remains an open question. This should be assessed by different methods, involving, for instance, direct measures of monetary policy and economic activity. Monthly data series do not seem to be appropriate for this exercise, but an investigation based on annual, possibly firm level, data that can somehow incorporate our findings on interest rate transmission, may shed light on this problem, too.

NOTES

The research was partly financed by a grant from the Hungarian National Science Fund (OTKA 293 'Gazdasági folyamatok elörejelzésének elméti kéredési'). Previous versions of this chapter have been presented at NBH seminars. The authors are grateful for helpful comments and suggestions by Loránd Ambrus-Lakatos, Norbert Élő, László Halpern, Álmos Kovács, Giancarlo Perasso and Charles Wyplosz. The views expressed are those of the authors, and are not to be interpreted as indicating the position of the NBH.

1 The history of Hungarian monetary policy can be followed from the various issues of the NBH *Annual Reports* and *Monthly Bulletins*; for more detailed accounts, see the OECD country studies on Hungary (OECD, 1995, 1997).

2 When speaking of 'operative targets', we do not claim that short-term rates have been operative targets used in the NBH's decision making procedures. Indeed, these procedures, too, have undergone changes, and we cannot regard any single interest rate as the operative target of the NBH in this stricter sense. Rather, we would like to argue that for an outside observer short-term rates could have been interpreted as operative targets of Hungarian monetary policy, in the sense that the monetary authorities wanted to control them, and were able, with some precision, to implement their wishes.

3 Also, expectations of realignments might have caused certain devaluations. The conclusion is unchanged, however.

4 It is interesting to note that the literature is usually silent on deposit rate transmission. In fact the effect of deposit rates on economic activity is something not easy to elucidate. On the one hand, since it is a savings instrument, a rise in deposit rates should lead to more saving, a 'normal' interest rate effect. On the other hand, as far as bank deposits provide transactions (money) services, larger bank deposits might act as a stimulant to economic activity.

5 As we want to apply this model to Hungary, we have to include this seemingly unnecessary complication with respect to mandatory reserves.

6 Strictly speaking, dichotomy also requires that (1) the two sides are separable in real inputs and, (2) in case of imperfect competition the elasticity of deposit supply is independent of lending rates, and the elasticity of credit demand is independent of deposit rates.

7 We speak of an adverse selection effect though, as is well known, moral hazard would account for the same conclusions.

8 In this general form, (4.2) is a far cry from the simple monopoly pricing formula except in one singular case. This singular case holds when the default probability (δ) is constant, and rL represents the demand for credit (in other words in the absence of the adverse selection effect). In that case, $p = \delta r$ with probability 1, and a modified version of the monopoly pricing formula follows:

$$\sigma r - r \frac{1}{E_L} = i$$

9 The retail deposit market must be very important for the transmission mechanism. We tried to estimate transmission equations for household deposit rates, based on panel data, but the results were not very illuminating.

10 All variables, except *WAGES* and *FATB* are directly from CSO publications. The *WAGES* series is due to István Hamecz (NBH).

11 We experimented with non-constant slope coefficients, too, but the terms involved proved to be insignificant.

12 For comparison, Cottarelli and Kourelis (1994) report lending rate transmission estimates for almost identical equations for 31 countries. The mean impact multiplier is 0.32 (0.33) for the level (differenced) estimates. The corresponding mean long-run multipliers are 0.97 (0.82).

13 We attempted to make the same correction for heteroscedasticity in the lending rate equations. The attempt was completely unsuccessful as fits became much worse.

14 The examination of household deposit rates indicated, if anything, an even higher degree of stickiness in the short term.
15 Among the Cottarelli and Kourelis (1994) estimates for developed countries, Japan has one of the smallest coefficients.
16 Cottarelli and Kourelis (1994) estimated a long-run coefficient of 0.88 (0.65) for Hungary in level (differenced) form equations. Their data was somewhat different from ours, and did not allow them to adjust for parameter change.

REFERENCES

Bardsen, G. (1989) 'The estimation of long-run coefficients from error-correction models', *Oxford Bulletin of Economics and Statistics*, **54**, 225–55
Bernanke, B.S. and A. Blinder (1988) 'Credit, money, and aggregate demand', *American Economic Review*, **78**, 435–9
  (1992) 'The Federal funds rate and the transmission of monetary policy', *American Economic Review*, **78**
BIS (Bank for International Settlements) (1994) 'National differences in interest rate transmission', BIS, Monetary and Economic Department, Basle (March)
Cottarelli, C. and A. Kourelis (1994) 'Financial structure, bank lending rates and the transmission mechanism of monetary policy', *IMF Staff Papers*, **41**
Darvas, Z. (1995) 'Exchange rate premia on the Hungarian foreign exchange market', paper presented at the Conference on 'Convertibility and Exchange Rate Policy', Sofia (September 22–23)
Engle, R.F. (1984) 'Wald, Likelihood Ratio and Lagrange Multiplier Tests in econometrics', in Z. Griliches and M.D. Intriligator (eds.), *Handbook of Econometrics*, vol. 2, Amsterdam: North-Holland
Gertler, M. and S. Gilchrist (1993) 'The role of credit market imperfections in the monetary transmission mechanism: arguments and evidence', *Scandinavian Journal of Economics*, **95**
Hannan, T.H. and A.N. Berger (1991) 'The rigidity of prices: evidence from the banking industry', *American Economic Review*, **81**, 938–51
Hutchison, D.E. (1995) 'Retail bank deposit pricing: an intertemporal asset pricing approach', *Journal of Money Credit and Banking*, **27**, 217–31
Jaffee, D. and J. Stiglitz (1990) 'Credit rationing', in B.M. Friedman and F.H. Hahn (eds.), *Handbook of Monetary Economics*, Amsterdam: North-Holland
King, S.R. (1986) 'Monetary transmission', *Journal of Money, Credit and Banking*, **18**, 290–303
Klein, M.A. (1971) 'A theory of the banking firm', *Journal of Money, Credit and Banking*, **3**, 205–18
Mishkin, F.S. (1995) 'Symposium on the monetary transmission mechanism', *Journal of Economic Perspectives* (Fall), 3–10
OECD (1995) *Economic Survey of Hungary*, Paris: OECD
  (1997) *Economic Survey of Hungary*, Paris: OECD
Romer, C. and D. Romer (1990) 'New evidence on the monetary transmission mechanism', *Brookings Papers on Economic Activity*, **1**
Schaffer, S. (1993) 'A test of competition in Canadian banking', *Journal of Money, Credit and Banking*, **25**, 49–61
Stiglitz, J.E. (1992) 'Capital markets and economic fluctuations in capitalist economies', *European Economic Review*, **36**, 269–306

Stiglitz, J.E. and A. Weiss (1981) 'Credit rationing in markets with imperfect information', *American Economic Review*, **71**
(1992) 'Asymmetric information in credit markets and its implications for macroeconomics', *Oxford Economic Papers*, **44**, 694–724
Taylor, J.B. (1995) 'The monetary transmission mechanism: an empirical framework', *Journal of Economic Perspectives* (Fall), 11–26

Discussion

GIANCARLO PERASSO

In their chapter 3, Világi and Vincze (hereafter, VV) tackle the very difficult issue – crucial for conducting economic policy – of whether policy-controlled interest rates influenced bank rates in Hungary in the early 1990s. Before reading the chapter, I was very sceptical about the possibility that even a thorough econometric analysis could lead to a conclusion relevant for the conduct of monetary policy. I am glad that my scepticism has been proved (partially) unfounded by the results the authors present.

The chapter starts with a brief but comprehensive description of the main principles guiding Hungarian monetary policy in the first half of the 1990s, which serves the purpose of setting the broad framework for analysing the interest rate transmission mechanism. VV go on to develop a simple model of Hungarian banks and then proceed to estimate single equation models of the transmission mechanism for both lending and deposit rates. The analysis is thorough, and reaches some interesting conclusions. I will concentrate my comments on three points.

The main conclusion of the chapter is that money market rates, which the authors show to be influenced by the interest rate policy followed by the Central Bank, determine bank rates. This result is reassuring and tells us that in a period of deep structural change the Central Bank can influence money market rates and that the transmission mechanism works, although not perfectly. The question is, thus, why does the transmission mechanism work imperfectly? Is it because of policy shortcomings, institutional features or something else, or is it because something is missing in the specification of the model? The authors themselves point out that their results indicate that 'something' is missing in their analysis that could help us understand why lending rates exhibit some degree of both short- and long-run rigidity, but they do not provide indications as to what might be missing. I would argue that the missing piece in the analysis is due to a modelisation of the Hungarian banking sector which does not capture some of its peculiar features. In particular, it is rather striking that the only costs for banks that are included in the model are those of collecting deposits and that there is no indication of the cost of provisioning for the stock of bad debts which would have allowed for a formal introduction of government intervention to cope with banks' bad debts. It has been calculated (OECD, 1997) that provisions for bad loans have played an important, albeit declining, role in determining interest rate spreads in the 1990s. The authors introduce a dummy variable once they find that there is a break in the series in 1993 which, they argue *passim*, captures the impact of the bank consolidation effort initiated in that year by the government. Aside from the fact that this is only a partial representation of the government effort to 'clean up' banks' balance sheets (different actions were, in fact, taken from 1991 to mid-1995 to relieve banks of the burden of their bad debts[1]), *ex post* rationalisation of the introduction of a dummy variable is somewhat unsatisfactory. In this specific case, one could argue that the break in the series could have been due to other factors: for example, 1993 was the first year of strong growth in aggregate demand since 1989. Hence, one could invoke (*ex post*) the strong increase in aggregate demand as the reason behind the break in the series. I am inclined to agree with the authors that the break is due to government action to clean up the banks' balance sheets, but I would have liked the model to be specified as to include bad loans rather than introducing them in an ad hoc fashion.

The authors point to credit rationing, or 'redlining', as a possible explanation of the low long-run adjustment of lending rates. This is a very important issue that deserves further thorough investigation. Real (PPI-deflated) bank credit has declined sharply since mid-1994 in Hungary and the causes of this decline are not clear. Credit rationing is the first possible explanation of this trend that comes to mind (Cornelli, Portes and Schaffer, 1996, found evidence of credit rationing in Hungary, but their analysis refers to 1992 only), but other factors may well explain the bankers' prudence in extending new loans: past experience; macroeconomic uncertainty, especially concerning inflation; staff inexperience in evaluating loan applications; the availability of adequate collateral.[2]

The analysis of the transmission mechanism for deposit rates is a welcome departure from the standard works on such a mechanism. It is, however, puzzling that the authors chose to concentrate on the rates for enterprise rather than for household deposits, which account for two-thirds of non-bank deposits in Hungary, or for total deposits. A comparison between the results obtained for the enterprise and household sectors could have shed more light on the degree of competition in the market for deposits. A thorough analysis of this issue seems necessary since there has been a concentration in deposits – the five largest Hungarian banks increased their share of total deposits from 62 to 75 per cent between 1992 and 1995 but, at the same time, the difference in deposit rates among different categories of banks narrowed (see OECD, 1997).

In conclusion, the authors deserve much credit for writing an interesting and stimulating chapter which represents a first solid area of research in this field. The rapid changes in both economic policy and the banking sector, especially its almost complete privatisation with strong foreign participation, should be a stimulus for the authors to continue their research work and provide us with further valuable material.

NOTES

The views expressed in the discussion are those of the author and do not reflect those of the OECD nor of its member countries.

1   See OECD (1995) for a detailed description of the financial measures taken by the authorities to aid banks.
2   See OECD (1997) for an analysis of the current situation of the banking sector in Hungary.

REFERENCES

Cornelli, F., R. Portes, and M.E. Schaffer (1996) 'The capital structure of firms in Central Europe', *CEPR Discussion paper*, 1392 (May)
OECD (1995) *Economic Survey of Hungary*, Paris: OECD
    (1997) *Economic Survey of Hungary*, Paris: OECD

4   The nature of Hungarian inflation

ISTVÁN HAMECZ, JÁNOS VINCZE AND
ISTVÁN ZSOLDOS

1   Introduction[1]

Hungarian inflation accelerated after 1990, the year normally considered as the start of transition, when import and price liberalisation made their largest impact on the economy. Beside these shocks, output dropped substantially in 1991 due to the collapse of East European trade, and to tight monetary policy that aimed at balancing external finances. The rate of unemployment began to increase rapidly in 1990, exceeding 10 per cent after 1991, while at the same time CPI inflation peaked around 40 per cent per annum. Through 1992 and early 1993 inflation fell below 20 per cent, but at the cost of an appreciation of the real exchange rate, and because the government kept some of the remaining administered prices within strict bounds. Inflation started to go up again in 1993; it was briefly stabilised, then in 1995 again approached 30 per cent and, after a year of a new stabilisation programme (begun in March 1995), has shown no obvious signs of abating.

Compared to many transitional economies inflation was never extremely high, there were no hyperinflationary episodes. Searching for reasons, one could point out that in Hungary late-socialist economic policies eliminated any monetary overhang that might have existed, that the country had been relatively open to foreign (i.e. 'western') trade and prices, or that Hungary had followed an 'evolutionary'-type policy (no shock therapy) in the early phases of transition.

Clearly the idiosyncrasies of Hungarian policy must have played a significant role in these developments, but with respect to relative price and real exchange rate developments one can guess that more fundamental forces were at play, too. The exchange rate regime before March 1995 was not easily classifiable – indeed, it was called a 'dirty' (or, euphemistically, 'adjustable') peg, where many small devaluations were interspersed among a few major ones (see Darvas, 1995). There was no clearly announced policy rule, but it was tacitly understood that maintaining some long-run real exchange rate target, defined by the PPI, was the government's goal. Since March 1995 a crawling peg with relatively generous bands (4.5 per cent in total) has been in effect, which has made exchange rates rather predictable, but interest rate differentials showed that the chance for a large devaluation was not far from the mind of the market, at least initially. (Though the system has been credible enough to generate continuously large capital inflows.)

On the other hand some salient features of the transition, including the appreciation of the real exchange rate, and a continuous gap between CPI and PPI inflation (see Dittus, 1993; Halpern and Wyplosz, 1995) emerged in Hungary, too. As a consequence certain 'real' measures behaved quite differently depending on which price index one employs for the calculation. For instance, the real exchange rate if measured by the CPI has definitely been appreciating, but if measured by the PPI it has been relatively stable. Large and volatile real interest rates and substantial swings in real wages also characterised the economy. In the latter case, the matter is complicated by the divergence between labour costs and net labour income, the former having increased faster than the latter.

What sort of theory can account for the facts of recent inflation in Hungary? Dornbusch and Fischer (1993) classify causes of inflation based on the presumption that inflation is basically the consequence of government action. From this point of view Hungarian inflation might have fallen into the category 'too costly to stop' – that is, after inflation jumped due to the transitional shocks of import liberalisation and privatisation, the authorities might have been reluctant to decrease inflation to lower levels because of the costs this might have involved.

Though it might satisfy us as a 'final' cause of the persistence of inflation, we should be curious about the details of the inflationary process. It is quite plausible to consider the PPI–CPI gap, and the appreciation of the real exchange rate as two facets of the same phenomenon. The CPI is an aggregate of prices that always contains some element of non-tradability, as final consumption inevitably involves the use of services. One cannot discount the possibility that the phenomenon has something to do with the peculiarities of the statistical system; consumer price statistics were overhauled in 1991, and indices can be really trusted only after 1992. Even a decent statistical system might be helpless in face of large and abrupt changes in the 'consumption basket' that characterised at least the first stages of the transition. A general increase in the level of the quality of goods and services might mean that the consumption good of today has quite different attributes than that of 1991, thus its price should reflect some of this change. We are not aware of the Hungarian Statistical Office having made any attempt to carry out any adjustment for this.

One line of reasoning has been followed by Halpern and Wyplosz (1995), who argue that the Balassa–Samuelson model that emphasises technological changes might partly be able to explain the (equilibrium) real exchange rate appreciation in practically every transitional economy. Analysing the CPI–PPI divergence Dittus (1993) points out the similarity with the Japanese and other Asian countries' experience, which is customarily attributed to income growth and the concomitant shift in favour of consumption goods which may be a proxy of the non-tradable sector. Another relevant historical case is the real exchange rate appreciation that has been widely observed in exchange rate-based stabilisations in Latin America and elsewhere. Calvo and Végh (1993) developed a theory that explains this phenomenon as a temporary feature, caused by the lack of credibility of the exchange rate policy, and working through intertemporal substitution effects. Certainly Hungarian Forint interest rates have sometimes shown large premia, which may have implied the presence of disbelief in the long-run sustainability of exchange rate policies. We will see in section 4 that some of our findings can be interpreted in terms of this theory, though our investigation provides no evidence to confirm or reject any of the other approaches.

In this study, we address various aspects of the inflationary process, focusing on problems that can lend themselves to econometric investigation. In section 2 we search for a money demand equation. In section 3 we turn to desegregated consumer price indices, where the analysis is purely descriptive and graphical. We provide several derived price series, and indicators of price variability and of real exchange rates are calculated by smoothing and decomposition. Then in section 4 we try to quantify the effect of exchange rates on consumer prices in panel models of price indices. Section 5 concludes with a view on some hot policy questions, that are, and will be for some time to come, on the agenda of monetary policy makers.

2 Money and prices

Inflation is a monetary phenomenon which means that although the price level can rise temporarily independently of money growth, other things being equal, a sustained increase of the price level is possible only with monetary accommodation. This observation makes the empirical money demand function an important tool for inflation analysis. A usual hypothesis for economies in transition is that the demand for money is unstable, making money unsuitable as a nominal anchor for policy purposes. This would put exchange rate or incomes (wages) policies in the forefront of policy makers' interests. Incomes policies might be difficult to administer in societies where liberalisation is a general principle of existence. We examine the role of exchange rates in section 4, while in this section we study the stability of money demand and the issue of real wage resistance.

2.1   Money demand

Estimating money demand functions for the transition economies is difficult because of the shortness of samples, the lack of observation on the relevant variables at the desired frequency, the high probability of structural change and the poor quality of the data. Keeping in mind these problems we engaged in the estimation of money demand functions.[2]

We did this for Hungary for the period 1989:4–1995:4. The choice of sample was motivated by the fact that market forces had exerted little influence on interest rates before late 1989. We chose the quarterly frequency because monthly series are too noisy, and we have only quarterly observations on certain monetary aggregates (like M1). Also we had to construct a GDP series, which would have been a formidable task with monthly data.

Previous estimates derived quarterly GDP with the help of quarterly industrial production data adjusted for the annual properties of GDP, although these estimates have two major shortcomings. First, industrial production series are gross output series while GDP is a value added concept. We have experienced in other contexts that the transitional restructuring of industry makes gross output and value added series so divergent as to make it misleading to use one to estimate the other. The second problem stems from structural change: a substantial fall in the share of industry in total value added can be observed due to the rapid growth of the previously under-developed service sector.

Given these problems, we tried to estimate quarterly GDP on an atheoretical basis from annual data. We used cubic spline interpolation to arrive at a quarterly series. This method produces a 'too smooth' series but we do believe that the properties of this series reflect those of the underlying series well enough. We also estimated a quarterly GDP deflator from the quarterly CPI and the annual GDP deflator. The method we chose for this estimation was to compare the annual properties of the CPI and the GDP deflator and adjust the existing CPI series in a way that its annual properties met those of the GDP deflator.

Because there was no noticeable gap between the two indices in the period covered, we think the bias of this procedure is negligible.

The first theoretical problem was the choice of a monetary aggregate that we could call money. In transition economies it is usually deemed advisable to use broad money (M2), as it includes foreign exchange deposits. Eventually we rejected this aggregate because, on the one hand, foreign exchange has never been used for transaction purposes in Hungary, and on the other our analysis showed that the part of M2 which is not in M1 has been driven mainly by the savings motive, and which, with the evolution of new financial instruments such as bank securities (included in M3) and government bonds (included in M4) has become relatively less important due to substitution effects. So we decided to use M1 as money in our analysis.

Johansen-type cointegration analysis suggested that there is a cointegrating relationship between real M1 and real GDP and that the coefficient of real income is 1. (The same analysis for the broader categories showed less appealing relationships. For example, in the case of M4 the estimated coefficient was negative – not surprising as in our period a substantial fall in real GDP was accompanied by the build-up of financial savings, probably due to precautionary motives.) Using this finding, we tried to estimate long- and short-run demand functions for real M1. In the estimation we have restricted the long-run coefficient of real income on money to 1, which means that we estimated an equation for the (log of) inverse velocity of M1 (*LIVELM1*). This equation gave very poor results, and examining the error term we hypothesised that a non-linear trend was present in the data. Re-estimating we get an acceptable estimate (see table 4.1), where we can consider the non-linear trend as a proxy for the shifts in real money demand. The coefficients indicate that in the first years of the transition (until 1993) we can observe an upward shift in money demand, followed by a drastic fall. Here *TB90* is the quarterly series of 90-day Treasury bill yields, and units of measurements are such that the 'long-run' effect of 1 percentage point change in the interest rate on the inverse velocity of real M1 is -0.9.

Using the error terms from the long-run equation we formulated an error correction model for the short-run money demand. As we can see from table 4.1 the short-run semi-elasticity of interest rate is -0.5, which is in line with the evidence from other countries. We cannot reject the null hypothesis that the income elasticity of money demand is not significantly different from 1 at the 10 per cent significance level. The relatively large coefficient on the error correction term implies that deviations from long-run equilibrium have strong short-term effects.

Table 4.1. Money demand equations

Name of equation	The long-run demand for real M1	The short-run demand for real M1	The long-run demand for household real M1	The long-run demand for corporate real M1
Dependent variable	LIVELM1	D(LRM1)	LIVELM1H	LIVELM1C
	C	C	C	C
Regressors (C stands	1.584218*	0.004434*	1.198592*	0.592536*
for constant, t-statistics in parenthesis)	(28.83841)	(2.73254)	(25.00545)	(10.85370)
	TB90	D(TB90)	TB90	TB90
	−0.008898*	−0.005131*	−0.013057*	−0.004913*
	(−6.780453)	(−2.120650)	(−8.633851)	(−3.766927)
	TREND	EC(−1)	TREND	TREND
	0.013193*	−0.459537*	−0.003697*	0.028064*
	(3.101184)	(−2.713080)	(−2.911558)	(6.637917)
	TRENDSQ	D(LGDP)		TRENDSQ
	−0.000964*	0.917627*		−0.001960*
	(−5.659436)	(1.830446)		(−11.57774)
Adjusted $R2$	0.901205	0.197368	0.761761	0.960262
D–W statistic	1.093633	1.504499	0.966228	1.492063

The findings of the above analysis may clarify some of the developments of inflation in the period. The rapid fall of inflation in 1992 can partly be explained by an upward shift in corporate money demand (see below). In 1992, inflation was 23 per cent, after having reached 35 per cent in 1991. Even though the M1:GDP ratio was the same in both years the monetary policy cannot be considered as accommodating because of this shift, the price shock of 1991 died out quickly.

Our hypothesis was that this pattern was due to two factors. The first is a rapid financial innovation both in retail and business banking, the second invokes the rapid growth of business units due to restructuring, bankruptcy laws and privatisation (see also chapter 6), and the resulting rise in the demand for liquidity. We tried to test our hypothesis by splitting M1 into household and corporate components. In the case of household M1 demand the long-run coefficient of interest rate was −1.3, and only a linear trend could be fitted, showing that household demand for M1, after accounting for changes in both incomes and interest rates, fell around a quarterly 0.4 per cent rate through the whole period. As far as corporate M1 demand is concerned the interest rate sensitivity is much smaller (about 0.5 per cent), and the non-linear trend reappears with the same characteristics as in the case of total M1 demand.

Our results would suggest that in 1994 and 1995 the modest growth rates of M1 compared to CPI do not necessarily mean that an anti-inflationary policy was put in place because a large downward shift in money demand, probably due to financial innovations, masked the link between money and inflation. 'Core' inflation did not change very much between 1992 and 1994, as will be shown in section 3 below.

We readily admit that our efforts can be regarded as a fitting exercise rather than the identification of a money demand function. Also we probably over-estimate the effects of financial innovations. The M1 measure probably needs a revision to take into account the new liquidity management techniques developed in the period, mainly repo facilities (see also chapter 2). The known shortcomings of the M1 series should not imply that we will have to switch to M2 or higher aggregates, because those aggregates, besides being influenced by other factors than pure money demand considerations, do not reflect the full range of financial innovations either.

3   Data analysis of disaggregated consumer prices

3.1   Disaggregated consumer prices

The Hungarian Central Statistical Office has published detailed consumer price indices since the beginning of 1992. The breakdown is into 160 subgroups, and both month-on-the-same-month-of-the-previous-year and month-on-previous-month-type indices are published. Taking these two series for 1992, it is possible to calculate the implied monthly inflation data for 1991, except for January 1991. Having done the calculations, some of the implied price indices showed suspiciously large swings, in which cases we treated the 1992 12-month inflation data points as missing observations, and replaced them with the average of the two neighbouring 12-month inflation data. Of course, as a result of this, 1991 figures are less reliable than the rest.

In this way we arrived at 160 price level indices (where January 1991 = 1) by chaining the monthly inflation rates. The natural logarithm of these price indices was taken as the starting point of all calculations. All subsequent references to the price level are to these indices.

Our goal was to pick out series amenable to statistical analysis. First we divided the 160 goods into four subgroups: regulated, foodstuffs, other tradables, non-tradables. We classified a good as 'regulated' wherever its price is set by the government, or a significant part of the price is made up by subsidies or excise taxes, whose changes are likely to be the consequence of fiscal policy. As weights we used the average yearly weights during the period 1992–5 as published by the Central Statistical Office, that applies Laspeyres-weighting based on the consumption structure of the previous year. The difference in weights, however, does not cause a great discrepancy between the inflation rates calculated by us and the CSO.[3]

The weights of the four subgroups are as follows:

'Regulated'	31.200
Foodstuffs	23.700
Tradables	28.925
Non-tradables	16.175

We disregard the 'regulated' group in econometric investigations. Then we tried to separate the effect of VAT increases. Because we do not know how the effect of a VAT increase is distributed between consumer price increase and producer price decline, in many cases it is difficult to determine the exact scope and magnitude of VAT increases. We decided to estimate the effects of VAT changes purely by statistical methods. We have taken first and twelfth differences of each 'unregulated' index, and run the following regression on the resulting series:

$$DSP_i = \alpha_1^* \text{constant} + \alpha_2^* DSP_i(-1) + \alpha_3^* DSP_i(-2) + \alpha_4^* DSP_i(-3)$$
$$+ \alpha_5^* MA(1) + \alpha_6^* MA(2) + \alpha_7^* MA(3) + \alpha_8^* DUMJAN93$$
$$+ \alpha_9^* DUMAUG93 + \alpha_{10}^* DUMJAN95$$

where DSP_i stands for the twice-differenced log price index of commodity group i and MAs represent moving-average terms. The last three variables are impact dummies for the three points in time when significant changes in VAT rates occurred (January 1993, August 1993, January 1995). We treated the coefficients of these dummy variables as the impact of the VAT changes, but if the estimated impact was higher than the whole of the VAT increase at that time then we limited it to the size of the VAT increase. This method has the drawback that in some cases it shows VAT impact even when we know for sure that there was no VAT increase in the case of the particular commodity group, but we stuck to this method for want of a better one. The aggregate effect of the VAT shocks was estimated as 2.2 per cent, 0.6 per cent and 0.3 per cent in January 1993, August 1993 and January 1995, respectively.

Table 4.2. Seasonal components of aggregate monthly inflation

	(%)
January	0.60
February	0.04
March	−0.06
April	0.07
May	−0.01
June	−0.56
July	−0.42
August	−0.54
September	0.36
October	0.32
November	0.11
December	0.08

For the deshocked series we examined whether they exhibited seasonality. We treated a time series as seasonal if the 12th autocorrelation coefficient was significant at the 5 per cent level, or if this coefficient was close to being significant, and the 24th autocorrelation coefficient was significant. We seasonally adjusted the deshocked price series with the X11 ARIMA method. From now on we treat the resulting seasonally adjusted series as the basis of our analysis. We arrived at the seasonal components in the overall monthly inflation rates shown in table 4.2.

It is interesting to have a look at some of the indices that can be derived from our adjusted data set. Figure 4.1 shows the decomposition of the adjusted aggregate monthly inflation rate into two components: changes in 'regulated' prices, and the rest which we will call 'core' inflation. We are sorry to possibly add to the confusion surrounding the concept of core inflation. We use inverted commas to indicate that we have no rigorous theoretical notion in mind. Rather our 'core' is defined with the aim of obtaining something that can be analysed by statistical methods. Subtracting the effect of 'large' government interventions basically means that we try to filter out discrete events the analysis of which would be practically impossible in such a short sample. This 'core' concept has apparently nothing to do with the recent theoretically-based analysis of core inflation by Quah and Vahey (1995), whose core inflation can be regarded as a dual to the notion of potential output.

It is striking that a good deal of the variance of inflation is a result of the variance of regulated price increases and VAT shocks – the 'core' is relatively smooth, and its contribution to the overall monthly inflation is around 1–1.3 per cent in the whole period. This is an important point to

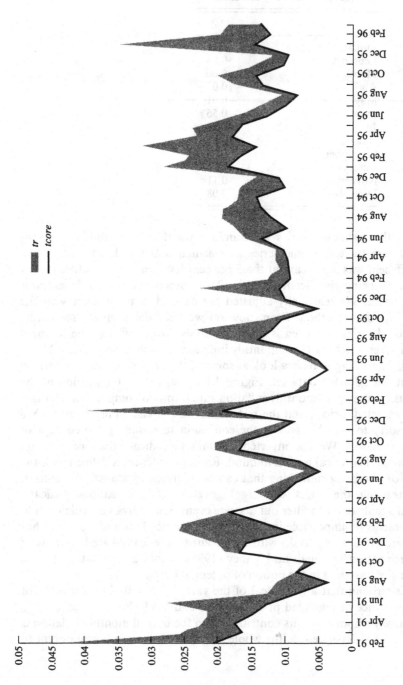

Figure 4.1 Decomposition of monthly inflation rate into 'regulated price' increase and 'core', February 1991–February 1996

emphasise because in economic analysis, and in the media, a great deal of attention is given to the CPI inflation, under which apparently lies a more stable 'core'. This underlying inflation has exhibited a (noisy) upward trend since the second half of 1993. The effect of the March 1995 policy package, which included real wage and budget deficit cuts as well as the new exchange rate regime (see chapter 2), is hard to assess, but clear signs of a trend reversal are not apparent.

Figure 4.2 shows that there was substantial variation across subgroups among 'unregulated' prices. The variability of food price inflation is high, even after removing the seasonal component. This argues in favour of calculating a separate non-food non-regulated price index, which would give an alternative, and presumably less noisy picture of the inflationary process. Figure 4.3 presents a version of this index, together with the inflation rate of food products.

3.2   The variability of prices

Economists have traditionally considered the variability of prices as one of the main costs of inflation (see Driffill, Mizon and Ulph, 1990). The concept of 'variability' can be understood either as the conditional variance of aggregate inflation, or as the (cross-sectional) variability of relative prices. There is a general expectation among economists of finding positive correlation between relative price variability and the level of aggregate inflation, and there exists an important literature (see, for instance, Cukierman, 1982) that formulated hypotheses with respect to the positive correlation between relative price variability and the variance of aggregate inflation. The conjunction of these two hypotheses involves the existence of ARCH effects (see Engle, 1983). Estimating aggregate inflation equations we have not found ARCH effects in the error process, which suggests that this sort of variability may not be our concern.

Relative price change distributions are usually found to be non-normal, and this is true for our sample, too. Thus it is advisable to create several indicators for relative price variability besides cross-sectional standard deviation. We computed four series: cross-sectional standard deviation (*STANDDEV*), the difference between the largest and smallest inflation rates (*DMINMAX*), the difference between the first and third quartile (*DQUART*), and the dispersion defined in Blejer (1983) (*DISP*), which is the average of pairwise absolute deviations:

$$DISP_t = (1/(n-1)) \sum_{i=1}^{n-1} \sum_{j=i+1}^{n} (w_i + w_j)^* |(DP_i - DP_j)_t|$$

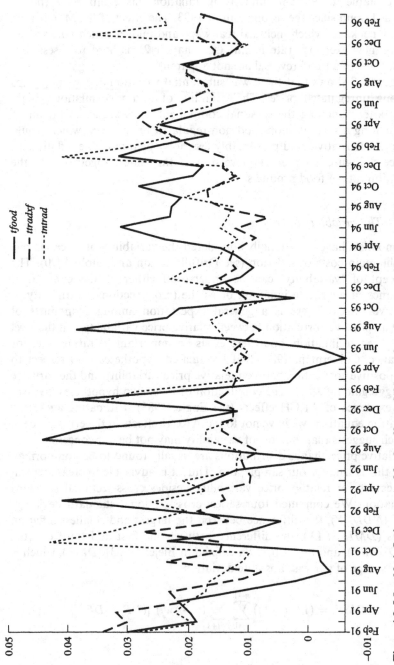

Figure 4.2 Monthly inflation rates of foodstuffs, tradable goods and non-tradable goods, February 1991–February 1996

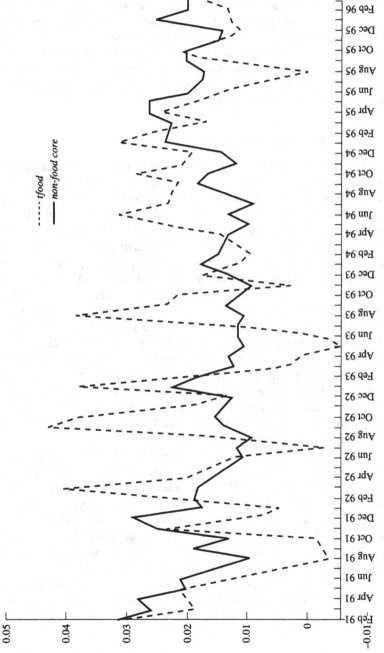

Figure 4.3 Monthly inflation rates of non-food, non-regulated goods, February 1991–February 1996

These indicators show similar pictures (see figures 4.4 and 4.5), perhaps with the exception of *DQUART*. The latter, which is less sensitive to outliers, suggests some decrease in dispersion by 1995.

If we graph quartile series (see figure 4.6) they suggest that dispersion was higher in the first two years of our period, whereas after 1993 different quartiles moved consistently together, and even the rise in inflation was not accompanied by any significant divergence. This suggests that the bulk of transitional relative price change was accomplished in the first couple of years. Since then the role of relative price changes in aggregate inflation must have diminished.[4]

3.3   Real exchange rate indicators

We can define several real exchange indicators from the disaggregated consumer price series (see figure 4.7). Here 'real exchange rate' means the price of foreign goods in terms of the home good, thus an appreciation must be understood as a fall in the real exchange rate indicator. We do not use foreign prices for these calculations, and our indicators can only capture the distinction between home and foreign goods. The first two indicators are the ratio of tradable (including food) prices to non-tradable prices (*RXCR*), and the ratio of non-food tradable prices to non-tradable prices (*RXCRXF*). Obviously the idea here is that tradable prices must follow more closely the prices of foreign goods, and non-tradables are a good approximation to home goods. The exclusion of food prices is intended to reduce the noise. The third index (*RXCRN*) is defined as the ratio of the nominal exchange rate to tradable prices, which is based on the idea of measuring price competitiveness by comparing changes in export and domestic prices in the tradable sector, where the nominal exchange rate serves as a proxy for export prices, assuming that the bulk of their variance must have come from changes in the exchange rate. (It must be true for Hungary.)

As we can see from figure 4.7 *RXCR* and *RXCRXF* exhibit downward trends, though there are signs that they stabilised after March 1995. *RXCRN* declines steeply in 1991–2, then seems to be stabilising, or even showing some slight increase. These phenomena can be explained by the theories discussed in the Introduction. If we take the theories based on either secular changes in technology (in favour of tradable goods), and/or that of changes in demand (in favour of non-tradables), both would imply such behaviour, quite irrespective of government policies.

In the case of Hungary specific transitional relative price changes must have occurred, too. If we look at the list of 'most increasing' prices over the period (for the list of commodities see appendix 4.1) we find

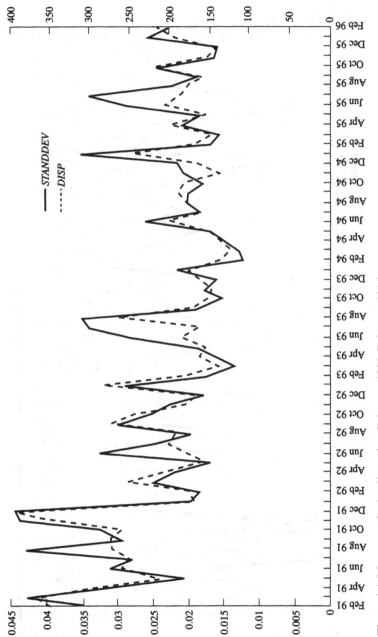

Figure 4.4 Measures of price dispersion, February 1991–February 1996

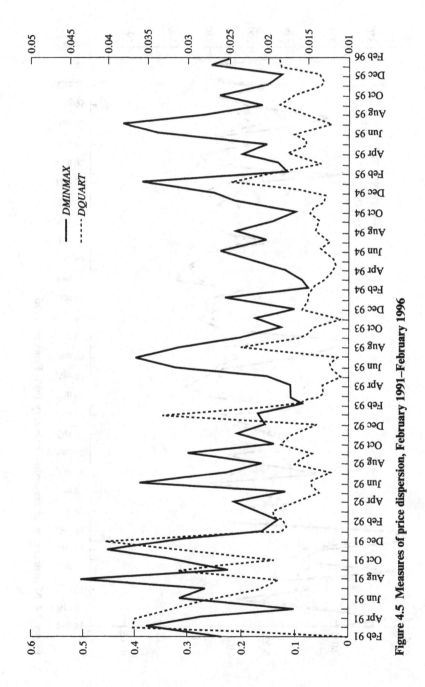

Figure 4.5 Measures of price dispersion, February 1991–February 1996

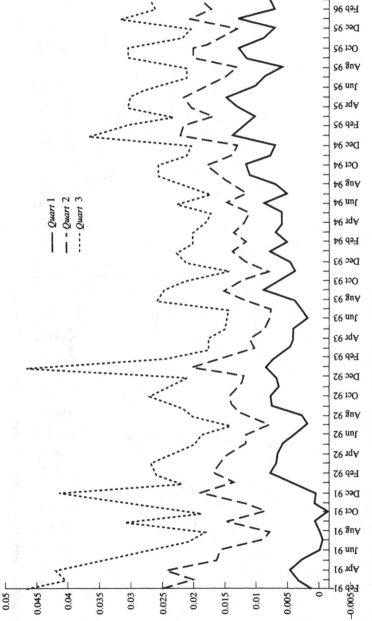

Figure 4.6 Quartile inflation rates, February 1991–February 1996

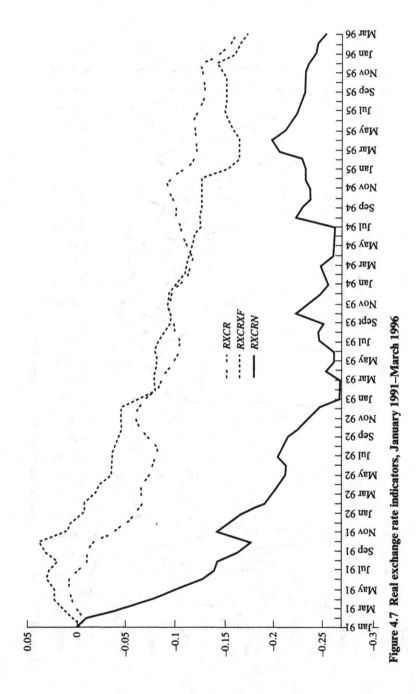

Figure 4.7 Real exchange rate indicators, January 1991–March 1996

commodity groups related to culture and education (books, school books, theatre tickets, newspapers), household energy, telephone, communal services, medicines – all belonging to once highly subsidised categories with rather restricted supply in several cases. The large increase in these prices is, most probably, due to the abolition of subsidies, and to market deregulation. Also telling is the case of bacon, traditionally the poor man's food in Hungary, the price of which leads the group of food prices. Transitional changes should have made their impact rather early, thus the continuing downward trends need some further clarification. It is also interesting to notice that $RXCRXF$ actually increased in 1991. This might reflect the effect of import liberalisation, which entailed the opening of many tradable goods markets, including cars, electronic equipment and household appliances, whose relative price increases might have been temporary, and a consequence of the inability of the statistical system to reflect quality differences. Many of these commodities belong to the 'least increasing' price category over the whole period.

One may guess also that the effect of monetary (exchange rate) policy must be looked for in deviations from trend. Fitting linear trends to these indicators $RXCRXF$ shows extra appreciation in 1992 when exchange rates were kept relatively unchanged, and an opposite deviation after March 1995. The behaviour of $RXCRN$ might be interpreted as showing that the adjustment of domestic tradable prices was accomplished by the end of 1992.

4   Exchange rates and prices

Hungarian exchange rates have, by and large, been determined by the government, and can be taken as predetermined. Strong exogeneity would probably be a wrong assumption, as some sort of real exchange rate targeting might have characterised the behaviour of the government at various times. Hungary being a relatively open, small economy, both common sense and theory suggests that the domestic price level should be influenced very much by the exchange rate, and in the long run inflation must follow very closely the rate of change in the exchange rate. However, as we noted in the Introduction, Hungary, like other transitional countries, has seen domestic consumer prices increase more than the rate of devaluation since 1990. In this section we attempt to give some estimates for the size of the 'autonomous' exchange rate appreciation (see definition below), and for the effect exchange rates had on the rate of inflation.

From basic economic theory, and common sense as well, one can assume that the price level in a small open economy should be rather closely related to the nominal exchange rate of the country in question. In a statistical sense, one would not expect cointegration to exist between these two variables, as world prices might not be stationary, and relative terms of trade might change due to the country's exceptional growth performance. These distortionary effects may be of much smaller magnitude for countries having relatively high levels of inflation than the size of exchange rates and price movements; thus picking up statistical relationships between price levels and exchange rates may prove to be a chimera. Still there is a better chance if one is willing to work with changes (growth rates) to estimate relationships with some precision, at the cost of giving up the probability of interpreting the price–exchange rate level. It seems more plausible for us to define exchange rate pass-through and appreciation in terms of first differences.

Let π denote the log change of some (domestic) price index, and e the log change of the nominal exchange rate. Then if we suppose that π can be approximated linearly as

$$\pi = \delta + \eta e \tag{1}$$

we will call δ the (approximate) autonomous real appreciation rate.

This relationship has a time dimension, and in principle one can identify δ and η parameter pairs for every time horizon.

Assuming zero foreign inflation, any given level of inflation and exchange rate devaluation defines the total real appreciation as $\pi - e$, and admits different δ and η parameters to be consistent with (1). The question of estimating these parameters has policy relevance, since the larger η the larger the impact exchange rate policy has on the rate of inflation. We can expect that over an infinite horizon, with no change in technology or preferences η will be unity and δ zero (with small foreign inflation close to zero). However, as we cannot assume that Hungary in the 1990s was even close to a state of long-run equilibrium, it is important to form a notion of how much, in the short-term, policy can affect prices by controlling the exchange rate, since the costs of using the exchange rate as a nominal anchor are clearly dependent on these parameters. With short- and medium-term ηs less than 1, nominal exchange rate devaluation has a positive effect on the real exchange rate, and only partially increases inflation. Looking at it from another angle, using the nominal exchange rate as a nominal anchor would in that case be only imperfectly effective.

We estimated several time series ADL equations linking various measures of CPI inflation with the rate of devaluation as the exogenous driving variable, and found rather poor results, irrespective of using levels or differences, the crude CPI, or its 'core' component as defined in section 3. Instead of the basic monthly data series we experimented with moving averages as well. One possible explanation for this failure is the presence of aggregation bias. Price movements are certainly better described by including autoregressive components than by using some distributed lag formulation. In our case there exists a possibility for aggregation bias as there is only a negligible chance that lagged inflation variables would have the same coefficients in each commodity group making up the CPI. Thus these considerations led us to apply the random coefficient model as developed by Swamy (1970) among others. (See also Greene, 1990, pp. 476–9.)

According to our general specification hypothesis the price index of group i can be written as

$$p_i = f_i(p_i(-1), \ldots, neer, neer(_1), neer(_2), \ldots, T) + \varepsilon_i \qquad (2)$$

where $neer$ is the nominal exchange rate, T is some time trend (see more on that later), and $\hat{\varepsilon}_i$ is white noise, uncorrelated with arguments in f_i. We assume also that the error terms pertaining to different groups, i and j, are independent of each other.

This expression represents a reduced form dynamic relationship between exchange rates and prices that cannot be construed in any sense as a structural equation. We include no other right-hand-side variable than the exchange rate, as we do not know of any that can be deemed to be orthogonal to it, and we want to measure the total effect of the exchange rate. (Neither do we have any group-specific variables that would capture group-specific cost or demand effects.)

In the following we always assume a linear form for f_is which we feel can only be justified as an approximation. As in other cases of time series analysis with trending variables it is important to pay attention to the specification of the trend.

Specification 1

$$\Delta p_i = A_i(L)\Delta p_i(_1) + B_i(L)\Delta e + C_i\varepsilon_i \qquad (3)$$

Here we assume that prices (a non-stationary series) are the 'consequence' of two non-stationary components, one of them observable (the exchange rates), the other non-observable. The non-observable components can be thought of as the mixture of factors invoked in the explanations of the transitional real exchange rate appreciation as described in the Introduction. The crucial assumption here is that the latter follows a random walk with drift – and what we want to do is to measure the effect of this 'underlying' drift – that is, the implied drift in the price index.

Specification 2

$$p_i = A_i(L)p_i(-1) + B_i(L)e + C_i^* t + D_i + \varepsilon_i \qquad (4)$$

Here the relationship is written in terms of levels.

D_is have no substantive meaning, they just fix the 'unit of measurement'.[5] The interpretation of C_is may be similar to the former case, though having deterministic trends for tastes and technology is somewhat too imaginative. Also an explanation involving the presence of bubbles may come to mind, with the trend representing the belief that real exchange rate appreciation will go on just because everyone expects it will do. The stochastic behaviour of an equation like (3) is different from one like (2). We will see indeed that there are substantial differences between the estimates of the two specifications.

There are 132 price indices included in the 'core' price series, with monthly observations running from 1991:2 to 1996:2. In models 1–3 (see appendix 4.3) we used the series with VAT interventions excluded, and in model 4 included. In the latter case we employed three impulse dummies in the equation specifications. We estimated a random coefficient model based on this panel of data. In other words, we assumed that individual equations have the same form, and the same size of parameter vector (β_i), which are randomly and independently drawn from a distribution with expected value β, and covariance matrix Γ. Our goal was to estimate these parameters. (See appendix 4.2 for details of the estimation procedure.)

In this type of model (see Pesaran and Smith, 1995) the consistency of the estimate of β can be achieved by estimating the individual equations separately (by OLS, for instance), and then forming some average of them. This might take the form of a simple unweighted average, or the GLS matrix weighted average as derived in Swamy (1970). The latter is more efficient, but requires a consistent estimate of the covariance matrix of the individual parameter OLS estimates. In case 2 (model 2) we have serious doubts that the conventional estimate would fulfil this condition, thus we applied the GLS estimate in all of the specifications in case 1, and the unweighted estimate in case 2.

We must stress that we do not want to interpret our estimates as giving information on the truly long-run behaviour of prices. However, for the (local) linear approximations we estimate, one can obviously compute 'long-run' coefficients in the usual manner. These 'long-run' coefficients have some merit as they give concise information on the local behaviour of prices. Thus we report our parameter estimates in this way, giving 'long-run' exchange rate effects and 'long-run' autonomous real appreciation parameters for each equation (see appendix 4.3). These long-run parameters can be calculated from different transformations of the same linear model, some of which have the desirable property of enabling one to read long-run effects directly from coefficient estimates, rather than requiring calculation. As Banerjee et al. (1993, pp. 62–4) prove, if we apply the Bewley transformation (see Banerjee et al., 1993, pp. 54–5), to (3) or (4), numerically the same long-run estimates can be obtained by IV using specific instruments, as when estimating the original equations by OLS and then computing the long-run effects. However, in our case of aggregating over different individual regression parameters the Bewley transformation has effects on the actual outcome, and should be viewed as an alternative hypothesis concerning the random process defining the coefficients. We applied this methodology to our data, too, and report estimates with the Bewley transformation as well.

After computing our estimates of average β (or functions thereof) we can form our best linear predictors of β_is from the initial estimates and the estimate of the average (see Greene, 1990, p. 478). With these predictors we can compute error series for each group which can be used for diagnosing specification failures, or comparing model specifications.

First we had to establish a common lag structure for our equations. We used traditional F-tests for lag exclusion in the individual equations starting with a lag of 5. We found that at lag length 3 in more than 10 per cent of equations the third lag was still significant, but at lag length 2 the last lag was significant only in less than 10 per cent of the total. Thus we opted for an ADL (3, 4), where we used a longer lag for the exchange rate in order to include in the sample the large devaluation in 1991:1, for which date we have no price indices. To capture potential temporal changes – which we indeed expected – in parameter estimates we estimated the model for three periods: (1) 1991:2–1995:2, (2) 1991:2–1996:2, (3) 1992:1–1996:2, where the lower dates refer to the last lag of the endogenous variables.

From Table 4A.1 in appendix 4.3 it appears that 'long-run' exchange rate coefficients are well below unity. We calculated the 'long-run' exchange rate coefficients in the customary way, namely we stripped the time subscripts of the variables and rearranged the equation so that on the right-hand side only the estimators were left, while on the left-hand side the dependent variable appears with a coefficient of unity. Then we added up the coefficients of the different lags of the exchange rate to arrive at the estimate of the long-run exchange rate coefficient. We denoted this estimate by LRB (long-run beta) in table 4A.1. We used a similar method for calculating the estimate of the long-run constant (denoted LRC) in table 4A.1, except that we did not have to deal with the lagged values of the constant only with the dependent variable when rearranging the equations.

The implied 'autonomous' real rate appreciation is above 10 per cent per annum for specification 1. For specification 2 the exchange rate coefficients are higher, but still less than 1, whereas autonomous real rate appreciation is negligible. At the same time parameters seem to change through time, in line with our expectations. The 'long-run' exchange rate effect increases through time indicating that the economy may have come nearer to long-run homogeneity. On the other hand, the slope parameter behaves strangely. 'Autonomous' appreciation even started to increase, then fell back to its former value. This finding may reflect the non-credibility of the 'no devaluation policy' in effect from the end of 1992 to mid-1993 (see figure 4.8 for the evolution of exchange rates) that was accompanied by a substantial decrease in short-term interest rates and a concomitant huge deterioration in external balance. The Calvo and Végh (1993) model can be invoked to give an explanation: a non-credible decrease in the rate of devaluation creates an expectation of an eventual rise in its rate, together with an increase in interest rates which, working through intertemporal substitution in consumption, leads to an increase in consumption, a negative balance of trade and an over-heating of the economy resulting in higher non-tradable inflation, i.e. an autonomous real exchange appreciation. An indirect proof for the applicability of this story for Hungary is presented by the behaviour of interest rates during this period. Though short-term rates first went down, longer-term lending practically came to a halt, the government was unable to issue longer-term fixed-coupon securities. Thus though the short-term ('instantaneous') interest rates declined more or less in line with the fall in the rate of devaluation, the eventual unsustainability of the regime was reflected in the steepness of the yield curve. The Hungarian 'hidden' exchange rate-based stabilisation – it was not announced as such – was a temporary phenomenon which, however, may distort our estimates.

How can we choose among models, and especially between specifications of the trend? We computed 'error' series from each aggregate equation (with full sample estimates), examined them with respect to normality and autocorrelation, and we also studied the distribution of individual parameter estimates (best linear predictors) (see table 4A.2 in appendix 4.3). On these measures it seems that estimates obtained from specification 2 (model 2) were definitely worse than the other estimates

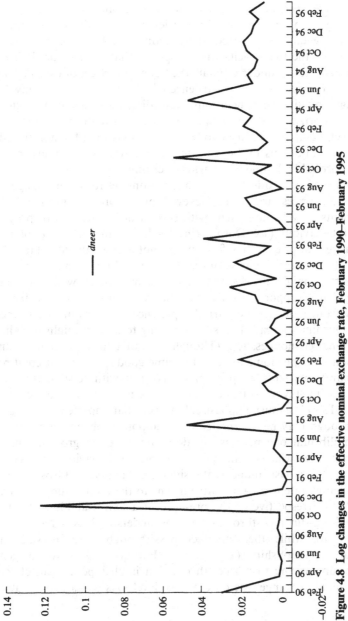

Figure 4.8 Log changes in the effective nominal exchange rate, February 1990–February 1995

dneer

belonging to specification 1. The estimates were relatively precise for this specification as shown by the standard errors for (1) in table 4A.5 in appendix 4.3. On the other hand we have no clear basis for preferring any of the remaining equations. Each of them exhibited rather significant error autocorrelation, which would suggest that possibly longer lags should have been necessary. Therefore we estimated an equation with longer lags, too, but 'long-run' coefficients showed the same features as those in the models reported in appendix 4.3. A comparison between estimates of the two specifications suggests that even if the differenced form specifications under-estimate the 'long-run' effect of exchange rates, we have no evidence for the existence of a bias so large as to invalidate our main qualitative conclusions, according to which in the short to medium horizon: (1) exchange rate pass-through has been rather imperfect; (2) it was stronger for tradable goods than for non-tradables; and (3) autonomous exchange rate appreciation was not insignificant, but has probably declined somewhat over time.

One may raise the question if such low estimates for the exchange rate's impact on prices are to be believed on theoretical grounds. These coefficients may be consistent with several novel theories of pricing to market behaviour (see Dornbusch, 1987, for an early example), that emphasise that price setting firms would not necessarily intend to achieve a perfect exchange rate pass-through. It is well known that monopolistic price setting might involve marginal cost multipliers well below unity. The evidence supporting pricing to market behaviour has so far come mainly from industrial countries' experience, and has not been unequivocal. Our findings can suggest that pricing to market might be valid for transitional economies, too. (Though note that third-order price discrimination – the phenomenon that the same good is sold at different prices on separate markets as price margins vary with local elasticities of demand – in 'favour' of poor countries is not a new idea; see Tirole, 1988, p. 137.) We must emphasise, however, that imperfect exchange rate pass-through may be interpreted as a temporary phenomenon. In long-run equilibrium one may expect domestic prices to grow in line with exchange rates whatever the particular pricing behaviour the economy exhibits. (It is a basic monetarist insight, see Adams and Gros, 1986, that the exchange rate is an alternative means to the money supply to fix the price level, irrespective of the presence of a non-tradable sector.) This perfect long-run pass-through must be understood as a reduced form relationship, while the imperfect pass-through may be valid as a structural relationship. (Though see Faruqee, 1995, for a general equilibrium pricing to market theory that implies permanent effects of the nominal exchange rate on the price level.) As we essentially attempt to estimate reduced form relations, our findings, if they are correct, are strongly in favour of pricing to market behaviour since in reduced form equations the exchange rate's impact should be higher than in a structural context.

Table 4A.4 in appendix 4.3 shows those commodity groups that have the highest (lowest) parameter estimates for the exchange rate effect. Our results largely accord with our expectations on the behaviour of tradable versus non-tradable prices. This conclusion is supported by table 4A.1 in appendix 4.3, where we report estimates separately for the tradable sector as well. This table shows that changing the nominal exchange rate had significant effects on the real exchange rate, in the short term at least, as the prices of tradable goods seem to have been more responsive to nominal exchange rate changes than those of non-tradable goods. However, none of our estimates suggests that these goods satisfy the definition of tradability employed in theoretical models, which would imply an instantaneous adjustment to foreign prices expressed in domestic currency, based on the idea of international commodity arbitrage under the conditions of free trade.

5   Summary and conclusions

Our measure of 'core' price index has properties that distinguish it from the crude CPI. It is much more stable, and it started to increase in 1993 – that is, earlier than the reported CPI. Subaggregates behave sufficiently differently to warrant analysis of disaggregated data. Analysis of quintiles suggests that the initial relative price changes, that were probably of a correcting nature, made their effect in 1991–2, but by the end of 1992 correction of former distortions was probably accomplished. Of course the initial burst of inflation might have been caused partly by these relative price changes, and an inflationary inertia might have developed. Our money demand equations contain non-linear trends, which suggests that they do not reflect stable relationships, being rather the result of a fitting exercise, thus calling into doubt the meaningfulness of using them as a basis for monetary policy. Our panel data estimates suggest that exchange rates have played only a partial role in the inflationary process, and the nominal exchange rate did have relative price effects, in the sense that tradable goods' prices reacted more strongly to exchange rate changes. Exchange rates appear to have become more influential in the inflationary process.

It seems that after 1992 relative price uncertainty diminished, and we have no clear evidence to judge the relationship between the predictability and the level of aggregate inflation. It then follows that the costs of inflation must be looked for in the generally high level of inflation, causing distortions in taxation and possibly adverse effects on growth. Thus the question whether the nominal exchange rate could be used as a nominal anchor should be raised. Our analysis suggests also that at the moment decreasing the preannounced rate of devaluation would not cause a rapid one-to-one fall in the inflation rate. Rather, it would cause higher real exchange rate appreciation. Thus fighting inflation should be complemented by action in other areas, like fiscal policy, or by decreasing domestic nominal demand. Even if it turns out that some real appreciation remains in the system it would not necessarily be bad, as it might possibly reflect the general tendency that non-tradables prices increase faster than tradables prices. Thus for economic policy it would be prudent to monitor relative price changes when judging the impacts of actions.

Appendix 4.1: 'most increasing' and 'least increasing' prices, 1991:1–1996:2

List of 'most increasing' prices during the sample period (1991:1–1996:2), average monthly price increase

	(%)
School books	4.35
Pharmaceuticals	4.02
Fuel oil	3.56
Telephone	3.17
Butane and propane	3.10
Briquettes, cake	2.98
Domestic holiday with holiday voucher	2.86
Books	2.76
Motorcycles	2.65
Local mass transport	2.58
Theatres, concerts	2.57
Bacon	2.53
Purchased heat	2.50
Sewage disposal fees	2.50
Newspapers, periodicals	2.47

List of 'least increasing' prices during the sample period (1991:1–1996:2), average monthly price increase

	(%)
Videocassette, headphones	0.53
Television sets	0.66
Holiday abroad	1.01
Vacuum cleaner, sewing machine	1.07
Bicycle	1.10
Children's coat	1.10
Potato	1.11
Washing machine, spin drier	1.11
Sugar	1.12
Canned meat	1.12
VCR, tape recorder	1.16
Women's hose, socks	1.20
Passenger car, used	1.21
Refrigerator, freezers	1.22
Passenger car, new	1.23

Appendix 4.2: estimation and prediction in the random coefficients model

This brief description is based on Swamy (1970, pp. 312–15), and Greene (1990, pp. 476–9).

Let i denote the ith group ($i = 1, \ldots, 132$). Then either specification 1 or 2 can be written as

$$p_i = X_i\beta_i + \varepsilon_i$$

$E(\varepsilon_i) = 0$, $E(\varepsilon_i^2) = \sigma_{ii}$ and $E(\varepsilon_i\varepsilon_j) = 0$ for different i and j, and all the ε_i, series are serially uncorrelated.

Here p_i is the price or inflation of the ith group (we suppress the time subscript), and X_i contains lagged values of p_i, contemporaneous and lagged values of the nominal exchange rate, a constant, and possibly a time trend. Thus in our case the X_i matrices differ only because of the presence of the lagged own price variables. We assume that

$$\beta_i = \beta + v_i$$

where $E(v_i) = 0$ and $E(v_i v_i') = \Gamma$

We also assume that ε_i and ε_j, as well as β_i and β_j are independent for each different i and j.

Then for given Γ the GLS estimator for β can be written as

$$\beta' = \Sigma W_i b_i$$

where b_i is the least squares coefficient vector of the ith equation, and W_i is a weighting matrix defined as

$$W_i = (\Sigma_i(\Gamma + V_i)^{-1})^{-1}(\Gamma + V_i)^{-1}$$

and V_i is the least squares coefficient 'covariance matrix' as computed in the usual way.

To make the estimation procedure feasible we need to replace Γ with an estimate of it. It can be done with the formula

$$G = (1/(n-1))(\Sigma_i b_i b_{i\prime} - n\, bb') - (1/n)\ \Sigma_i V_i$$

where $b = (1/n)\Sigma b_i$

It is possible that G is not positive definite, in which case we used the suggestion in Greene (1990), and dropped the last term.

The best linear predictor of β_i can be defined as

$$\beta_i' = (\Gamma^{-1} + V_i^{-1})^{-1}(\Gamma^{-1}\beta' + V_i^{-1}b_i)$$

Appendix 4.3: results of panel data estimation

LRC stands for 'long-run' constant (see text for definition). LRB stands for 'long-run' beta ('long-run' exchange rate effect – see text for definition).

Table 4A.1. Estimation period: 1991:2–1996:2

No.	Sample	Level/ Change	Method (weighting)	LRC	LRB
1	Whole sample	Change	Random coefficients	0.012975	0.239105
2	Tradable goods	Change	Random coefficients	0.010414	0.341689
3	Whole sample	Level	Random coefficients (consumer basket weights)	0.002374	0.366794
4	Tradable goods	Level	Random coefficients (consumer basket weights)	0.001090	0.720245
5	Whole sample	Change	Random coefficients (instrumental variables)	0.013175	0.216538
6	Tradable goods	Change	Random coefficients (instrumental variables)	0.010952	0.295106

No.	Sample	Level/ Change	Method (weighting)	LRC	LRB
7	Whole sample	Change	Random coefficients (series containing VAT shocks)	0.0116	0.307631
8	Tradable goods	Change	Random coefficients (series containing VAT shocks)	0.010472	0.353893
9	Whole sample	Change	Random coefficients	0.013123	0.182953
10	Tradable goods	Change	Random coefficients	0.011315	0.179063
11	Whole sample	Level	Random coefficients (consumer basket weights)	0.003127	0.289623
12	Tradable goods	Level	Random coefficients (consumer basket weights)	0.002417	0.332998
13	Whole sample	Change	Random coefficients (instrumental variables)	0.013724	0.117108
14	Tradable goods	Change	Random coefficients (instrumental variables)	0.012324	0.085502
15	Whole sample	Change	Random coefficients (series containing VAT shocks)	0.260189	0.011718
16	Tradable goods	Change	Random coefficients (series containing VAT shocks)	0.225679	0.011085
17	Whole sample	Change	Random coefficients	0.013448	0.182743
18	Tradable goods	Change	Random coefficients	0.008855	0.399004
19	Whole sample	Level	Random coefficients (consumer basket weights)	0.002914	0.317285

No.	Sample	Level/ Change	Method (weighting)	LRC	LRB
20	Tradable goods	Level	Random coefficients (consumer basket weights)	0.001605	0.592778
21	Whole sample	Change	Random coefficients (instrumental variables)	0.013320	0.185361
22	Tradable goods	Change	Random coefficients (instrumental variables)	0.008983	0.384154
23	Whole sample	Change	Random coefficients (series containing VAT shocks)	0.011402	0.293460
24	Tradable goods	Change	Random coefficients (series containing VAT shocks)	0.008753	0.420944

Statistics of model 1

Properties of the residuals calculated as a difference of (observed) aggregate inflation and its prediction, using the coefficient estimates of model 1, are shown in table 4A.2.

Table 4A.2

Lags	AC	PAC	Q-stat	Prob
1	0.248	0.248	3.7487	0.053
2	−0.197	−0.275	6.1554	0.046
3	−0.093	0.044	6.6972	0.082
4	−0.011	−0.056	6.7054	0.152
5	−0.069	−0.079	7.0218	0.219
6	−0.070	−0.039	7.3472	0.290

Jarque–Bera test of normality (probability in brackets): 1.413066 (0.493352)

Long-run exchange rate effects, cross-sectional distribution, model 1 are shown in figure 4A.1.

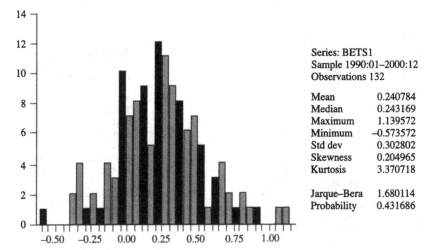

Series: BETS1
Sample 1990:01–2000:12
Observations 132

Mean	0.240784
Median	0.243169
Maximum	1.139572
Minimum	−0.573572
Std dev	0.302802
Skewness	0.204965
Kurtosis	3.370718
Jarque–Bera	1.680114
Probability	0.431686

Figure 4A.1 Long-run exchange rate effects, cross-sectional distribution, model 1

Statistics of model 3

Properties of the residuals calculated as a difference of (observed) aggregate inflation and its prediction, using the coefficient estimates of model 3, are shown in table 4A.3.

Table 4A.3

Lags	AC	PAC	Q-stat	Prob
1	0.374	0.374	8.6636	0.003
2	−0.003	−0.166	8.6642	0.013
3	0.116	0.215	9.5302	0.023
4	0.130	−0.007	10.635	0.031
5	0.018	−0.013	10.655	0.059
6	0.033	0.048	10.730	0.097

Jarque–Bera test of normality (probability in brackets): 1.37547 (0.502713)

Long-run exchange rate effects, cross-sectional distribution, model 3 are shown in figure 4A.2.

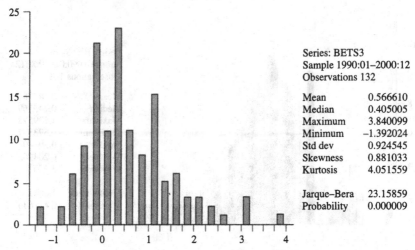

Series: BETS3
Sample 1990:01–2000:12
Observations 132

Mean	0.566610
Median	0.405005
Maximum	3.840099
Minimum	−1.392024
Std dev	0.924545
Skewness	0.881033
Kurtosis	4.051559
Jarque–Bera	23.15859
Probability	0.000009

Figure 4A.2 Long-run exchange rate effects, cross-sectional distribution, model 3

Statistics of model 7

Properties of the residuals calculated as a difference of (observed) aggregate inflation and its prediction, using the coefficient estimates of model 7, are shown in table 4A.4.

Table 4A.4

Lags	AC	PAC	Q-stat	Prob
1	0.218	0.218	2.8525	0.091
2	−0.172	−0.230	4.6575	0.097
3	−0.107	−0.012	5.3771	0.146
4	0.007	−0.001	5.3803	0.250
5	−0.067	−0.105	5.6670	0.340
6	−0.076	−0.037	6.0499	0.418

Jarque–Bera test of normality (probability in brackets): 1.37547 (0.502713)

Long-run exchange rate effects, cross-sectional distribution, model 7 are shown in figure 4A.3.

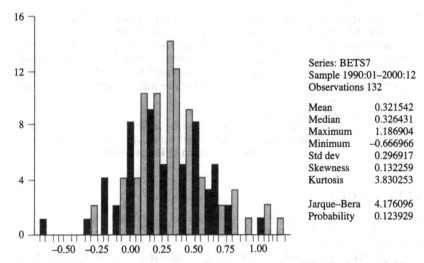

Series: BETS7	
Sample 1990:01–2000:12	
Observations 132	
Mean	0.321542
Median	0.326431
Maximum	1.186904
Minimum	–0.666966
Std dev	0.296917
Skewness	0.132259
Kurtosis	3.830253
Jarque–Bera	4.176096
Probability	0.123929

Figure 4A.3 Long-run exchange rate effects, cross-sectional distribution, model 7

An illustration of the coefficients and 'standard errors' from the random coefficient estimation (1) is given in table 4A.5.

Table 4A.5

Regressor	Betas	Std err.
dneer	0.030959	0.024776
dneer(−1)	0.045285	0.032308
dneer(−2)	0.046882	0.026349
dneer(−3)	0.034540	0.022714
dneer(−4)	0.027163	0.015909
dp(−1)	0.178324	0.025251
dp(−2)	−0.007582	0.019086
dp(−3)	0.056255	0.017063
Constant	0.010030	0.000849

NOTES

The views expressed herein are those of the authors, and are not to be interpreted as indicating the position of the National Bank of Hungary.
1   The financial support of the ACE Project *Econometric Inference into the Macroeconomic Dynamics of East European Economies* (MEET-III) is gratefully acknowledged. An earlier version of this chapter was discussed in an NBH Seminar. Participants both here and at the MEET-III Conference held in Leicester (7–8 June 1996) offered valuable comments. Particular thanks are due to Gábor Körösi for his help with the final version.

2 All statistical calculations reported in this chapter were carried out with Eviews. All variables with identifiers beginning with L are lagged.
3 It is interesting that the average weights *under-estimate* the inflation rates of later years. If the substitution effect had dominated, then the weights of goods that had become relatively more expensive would have declined, and using period average weights we would have got *higher* inflation rates than by using actual weights.
4 Quintile series show very similar tendencies.
5 As both the price and exchange rate series are logs of arbitrarily-'based' indices, the constant term can assume any numerical value, and cannot be compared either across equations or estimates based on different sample periods.

REFERENCES

Adams, C. and D. Gros (1986) 'The consequences of real exchange rate rules for inflation', *IMF Staff Papers*, 33 (September), 439–76
Banerjee, A., J. Dolado, J.W. Galbraith and D.F. Hendry (1993) *Co-Integration, Error Correction, and the Econometric Analysis of Non-Stationary Data*, Oxford: Oxford University Press
Blejer, M.I. (1983) 'On the anatomy of inflation (The variability of relative commodity prices in Argentina)', *Journal of Money, Credit, and Banking*, 15 (November), 469–82
Calvo, G.A. and C. Végh (1993) 'Exchange rate based stabilisation under imperfect credibility', in A. Wörgotter and H. Frisch (eds.), *Open Economy Macroeconomics*, London: Macmillan, 3–28
Cukierman, A. (1982) 'Relative price variability, inflation and the allocative efficiency of the price system', *Journal of Monetary Economics*, 9, 131–62
Darvas, Z. (1995) 'Exchange rate premia on the Hungarian foreign exchange market', paper presented at the conference on 'Convertibility and Exchange Rate Policy', Sofia (22–23 September)
Dittus, P. (1993) 'Consumer prices outpacing producer prices: a problem?', *Bank Review*, 4, 45–57
Dornbusch, R. (1987) 'Exchange rates and prices', *American Economic Review*, (March), 93–106
Dornbusch, R. and S. Fischer (1993) 'Moderate inflation', *World Bank Economic Review*, 7, 1–44
Driffill, J., G.E. Mizon and A. Ulph (1990) 'The costs of inflation', in B.M. Friedman and F.H. Hahn (eds.), *Handbook of Monetary Economics, II*, New York: Elsevier
Engle, R.F. (1983) 'Estimates of the variance of US inflation based upon the ARCH model', *Journal of Money, Credit, and Banking*, 15 (August), 286–301
Faruqee, H. (1995) 'Pricing to market and the real exchange rate', *IMF Staff Papers*, 42 (December), 855–81
Greene, W.H. (1990) *Econometric Analysis*, London: Macmillan
Halpern, L. and C. Wyplosz (1995) 'Equilibrium exchange rates in transition economies', *IMF Staff Papers*, 44(4), 430–60
Pesaran, M.H. and R. Smith (1995) 'Estimating long-run relationships from dynamic heterogeneous panels', *Journal of Econometrics*, 68, 75–113

Quah, D. and S.P. Vahey (1995) 'Measuring core inflation', *Economic Journal*, **105** (September), 1130–44

Swamy, P. (1970) 'Efficient inference in a random coefficient regression model', *Econometrica*, **38** (March), 311–23

Tirole, J. (1988) *The Theory of Industrial Organisation*, Cambridge, MA: MIT Press

Discussion

RATNA SAHAY

Chapter 4 attempts to analyse a key question facing Hungary, namely the factors explaining the persistence of moderately high inflation in the first half of the 1990s. While clearly of importance for policy makers in Hungary, this phenomenon is also of general interest to academics working on transition economies. This interest derives from the fact that, in contrast to Hungary, most other transition economies of Eastern Europe and the Former Soviet Union (FSU) have been successful in consistently reducing inflation rates over time, albeit from much higher levels than what Hungary faced at the start of the transition process.

To understand the inflationary process, the authors pursue three quantitative investigations: they estimate a money demand function, look at the evolution of several price indices and their variability and analyse the effect of exchange rates on consumer prices. Broadly speaking, the authors find that the contribution of relative price changes to inflation declined over time and that nominal exchange rate movements were only partly able to 'explain' inflation.

In addition, on the basis of the demand for money function that is estimated, the authors find evidence of a gradual loosening of monetary policy over the period under consideration (the first half of the 1990s). While all three results contribute to our understanding of the Hungarian inflationary process, I have some concern regarding the assumptions made and the approaches taken in conducting some of the analysis.

A fundamental problem with attempting to estimate a money demand equation for Hungary is that the sample period is much too short and the noise:signal ratio much too high due to the rapid structural transformations taking place during this period. Thus, *a priori*, it would be difficult to say anything meaningful about long-run relationships and, therefore, to put sufficient confidence in the reported results. While the authors acknowledge that their 'efforts can be regarded as a fitting exercise rather than the identification of a money demand function', they go ahead and interpret macroeconomic developments in Hungary on the basis of these results.

Given the fragility of the money demand estimates, it may have been useful to conduct a more thorough exercise. Several questions come to mind. How stable are the estimated coefficients when the sample period is shortened or lengthened? Are the 90-day Treasury Bill yields the most appropriate measure of the opportunity cost of holding money – what happens if these are substituted by other types of interest rates? How do the results change if the GDP series is substituted by industrial production? Unlike the GDP series, observations on industrial production are available at quarterly intervals and do not need to be interpolated. The justifications for using M1 and no other monetary aggregate are not fully convincing – where is the evidence that quasi-money was solely driven by the savings motive or that it does not reflect a fuller range of financial innovations? In fact, broader money aggregates, while admittedly less useful in policy, are typically more closely related to inflation. A simple correlation between prices and money in Hungary during the 1990–5 period shows that inflation moved more closely with M2 rather than M1 (table D4.1). The presence of a non-linear trend is also worrisome as it implies that, at best, one is empirically unable to explain the factors causing shifts in money demand during this period or, at worst, that the equation is misspecified. As a consequence, the monetary policy stance cannot be judged with reasonable certainty by looking at M1 growth rates, since there were considerable shifts in the money demand function. To the authors' credit, they have tried to build a consistent story regarding the possible shifts and direction in money demand which would have been somewhat more convincing had more direct evidence been presented (for example, regarding financial innovations) or had the estimated results been shown to be more robust.

The data analyses of disaggregated consumer prices are a well thought out and worthwhile exercise. It is revealing to see that a large part of the variance in inflation is accounted for by regulated price changes and VAT shocks. This finding is important because it shows the contribution of pure price level jumps relative to macroeconomic policy variables to measured inflation. The authors also find that the role of relative price changes in aggregate inflation declined substantially after 1992. This result re-confirms the findings of Coorey, Mecagni and Offerdal (1996)

Table D4.1. Inflation and money growth: correlation matrix, 1990–5 (annual data, end of period)

	Inflation	M1 growth	M2 growth
Inflation	1.000		
M1 growth	0.421	1.000	
M2 growth	0.758	0.816	1.000

Source: IMF, *International Financial Statistics.*

that relative price variability in 21 transition economies had a sizeable effect during initial liberalisation and a small effect later on.

The authors find that the PPI and the CPI diverged during their period of analysis (1990–5), and suggest that this may have something to do with shortcomings in the statistical system. While measurement problems may be an issue, the PPI–CPI gap phenomenon was not uncommon in other transition economies and can be readily explained by the gradual decline of subsidies to the non-tradables sector (for example, housing) and by the boom in the services sector. Moreover, if some form of a real exchange rate target rule based on the PPI was used (as is suggested in chapter 4, p. 89), it is no surprise that the authors find that the real exchange rate was relatively stable when measured by the PPI, but not when the CPI was used.

The links between the nominal exchange rate and the inflation rate are also not straightforward. On the one hand, the authors acknowledge that it was not easy to describe the exchange rate regime before March 1995 and that a real exchange rate rule was possibly followed, while on the other hand, they assume the nominal exchange rate to be an exogenous variable when determining the behaviour of the inflation rate. The fact that the Hungarian exchange rate has been 'determined by the government' (p. 105) does not imply that this variable is exogenous. If a real exchange rate target was followed, the government was using some feedback rule whereby the domestic inflation rate determined the nominal exchange rate. In this light, the equation on p. 106 may be misspecified and the interpretation of the intercept term to be the 'autonomous real appreciation rate' somewhat misleading. A more likely scenario is one where both exchange rate changes and inflation affected each other.

An examination of the short-run dynamics of money, inflation and the exchange rate should shed some light on the issue of whether exchange rate policy reacts to or leads inflation and money growth. To see whether

Table D4.2. VAR-based Granger-causality-tests, 1989:4–1995:4

Money aggregate	Appropriate lag length (quarters)	Monetary rowth[a]	Inflation[a]	Exchange rate change[a]
M1	1	**	–	–
M2	5	**	**	*

Notes:
[a] Significant at
** 1 per cent level
* 5 per cent level
– Not significant at 1 per cent and 5 per cent level
Sources: IMF, *International Financial Statistics* and discussant's calculations.

money growth leads or lags inflation, I conducted Granger-causality-tests by running vector autoregressions (VARs) in a three-variable system, containing the CPI inflation rate, nominal exchange rate (percentage change), and money growth. The data consisted of quarterly series on these three variables during 1989:4–1995:4. I first ran an unrestricted VAR and then ran a series of restricted VARs by excluding each variable, one at a time, from the equations for the other two variables (still in the three-variable system) and conducted Chi-squared-tests to see whether the exclusion of these variables is rejected. Table D4.2 presents the results of the three-way Granger-causality-tests. (The standard *F*-test rejected the presence of seasonal dummies in the unrestricted VAR regression. The most appropriate lag length was chosen on the basis of the *F*-test.) Interestingly, the results indicate that when narrow money (M1) is used, narrow money growth Granger-causes exchange rate changes and inflation. When broad money (M2) is used, all three variables influence each other, but even in this system the exchange rate variable is the least important one. Thus, narrow money, rather than the nominal exchange rate, seems to be the more likely 'exogenous' policy variable. It may be worthwhile for the authors in their future work to extend this exercise to include nominal wage growth and PPI-inflation (I could not pursue it for lack of data) in the VAR system to see whether these variables are important in leading inflation or the exchange rate movements.

Overall, I believe that chapter 4 makes an important first step in attempting to understand the post-transition inflation behaviour in Hungary. However, for methodological reasons as well as the results presented, one is still left wondering as to what were the key factors that led to the persistence of the moderately high inflation rates. On the basis of the results presented in the chapter and my own tentative investigations, the monetary policy stance seems to be the most likely explanation. Unfortunately, since little confidence can be put on the money demand estimations, I would tend to agree with one of the policy conclusions in the chapter (albeit for different reasons) that the nominal exchange rate should be more actively used as a nominal anchor at this time. With the passage of time and with more data, richer analyses will be made possible.

REFERENCE

Coorey, S., M. Mecagni and E. Offerdal (1996) 'Disinflation in transition economies: the role of relative price adjustment', *IMF Working Paper*, **WP/96/138**, Washington, DC: International Monetary Fund

5 The hidden economies of Visegrád countries in international comparison: a household electricity approach

MÁRIA LACKÓ

1 Introduction[1]

The hidden economy is universal: one can find it in any society, in any strata, any sector and any economic system. It therefore seems surprising that the prominent experts on this topic still find that little attention has until quite recently been paid to this phenomenon (cf. Tanzi and Shome, 1993, p. 807). In the last 10–15 years this deficiency has slowly been repaired: attention has gradually been directed to the hidden economy both in the market system and in planned and post-socialist societies.

In market economies, it is usually increasing budget deficits and the ensuing difficulties that have turned the interest of policy makers and researchers towards this not easily discernible part of the economy. In the socialist countries, the hidden economy (or to use another term, the second economy) was mostly associated with the pervasive shortage situation. The study of this sector commenced when the deficiencies of the state-owned sector surfaced and systematic empirical research started to discover the actual working of the state sector and its informal supplements. In post-socialist societies the analysis of the hidden economy came on to the agenda because of the rapid increase of budgetary deficits (partly associated with taxpayers concealing their revenues) and the grave output decline registered in official statistics.

This chapter first gives a brief survey of alternative definitions of the hidden economy. Section 3 clarifies the distinct causes of hidden activities in different economic systems, namely market, socialist and post-socialist societies. The following sections are devoted to a new comparative estimation method based on household electricity consumption. Section 4 presents the basic cross-sectional model, section 5 gives an estimation of the size of the hidden economy in terms of share of GDP. Section 6 investigates the connection between the development of the hidden economy and the currency ratio. While these sections focus on market economies section 7 applies the results for selected post-socialist countries. Section 8 summarises some important characteristic features of the transition process and their connections with the hidden economies in the post-socialist countries investigated. The chapter closes with a summary and conclusions.

2   Alternative definitions of the hidden economy

Different authors give different definitions for the concept of the hidden (underground, shadow, informal, irregular, black, second, etc.) economy. In the widest sense the hidden economy comprises all the economic activities that are not registered (Feige, 1979). This definition in fact covers the activities which are not taken into account in the calculation of the GDP of the country, either by convention or because they escape registration. Other scholars use a narrower definition: according to Tanzi (1980) and Macafee (1980) the hidden economy is an economy that generates revenues that the official statistics do not register, although they should do.

Following the widest definition Carter (1984) calls the first part of the hidden economy the 'informal' economy; this, as a rule, is not covered by the definition of GDP, and accordingly, no attempt is usually made to measure it. Activities belonging to this category include the production in households, do-it-yourself activities, reciprocal transactions between individuals, etc. (The growing importance of households' production is emphasised by Burns, 1977; Gershuny, 1979; Mattera, 1985.) The second part is usually called the 'underground' economy, and comprises activities that are assumed to be measured but escape from official registration or measurement. On the one hand, this category covers the activity of registered economic agents who do not report a part of their income and/or costs in order to evade taxes or circumvent licensing obligations. On the other hand, it covers the operation of non-registered economic agents who do not report their revenue from their production or servicing activity at all. A large part of the latter category of the underground economy takes place in households or earns revenues directly for households. Households also play a pivotal role as a workplace for important categories of registered business: the self-employed often use their home for work, and firms providing services for households also often exercise their activities on the spot.

The part of the underground economy which is based on breaking fundamental laws (not only compulsory registration and tax payment) is called the 'criminal' economy, and lends itself even less to economic analysis.

The borders between the informal and the underground economy, as well as between different activities within the underground economy are blurred; different parts of these economies are also strongly interrelated.

3   The causes of the hidden economy in market economies and in socialist/post-socialist economies

The general reason to hide economic activity is to avoid being recorded by the authorities in order to make possible some activities otherwise impeded, and/or maximise the income from them otherwise reduced by existing laws or rules of ad hoc intervention.

The literature on the hidden economy analyses the factors which are considered to be the most important in giving rise to hidden activities.

3.1 Market economies

In *market economies*, these factors can be summarised as follows:

(1) *Tax rates* (corporate tax, VAT, payroll tax, etc.): the higher they are the more incentives appear for moving activity to, or starting it, in the hidden economy.

(2) The burden of *regulation* by the state:
   (a) The more onerous this regulation is, the more agents find it reasonable to escape from the official economy.
   (b) The more control and the stronger the sanctions imposed on those evading taxes and against black workers, the less room is left for being engaged in the hidden economy. But at a given level of control and sanctions, the larger the number of entrepreneurs the more difficult will be the control.

(3) Possibilities of *being employed* in the official economy:
   (a) The lower the participation rate is kept by hiring policies, the higher the probability that labour not employed in the official economy will join the hidden economy.
   (b) The length of the working hours in the official economy – the shorter the working hours are, the higher the possibility of participation in the hidden economy.

(4) *Tax morality*: the higher this morality, the fewer people and enterprises evade taxation and operate in the hidden economy.

We have to note that some of the factors listed above are not only causes of the hidden economy but also its effects. For example, tax rates are high in some countries partly as a response to the large size of the hidden economy; the participation ratio can be low because of normal reasons (demographic trends, state of the labour market), but also because of the high ratio of the hidden economy.

3.2 Socialist economies

The causes of emergence and perpetuation of the hidden economy in *socialist economies* were entirely different from those in market economies. In fact, the habitual factors of market economies could not be significant in the socialist environment because of the extremely narrow scope of formal taxation and, in principle, the full employment of the labour force. Major factors triggering the expansion of the hidden economy in socialist countries were the pressure of permanent shortages, the negligible size of the legal private economy, the low level of services provided by the state and the lack of competition. In the socialist countries both parts of the hidden economy – household production and the activities in the underground economy – were extensive. To obtain the products and services in chronic shortage the consumers of the socialist economy used the hidden economy: they placed orders that were to be accomplished through moonlighting, paid tips or gratitude sums to the sales clerks of state shops and service places, or simply did the job themselves. Almost every consumer was also a producer in the hidden economy. Their commitment to accomplish this work well and efficiently was high, since the efficiency of their work here counted much more than in the visible (state) sector. In most cases the working time in the state sector was abundant enough to host also the activities in the hidden economy, and usually even the premises, machines and materials of the state sector could be used without any inconvenience.

3.3 Post-socialist system

In the *post-socialist system*, a gradual restructuring of the factors that trigger the hidden activities takes place: the factors that had been characteristic of the socialist system lose importance, while those characterising the market system gain ground. Major new developments, such as the disappearance of shortages, the emergence of competition, a gradually expanding market for services and the growing role of the legal private economy have all led to the disappearance of earlier traditional causes of a hidden economy and have given way to the traditional causes in market economies such as tax evasion and black labour by the unemployed and other inactive people.

In centrally planned economies the participation rate was traditionally very high. One should not infer from this, however, that there was no labour potential to feed the hidden economy. In these countries, most of the hidden activity was carried out by the relatively numerous active earners. In the course of transition this situation has changed and employment proportions of comparable market economies have been achieved very fast: in Hungary, for instance, the number of dependants and inactive earners per 100 active earners was 119 in 1989, and reached 183 by 1995. (For comparison: this number was 157 in Spain in 1991 and 153 in Greece in 1990.)

Taxation was also neither a traditional source of budgetary revenues nor a frequently used regulator in socialist economies. There was no widespread use of taxes until the last years of socialism and the first years of transition. After bold liberalisation of prices and radical cuts in subsidies taxes started to play the same decisive role for the state budget as in long-established market economies. In post-socialist countries, the efforts of the state to enforce tax collection are still weak and cannot be appropriately represented by the same indicators used in market economies. Tax enforcement is a new task, that demands new institutions, which are only just being established in the transition economies.

4   New estimation method for the size of the hidden economy: the household electricity approach

From the literature measuring the hidden economy the view that the relative size of the hidden economy in the socialist/post-socialist countries is larger than in developed market economies seems to be confirmed. However, different definitions and different measurement methods in the literature allow only cautious comparisons even among market economies, let alone comparisons between market economies and socialist/post-socialist countries.

A method of estimation that helps to order various countries according to the share of a certain part of their hidden economy in the total economy is now presented. This part of the hidden economy is associated with the household consumption of electricity.[2] It comprises, among others, that part of household production, do-it-yourself activity and other non-registered production and services which need the use of electricity. This relatively broad section of the hidden economy does not involve the following activities or incomes: tips, corruption, smuggling and generally the hidden activity not associated with the consumption of household electricity. One can assume, though, that in the countries where the section of the hidden economy associated with household electricity consumption is high, the rest of the hidden economy, i.e. the part we cannot measure, will also be high.

We start with the determination of total electricity consumption of households. We assume that electricity consumption of households in a country is determined not only by such visible factors as the size of population, the level of economic development, the country's geographical location (climate and weather), the relative price of electricity and the access to other energy sources, but also by the intensity of the hidden economy.

The model is described by the following equations:

$$\ln E + i = \alpha_1 \ln C_i + \alpha_2 \ln PR_i + \alpha_3 G_i + \alpha_4 Q_i + \alpha_5 H_i + \alpha_6 \qquad (1)$$

$$H_i = \beta_1 T_i + \beta_2 (S_i - T_i) + \beta_3 D_i$$
$$\beta_1 > 0 \quad \beta_2 < 0 \qquad \beta_3 > 0 \qquad (2)$$

where

i : the number assigned to the country

E_i : *per capita* household electricity consumption in country i in Mtoe

C_i : *per capita* real consumption of households without the consumption of electricity in country i in US dollars (at purchasing power parity)

PR_i : the real price of consumption of 1 kwh of residential electricity in US dollars (at purchasing power parity)

G_i : the relative frequency of months with the need of heating in houses in country i

Q_i : the ratio of energy sources other than electric energy to all energy sources in household energy consumption

H_i : the *per capita* output of the hidden economy

T_i : the ratio of the sum of paid personal income, corporate profit and taxes on goods and services to GDP

S_i : the ratio of public social welfare expenditures to GDP

D_i : the sum of number of dependants over 14 years and of inactive earners, both per 100 active earners

In (1) *per capita* residential electricity consumption depends on the positive effect of the *per capita* private consumption, the negative effect of the price of residential electricity, the positive effect of heating, the negative effect of the other energy sources and the positive effect of the size of the hidden economy.

(2) determines the size of the hidden economy. It states that the hidden economy is a function of three indicators:

(1) *Tax burden*: the higher the tax rate the more incentive to evade paying taxes and to earn income in the part of the economy which is not scrutinised by the authorities.

In (2) we use the ratio of taxes on personal incomes, corporate profits and goods and services to GDP. This implies the assumption of a positive correlation between the tax rates and tax payments despite the impact of the hidden economy, pervasive tax avoidance and tax evasion. We do not use explicit tax rates for various reasons: first, not all respective rates were available for the subsequent estimations, second, it is not easy to create a single index from complicated tax schedules. A third reason is that statutory rates are usually 'contaminated' with the effects of tax evasion: statutory rates have often been increased to compensate for the revenue losses associated with tax evasion. It is worth citing Tanzi and Shome here who recalled the remark that the prominent public finance scholar Luigi Enaudi once made: 'if all the Italian tax laws on the books were fully enforced the Italian level of taxation would be 120 percent of national income' (Tanzi and Shome, 1993, p. 821).

(2) *Tax enforcement*: Tax evasion or cheating the tax authorities does not depend only on the size of tax rates, but also on the enforcement of tax payments.

The variation in tax enforcement across different countries could be measured in various ways, for instance by the costs used for tax collection, or the frequency of tax inspections. Unfortunately, no data could be collected on these phenomena in a uniform and comparable form. Therefore, as an alternative, an indirect indicator had to be chosen and this is the difference between the welfare expenditures and tax payments in the given country, both expressed as a ratio of GDP. The use of this indicator assumes that the higher the above difference, the stronger efforts are made by the state to collect outstanding taxes. These efforts of the state reduce, *ceteris paribus*, the size of the hidden economy.

(3) *Participation (in fact, non-participation) rate*: the less the employment participation in the activities of the visible (official) economy, the higher the probability that the non-participatory workforce will seek employment in the hidden economy.

In (2) we use the number of dependants over 14 years and of inactive earners per 100 active earners as the indicator for non-participation. The category 'inactive earners' comprises the group of unemployed (whether short-term or long-term), and also those who became discouraged, lost entitlement for unemployment benefits, lived on welfare and gave up searching for employment. Disabled, who do not join official employment for health reasons also belong to this category.

This indicator of non-participation contains an important effect which complements the relationship described in (3) above. The higher the share of non-participants, the higher the possibility of having many self-employed, and a large number of small entrepreneurs who are not easy to control as taxpayers. According to our own calculations the less developed an OECD country, the higher is the ratio of the dependants and inactive earners to the active earners, and also the higher is the ratio of the self-employed.

The behavioural relationships listed in (1)–(3) above could in principle work through different lags. For the sake of simplicity, and because of paucity of data, we assumed no lags. The estimation of the respective parameters is carried out on (3) which is derived from (1) and (2) through substitution

$$\ln E_i = \Gamma_1 \ln C_i + \Gamma_2 \ln PR_i + \Gamma_3 G_i + \Gamma_4 Q_i + \Gamma_5 D_i + \Gamma_6 T_i$$
$$+ \Gamma_7 S_i + \Gamma_8 \tag{3}$$

where

$$\Gamma_1 = \alpha_1 > 0, \Gamma_2 = \alpha_2 < 0, \Gamma_3 = \alpha_3 > 0, \Gamma_4 = \alpha_4 < 0, \Gamma_5 = \alpha_5\beta_3 > 0$$
$$\Gamma_6 = \alpha_5(\beta_1 - \beta_2) > 0, \Gamma_7 = \alpha_5\beta_2 < 0, \Gamma_8 = \alpha_6$$

The parameters of (3) were estimated on a panel data set of 19 OECD countries for the years 1989 and 1990 by the method of OLS. The results are presented in table 5.1 As the results indicate, the parameters of the regression equation are significant, the signs coincide with the expected ones. These support, or at least do not reject, our assumptions about the determinants of household electricity consumption, including the impact of the hidden economy. The standardised regression coefficients in column (2) of table 5.1 indicate the relative weight of each of the independent variables.

In the course of estimating (3) two dummy variables were used. The dummies *duUSA* and *duSp* indicate that for the USA and in Spain some special considerations had to be taken into account. In the USA the *per capita* electricity consumption of households is much higher than in the other OECD countries; this is why *duUSA* has a positive sign. One reason for the higher household electricity consumption may be the widespread use of air conditioning in large regions of the USA. Another reason may be that household electric appliances are relatively cheap in the USA. The specific feature of Spain is that here the energy consumption of households other than electricity is overwhelmingly based on oil. Since the price of oil is unusually cheap relative to electricity there is a high incentive for substituting oil for electricity. This feature explains the negative sign of *duSp*.

Table 5.1. Estimation for *per capita* household electricity consumption: regression results on (3)

Dependent variable: *per capita* consumption of residential electricity

	(1) Regression coefficients	(2) Standardised regression
Per capita private consumption	0.6013	0.2435
(ln C_i)	(6.75)	
Price of residential electricity	−0.6642	−0.4361
(ln PR_i)	(9.94)	
Ratio of other energy	−0.0183	−0.4099
(Q_i)	(10.85)	
Heating frequency	1.0494	0.3597
(G_i)	(8.67)	
Taxes	0.02024	0.2122
(Ti)	(4.78)	
Social expenditure	−0.0164	−0.1473
(S_i)	(3.31)	
Ratio of inactives to actives	0.0071	0.2143
(D_i)	(4.83)	
Dummy for Spain	−0.3304	−0.1151
($duSp$)	(3.68)	
Dummy for USA	0.5001	0.1733
($duUSA$)	(5.24)	
Constant	5.3272	
	(17.96)	
R^2	0.975	
F	158.8	
RMSE	0.1037	
MAPE	1.47	
RESET y2	0.68	
RESET y3	1.04	
Heteroscedasticity		
LMI	13.3	
	(21.66)	
LMII	26.9	
	(32.0)	
Chow	0.2	

Notes:
Method of estimation: OLS method. Number of observations: 38.
In brackets are t-statistics, for heteroscedasticity critical values of hi^2 distribution.
R^2: adjusted R^2.
RMSE: Root mean square error.
MAPE: Mean of absolute percentage error.
RESET y^2: Ramsey-test, where the square of fitted values was put into the additional regression.

RESET y3: Ramsey-test, where the square and cube of fitted values were put into the additional regression.
LMI: the explanatory variables of the original equation were put into the additional regression.
LMII: the explanatory variables and their square values were put into the additional regression.

The results of the diagnostic analysis of the regression function (3) are now analysed.

(1) The *LM*-tests for heteroscedasticity are not significant, so we cannot reject the null hypothesis of homoscedasticity. In the *LMI*-test the explanatory variables of (3) were put into the complementary regression, while in *LMII* the square values of these variables were used too.
(2) The *RESET*-tests (using the squares and cubics of the estimated values of the dependent variables) do not turn out to be significant either, i.e. they do not indicate the presence of specification errors.
(3) The Chow-test does not show a break point between the two years that were used for the panel estimation.
(4) Multicollinearity was checked by the matrix of pairwise correlations between the estimated regression coefficients. The correlations turned out moderate, so they did not show much evidence of multicollinearity.

The results of the estimation of (3) can be used to establish the ranking of the countries in respect to electricity use in their hidden economies. We decompose the estimated (3) into two parts:

$$\ln \hat{E}_{i1} = \hat{\Gamma}_1 \ln C_i + \hat{\Gamma}_2 \ln PR_i + \hat{\Gamma}_3 Q_i + \hat{\Gamma}_4 G_i + \hat{\Gamma}_8 \tag{4}$$

$$\ln \hat{E}_{i2} = \hat{\Gamma}_5 D_i + \hat{\Gamma}_6 T_i + \hat{\Gamma}_7 S_i \tag{5}$$

where

$$\ln \hat{E}_i = \ln \hat{E}_{i1} + \ln \hat{E}_{i12} \tag{6}$$

With the use of these parts we define the h_i index in two equivalent forms:

$$h_i = \frac{\ln \hat{E}_{i2}}{\ln \hat{E}_i} \tag{7a}$$

$$h_i = \frac{\ln \hat{E}_i - \ln \hat{E}_{i1}}{\ln \hat{E}_i} \tag{7b}$$

By using (7a) or (7b) we can get indicators for each country showing *per*

Table 5.2. The shares of the hidden economy (percentages), 1978–90

	Household electricity approach				Soft modelling method[a] in GDP	Currency-ratio method[b] in GDP	Other methods in GDP
	(1A) In electricity consumption		(1B) In GDP				
	1989	1990	1989	1990	1978		1990
Australia	11.5	11.3	15.4	15.1			
Austria	10.9	11.6	14.5	15.5	8.9	5.3 (1991)	
Belgium	18.2	14.8	24.2	19.8	12.1	20.8 (1980)	
Canada	8.7	8.7	11.7	11.7	8.7	11.2 (1980)	
Denmark	14.0	12.6	18.7	16.9	11.8	10.2 (1980)	
Finland	9.9	10.0	13.2	13.3	7.6		
France	9.4	9.2	12.6	12.3	9.4	6.7 (1978)	
Germany	12.0	10.9	16.1	14.6	8.6	11.2 (1980)	
Greece	15.4	16.3	20.6	21.8			
Ireland	15.6	15.5	20.8	20.6	7.2	8.0 (1980)	
Italy	14.7	14.7	19.6	19.6	9.2	30.0 (1978)	15–20[c]
Japan	10.6	9.9	14.1	13.2	4.1		
Netherlands	10.5	10.0	14.0	13.4	9.6		
Norway	6.4	6.9	8.6	9.3	9.2	10.9 (1980)	
Portugal	14.9	10.3	19.8	13.8			
Spain	18.6	17.1	24.8	22.9	6.5	23.0 (1978)	
Sweden	7.9	8.3	10.5	11.0	13.2	12.4 (1980)	
Switzerland[e]	7.6	7.6	10.2	10.2	4.3	6.5 (1980)	
UK	10.7	9.8	14.3	13.1	8	11.0 (1980)	
USA	7.9	7.9	10.5	10.5	8.3	6.1 (1980)	10–11[d]

Notes:
[a] Method elaborated by Frey and Weck (1984). Data are cited in Schneider (1994), p. 200.
[b] Estimations by currency ratio method are in Schneider (1994), p. 200.
[c] Bordignon (1993).
[d] Morris (1993).
[e] Because of lack of data a rough estimation was made.

capita household consumption of electricity related to their hidden economy as a share of total per capita household consumption. These shares for 20 countries are listed in column (1A) of table 5.2.

As table 5.2 indicates, the largest shares of hidden economy can be found in Spain, Greece, Ireland, Belgium, Italy and Denmark, the smallest in Norway, Switzerland and the USA. Because of lack of some data, notably S, Switzerland was not used in our sample. We made a rough estimation for its indicator h: assuming that

$$\ln E(\text{Switzerland}) = \ln \hat{E}(\text{Switzerland})$$

and applying formula (4) to calculate

$$\ln \hat{E}_1$$

with the proper data (C, PR, Q and G) of Switzerland (7b) gives value h for Switzerland. (This calculation does not take into account the error term of the estimated equation.)

5   Calculating the share of the hidden economy in GDP

The estimations in the previous section did not lead to the determination of the hidden economy's contribution to GDP in the individual countries. For the calculation of this crucial index, in addition to the calculations already accomplished, we need to know how much GDP is produced by 1 unit of electricity in the hidden economy of each country. Since these data are not known, we opted for the method followed by Frey and Weck in their study (Frey and Weck, 1984). We take the result of one of the known estimations that were carried out for a market economy with another approach for the early 1990s and apply this proportion to the other countries. According to Morris (1993) in the early 1990s, in the USA the contribution of the hidden economy to the GDP was 10–11 per cent. Using this result and taking 10.5 per cent as a base we can determine the share of the hidden economy in GDP for all the countries (see column (1B) of table 5.2). Since the US base data do not include household production, the indices obtained for the other countries also represent the hidden economy without household production.

According to the results in table 5.2 the share of the hidden economy in GDP varies between 9 per cent and 23 per cent in the OECD countries under investigation.

While admitting that our results are preliminary and of an indicative nature, it seems worthwhile to compare these estimates with the results obtained from calculations based on different methods. In columns (2), (3) and (4) of table 5.2 these alternative indicators are listed. A direct comparison can be accomplished for two countries only – i.e. for Italy and Austria – since there are no other countries for which alternative estimations exist for the early 1990s (except the USA, but that result was already used as a base). When comparing these data with our results in table 5.2, we find no substantial discrepancy for Italy. For Austria, however, our estimation shows a considerably higher share than the alternative result, the outcome of Schneider's calculation based on the currency-ratio[3] method.

Since the rest of the alternative estimates were obtained for different periods before 1990 such a comparison is possible only where the indices are placed into a ranking of the countries irrespective of the period they refer to. In estimations with the 'currency-ratio method' for the period 1978–80 distinctly high ratios of the hidden economy (20–30 per cent of GDP) were found for Italy, Belgium and Spain, while the smallest ratios (5–7 per cent) were found for the USA, Switzerland and Austria.

With the 'soft modelling method'[4] a relatively extensive hidden economy was detected for Belgium and Italy, but also for Sweden, Norway and Denmark in the year 1978. This approach produced the smallest values for Japan and Switzerland.

If we compare the results of my own current estimations (column (1B)) with these findings (column (2), (3)), we see Ireland, Sweden and Norway as the countries that are positioned substantially differently in the two columns. In all earlier estimations Ireland was found in the middle, while Sweden and Norway were positioned fairly high. In contrast, in my estimation Ireland stands near the top, while the other two are at the bottom.

The divergence between the results produced by the different models is a logical consequence of their different specifications. In the currency method the tax burden is the sole explanatory variable, while in the soft modelling method there are more explanatory variables (tax burden, participation rate), but the impact of taxation is higher than that of the participation rate, because the exogenously inserted data ensure it. Consequently, in both of these models those countries show a high hidden economy where the tax rates are high. The method developed in this chapter, the household electricity method, does not make use of predetermined weights: it lets the weights of the different causes of the hidden economy be determined in the course of the estimation.

6   Indices of the hidden economy and the currency ratios

When reviewing the literature we can see that one of the most popular indirect estimation methods of the size of the hidden economy is the currency-ratio model. All variants of this model have the common assumption that a large part of the hidden economy is managed by cash. The question then arises whether our indices for the hidden economy support or contradict this popular assumption. To get a short answer to this question is not easy since our model is based on cross-section analysis of different countries, while the currency-ratio models usually analyse time series data of single countries.

Comparing currency:GDP ratios of different countries is rather complicated since one has to allow for the different definitions of money, different levels of development of bank services and variations in monetary regulations in the individual countries. Despite these difficulties, I attempt to define and estimate a function which can explain, on an acceptable level, the differences among the currency:GDP ratios of the individual countries. In the course of the estimation several dummy variables have to be used in order to represent the impact of some countries' specificities.

The differences in the currency:GDP ratios are explained by the following factors:

(1) *The velocity of broad money (GDP/M2)*: the smaller this velocity, the larger is, *ceteris paribus*, the stock of broad money, and this has direct positive consequences on the stock of currency within the stock of broad money
(2) *The nominal interest rate*: a higher nominal interest rate decreases, *ceteris paribus*, the currency stock that the consumers want to keep
(3) *The inflation rate*: a higher inflation rate increases the currency the consumers need for transaction purposes
(4) *The size of the hidden economy*: the larger the hidden economy, the larger is, *ceteris paribus*, the currency stock.

Expressing the impact of all these factors in a function:

$$\ln C_i = \omega_1 \ln v_i + \omega_2 r_i + \omega_3 p_i + \omega_4 h_i + \omega_5$$
$$\omega_1 < 0 \quad \omega_2 < 0 \quad \omega_3 > 0 \quad \omega_4 > 0 \tag{8}$$

where

c_i : the currency:GDP ratio in country i
v_i : the velocity of broad money in country i
r_i : nominal interest rate in country i
p_i : inflation rate in country i
h_i : index (size) of the hidden economy in country i

The estimation of (8) was carried out on a panel data set of 19 OECD countries for the years 1989 and 1990 by the OLS method. The h_i indices were taken from our estimation (column (1A) of table 5.2). The results are summarised in table 5.3.

142   Mária Lackó

Table 5.3. Estimation for currency ratio: regression results on (8)

Dependent variable: ratio of currency to GDP

	Regression coefficients	Standardised regression coefficients
Velocity of broad money	−0.7241	−0.4013
(ln v_i)	(5.05)	
Interest rate	−0.0299	−0.2676
(r_i)	(1.92)	
Inflation rate	0.0471	0.4019
(p_i)	(2.93)	
Index of hidden economy	4.9414	0.3482
(h_i)	(4.83)	
Dummy for Denmark	−0.6480	−0.3205
(duD)	(4.82)	
Dummy for Finland	−1.0405	−0.5146
(duF)	(7.24)	
Dummy for UK	−0.8804	−0.4354
($duUK$)	(6.05)	
Constant	1.4771	
	(10.85)	
R^2		
F	0.85	
RMSE	30.8	
MAPE	0.1775	
RESET y^2	8.08	
RESET y^3	0.00	
Heteroscedasticity	0.00	
LMI	5.31	
LMII	(18.48)	
	21.07	
Chow	(24.73)	
	0.07	

Notes: Method of estimation: OLS method.

Number of observations: 38.

In brackets t-statistics, for heteroscedasticity critical values of hi^2 distribution.

R^2: adjusted R^2.

RMSE: Root mean square error.

MAPE: Mean of absolute percentage error.

RESET y^2: Ramsey-test, where the square of fitted values was put into the additional regression.

RESET y^3: Ramsey-test, where square and cube of fitted values were put into the additional regression.

LMI: the explanatory variables of the original equation were put into the additional regression.

LMII: the explanatory variables and their square values were put into the additional regression.

In table 5.3 we can see that the results of the estimations are reasonably good, the parameters have the expected signs and they are significant. In the course of the estimation dummy variables had to be used for Denmark, Finland and the UK, since in these countries the actual levels of the currency:GDP ratio were much smaller than the levels explained by (8).

The statistical test of the estimation showed the following results:

(1) The *LM*-tests for heteroscedasticity are not significant, so we cannot reject the null hypothesis of homoscedasticity. In the *LMI*-test the explanatory variables of (8) were put into the complementary regression, while in *LMII* the square values of these variables were used, too.

(2) The *RESET*-tests (using the squares and cubics of the estimated values of the dependent variables) do not turn out to be significant either, i.e. they do not indicate the presence of specification errors.

(3) The Chow-test does not show a break point between the two years that were used for the panel estimation.

(4) Multicollinearity was checked by the matrix of pairwise correlations between the estimated regression coefficients. Not surprisingly, a linear relation was found between the inflation rate and the nominal interest rate. This relation, however, was not so strong that it spoiled the *t*-statistics of the two variables. The *t*-statistics of the estimated value of the interest rate, for instance, are significant at the 6 per cent level. (An alternative calculation for (8) was also made with the difference between the nominal interest rate and the inflation rate; in this calculation the coefficients were only slightly different from the original ones.)

The estimation results of the currency-ratio equation indicate that the indices of hidden economy calculated by the household electricity model show a significant relation to the currency ratios.

7   The position of Hungary, the Czech republic, Slovakia and Poland as determined by the model

Can the models of the hidden economy developed for industrialised market economies be used for the investigation of socialist countries and economies in transition from plan to the market? In section 3 we reviewed the differences between the causes of hidden activities in market economies in socialist and post-socialist countries. Considering these substantial differences, we come to the conclusion that in the mid-1990s it is impossible to accomplish an exact analysis of the hidden economy in socialist countries and post-socialist countries with the help of our model used for OECD countries above. Changes in conditions of the transition economies may perhaps make possible this exercise in 5–10 years' time: this seems too long a period to be lacking any internationally comparable measure about the size of the hidden economies in post-socialist countries.

In fact, with some assumptions and modifications the model can place Hungary, the Czech republic, Slovakia and Poland into the ranking of market economies according to the size of their hidden economies. With this exercise we can also test the earlier proposal that the ratio of the hidden economy in socialist/post-socialist economies has been higher than in developed market economies.

For this estimation we use the following formula:

$$h_i = \frac{\ln \hat{E}_i - (\hat{\Gamma}_1 \ln C_i + \hat{\Gamma}_2 \ln PRi - \hat{\Gamma}_2 \ln PB/PR + \hat{\Gamma}_3 Q_i + \hat{\Gamma}_4 G_i + \Gamma_8)}{\ln E_i} \quad (9)$$

(9) differs from (7b) in the following respects:

(1) It is assumed that

$$\ln E_i = \ln \hat{E}_i$$

since one can assume that also in post-socialist economies E_i can be decomposed into two parts: one which is related to the hidden economy and one which is not related to it. (Here the error term of the estimation was not taken into account.)

(2) It is assumed that for the post-socialist economies the household electricity consumption which is not related to the hidden economy can be determined by the coefficients estimated for the market economies with some modification of the price effect.

(3) The price effect is modified. If the price of electricity used by the legal private business sector is much higher than the price applied for household use (a relation usual in socialist and post-socialist countries), then a part of the electricity consumption of the private business sector is transferred to the households' electricity consumption, and through this the hidden economy expands.

If there were no such transfers, the price elasticity of household electricity consumption would be higher than it is: free from the transfer effect, a given increase in the price would decrease more, *ceteris paribus*, the electricity consumption in the household sector, than in the presence of the transfer effect. To catch the impact of the price difference we divide the actual price effect by the use of an identity and assume that the second part of the right-hand side is connected with the hidden economy

$$\hat{\Gamma}_2 \ln PR = \hat{\Gamma}_2 \ln PB - \hat{\Gamma}_2 \ln \left(\frac{PB}{PR}\right) \tag{10}$$

where

PB : the price of the electricity used in the legal private business sector
PR : the price of electricity used by households (residential sector)
$\hat{\Gamma}_2$: estimated parameter of the price variable in (3).

After estimating h_i according to (9), the ratio of the hidden economy to GDP can be calculated the same way as in the case of developed market economies.

The results of the estimations for Hungary, the Czech republic, Slovakia and Poland for 1990–4 are summarised in table 5.4, which also lists alternative estimations that scholars have made with alternative approaches.

Table 5.4 shows that our own calculations resulted in shares of the hidden economy for Hungary and Poland which are approximately twice as large as the average in the market economies. In contrast, the size of the hidden economy in the Czech and Slovak republics coincides with the average of the market economies.

With these results we got a plausible ranking among the post-socialist countries: at the beginning of the 1990s Poland had the largest hidden economy, followed by Hungary and, at a substantial distance, the Czech republic and Slovakia (at that time still in a common federate state). Anecdotal evidence on the prevalence of multiple employments and illegal trade practices, as well as the relative tolerance of the authorities toward these activities confirm that the hidden economy was rather high in Poland and Hungary, while in the Czech republic and Slovakia these activities were considerably restricted. As a control we can compare the results for Hungary and the Czech republic with estimates made according to other methods. We can see that our results, especially in the case of Hungary, are close to the alternative indices.

As far as the currency-ratio equation (8) is concerned, the actual currency ratios of the post-socialist countries are smaller than those estimated by (8), which was set up on data for developed market economies. The reason for this difference is connected with the much higher inflation in the early transition period in post-socialist economies. When setting up (8) we assumed that increasing inflation leads to increasing holding of currencies; it is true, however, that above some level of inflation business and the public try to get rid of currency. This high-inflation effect was not considered in (8), which is why it is not applicable for post-socialist countries for the early transition period.

It is also worthwhile following the development of the size of hidden economies in time, i.e. between 1990 and 1994. In Hungary, the hidden economy shows a substantial expansion in 1990–2 (8.1 percentage points) which is followed by a smaller decline (3.8 percentage points) in 1993–4. The same pattern can be found in Poland, however with smaller growth and smaller decline (2.8 and 0.8 percentage points, respectively). A one-time increase can be seen also in the Czech case, but the share of the hidden economy mostly stays around 15 per cent. Finally, Slovakia shows a distinct pattern: the share of the hidden economy increases steadily between 1991 and 1994 and by the largest scale in the four countries (11 percentage points).

8   Unemployment, self-employment and the hidden economy in post-socialist countries

The index of the size of the hidden economy can be used for the analysis of various relationships. For instance, it can be shown that in developed market economies the size of the hidden economy has a positive relationship with the rate of unemployment and the share of the self-employed (see table 5.5, p. 149). These relationships are more or less implications of the household electricity model that were used in our calculations: the ratio of adult inactives to 100 active earners was one of the explanatory variables in that model, and this variable has obvious close positive relations to the rate of unemployed and the ratio of self-employed.

The question arises whether these relationships, characteristic of the developed market economies, are already relevant in the post-socialist countries. As statistical data show, since the start of transition both the rate of unemployment and the ratio of self-employed increased fast in the post-socialist countries, albeit at different rates (see table 5.4). In the period 1990–4 the expansion of the hidden economy, however, was not as spectacular as the growth of these two employment indices. The explanation for the slower growth is the transformation of the hidden economy itself. As discussed in section 3 above, the hidden economy already existed in the socialist era, and the transition to the market brought about a structural shift in the hidden activities. The factors traditionally giving rise to hidden activities in the socialist system (shortages, low level of services, administrative restrictions on private business, etc.) gradually lost their relevance and have been replaced by

Table 5.4. Hidden economy, unemployment and self-employment in Visegrád countries, 1990–4

		Share of hidden economy in GDP		Unemployment rate	Ratio of non-agricultural self-employment
		Electricity approach	Other estimation		
Hungary	1990	26.7		1.9	6.6
	1991	32.4	26–32[a]	7.8	7.9
	1992	34.8		13.2	9.4
	1993	32.8		12.6	11.1
	1994	31.0		10.9	13.4
Poland	1990	30.8		6.3	5.1
	1991	29.7		11.8	6.8
	1992	33.0		13.6	8.2
	1993	33.6		16.4	9.1
	1994	32.8		16.0	10.2
Czech rep.	1990	n.a.		0.8	0.8
	1991	15.2		4.1	4.8
	1992	19.9		2.6	6.6
	1993	14.4		3.5	8.6
	1994	15.4	8–10[b]	3.2	9.6
Slovakia	1990	n.a.		1.6	0.0
	1991	11.2		11.8	3.5
	1992	4.7		10.4	5.2
	1993	15.0		14.4	6.0
	1994	22.3		14.8	6.5
Former CSFR[c]	1990	n.a.		1.1	0.5
	1991	13.8		5.4	4.4
	1992	18.1		5.5	6.1
	1993	14.6		7.2	7.7
	1994	17.7		7.1	8.4

Notes: [a] Árvay and Vértes (1994).
[b] Kadera (1995).
[c] Weighted average, weighted by Czech and Slovak population ratios.
n.a. = not available.
Sources:
Source of unemployment data: *Countries in Transition* (1996). Source of self-employment data: *OECD Observer*, **198** (February–March 1996).

those factors that are the usual reasons for hidden activity in market economies (unemployment, self-employment, burden of taxes, etc.).

With the calculation of simple correlations one can check how far the post-socialist countries have gone in this structural change, i.e. how strong the relationship is between the traditional market economy factors of the hidden economy and the size of the hidden economy in the post-socialist countries in 1990–4. Table 5.5 gives data for the sign and strength of the relationship between the size of the hidden economy (ratio to GDP) on the one hand, and the rate of unemployment and the ratio of self-employed, on the other, in the post-socialist countries. A comparison between developed market economies and post-socialist economies is also possible.

According to these results, in the four post-socialist countries the size of the hidden economy is positively related to both variables, especially to the rate of unemployment, although these relations are to some extent weaker than in developed market economies.

9   Summary and conclusions

This chapter attempted to identify the size of the Hungarian, Czech, Slovak and Polish hidden economy in 1990–4 in international perspective. The recent literature about hidden/underground economies provides numerous estimations about the size of the hidden economy in different countries. The comparison of these results with each other was unwarranted until now since the different estimations were based on different definitions of the hidden economy and diverse methods of measurement. To compensate for the lack of common ground needed for inter-country comparisons the chapter elaborated and used a new estimation method for the size of the hidden economy: this method is based on a single definition of hidden activities, applies an identical method of estimation for all the countries, and uses relatively easily accessible and uniformly defined data.

The analysis of household electricity consumption in 19 OECD countries led to the separation of that part of household electricity consumption which was closely related to the hidden economy from that part which was independent of it. With the help of this method 20 developed OECD economies and four East European transition countries could be ranked in respect to the size of household electricity consumption in their hidden economy. Subsequently these electricity consumption ratios were converted to indices that show the share of hidden economy (free of household production) in GDP.

As opposed to earlier approaches used by analysts, this method has the

Table 5.5. Pairwise correlations between the size of the hidden economy, unemployment, and non-agricultural self-employment, 1990–4

Size of hidden economy based on household electricity approach

	In developed market economies	In post-socialist economies		
Unemployment	0.73^a	0.65^b	0.8^c	0.41^d
Self-employment	0.73	0.51	0.51	0.57

Notes:
[a] 19 OECD countries, 1990.
[b] Hungary, Poland, Former Czechoslovakia, 1990–4.
[c] Hungary, Poland, Czech republic, 1990–4.
[d] Hungary, Poland, Czech republic, Slovakia, 1990–4.

advantage of taking into account several factors that give rise to the hidden economy, and in such a way that the weights of these factors are endogenously determined in the course of the estimation. Another advantage is that the method can be used for the analysis of the hidden economy not only in market economies but, with some assumptions, in socialist and post-socialist economies as well. The drawback of the method is that it focuses on the investigation of only that part of the hidden economy which is associated with the use of household electricity.

The results show that the hidden economy is relatively large in Spain, Greece, Ireland, Belgium, Italy and Denmark (17–25 per cent of GDP), of medium size in Portugal, Austria, Australia, Germany and the Netherlands (14–16 per cent), while in Canada, Sweden, Finland, France, the UK, Japan, the USA, Switzerland and Norway its share is lower (9–13 per cent).

The specific position of the hidden economy in post-socialist countries was examined using the example of the Czech republic, Slovakia, Hungary and Poland. In the early 1990s, the size of the hidden economy could be considered large in Poland and Hungary (26–36 per cent of GDP): these values were higher than in any of the market economies in the OECD sample. The share of the hidden economy in the Czech republic and Slovakia was smaller (15–22 per cent of GDP). The results show that the size of the hidden economy is in positive relation with the rate of unemployed and the ratio of self-employed not only in market economies but also in the post-socialist countries.

NOTES

1   The final version of this chapter was written during the author's PHARE/ ACE Fellowship No. P95–2776–F at the International Institute for Applied

Systems Analysis (IIASA), Austria. The author is grateful to Nebojsa Nakicenovic (IIASA), Leo Schrattenholzer (IIASA) and Friedrich Schneider (University of Linz) as well as the editors of this book for their valuable comments. All errors remain the responsibility of the author.

2   A 'macroelectric' method was worked out by Dobozi and Pohl (1995) and Kaufmann and Kaliberda (1996) to measure the changes in the size of the hidden economy for post-socialist countries. According to that method, the difference between the growth rate of registered GDP and the growth rate of total electricity consumption can be attributed to the growth of the hidden economy. Elsewhere I question this method, because I found that not only the growth of the hidden economy, but also the differences in branch level structural changes in the registered production had effects on total electricity consumption in transition countries after 1989 (see Lackó, 1996b). In contrast to Dobozi and Pohl (1995) and Kaufmann and Kaliberda (1996) in my investigations I do not use total electricity consumption but household electricity consumption data.

3   The method is based on the ratio of currency to demand deposits and assumes that the size of the hidden economy is reflected in this ratio. Supporters of this method assert that there is a stable quantitative relation between the currency held by the private sector and the demand deposits owned by private entrepreneurs. The technique assumes that in a given base period no hidden economy exists, and the measured ratio between the currency and demand deposits is stable. Following the calculations by Cagan (1958), Gutmann (1977) and Feige (1979) the method was improved by Tanzi (1980). The latter showed that the stock or ratio of currency is influenced by several factors, one of these being the size of taxes. Tanzi argued that the increment in currency stock related to taxes can be in essence considered the reflection of the hidden economy. With the separation of the tax-related component and by assuming that the velocity of money is the same in the visible and hidden economies, Tanzi managed to determine the size of the hidden economy as a share of GDP.

When examining the hidden economy in Austria Schneider (1994) made a step forward compared to Tanzi: in addition to the tax rates he also took into account the burden of administrative regulation. In his model he assumed that the higher the burden of regulation, the larger is, *ceteris paribus*, the hidden economy. (For the construction of the index of the burden of regulation two proxies were used by Schneider: the number of pages of the new laws prescribing different regulations, and the number of employees of various state administrative institutions.)

4   The soft modelling method attempts to combine several causes and indicators of hidden economy in the course of the estimation of the hidden economy's size. By using the soft modelling approach Frey and Weck (1984) made a cross-section and time series analysis of 17 OECD countries. The following explanatory variables were taken into account: tax rates, burden of regulation by the state (represented by the number of employees in state bureaucracy), tax morality (countries were ranked on the evidence found in the literature), rate of participation in the official economy, weekly working hours, and the ratio of guest workers to total employed. The system of weights attached to the individual causes and indicators was developed independently from the model. According to this system the most significant weight was given to tax

rates, then descending weights were applied to tax morality, burden of regulation by the state, participation rate and working hours, and the ratio of guest workers to non-guest workers.

REFERENCES

Árvay, J. (1993) 'Methods of measuring the hidden economy in the transition countries', Paris: OECD, manuscript
Árvay, J. and A. Vértes (1994) 'Rejteni, ami rejthető...' (To hide, that can be hidden...), *Figyelő* (24 February)
Bordignon, M. (1993) 'Taxing lessons from Italy', *International Economic Insight*, IV, 10–14
Burns, S. (1977) *The Household Economy*, Boston: Beacon Press
Cagan, P. (1958) 'The demand for currency relative to total money supply', *Journal of Political Economy*, 66, 303–29
Carter, M. (1984) 'Issues in the hidden economy', *Economic Record*, 60, 209–11
Countries in Transition 1994, 1995, 1996, WIIW Handbook of Statistics, Vienna: Vienna Institute for Comparative Economic Studies
Dobozi, I. and G. Pohl (1995) 'Real output declines in transition economies – forget GDP, try power consumption data', *Transition*, 6
Ékes, I. (1993) *Rejtett gazdaság – Láthatatlan jövedelmek tegnap és ma* (Hidden economy – Invisible incomes yesterday and today), Budapest, author's own publication
Energy Prices and Taxes 1991, 1992, 1993, 1994, Paris: OECD
Feige, E.L. (1979) 'How big is the irregular economy?', *Challenge*, 22, 5–13
Feige, E.L. (ed.) (1989) *The Underground Economies: Tax Evasion and Information Distortion*, Cambridge, MA: Cambridge University Press
(1993) 'The myth of the cashless society', *International Economic Insights*, IV, 2–4
Frey, B.S. and H. Weck (1983a) 'What produces a hidden economy? An international cross-section analysis', *Southern Economic Journal*, 49, 822–32
(1983b) 'Estimating the shadow economy: a naive approach', *Oxford Economic Papers*, 35, 23–4
(1984) 'The hidden economy as an unobserved variable', *European Economic Review*, 26, 33–53
Gershuny, J.I. (1979) 'The informal economy: its role in post-industrial society', *Futures*, 11, 3–15
Gutmann, P.M. (1977) 'The subterranean economy', *Financial Analysts Journal*, 33
International Financial Statistics 1992, Washington, DC: International Monetary Fund
Kadera, V. (1995) 'The importance and role of the shadow economy in the transformation period of the Czech republic: economic trends', *Komercni Banka*, 4
Kaufmann, D. and A. Kaliberda (1996) 'Integrating the unofficial economy into the dynamics of post-socialist economies: a framework of analysis and evidence', in B. Kaminski (ed.), *Economic Transition in Russia and the New States of Eurasia*, Armonk, NY: M.E. Sharpe
Klovland, J.T. (1983) 'Tax evasion and the demand for currency in Norway and

Sweden: is there a hidden relationship?', Norwegian School of Economics and Business Administration, *Discussion Paper*, **07/8(3)**, mimeo

Lackó, M. (1995) 'The Hungarian hidden economy in international comparison: estimation method based on household electricity consumption and currency ratio', *Discussion Paper*, **25**, Institute of Economics, Hungarian Academy of Sciences, Budapest

(1996a) 'Hidden economy in East-European countries in international comparison', Laxenburg: IIASA, mimeo

(1996b) 'Do power consumption data tell the story? Electricity intensities in the post-socialist countries between 1989 and 1994', Laxenburg: IIASA, mimeo

Macafee, K. (1980) 'A glimpse of the hidden economy in the national accounts', *Economic Trends*, **316**, 81–7

Magyar Statisztikai Évkönyv 1992 (*Hungarian Statistical Yearbook*), Budapest: KSH

Marrelli, M. (1987) 'The economic analysis of tax evasion: empirical aspects', in J.D. Hey and P.J. Lambert (eds.), *Surveys in the Economics of Uncertainty*, Oxford: Blackwell

Mattera, P. (1985) *Off the Books*, London, Pluto

Morris, B. (1993) 'Editorial statement', *International Economic Insights*, **IV** *Nemzetközi Statisztikai Évkönyv* (International Statistical Yearbook, 1989) Budapest: KSH

Novotny, E. and G. Winckler (1994) *Grundzüge der Wirtschafts Politik Österreichs*, Wien: MANZ

OECD (1992a) *Electricity Information 1992*, International Energy Agency, Paris: OECD

(1992b) *Energy Statistics and Balances of Non-OECD Countries 1989–1990*, Paris: OECD

(1994a) *New Orientation in Social Policy*, Paris: OECD

(1994b) *The OECD Job Study, Evidence and Explanations I, II*, Paris: OECD Paris.

(1996a) *Energy Statistics and Balances of Non-OECD Countries 1993–1994*, Paris: OECD

(1996b) *OECD Observer*, **198**

Schneider, F. (1994) 'Measuring the size and development of the shadow economy. Can the causes be found and the obstacles be overcome?', in H. Brandstatter and W. Güth (eds.), *Essays on Economic Psychology*, Berlin and Heidelberg: Springer Verlag, 193–212

Tanzi, V. (1980) 'The underground economy in the United States: estimates and implications', *Banca Nazionale del Lavoro Quarterly Review*, **135**, 427–53

(1982) *The Underground Economy in the United States and Abroad*, Lexington, MA: D.C. Heath

(1983) 'The underground economy in the United States: annual estimates, 1930–1980', *IMF Staff Papers*, **30**, 238–305

Tanzi, V. and P. Shome (1993) 'A primer on tax evasion', *IMF Staff Papers*, **40**, 807–25

US Department of Commerce (1994) *World Weather* Records, R.M. Steurer (ed.), National Oceanic and Atmospheric Administration (NOAA), National Environmental Satellite Data and Information Service, National Climatic Center, Washington DC

Discussion

MICHAEL A. LANDESMANN

Mária Lackó's chapter 5 is a professionally executed study estimating the size of the 'hidden' economy in some Central and Eastern European (CEE) countries (Hungary, Poland, the Czech republic and Slovakia). The methodology she adopts is that of estimating a model of household consumption of energy for OECD economies and then applying this model with some modifications to the CEE economies. The concept behind this model is that household energy consumption accounts for a part of the 'non-registered' economic activities in both market and transition economies and hence Lackó's approach is to decompose overall energy demand by households into two components, one which proxies energy demand for registered household activities, the other for non-registered household activities. The part of the non-registered household activities is assumed in the model to be a function of the overall tax burden in an economy, of the pressure on state finances to collect taxes (proxied by the difference between state expenditure for social welfare and tax income) and of the number of people over 14 years old who are not in registered employment. These variables and the decomposition allow Lackó to develop an operational model which could be estimated across the range of OECD and transition economies and come up with a plausible ranking of both OECD and transition economies in terms of the size of their 'hidden' economy.

The size and role of the 'hidden' economy has attracted a lot of attention both in market economies and in former socialist economies (where it was commonly assumed that the size of the 'hidden' economy exceeded that in comparable market economies). In transition economies the size of the 'hidden' economy is again of scientific interest, as it reflects the change in the behavioural and institutional regime which characterises the transition, and it is of great policy relevance as well. The policy relevance stems from the fact that the evolution of 'non-registered activities' can, firstly, be seen in a number of ways to reflect the relative success of the transition itself and has, secondly, severe implications for the fiscal policy constraints a government faces in the (economically and politically) rather unstable period of transition.

Lackó discusses the differences which characterise the reasons for the emergence of a 'hidden' economy in market economies and in the previous 'socialist' economies. She is much briefer in her discussion of the particular characteristics of these activities in the period of transition itself; she maintains that this period is basically characterised by a gradual changeover from a regime in which the set of reasons which caused the existence of 'non-registered activities' in formerly socialist economies (the features of a 'shortage economy', the ability to use capacities and materials from the official economy for private activities, the under-utilisation of work in official jobs, corrupt practices, etc.) gives way to another set which are usually seen as accounting for unregistered activities in market economies (avoidance of tax, uneven degree of tax enforcement, lax tax morality). In my view, this view of the transition as a simple 'traverse' from one set of behavioural rules to another is too superficial and does not bring out the interesting singular features of the transition itself, especially since the evolution of the 'hidden' economy in this crucial and unstable period could itself be an important indicator of whether or not the transition is successful.

First, there is the severe weakening of the authority of the state itself during the transition; this is accompanied by a severe drain of resources and skilled personnel from state administrative bodies. This means a drop in the efficiency and effectiveness with which the state can pursue its various operations, including the enforcement of a particular tax regime. Secondly, the period of transition – particularly its early phase – is characterised by a constant flux in the legal framework and in the institutional arrangements in which state operations take place, and this also weakens the effectiveness of tax enforcement. Thirdly, there are attitude changes, adjustments to a new relationship between the (potential) taxpayers and the tax authorities which went through a major phase of delegitimisation and decline in the instruments of compulsion in the shift from an authoritarian to a parliamentary state. All these factors could indicate a dramatic temporary loss of control over part of the economy on which the tax base could be built. They all indicate that, just as the changeover in the basic mechanisms of resource allocation which the transition from state directed to market oriented economic activity led to a deep (though temporary) 'transformational recession' (Kornai, 1995), so also would the change in state–household relationships in the realm of tax regulation, tax enforcement and tax legitimisation follow a 'U-shaped pattern'. High levels of 'hidden' economy activities would – if the transition in this sphere proceeded successfully – be followed by a period in which the size of the 'hidden' economy would start to approach that of well functioning market economies when the state has regained a level of legitimacy and efficacy of operation and when behavioural rules followed by households and in businesses have adjusted to a new long-term relationship between state and private economic agents.

Lackó's model does not attempt to encompass the specific features of the 'transition' which would – as argued above – be of relevance to understanding and also projecting the nature and evolution of the 'hidden' economy during the various phases of the transition. However, this might – as Lackó notes at one point – be too ambitious a task given the short time series available. Nonetheless, an attempt to get at these features in a systematic and quantitative way would not only be important to track the 'U-shaped pattern' in the development of the 'hidden' economy in the more successful transition economies (not fully, but mostly congruent with Lackó's sample) but also to understand some of the failures of a successful transition – i.e. the fact that legitimacy and effectiveness of state–administrative operations as well as behavioural adjustments to a new long-term regime of state–private agents relationships have not taken place, with all the implications that this entails for microeconomic efficiency and constraints upon macroeconomic policy making.

Let me now briefly return to Lackó's model. Does it, in spite of its more limited conceptual scope (but enhanced operationality), yield useful rough estimates of at least a part of the unrecorded economic activities in CEE economies? This very much hinges upon the question of whether the decomposition technique which usefully segments the factors which give rise to registered versus non-registered types of economic activities for OECD economies can usefully give first proxies of the main reasons for the emergence of non-registered activities. These factors are: a variable which proxies the incentives of private agents to accept the risks of non-registration, i.e. the size of the fiscal burden in an economy; the incentive of the state to enforce tax laws proxied by the severity of budgetary pressures; a measure of the pool of a potential labour force upon which non-registered economic activity can draw; and, lastly, a factor introduced specifically by Lackó to account for an additional reason which induces businesses in CEE countries to conduct activities under the disguise of being households: the fact that energy has traditionally been supplied at considerably lower rates to households than to enterprises, inducing a shift of recorded energy consumption towards households and away from businesses.

All these factors can indeed play a role, and possibly a major role, in transition economies just as they do in fully adjusted market economies to account for the size of the 'hidden' economy. They do not take into account the additional behavioural and institutional turmoil described above, which 'transition' implies unless there is a close correlation between the two. Indeed, one could argue that, say, budgetary pressures in the transition are to a significant degree caused by the dwindling tax base due to tax evasion and this, in fact, reflects the institutional and behavioural turmoil characteristic of the early phase of the transition. Similarly, evidence for particularly high nominal tax rates and high dependency ratios would also be a reflection of a large unrecorded sector of the economy and hence the correlation between the variables used in the regression and the 'transition-specific' factors would be rather high. The trouble with this argument is that while we could accept the important positive aspect of the exercise – namely that the estimates from the regression concerning the 'size' of the 'hidden' economy would remain reliable even for the period of the transition – we could, firstly, not be sure of that (in the sense that the correlations are not explicitly tested for) and, secondly, as Maria Lackó also acknowledges, the causality relationship would have been turned around. Our explanatory variables (tax burden for the 'recorded activities', budgetary pressures, etc.) would have become the dependent variables and hence the explanatory framework for analysing the specific causes for the emergence (and, possibly, later disappearance) of unusually high levels of 'black' economies in economies of transition would still be missing. Hence, Maria Lackó's chapter provides a good first shot at an empirical estimate of the size of the 'hidden' economy in transition economies if one could indeed assume that the particular factors of the transition would no longer apply, but it still leaves open both the theoretical and empirical tasks of a deeper analysis of the role and evolution of 'unrecorded activities' during the turbulent and interesting period of the transition itself. Since that phase is far from successfully completed for a large number of transition economies both in Eastern Europe and Asia these remain compelling issues not only from an historical but also a current policy point of view.

REFERENCE

Kornai, J. (1995) 'A magyar gazdaságpolitika dilemmái' (Dilemmas of Hungary's economic policy), *Kőzgazdasági Szemle*, **1995/7–8**

Part Two
Industrial structure

6 Corporate governance in the transition – the case of Hungary: do new structures help create efficient ownership control?

ÁDÁM TÖRÖK

1 Introduction

Corporate governance (CG) is one of the genuinely key issues of the microeconomic aspect of the transition process. The problem becomes really interesting in those countries including Hungary where the legal and organisational framework for CG has existed for several years and the functioning of CG structures as well as their adaptability to the conditions of a transition economy can be tested.

The Hungarian economy of the mid-1990s seems to be such a testing ground. This is mainly due to the temporary coexistence of private firms in domestic and foreign ownership with state firms and cooperatives in Hungary. Legislation makes it inevitable for all forms of entrepreneurship with a legal personality (i.e. legal entities) to have CG structures. Therefore a comparative approach can be taken in order to identify the key differences between CG structures of Hungarian firms in different ownership forms and also to see the extent to which the apparent convergence of the economy's institutional development with that of EU countries is reflected in the pattern of CG development in Hungary.

Finally, conspicuous recent stock market development in Hungary is likely to make the country an increasingly attractive target for institutional investors. The effectiveness of CG in Hungary is undoubtedly one of the key factors in the decisions of these investors as well as others considering setting up physical capacity in the country.

2 Models of CG

2.1 Historical and definitional issues

The role of CG in the ownership and the management of various forms of corporations has been widely discussed in the economic and manage-

159

ment literature. It would be very difficult to find the origins of CG structures; certainly, the institutions of early nineteenth-century European (more precisely, British) capitalism were based on such an enterprise structure in which

> The unit of . . . private-property economy was the firm of medium size. Its typical legal form was the private partnership. Barring the 'sleeping' partner, it was typically managed by the owner or owners, a fact that is important to keep in mind in any effort to understand 'classic' economics. The facts and problems of large-scale production and, in connection with them, those of joint stock companies were recognized by economists after anyone else had recognized them. They received textbook status at the hands of J.S. Mill, who duly blamed A. Smith for his narrow views on corporate business. (Schumpeter, 1954, p. 545)

In other words, the early nineteenth-century British firm may have been a *company*, but in most cases it wasn't a *corporation*. We understand by the term 'corporation' 'An artificial being, invisible, intangible, and existing only in contemplation of law. It is exclusively the work of the law, and the best evidence is the grant of corporate powers by the commonwealth' (Donnell, Barnes and Metzger, 1983, p. 934).[1]

Three main types of corporations can be distinguished (Donnell *et al.*, 1983, p. 362): (1) governmental or municipal corporations; (2) non-profit corporations; (3) for-profit corporations. The latter group can still be divided into (a) close (e.g. family-owned) and (b) publicly held corporations. Although CG must and does exist in types (1), (2) and (3a), we deal only with CG in publicly held corporations.[2]

In a very general approach, 'corporate governance issues arise in an organisation when two conditions hold: an agency problem and sufficiently high transactions costs to rule out dealing with the agency problem via a contract' (Greenaway, 1995, p. 676). Most modern legal systems do not follow this approach: they simply make the creation of CG structures one of the prerequisites for establishing a for-profit corporation – without respect to agency and transaction cost problems. Suffice to mention the German, Austrian or Hungarian practice: limited liability companies (above a certain size limit – 300 employees in Hungary) must have Supervisory Boards. Companies limited by shares are obliged to have both boards of directors and Supervisory Boards (cf. Sárközy, 1994; Török, 1994, pp. 14–15).

Before tackling some theoretical issues of CG analysis, one more definitional comment needs to be made. It is important to appreciate that the use of Anglo-Saxon legal and/or case study material can have only a limited relevance for an assessment of the Hungarian or, in a broader sense, the entire East European transitional experience related to CG issues.

The main reason for this relative lack of relevance is the *systemic difference* between Anglo-Saxon and continental corporate legislations.[3] This difference between the levels of individual responsibility does not mean, of course, that shareholders may carry any liability for their corporation in the Anglo-Saxon system beyond the market value of their shares. On the other hand, many details can be found in continental and Anglo-Saxon systems of corporate legislation to pinpoint the nature of this difference. For example: the Hungarian corporate law does not contain *expressis verbis* the Anglo-Saxon principles of 'business judgement rule' and 'due care and prudence', but their application in cases of litigation involving Board members cannot in the future be excluded (cf. Leloczky, 1993, p. 138).

For the sake of analytical precision, a final definitional remark seems inevitable. A clear distinction has to be made between (1) CG itself, and (2) CG structures, as we call the Board of Directors, the Supervisory Board and, (3) last but not least, the General Assembly of the corporation.

It is very important at this point that any confusion over the understanding of terms be avoided. The terms 'Board of Directors', 'Supervisory Board' and 'General Assembly' are English translations of Hungarian expressions without any direct counterpart in the English-speaking world (see in detail, Charkham, 1994).

The Hungarian *Board of Directors* is the equivalent of the *Board* in the USA and the UK (with somewhat different functions), the *Board of Directors* (with a different content again) in Japan, and the *Vorstand* (the most similar of all, but not the same) in Germany. The Hungarian *Supervisory Board*'s counterpart in the USA may be only the so-called *Audit Committee* of the Board (required for companies quoted on the NYSE) and also in the UK, the *statutory auditors* (*Kansayaku*) in Japan, and the *Aufsichtsrat* in Germany. Although the latter is quite similar in scope to that of Supervisory Boards in Hungary, its powers are much more extensive: the Chairman and the members of the Board, for example, are nominated by the Supervisory Board in the German system (Charkham, 1994, p. 22).

In fact, among the big industrial countries only Germany has the fully two-tier CG system that exists in Hungary. France has two parallel CG systems for companies limited by shares. One of these systems has boards (*directoires*) and supervisory boards (*conseils de surveillance*) while the other, based on the strong leadership of the *President Directeur Général*, does not have any (Charkham, 1994, pp. 133–5).

CG itself is understood as an abstract term referred to in the literature as a kind of superstructure of the firm ensuring effective ownership control and the coordination of interests between the players of the corporate game, and creating an efficient link between owner (the 'principal') and management (the 'agent'). CG structures, on the other hand, are groups of persons selected by the owners to act on their behalf and, therefore, to be considered their 'proxies' except if they are the *owner* or *owners* themselves. Because of this distinction, the 'functioning of CG' is a contradiction in terms, and only the functioning of CG structures can be analysed.

2.2   The functions of CG structures

CG problems have to be understood as problems of the multilateral relationship linking the following players of the 'corporate game' to each other: (1) owners, (2) employees, (3) suppliers, (4) customers, (5) the community[4] and (6) the management. This scheme has been taken from Oliver Williamson who gives a detailed analysis of why all these groups of players must be included in the model (cf. Williamson, 1985, pp. 302–11). Williamson's explanation makes it clear why it would be mistaken to limit the number of participants in CG models to only three players (i.e. owners, employees and management) following the widespread common belief. In fact, each of the six groups has *legitimate interests* which have to be represented in and/or taken care of by the CG structures.

Participation in CG structures can take two basic forms: (1) *voting membership* which entails the possibility of and the right to 'the ratification of corporate decisions and the follow-on monitoring of corporate performance';[5] (2) informational participation which allows the members of CG structures 'to observe strategic planning and to be apprised of information on which decisions are based, but allows no vote on investments or management' (Williamson, 1985, p. 302). It is not clear from available literature whether (2) implies any financial compensation and/or legal responsibility (liability) of members of CG structures. It is important to note that *financial compensation* of members of CG structures (boards) is not obligatory.

A Hungarian case in point is GE-Tungsram where Board members are not paid. There is no known case in Hungary of informational participation of formal Board members in CG structures. On the other hand, the so-called 'legal persons' membership' of representatives of state holding (asset management) companies[6] on the Boards of Directors of state-owned firms makes it possible for a number of employees of these holdings to become *de facto* informational participants of the CG structures of state-owned firms.

Anglo-Saxon practice is very varied:

> In times past, the corporation had no duty to compensate directors for their services . . . Today, although many corporations still pay their directors little or no compensation for their services, an increasing number of corporations do pay hefty sums to them. Since directors today often are not substantial shareholders and since they are subject to ever-expanding duties and concomitant possibilities for liability, compensation seems defensible. (Davidson *et al.*, 1989, p. 903)

This approach rightly links the compensation of Board (and Supervisory Board) members to their liability, although most legal systems define the content and the limits of the liability of Board (and Supervisory Board) members in a rather vague way. This vagueness exists especially in the Hungarian case which has been referred to earlier with respect to litigation issues involving Board members (cf. Leloczky, 1993, p. 138). The Anglo-Saxon legal system also leaves much room for a generous concept of 'liability' in this case.

This generosity is based on the doctrine of *respondeat superior*, which stipulates that an 'officer' (i.e. not only an *employee*) of a company can be made liable for a tort in which he actively participated, but the company (his 'superior') can be made liable as well (Davidson *et al.*, 1989, p. 907).

Thus far, we have concentrated on a survey of 'non-mainstream' CG structures from which at least one of the following attributes of 'mainstream' CG structures was missing: (1) directors (Board members) and/or Supervisory Board members represent owners and, eventually, other parties interested in a smooth functioning of the firm; (2) they get compensation for their services rendered to the company; (3) they are legally liable for any tort or damage they may cause to the company; (4) they exercise control over management, and have access to a large amount of company-specific information.

Special conditions of a firm may make it necessary to create 'non-mainstream'-type CG structures in which not all of these four attributes exist. But it seems evident from the international literature and Hungarian experience that most currently existing CG structures belong to what we have called the 'mainstream' type.

Oliver Williamson's seminal book (Williamson, 1985) focuses on the Board of Directors as the key element of CG structures. As a matter of fact, Williamson does not even touch upon the functions of Supervisory Boards in his book, and General Assemblies are also left aside in the analysis.[7] The explanation for this apparent anomaly in the American literature seems quite simple: the functions of the boards of directors in the USA (and probably also in the entire Anglo-Saxon legal system) include a role of control over management in the broad sense, and therefore Supervisory Boards have no room in the system (although, as was mentioned earlier, some of their functions are performed by Auditing Committees, see Charkham, 1994 – USA, pp. 191–2, UK, pp. 274–5). Neither the continental nor the Anglo-Saxon system leaves control over management entirely to the Boards of Directors.

The continental system widely applies the institution of Supervisory Boards in both companies limited by shares and limited liability companies as the main instrument of ownership control[8] over both the Board of Directors and management. The Anglo-Saxon system has several mechanisms of ownership control over management. One of these is the Board of Directors itself, and the literature describes at least three more control mechanisms (cf. Hart, 1995, pp. 681–6; Phelps *et al.*, 1993, pp. 18–19). For example, Oliver Hart's scheme of control mechanisms consists of the following elements (Hart, 1995, pp. 681–6):

(1) *The Board of Directors*: Most boards seem to have more theoretical than practical efficiency for several reasons (Hart, 1995, pp. 681–2). Executive directors are members of the management team, and therefore not disinterested in the consequences of evaluating the company's and its management's performance. Non-executive directors are mostly busy outsiders without much direct interest in the performance of the company, although some of them may represent important suppliers or customers of the firm. It is nevertheless likely that good Boards should have a structured balance between 'execs' and 'non-execs'.[9]

(2) *Proxy fights*: This somewhat vague term means that under-performing Board members can be replaced by candidates put up by certain shareholders, and this replacement usually takes place through conflicts (fights) between different groups of shareholders. While such a change can be easily accomplished by a majority shareholder, shareholders with smaller equity stakes will have to undertake costly and time-consuming action to persuade other shareholders to vote for the change. Therefore this instrument of ownership control can be efficient only for majority owners or strong shareholders.

(3) *Large shareholders*: It has been suggested for the above reason that the performance of CG structures be improved by the obligation that each joint stock company have at least one major shareholder (Hart, 1995, p. 683). This is, of course, a quite outlandish idea, but it has a grain of truth. A large shareholder may develop an aggressive and oppressive behaviour towards smaller ones in order to reduce their

degree of effective ownership control, but a large shareholder is undoubtedly an owner who is able to represent his strong interest in the good performance of the company. There is evidence from Japan that large shareholders play an important role in improving firm performance by replacing Board members with outsiders ('outside succession') (Kang and Shivdasani, 1995). On the other hand, 'succession planning' is mostly the task of the management teams in American firms, with the Board of Directors reserving the right to plan the succession of the CEO in office (Leibman and Bruer, 1994, p. 28).

(4) *Hostile takeovers*: Simply put, the danger of these is a permanent challenge to management. The reason is that the inadequate performance of management may show the company's current value on the stock market to be lower than it could be under a better management team. Therefore, in theory at least, a corporate raider may realise a significant gain by buying a firm under-valued only owing to poor management and selling it more expensively after installing a new management team. In reality, the presence of the free-rider problem as well as competition from other bidders may prevent the hostile takeover (Hart, 1995, p. 684). A further safeguard may be, of course, the attention of management toward any intention of hostile takeovers (Hart, 1995, p. 685). Finally, so-called 'poison pills'[10] could also be used.

It has to be borne in mind that the danger of hostile takeovers is a means of indirect control of management only in such countries where the shares of most big firms are openly traded. Germany and Japan do not belong to this group, and France does so only to a limited extent (Charkham, 1994).

While the above mechanisms of control over management can work well in Anglo-Saxon countries, most continental systems have much more rigid institutional elements of control. By far the most important of these is the Supervisory Board (*Aufsichtsrat, conseil de surveillance, Felügyelő Bizottság*). This element of continental CG structures has roughly the same functions in each country where it exists, but its strategic role varies quite markedly.

One extreme is where the Supervisory Board or its equivalent is merely a duplicate of, or a link between, internal and external auditors and its responsibilities do not go beyond financial control. This is the case of the Statutory Auditors (*Kansayaku*) elected by shareholders in Japan (Charkham, 1994, pp. 92–3). At the other extreme, Supervisory Boards (*Aufsichtsräte*) have a very broad authority in Germany.[11] This is contested by some authors, who think that the German concept of trying to better integrate the firm into society through its CG structures may eventually become a stumbling block to the 'Europeanisation of the firm'. This 'Europeanisation' is also supposed to include the creation of a unique EU-wide CG system (cf. Coutinho de Abreu, 1995, p. 20).

The French case is distinctive again: in companies where '*conseils de surveillance*' exist, their members do not carry legal liability, unlike Board members (Charkham, 1994, p. 137).

It is a prerequisite of setting up Supervisory Boards in the continental system that their membership may not overlap with Board membership. Their members should not be members of the management team either, but it occurs quite frequently in Germany that employee representatives are managers only a few levels below the top. In any event, Supervisory Boards have to exert legal and financial control over the operations of management, but they should avoid any strategic interference with the Board. Supervisory Boards are the *ultimate institutional guarantee of the normal functioning of the company for the shareholders*. It is probably for this reason that Supervisory Board members in France have to be holders of qualifying shares (Charkham, 1994, p. 134).

3   CG and economic transition

3.1   The evolution of CG in Hungary

As an element of the pre-1989 economic reforms, the government ruled in 1984 that most state enterprises should create so-called bodies of self-governance (or self-management). This system was somewhat similar to the Yugoslav scheme of enterprise self-management (for details cf. Sárközy, 1993, pp. 20–2). State firms were divided in three categories according to their new form of 'enterprise governance':

(1) *Enterprise boards* at about 75 per cent of state firms. Half of the members of this Board were elected by employees, one-third delegated by the managers of organisational units and one-sixth appointed by the CEO. This Board, with a right to formulate enterprise strategy, also had the right to appoint the CEO but, in turn, its members (and their bonuses) depended on the CEO as well.

(2) *General Assemblies at the enterprise* were created at about 5 per cent of state firms (SMEs). All members of these were elected by the employees. The decision making powers of this Assembly were quite limited.

(3) *State firms under government supervision* (20 per cent of state

enterprises) were controlled by Supervisory Boards appointed by the founding ministries (Török, 1993–4, pp. 73–4). These Supervisory Boards were *not, in any sense, CG bodies in the current meaning of the term.* Their existence was not rooted in corporate legislation, but they did not have Boards of Directors to deal with either. These very special 'Supervisory Boards' were created to facilitate enterprise transformation and to establish an indirect linkage between the government and the management of the firms. After the legal transformation of the firms, many members of these Supervisory Boards were delegated to the boards of state-owned companies limited by shares.

Modern CG structures were created by the Law on Economic Associations (VI/1988). The Law on Enterprise Transformation (XIII/1989), the Law on the State Property Agency (VII/1990) and the Law on the Protection of State-owned Assets (VIII/1990) also made important contributions to the clarification of the rules of setting up CG structures (Brada *et al.*, 1994, pp. 13–15).

These three pieces of legislation were later replaced by (or, more accurately, amalgamated in) the so-called Privatisation Act (LIV/1992). The legislation replacing the latter in 1995 (XXXIX/1995, Law on the Sale of Entrepreneurial Assets Owned by the State) left all legal rules defining and governing CG practically untouched.

3.2   How does CG work in Hungary?

CG structures can be created in three ways in Hungary. The 'mainstream' possibility, exclusively governed by the Law on Economic Associations, is the creation of a company with legal personality (company limited by shares or limited liability company). In this case, the law precisely defines which bodies belong to which form of company. *Companies without a legal personality* (e.g. partnerships) *do not need any form of CG outside of management.*[12] The two other possibilities are linked to privatisation.[13]

The second possibility has been the *legal transformation* of a state enterprise into a company.[14] Formal prerequisites of legal transformation include corporate statutes, an audited asset evaluation and an audited balance sheet, and the definition of the ownership structure by the Corporate Charter of the firm. A firm transformed but not yet privatised can be 100 per cent state-owned.

A special way of creating companies and CG structures from scratch has been the so-called 'spinoff' or 'asset-protection'-type privatisation. Such privatisations have involved the sales of assets of not yet transformed state enterprises to other firms, including the separation of such organisational units from the 'mother company' to become new firms in the legal sense. Such cases are, though, *not legal transformations.* They are therefore governed by the Law on Economic Associations, albeit that strict rules determine the transfer of SOE assets to private firms.

The Hungarian Law on Economic Associations has uniform general rules for the CG of joint stock companies. Each has to set up a Board of Directors and a Supervisory Board. The members of these bodies carry a liability of all their personal wealth for any negative consequences their bad decisions cause to the firm. Limited liability companies are obliged to have Supervisory Boards only, and only above a quite high company size limit. CG at these companies is therefore jointly assured by the Managing Director and the Supervisory Board.

This feature of CG in Hungary also proves that the system is formally quite similar to the one functioning in Germany. On the other hand, Supervisory Boards in Hungary have a much weaker role than in Germany since they have no input concerning the nomination or replacement of directors (Board members) and they can in no way be regarded as the highest instance of CG at the firm.[15] Hungarian Boards tend to be much smaller than in Germany with usually fewer than 10 directors and no more than five members in Supervisory Boards. The highest instance of CG is the General Assembly of the owners of a company limited by shares (or the assembly of the owners of a limited liability company). The functioning of the General Assembly depends on the character of shares.

Shares offering special rights to their owners are quite rare in the Hungarian practice.[16] One possible explanation of this could be a legal problem: the Law on Economic Associations (VI/1988, par. 243) determines the category of shares with special rights, but it does not distinguish them from non-special, 'base' shares in a suitably precise way. This lack of precision causes problems because the Hungarian law allows only equal face values for the same kind of shares (cf. Szegediné, 1994, p. 2). In practice, however, some owners of 'base' shares have been recompensed for their lack of special rights at the expense of other holders of the same type of shares.

The specification of special rights linked to shares is as yet rarely used as a tool of special ownership control over the firm. There are, however, some challenging exceptions. A very interesting case in point was Alitalia's minority buyout of the Hungarian airline MALÉV. The very special definition of some shares in that case gave rise to an antitrust dispute that was finally settled peacefully.

Another recent case in point was the issuance of 'golden shares' of regional gas companies privatised in late 1995. These golden shares belong to the former majority owner, the state holding (ÁPV Rt) giving it a decisive vote in several major issues (changes in the equity capital, nominations to the Board, resale of the company, etc.) but not entitling it to a dividend. The existence of these golden shares is contested by a number of legal experts stating that the Law on Economic Associations (VI/1988) explicitly links voting rights to ownership shares. Literature on this debate in Hungary is not yet available.

Non-voting shares are usually issued in ESOPs, although ESOP shares need not be non-voting. Such shares can be physically distributed among their owners according to the repayment of credits for ESOP by these owners.

Minority foreign investors in 'spinoffs' of state-owned holdings eventually accept non-voting shares.[17] These shares should be available cheaply with a good option for the further participation of the non-voting minority shareholder in privatisation.

It is known from international literature that voting rights of shareholders are a key element in CG,[18] but there is much less evidence of how voting rights work within Boards themselves. To be more precise: there is evidence on the (lack of) use of voting rights in such countries where CG structures function either in a formal way, or there are such hierarchical relationships within Boards that they virtually exclude the effective use of voting rights.

An appropriate example is Japan (Charkham, 1994, pp. 70–118). An important explanation of the quite formal voting procedures within Japanese boards lies in the high value the Japanese traditionally attach to consensus.[19] It is important to note at this point (the credit for this observation belongs to Sweder van Wijnbergen) that the functioning of CG structures in Japanese corporations lacks transparency and controllability. Therefore Hungarian firms should be extremely careful if they eventually try to follow the Japanese pattern of 'informal' CG. On the other hand, the Japanese pattern of 'informal' CG seems to be able, at least in the Japanese social and economic context, to serve well defined efficiency criteria at the company level (Matsumoto, 1991, pp. 142–3).

Voting is rarely decisive at boards of Hungarian firms. In most cases there is an extensive bargaining process on sensitive issues at Board meetings. Consensus, or at least the changing of one camp's 'yes' or 'no' votes into abstention, is very often achieved. This effort to reach consensus seems to have several explanations (mostly quite different from those valid for the case of Japan):

(1) *Sharing responsibility* among Board members (cf. their financial liability).
(2) *The problem of asymmetric information.* Most Boards at industrial firms have two or three 'insider' members (the CEO and one or two of his deputies) and usually more 'non-execs'; these are mainly not from banks (as in Germany) or from other firms of related industries (as at several companies in Anglo-Saxon countries).

Most of these Board members are usually independent experts on the industry (university professors, economic analysts, management consultants, sometimes lawyers or technical experts), and many of them actually represent owners. At state firms (including those with minority state ownership) the government's privatisation agency is also represented on the Board.

Prior to June 1995 the government had two privatisation agencies, the SPA (ÁVÜ) and the SAMC (ÁV Rt).[20] Since June 1995 the SPAMC (ÁPV Rt) has exerted the ownership rights of the government with its staff members sitting on the Boards of firms with state ownership. This practice is considered incompatible with Hungarian corporate legislation by some legal experts (cf. Czuczai, 1994, pp. 46–8). The new Law on Privatisation (XXXIX/1995.tv), like the former one, does not include any explicit regulation with respect to this practice either.

'Insiders' have better access to company-related information and it is relatively rare that discussion materials prepared by them for the Board lead to very strong antagonisms.
(3) *Possible financial reasons.* Board memberships at big firms entitle their holders to fees commonly equal to or higher than the monthly salary of a tenured university professor. These incomes can lead to *opportunism* in a number of cases. On the other hand, Board members strongly interested in keeping these posts usually show conservative and risk avoiding attitudes at important Board decisions.

The actual functioning of the Boards strongly depends on the statutes of the company and on the Chairman of the Board. He is obliged by law to prepare the schedule and the work programme of the Board, and he has to present the Board's account of the company's previous business year, as well as its business plan to the regular annual General Assembly which must meet before 31 May each year.[21]

Supervisory Boards usually have three or four members, out of whom at least one has to be an employee delegate at state firms, following the German example of codetermination by employee representation in CG (Charkham, 1994, pp. 17–25). These CG bodies usually meet three or four times a year. Their most important task is to accept and countersign the balance sheet, the income statement and the auditor's report before the General Assembly, and they have to give an evaluation of these documents at the General Assembly.

Supervisory Boards are a complementary tool of the owners to control management and keep the Board of Directors in check. If there is a possibility of a lack of due diligence by management or the Board of Directors, or both, the owners first ask the Supervisory Board for an evaluation of responsibilities.

While the Board of Directors continuously monitors management and formulates the company's strategy, Supervisory Boards do not have any *strategic role*. On the other hand, the Chairman of the Supervisory Board is usually invited to Board meetings without a voting right. Consensus-based working practices of Boards of Directors very often include a consultation with the Chairman of the Supervisory Board prior to important Board decisions.

The effective role of CG bodies in designing and executing company strategy differs widely across Hungarian firms. In order to clarify the sample of firms from which we have drawn our conclusions a brief methodological detour is inevitable at this point.

3.3   The enterprise sample

Our analysis is based on about 40 cases of Hungarian enterprises. 30 of these case studies were prepared in a project sponsored by the World Bank and the Government of Portugal (the first selection of these cases was published in Estrin *et al.*, 1995). 10 (unpublished and mostly confidential) others were prepared for other purposes by the author.

The cases cover only the Hungarian industry (food, manufacturing and energy) with ownership forms including full, majority and minority foreign and domestic private ownership, full, majority and minority state ownership and cooperatives. Legal forms include joint stock companies, limited liability companies and cooperatives. A few firms did not give their consent to having their names published even in a coded form. Others permitted only the use of code names. The list of firms covered (code-named firms are referred to in *italics*) will be found in appendix 6.1 (p.184).We have to agree with Sweder van Wijnbergen that this case study-based approach raises some methodological problems, first of all that of biased or deliberate (mis)interpretation of selected facts. On the other hand, the choice lies between in-depth analyses of a limited number of cases and a more superficial analysis of a much broader sample. We had to take the first option mainly because only this kind of company level information was available to us, and this approach made it possible to make use of the substantial amount of qualitative information collected. It would require a considerable effort to collect comparable qualitative and quantitative data on CG structures of a broader sample of Hungarian firms. If this research is continued, the current results will be compared with findings from a cross-section-type analysis.

3.4   Patterns of ownership and CG

There are several examples among the case studies we have used (cf. Török, 1994) where private owners (domestic and foreign) with a great sense of responsibility leave only a more or less formal role to the Board or its members. At Rolitron, for example, they have only a nominal role. At Gamma Technical Ltd, they mostly influence only technology and R&D management. At Matra Beghin-Say the French members of CG structures leave a very high degree of freedom to the Hungarian management. At GE-Tungsram the quite formal role of the Boards is underlined by the fact that their members receive no compensation. At state-owned firms already transformed into companies limited by shares several cases speak of useful work at and outside Board meetings, but with a very strong emphasis on preparing privatisation. This was the case of DKG Rt, DKG-East, EGIS and an electronics firm code named Radion.

Well connected and competent Board and Supervisory Board members could help their firms much more by supporting their privatisation effort with advice and lobbying rather than with trying to play a direct role in their restructuring or crisis management. According to this approach, the CG structures in Hungarian industry can, besides exerting ownership control and having a certain role in enterprise strategy, usefully serve their firms as interfaces connecting the companies to government bodies, possible investors and consulting firms preparing privatisation.

The most frequent case seems to be when CG structures exist but do not have a real influence on the company's *strategy*, let alone *everyday management*. The reasons for this apparent anomaly have to be identified, in all probability, with some special characteristics of the firms' owners. The relationship of private owners to CG has taken the following forms in Hungary:

(1) The *'too strong owner'*: he needs CG only for legal reasons and eventually in an advisory role, but not for effective ownership control.

This can be observed at two private 'greenfield' high-tech companies, Nivelco and Rolitron, at the DMV Holding, some subsidiaries of the BRG Holding but also, probably to a lesser extent, at GE-Tungsram. This 'strong owner' is either one Hungarian individual (or a strongly coherent group of them) or a huge multi-national firm with world-wide operations but a very centralised structure.[22] 'Strong' owners seem to think they do not really need the usual CG tools for their control of the firm or subsidiary (subsidiaries) in Hungary. Their direct supervision of the management is perhaps more effective and does not lead to conflicts of competence or interest.

A special case is DMV Holding (and to a lesser extent BRG Holding). Here the 'empty shell's' ownership control of the subsidiaries is exerted through the very strong participation of the managers of the holding in the CG structures of the subsidiaries and also in their management. This strong personal control ensures, in fact, that the everyday management of the subsidiaries of these holdings is *ensured by the holdings themselves*. The same phenomenon was observable in most holding-based enterprise groups created out of big state firms in 1988 and 1989 (Videoton Rt, Ganz Danubius, Medicor, etc.).

(2) The *'negligent owner'*: this is, in almost all of our cases, a foreign minority owner of a joint venture in Hungary (Matra Beghin-Say and at least one subsidiary of BRG Holding, BRG Rádiótechnika). This owner cooperates in the CG structures of its Hungarian subsidiary with a Hungarian majority owner (the state privatisation agency or a state-owned holding). The strategic interest of the latter is the full privatisation of the joint venture.

This type of foreign owner does not show much interest in running the Hungarian firm or in its CG for the following reason.[23]

The Hungarian majority owner seems to go for privatisation in which the foreign minority owner will very likely have an option. The latter wants to keep this option open. Prior to his takeover of the firm, though, he does not want to make any commitment to any action taken by the current management or the Board of the firm.

Our assessment of this behavioural pattern is as follows. Such a commitment could eventually compromise the foreign co-owner's chances of a successful takeover. If it is, for example, a major investment decision, accepting that decision by the minority owner would mean a possible increase in the takeover price of the firm.

Another sort of 'negligent' owner could be found at Glasunion where the representatives of the holding created by the creditor banks constituted the CG in 1993 and 1994. This 'negligence' could be probably linked to the fact that the owners considered their investment a tactical one. Their major motive in this tactical investment was the extremely low-price conversion of 'sunk' credits into still valuable assets.

A foreign owner in a minority position is not necessarily 'negligent'. At SVT-Wamsler, for example, the German owner with only 30 per cent of the shares is probably the strongest participant in the company's CG. *A minority owner is not necessarily 'negligent', and a seemingly 'negligent' owner is not necessarily incompetent or irresponsible.* He simply wants to postpone major management decisions until becoming a majority owner. He probably thinks any too strong activity in the CG structures of the firm would eventually compromise his subsequent chances of a full takeover.

(3) *'Partial CG'* : this is the case where a few sectors of the company's strategy are strictly delimited. CG can have a decisive word only in these sectors.

Gamma is a good example of this case. Gamma's Board of Directors consists of several university professors with a good reputation in research concerning the technological problems in the field. It can be supposed these professors offer technical consultancy to the management as members of the Board which satisfies both them and the owners.[24]

The above three CG behavioural patterns of private owners did not include a fourth, 'normal' or 'mainstream'-type behaviour. Examples of this do not abound in the cases known to us, but this may be just a shortcoming of the sample. It contained only a few private firms with a sufficiently long record of private ownership, thus we have had only a very small number of examples with established CG structures. The functioning and the role of CG is undergoing widespread change in Hungary. The direction and the content of that change now have to be scrutinised.

4   Evolution or bifurcation?

4.1   The players of the CG game

Williamson's (1985) model of the parties interested in CG should be recapitulated briefly. The six theoretical participants of the game include

(1) owners, (2) employees, (3) suppliers, (4) customers, (5) the community and (6) the management (Williamson, 1985, pp. 302–11).

It would be an exaggeration to say that the model is not valid in its original form for firms in transition economies such as Hungary. Still, the role of some players is certainly as yet quite modest. For example: we haven't found any evidence of the participation of major suppliers or customers in the CG structures analysed. This is a major difference from Germany where an array of big manufacturing firms have representatives of their suppliers, their customers, let alone their competitors in their CG structures.

According to a survey of Supervisory Boards of big German manufacturing firms made in 1993 (Charkham, 1994, pp. 61–9), *BMW AG* had representatives of Philips, Linde and of Maschinenfabrik Goebel on its Board, *Daimler Benz AG* had Board members from Deutsche Shell, Bayer and AEG. *BASF AG*'s Board included people from Robert Bosch GmbH, Unilever, and Kali und Salz AG. *Hoechst AG* had members of its Board from Mannesmann and Petrochemical Industries Kuwait, while *Volkswagen AG*'s Board had representatives of Robert Bosch GmbH and Ruhrgas AG.

Hungarian CG legislation has followed the German pattern quite closely, but a major difference is the much stricter rules of incompatibility. Representatives of other firms active in the same field of business (a definition understood quite differently by several Commercial Courts across the country) are not allowed to be elected to CG structures. High-level government officials including Deputy State Secretaries (and upwards) are completely banned from participation in Boards or Supervisory Boards (XXXIII/1990 par. 11). This is again not the case in Germany where, for example, the Bundesland of Lower Saxony as a 20 per cent owner of Volkswagen AG is represented by several members of its government in the CG structures of the firm.

Strict compatibility rules are probably the most important explanation for the usually very poor representation of industry in the CG structures of Hungarian manufacturing firms. Therefore groups (3) and (4) from Williamson's scheme do not have much practical validity for Hungary.

The role of 'community' is different. It is usually represented by government officials, privatisation agency staff members and people appointed by municipalities if the latter are important shareholders of the firm. Government officials belong mostly to the ministry dealing with the sector where the firm is active (this means the Ministry of Industry and Trade for manufacturing firms). They may keep their seats even if the company is completely privatised, or remain over-represented in its

CG structures when the state is no more a majority owner.[25] In contrast, agency officials leave CG completely after privatisation.

There is a marked difference between the role of privatisation agency and sectorial ministry officials in the CG of Hungarian firms. Privatisation agency representatives usually act as a proxy for the agency at the firm, and they act and/or vote on behalf of the owner. Sectorial ministry officials usually represent themselves as experts of the sector in question. Owing to their competence and the high quality of their sources of information, a number of new private owners keep them on the boards.

The development of CG in Hungary will be certainly much more influenced by the attitudes of the three other groups of players in Williamson's scheme: owners, employees and managers.

4.1.1 Incumbent owners and outside investors

The *strong control of incumbent private owners* over CG is evident from almost all the cases known to us. Outside investors influence CG, in many cases, before they actually acquire the firm and become incumbent owners. Most state-owned Hungarian firms have privatisation as their main strategic objective. Therefore their Board of Directors and their management try to learn as much as possible about potential investors by making contact with them.

At those firms where there is only one strong candidate for investment the behaviour of management and the Board of Directors can be strongly influenced by the strategic interests of this possible new owner. This has been the case at the DKG Group where the close cooperation between DKG-East and its minority Russian owner helped DKG Rt, a state firm until February 1994, to prepare for its takeover by the same Russian investor.

Most outside investors restructure the firm, and this usually brings efficiency improvement to the company, albeit sometimes with some years of delay (cf. Hamar, 1993, p. 54). After a certain 'learning period' for the new owners, the former management can be got rid of since its *company-specific knowledge is no longer a valuable asset*. The GE-Tungsram or the Lehel-Electrolux case are good illustrations of such a development. The Rolitron example is similar. Management was reshuffled several times at that firm. This was a consequence of the urgent need of adjustment in response to an apparently not very successful ownership change. These changes were carried out by the original 'strong' Hungarian private owner.

The CG structures usually change after ownership change. A number of examples (Gamma, GE-Tungsram, Matra Beghin-Say, Herend China Factory, MMG AM, etc.) show that direct representatives of the new owners may be apparently under-represented. The reason is that strong foreign investors in Hungary have other tools to control their subsidiary in Hungary than the CG structure alone. On the other hand, state firms privatised in ESOPs may have such new owners who prefer to have 'heavyweight', widely known persons on their Boards. In several cases pre-privatisation external Board members keep their seats after ESOP privatisation due to their support of the takeover by employees.[26] The really effective tool of ownership control is the General Assembly of the shareholders. The majority owner can immediately replace any member of the Board or of the management at this meeting of owners.

The under-capitalisation of most state-owned Hungarian firms has made it crucial for them to find a financially strong private, possibly foreign investor. Neither their managements nor the privatisation agency had much choice if there was only one strong candidate. Ownership change from the state to a majority foreign owner almost always means a *much stronger ownership control* in Hungarian industry. A certain marginalisation of the CG structures cannot be ruled out thereafter.

4.1.2 Employees

The direct role of employees in CG is not strong in Hungary in general. One member of the Supervisory Board is appointed by the employees at state firms, but private firms need not adopt even this requirement. There is no example of any substantial influence on CG of the employee representative on the Supervisory Board. Furthermore there is no evidence of any other form of employee representation exerting a considerable influence on management and CG.

4.1.3 Managers

The role of managers in decision making, management and CG is quite strong at most firms surveyed. CEOs are usually members of the Boards of Directors, but President-CEOs (or CEOs also acting as Chairmen of the Board) exist only at some private companies. New foreign owners tend to keep the former Hungarian top manager at the firm, recognising his or her *de facto* monopoly of information. Once this monopoly has disappeared, this Hungarian CEO may be replaced, but there are quite a few foreign CEOs at the firms surveyed. At some of them (e.g. at Lehel-Electrolux, formerly at GE-Tungsram, or at Pécs Brewery) such foreign CEOs are or were ethnic Hungarians.

Management is usually also strong at transformed but non-privatised firms where the state privatisation agency as the owner concentrates on privatisation. The mostly strong position of the managers should be linked first of all to *asymmetric information* also if faced with the state as the owner.

The state privatisation agency is still overwhelmed with firms to be privatised, and has desk officers responsible for several companies. Most of these desk officers are unable to acquire an in-depth knowledge of the firms they are responsible for. Government officials have a much less direct contact with firms than a few years ago, because government interference with the affairs of state firms has strongly decreased.

Most enterprise cases show that the former Hungarian top management is usually accepted by the new owners. A quite frequent change in top management includes the appointment of either a foreign or a new Hungarian financial director, but the CEO's job is left untouched. It remains to be seen how management changes when the privatised company becomes an established private firm, but only quite poor empirical evidence is available on this problem at the moment.[27]

4.2   The future role of CG at Hungarian private firms

The exact role of CG at an established private firm is subject to much controversy. An integrative description of sometimes very divergent viewpoints is provided by Oliver Williamson (Williamson, 1985, ch.12): 'Management's presence on the Board can improve the amount and quality of information and lead to superior decisions. But such a presence should not upset the board's basic control relation with the corporation' (Williamson, 1985, p. 324).

The first part of the problem, the presence of management in CG, seems quite clear in Hungary. *Top management is practically always represented on the Board of Directors at companies limited by shares which are obliged to have such Boards.* In limited liability companies Supervisory Boards are the only permanently functioning CG body, but their role is usually quite formal. At such firms, however, managers can usually influence company strategy at the Assembly Meetings of the owners.

The second part of the problem, 'the Board's basic control relation with the corporation' is much less transparent from empirical evidence. At almost each firm surveyed CG seems to be the *weakest element* in the chain ownership–CG–management.

Legal transformation and privatisation have created such CG structures at Hungarian industrial firms which closely correspond to Western institutional CG patterns, but their real content in terms of influence on decision making as well as corporate control is mostly missing.

Perhaps the lack of a really well functioning and diversified capital market has to be blamed for the situation shown by our case study experience: 'strong' owners are the absolute majority among the owners of Hungarian private firms, and they are strong to such an extent that they can easily bypass CG. Ownership is strongly concentrated at most private firms surveyed.

This somewhat disappointing picture should not suggest that setting up CG structures in Hungary was premature, and one would have to accept that CG structures will continue to have a more or less formal character. The role of these structures is bound to change, but the direction of this change is not clear yet. Three scenarios can be distinguished:

(1) The development of CG in Hungary will follow the patterns of West European and American firms (the 'evolutionary' model). Literature shows (e.g. Cadbury, 1992; Pound, 1995) that these patterns are likely to undergo significant transformation in the years to come. This transformation may include the following US elements (cf. Pound, 1995, p. 93):

The role of the Board of Directors will take on a more strategic character. This would mean less direct involvement in issues of replacement and appointment as well as less direct monitoring of the management. On the other hand, the Board should become capable of creating 'value added' for the company through fostering effective decisions and eventually reversing failed policies. Such a transformation could eventually be a first step towards creating European-style two-tier CG structures overseas, since the idea seems to be less monitoring and more strategic decision making at Board level.

– The separation between Board and management will be less formal. Non-executive directors should include more experts on industry and finance and fewer lawyers or, if this is still the case, politicians or lobbyists. Both the time commitment and the remuneration of outside directors should increase substantially. Boards should monitor policies and strategies, not persons or teams.

– Interaction between Board and shareholders should become more frequent, direct and informative. Our interpretation of Pound's concept is that the Board should act as a kind of 'feeler' for both management and the shareholders. This means supporting strategic thinking at Board level with outside information, and helping shareholders with information from within the firm.

If this concept is transferred to Hungary, not all of its elements can be retained, of course. The most important difference is that the CG monitoring function is already present at the Supervisory Board level in Hungary. The role of Boards of Directors could also include an element of strategic decision making in the future, and the advisory function of Boards could be greatly strengthened.

More time commitment for Board members would mean research and/or analytical tasks for individual Board members, of course only for use within the Board. The introduction of such tasks for Board members would also mean less rigid rules of remuneration and compatibility.

Supervisory Boards could also develop a less formal role in monitoring management and the company's affairs. This would also mean more presence for Supervisory Board members at the firm's premises including, for example, preliminary audits of quarterly balance sheets.

(2) The development of CG in Hungary could also lead to the creation of a more Japanese-style system at most firms (the 'integrative' model). As has been pointed out in this chapter, the current functioning of CG structures in Hungary shows some parallels with the Japanese model. Such parallels include a widely observable effort to reach consensus before voting and, firstly at state-owned firms, the important role in the setting up and running of Boards of personal relationships created during former careers in government service (cf. Charkham, 1994, pp. 94–5). An important difference between the Hungarian and the Japanese system is, however, that there are usually few 'non-execs' in Japan.

In any event, the main function of the Board would have a more political than strategic character in the Hungarian 'integrative' model. According to this scenario, the Board should help integrate all interests linked to the development of the firm, and also act as an interface between the government and the company. Should this model prevail in Hungary, the composition of CG structures would probably change much less than in model (1). Lawyers, politicians, lobbyists and people linked to trade unions would take (or keep) seats on Boards, and industrial strategists or financial experts would be pushed into the background.

The dangers of a 'Japanese-style' development of CG in Hungary have to be reiterated. Any development towards an 'integrative' model has to be based on legal guarantees ensuring a level of transparence and accountability according to American or West European standards. Eventual clarifications to this effect could be considered to be included in a new Amendment of the Law on Economic Associations (VI/1988).

(3) Mixed scenarios always make an impression of being more realistic

than pure ones. The 'bifurcational' model is, however, more than just a blend of models (1) and (2). It is represented by firms with either frequent ownership changes (cf. Kanizsa Brewery, Rolitron, Gamma Technical Ltd, Glasunion and to a certain extent Radion) or by firms where the profile of CG has been shifting back and forth between the evolutionary and the integrative model. This could be observed during the gradual reunification of DKG Rt and DKG-EAST following the acquisition of the former company by the Russian minority owner of the latter or, in a special form, in August–September 1995 at the regional gas firms.[28]

The bifurcational model may be observed at some firms whose owner wants to have CG structures with the positive elements of both the evolutionary and the integrational model. The problem is that the size of CG structures is limited by Hungarian law to less than half that of large German and Japanese Boards of Directors, and Supervisory Boards in Hungary can have only a quarter of the members of big Supervisory Boards in Germany. Therefore it is very difficult to have, with some simplification, a sufficient number of both 'strategists' and 'lobbyists' aboard.

The bifurcational model is, in fact, a CG model in which the owner does not want to yield effective decision making power to the Board, but he (she) does not want to have its members just because this is a formal legal requirement. Therefore the owner repeatedly tries to give the Board a well specified role and tasks. He may fail in such efforts either because of a lack of consensus over which direction the Board should really follow, or due to the wish of a majority of Board members to regard their task merely as a formal one.

The bifurcational model can be only partly understood as a pattern of shifting between the evolutionary and the integrational model. The problem is these two models are not really substitutes. The evolutionary model is a *dynamic one* still developing even in mature market economies, whereas the integrative model has a substantially more *rigid* character. On the other hand, having integrative-type CG structures requires much less effort from the owner with much less benefit, of course, from strategic interaction between Board, owner and management.

As we have observed really effective CG structures are not frequent in Hungarian private firms. On the other hand, the still quite scattered evidence from literature on the problems of CG in other transition economies seems to show that these problems do not really arise there at the firm level, or less so than in Hungary. The question whether CG

could be made effective arises in some other transition countries more at
the level of financial intermediaries and privatisation funds than at
company level as is the case in Hungary.

For example: the mass privatisation schemes applied in Russia, the
former Czechoslovakia and Poland laid emphasis on (or at least gave a
green light to) the creation of holders of large blocks of shares
('blockholders') as a CG tool at the firm level for the financial
intermediaries representing the ultimate owners (Phelps *et al.*, 1993, pp.
22–3), but the latter were apparently not meant to have a direct access to
CG at the firm level.

In Romania, the core of the CG problem lies in the CG structures of
POFs (Private Ownership Funds). These CG structures are based on
'Councils of Administration', each with seven members nominated by
the government and approved by the National Assembly and the Senate
(Earle and Sapatoru, 1994, pp. 68–9). This source does not refer to CG
at the firm level at all.

The possibility of the evolutionary model of CG in Hungary gaining
considerable ground is not a high-probability outcome in the case
studies surveyed in our research. On the other hand, it may be
considered a moderately positive sign that the problem of effective CG
structures can be examined at the firm level at all. The simple reason is
that these structures exist at the firm level, and they are not replaced by
CG 'above the firms', i.e. in *privatisation funds* or *financial intermediaries*.

5   Conclusions for legislation and policy

Privatisation is expected to be completed in Hungary by 1998. The
speed and breadth of the expansion of private ownership is undoubtedly
one of the success stories of recent Hungarian economic development,
and the creation of a quite stable legal and institutional framework for
the smooth functioning of the market economy is another. The
unfolding of modern CG structures is the intersection of these two
trends and its content has been analysed in this chapter. Our conclusions
are based on our understanding of CG as one of the key factors making
the micro level of the capitalist economy simultaneously transparent and
efficient.

Our analysis of CG in Hungary has shown that the Hungarian CG
system has firm legal foundations and is therefore comparable with the
systems currently in operation in the major industrial countries. Its
content, however, varies according to the companies using it. There is no
direct relationship between the efficiency of CG and the company's

ownership form: private firms may very well have formal or just façade-like CG structures. Transparence is incomplete at many firms observed, but the reasons for this seem to be very different from the reasons in Japan. While the typical Japanese company has several features Europeans or Americans might call 'corporatist', Japanese authors tend to explain the complex web of cooperative relationships between owners, managers and employees as related to their common long-term interests.

In contrast, those Hungarian companies where the transparence of CG stuctures seems to be inadequate are usually controlled by very strong owners. These strong owners are mostly the products of the Hungarian way of 'privatisation on the market', and Hungarian capitalism will probably be characterised by a widespread presence of such firms at which *owners and key members of the management are identical.*

A distinction has also to be made between the effectiveness of Boards of Directors and Supervisory Boards at Hungarian joint stock companies. Boards of Directors usually play a certain role in strategic management, but current legislation puts strong restraints on the real influence of Supervisory Boards on management. Their role basically consists of monitoring the conformity of the company's functioning with the law and of approving the documents to be presented to the annual General Assembly. Supervisory Boards may play a really important role at the company only if they are requested by the owners to carry out a investigation of any financial or legal wrongdoing by the Board of Directors or the management. Despite this, Supervisory Boards do not have a decisive role in the company's affairs, and Boards of Directors do not depend on them in any real sense. Responsibility towards the owners is not really shared between the two bodies, Supervisory Boards rather being formal elements of the CG structure. Supervisory Boards should therefore be upgraded to give them some real control over Boards of Directors; we suggest taking over a further element of the German CG system.

The Supervisory Board should be entrusted with and made responsible for selecting the members of the Board of Directors, and appointing its Chairman. The Chairman, the highest ranking position in the company hierarchy, should also be responsible to the Supervisory Board on a regular basis instead of depending on the General Assembly, which can be convened only with a considerable delay, and on the Board of Directors which has the formal right to elect him or her.

This legal change would not at once turn inefficient CG structures into efficient ones, but it would certainly help to put Supervisory Boards on an equal footing with Boards of Directors. This could be a first step towards transforming CG structures into real tools of efficient ownership control instead of using them only as monitors of fulfilment of the obligations enshrined in corporate legislation.

The real choice now lies between completely formal- or integrative-type CG structures, and the ultimate choice has to be made by the owners of firms. Only further discussion will eventually make it possible to decide whether the integrative CG model would really be better for Hungary – not only from the sterile viewpoint of microeconomic theory but also for the six groups of players most interested in the smooth and profitable functioning of the firm.

Appendix 6.1: the enterprise sample

Bakony Metal and Electrical Appliance Works (car components)
BRG Holding (electronics)
Budapest Handicraft Enterprise (handicraft and folk-art products)
DKG Rt (oil and gas industry equipment)
DKG-East Kft (petroleum drilling equipment)
DMV (agricultural machinery)
EGIS (pharmaceuticals)
Elegant Charm (textiles)
FMV (electronics)
Gamma Technical Ltd (electronics)
GE-Tungsram (lighting equipment)
Glasunion (glass)
Hungaroplast (plastics)
Hungartextile Holding (textiles)
Intercsokoládé (sweets and coffee)
Kaniza Brewery (beer)
Lehel-Electrolux (white goods)
LOG Rt (oil and gas industry equipment)
Matra Beghin-Say (sugar)
Nivelco (measuring equipment)
OKGT (later MOL, oil and gas)
Plaingas Rt (natural gas)
Radion (electronics)
Rekard (agricultural machinery)
Rolitron (electronics)
Salgglas (glass)
SVT-Wamsler (household appliances)
Terta (electronics)
Theta Works (defence industry)
Videoton Rt (electronics)

Appendix 2: list of major laws related to CG and privatisation

XXXVII/1875 Commercial Law (predecessor of the Law on Economic
 Associations, VI/1988)
VI/1977 Law on State Enterprises
2(2)/1984 Government Decree with the Status of Law on Enterprise Self-
 management
VI/1988 Law on Economic Associations
XXIV/1988 Law on Foreign Investment (in Hungary)
XIII/1989 Law on Enterprise Transformation
XIV/1989 Amendment of the Law on State Enterprises (VI/1977)
LXXIV/1990 Law on Pre-privatisation (i.e. long-term leasing of small retail
 shops)
V/1990 Law on Individual Entrepreneurship
VII/1990 Law on the State Property Agency
VIII/1990 Law on the Protection of State-owned Assets
IL/1991 Law on Bankruptcy
LI/1991 Law on Receivership, Bankruptcy and Liquidation
LXIX/1991 Law on Banks
XLIV/1991 Law on ESOPs
XVI/1991 Law on Concessions
XVIII/1991 Law on Accounting
XXV/1991 Law on Recompensation (for confiscated property)
XXXIII/1991 Law on the Transfer of State-owned Assets to Municipalities
I/1992 Law on Cooperatives
LIII/1992 Law on Assets Under Long-Term State Management
LIV/1992 Law on Privatisation
LXXXI/1993 Amendment of the Law on Bankruptcy (IL/1991)
XXXIX/1995 Law on the Sale of Entrepreneurial Assets Owned by the State
 (Law on Privatisation)

NOTES

The author wishes to thank Sweder van Wijnbergen, Koji Matsumoto, Judit
Karsai, Judit Ványai and two anonymous referees for their helpful comments,
but all the remaining errors are his own. Other usual caveats also apply.
1   The same source also states that

> a *corporation* is treated by the law as an *intangible being* that is separate
> from its members; its life is not affected by their death . . . The early
> corporations were municipalities, churches and the guilds of tradesmen
> in the Middle Ages. The business corporation is a much later
> development. In English–American law it had its beginning with the
> large joint-stock trading companies chartered by the king or the queen
> beginning in 1600. These companies were given an exclusive right to
> establish settlements and to trade in a certain part of the world. Their
> powers were governmental as well as commercial. They were given the
> right to have a military force and sometimes even to coin money. One of
> these, the Hudson Bay Company, still operates in Canada. (Donnell *et
> al.*, 1983, p. 361)

This description of early *semi-governmental* corporations does not seem to conflict with Schumpeter's analysis of the *typical private* firm in nineteenth-century British capitalism.

2 The exclusion of close corporations from the analysis is based on the fact that 'close corporations are like partnerships in that the controlling shareholders actively take part in the day-to-day management of the corporation' (Davidson *et al.*, 1989, p. 888). We shall see, though, that such cases exist in Hungary where *de jure* publicly held corporations become *de facto* close corporations with *pro forma* structures of CG.

3 The distinction used by several French authors may shed some light on this problem. The so-called 'Rhenish' legal and social systems common on the European continent try to integrate the idea of market economy with a certain sense of collectivism through putting some limit on individual responsibility. 'Saxon' systems used in English-speaking countries push individual responsibility in economic affairs to the possible maximum (Champaud, 1993, p. 82).

4 Or, in our 'continental' understanding, the entire society including the business community. The good functioning of CG is in the interest of the community for two main reasons: (1) externalities (e.g. pollution) not regulated by contractual relationships; (2) the hazards of expropriation (Williamson, 1985, pp. 310–11). In our view, the latter can be considered such special externalities (e.g. in the case of publicly financed infrastructure made use of and also abused by the firm in question) from which the firm can earn a free benefit financed indirectly by the community. Example: the use of community roads by heavy trucks; this is analogous to pollution, but not identical with it.

5 Cf. Fama and Jensen (1983), quoted by Williamson (1985, p. 302).

6 Before June 1995: ÁV Rt (State Assets Management Corporation), after June 1995: ÁPV Rt (State Privatisation and Assets Management Corporation) in Hungary.

7 There are eight references to the term Board of Directors in the subject index of the book (Williamson, 1985, pp. 442–50) and three of them are long discussions of the subject. Neither Supervisory Boards nor General Assemblies are mentioned. Similarly, both the *Dictionary of Banking Terms* (Fitch, 1990) and the *Dictionary of Finance and Investment Terms* (Downes and Goodman, 1987) describe only Boards of Directors without mentioning Supervisory Boards or General Assemblies as CG structures. These facts show that the literature quoted does not take 'continental-type' two-tier CG systems into consideration.

8 Or PLCs (limited companies) and LLCs (limited liability companies) in the UK. An important detail for understanding the British terminology is that:
> companies limited by shares . . . are divided into two types, 'Limited' and 'Public Limited', and the [1985 Companies] Act provides that their names shall end with Ltd. or PLC respectively. Contrary to what is sometimes believed, being a PLC does not mean that the company's shares are publicly quoted on a stock exchange. (Charkham, 1994, p. 261)

9 The Cadbury Report (1992) has several suggestions concerning the probably best available structure of boards (at least in the UK). For example: the chairman of the board should be independent, there should be a formal

selection procedure for non-executive directors, and audit and remuneration committees should consist mainly of non-execs (Hart, 1995, p. 682). It has to be noted again at this point that several control functions of continental Supervisory Boards are performed by *ad hoc* or *permanent committees* for audits and remuneration-related board decisions in the UK and the USA.

10   Beleaguered corporate management cast around for ways of defending itself, and the ingenious legal profession produced some brilliant answers. In essence they were all based on a single principle. A company would set in place an arrangement which in normal times would lie dormant. Only a tender offer would activate it. Then, once the alarm bells rang, management could set the machinery in motion to change, grant extra shares, etc., etc., the result of which would be to make it impossible for the bidder to succeed. These were the so-called 'poison pills'. (Charkham, 1994, p. 217)

11 They cover: (1) the company's accounts for the financial year or each quarter; (2) major capital expenditure, acquisitions, closures; (3) appointments to the Board of Directors (the *Vorstand*); (4) approving the dividend (Charkham, 1994, p. 22). The Supervisory Boards of big German firms are usually 15–20 strong with quite impressive employee representation. Main banking partners are inevitably represented, as are major industrial partners, and locally or regionally influential political groups.

12 Strictly speaking, management is in no sense a legal substitute for CG or comparable bodies.

13 For the theoretical background of the problem of CG structures created by privatisation, cf. Vickers and Yarrow (1988, pp. 7–44).

14 For a concise comparative analysis of enterprise transformation cf. Major (1993, pp. 82–3).

15 Hungarian Supervisory Boards usually have a triple role: (1) supervision of and guidance to the internal auditing unit of the firm; (2) continuous legal control of board and management; (3) commenting on the balance sheet for the General Assembly (Annual Meeting) of the owners of the firm and eventually proposing its acceptance.

16 For a survey of recent literature on dual class equity structures and CG problems in these structures, cf. Moyer *et al.* (1992, pp. 35–6). The study offers a highly interesting analysis of how the owners of non-voting shares can be compensated for their lack of influence on CG in the USA.

17 One enterprise example for this is BRG Holding, the consumer electronics firm privatised in a two-tier, holding-based structure.

18 One good example is the 'Corporate Governance Compact' issued by the Working Group on Corporate Governance in the USA in 1991. It explicitly states that shareholders have to act as owners, not just as investors, and they should play an active part in continually evaluating the performance of directors. Moreover, a comment on the report emphatically argues for a more active role of shareholders in voting for directors. Nevertheless, coming up with candidates for board seats supported by shareholder groups should not become a widespread practice. 'This tactic . . . turns the elective process into a free-for-all, and an expensive one at that' (Wharton, 1991, p. 138).

19   Japanese companies have certain practices related to decisionmaking. In the *ringi* system, for example, written proposals are passed around to

relevant people for their comments and acceptance. By the time the proposal reaches the person with the authority to accept or reject it, it has thus already been seen by a number of other people. There is also *nemawashi*, where those concerned unofficially discuss a matter to pave the way for its later approval at an official meeting. Meetings are frequently held that do not always seem to be tied directly to decision making, but which nonetheless serve an important purpose. In such ways, voluntary adjustments are made among corporate employees in Japanese companies in an organized way. Information is exchanged, and viewpoints are integrated. (Matsumoto, 1991, p. 146)

20 On the policy of the SAMC regarding CG see Voszka (1995, pp. 128–33). She also states that this policy was not regulated by former privatisation legislation.

21 31 May is the legal deadline for submitting the balance sheet, the income statement and the account of the previous business year to the Commercial Courts.

22   The multidivisional [MD] organisation takes two or more functional organisations and places them under the supervision of a single top executive . . . Naturally enough, the more diversified a firm's activities, the more likely that it employs MD organisation. (Caves, 1982, pp. 74–5)

We think GE is a typical MD organisation in which GE-Tungsram as one of the subsidiaries does not really have much room for its own CG. Our knowledge of GE-Tungsram comes from Paul Marer's excellent but as yet unpublished in-depth case study of the firm.

23 In one case (BRG Rádiótechnika) the foreign minority owner even accepted non-voting shares for the transitional period before full privatisation.

24 'The representative of the shareholders is exerting financial control while the professors give professional guidance' (Gamma case study, p. 11).

25 Such cases included or include: Siemens Telefongyár Rt, Herend China Factory, DKG-EAST Rt and LOG Rt. The Ministry has at least one seat on the Board of each big infrastructural firm.

26 Not a proof, but an interesting side effect of the usually weak role of employees in CG is the fact that there have been relatively few ESOPs in Hungary (122 in 1993 and 38 in the first half of 1994, information from Judit Karsai). An example of a failed ESOP is Kanizsa Brewery, thus far successful ones include MMG AM and Herend China Factory.

27 Evidence from international literature seems to suggest that negative incentives (e.g. firing under-performing managers) do not improve, in general, the relationship between owners and management to the expected extent. Cf. Phelps *et al.* (1993, pp. 18–19). On the other hand, the role of privatisation in changing incentive structures for managers is a promising topic for research in the microeconomics of transition. For an initial approach to the topic see Choi (1993).

28 This strange story is not yet known in detail. The state privatisation agency prepared a far-reaching reshuffle of the CG structures of regional gas firms in July–August 1995. This reshuffle would have meant a change from the evolutionary towards the integrative model, allegedly in order to serve subsequent privatisation. In September, however, it was decided that privatisation would be better served with CG structures left almost untouched

at these firms. The only important changes consisted in dismissing the CEOs of four firms out of five from the Boards, and the appointment of 'General Deputy CEOs' to the company and to the Board.

REFERENCES

1995: XXXIX.tv. (1995) Az állam tulajdonában levõ vállalkozói vagyon értékesítésérõl (The Law on Privatisation), Magyar Közlöny, **1995/38**, Budapest (17 May)

Brada, J.C., I. Singh and Á. Török (1994) *Firms Afloat and Firms Adrift: Hungarian Industry and the Economic Transition*, Armonk, NY: M.E. Sharpe

Cadbury (1992) Committee Report, *The Financial Aspects of Corporate Governance*, London: Gee

Caves, R.E. (1982) 'Multinational enterprise and economic analysis', *Cambridge Surveys of Economic Literature*, Cambridge: Cambridge University Press

Champaud, C. (1993) 'L'entreprise se lève a l'Est', in *Droit et gestion de l'entreprise: mélanges en l'honneur du doyen Roger Percerou*, Paris: Vuibert Gestion, 75–92

Charkham, J.P. (1994) *Keeping Good Company. A Study of CG in Five Countries*, Oxford: Clarendon Press

Choi, Y.K. (1993) 'The choice of organisational form: the case of post-merger managerial incentive structure', *Financial Management*, **22**, 69–81

Conyon, M.J. and D. Leech (1993) 'Top pay, company performance and CG', *Warwick Economic Research Papers*, **410**, University of Warwick (June)

Coutinho de Abreu, J.-M. (1995) 'L'européanisation du concept d'entreprise', *Revue Internationale de Droit Economique*, **1995/1**, 9–30

Czuczai, Jenõ (1994) *A magyar privatizáció alulnézetbõl. Múltja, jelene, jövõje* (Hungarian privatisation seen from below. Its past, present and future), Budapest: Agrocent Kiadó

Davidson, D.V., B.E. Knowles, L.M. Forsythe and R.R. Jesperson (1989) *Comprehensive Business Law: Principles and Cases*, Boston: Kent Publishing Co.

Donnell, J.D., A.J. Barnes and M.B. Metzger (1983) *Law for Business*, Homewood, IL: Irwin

Downes, J. and J.E. Goodman (1987) *Dictionary of Finance and Investment Terms*, New York, London, Toronto and Sydney: Barron's Financial Guides

Earle, J.S. and D. Sapatoru (1994) 'Incentive contracts, CG and privatisation funds in Romania', *Atlantic Economic Journal*, **22**, 61–79

Estrin, S., J. Brada, A. Gelb and I. Singh (eds.) (1995) *Restructuring and Privatisation in Central Eastern Europe: Case Studies of Firms in Transition*, Armonk, NY and London: M.E. Sharpe

Fama, E.F. and M.C. Jensen (1983) 'Separation of ownership and control', *Journal of Law and Economics*, **26**, 301–26

Fitch, T. (1990) *Dictionary of Banking Terms*, New York, London, Toronto and Sydney: Barron's Business Guides

Greenaway, D. (1995) 'Policy forum: corporate governance. Editorial note', *Economic Journal*, **105**, 676–7

Hamar, J. (1993) 'Külföldi mûködõtõke-beáramlás és privatizáció Magyarországon' (The inflow of foreign direct investment and privatisation in Hungary), *Külgazdaság*, **1993/12**, 49–61

Hart, O. (1995) 'CG: some theory and implications', *Economic Journal*, **105**, 678–89

Journal of Business Strategy (1994) '100 strategists to watch', *Journal of Business Strategy*, **15**, 37–49

Kang, J.-K. and A. Shivdasani (1995) 'Firm performance, corporate governance and top executive turnover in Japan', *Journal of Financial Economics*, **38**, 29–58

Leibman, M.S. and R.A. Bruer (1994) 'Where there's a will there's a way', *Journal of Business Strategy*, **12**, 26–35

Leloczky, K. (1993) 'Az igazgatóság felelőssége a részvényesekkel szemben' (The liability of Board members towards the holders of equity shares), *Külgazdaság*, **1993/9**, Legal Supplement, 139–43

Major, I. (1993) *Privatisation in Eastern Europe: A Critical Approach*, London: Edward Elgar and Budapest: MTA KTI

Major, I. and P. Mihály (1994) 'Privatizáció – hogyan tovább?' (Privatisation – how to continue?), *Közgazdasági Szemle*, **41**, 214–28

Matsumoto, K. (1991) *The Rise of the Japanese Corporate System: The Inside View of an MITI Official*, London and New York: Kegan Paul International

Moyer, C., R. Rao and P.M. Sisneros (1992) 'Substitutes for voting rights: evidence from dual class recapitalisations', *Financial Management*, **21**, 35–47

Nuchelmans, D. (1992) 'Privatisation et mécanismes du marché dans le secteur des télécommunications: dérégulation . . . rérégulation?', *Revue Internationale de Droit Economique*, **1992/2**, 191–204

Phelps, E.S., R. Frydman, A. Rapaczynski and A. Shleifer (1993) 'Needed mechanisms of corporate governance and finance in Eastern Europe', *EBRD Working Paper*, **1**

Pound, J. (1995) 'The promise of the governed corporation', *Harvard Business Review* (**March–April**), 89–98

Sárközy, T. (1994) *A privatizáció joga Magyarországon, 1989–1993* (Privatisation legislation in Hungary, 1989–1993) Budapest: Akadémiai Kiadó

Schumpeter, J.A. (1954) *The History of Economic Analysis*, Oxford and New York: Oxford University Press

Szegediné, S.K. (1994) 'A részvény és névértéke, a közös tulajdon, a saját és a dolgozói részvény' (The share and its face value, joint stock, own and employee-owned shares), *Külgazdaság*, **1994/1**, Legal Supplement, 1–10

Török, Á. (1993–4) 'Hungarian industry in 1992: an assessment of trends and behaviours', *Eastern European Economics*, **31**, 66–80

(1994) 'Performance and corporate governance in Hungarian industry (1989–1994)', Country Overview Paper for the World Bank Project 'Enterprise behaviour in the transition', Unpublished manuscript, first draft, Budapest (July)

Vickers, J. and G. Yarrow (1988) *Privatisation: An Economic Analysis*, Cambridge, MA: MIT Press

Vince, P. (1993) 'Az állami szerepvállalás változatai' (Variations of the ownership role of the state), *Külgazdaság*, **1993/9**, 15–24

Voszka, E. (1995) *Az agyaglábakon álló óriás. Az Állami Vagyonkezelő Részvénytársaság felállítása és működése* (The tottering giant. The setting up and the functioning of SAMC), Budapest: Pénzügykutató Rt

Wharton, C.R., Jr. (1991) 'Just vote no', in 'Advice and dissent: rating the CG compact', *Harvard Business Review* (November–December), 136–43
Wiesendanger, B. (1995) 'Shrink rap', *Journal of Business Strategy*, **16**
Williamson, O.E. (1995) *The Economic Institutions of Capitalism: Firms, Markets, Regional Contracting*, New York and London: Free Press

7 Corporate performance in the transition: econometric analysis of Hungarian exporting firms, 1985–1994

LÁSZLÓ HALPERN and GÁBOR KŐRÖSI

In a small open transition economy the behaviour of exporting firms has a decisive effect on the economic performance of the country. In a previous paper (Halpern, 1993) it was shown that in a period of radical change (reorientation from rouble to dollar trade) microeconomic efficiency had deteriorated in the late 1980s. Since that time other – even more radical – change has come in the form of commercialisation, privatisation and the steady increase of foreign ownership (see chapters 6 and 8). It is important to assess the effect of these changes on enterprise performance.

Theoretical description of the behaviour of firms in transition economies is developing quite rapidly. Aghion *et al.* (1994) explores the ways to promote restructuring by improving managerial incentives. Katsoulacos (1994) examines how alternative corporate objectives affect incentives in a mixed oligopoly where a public firm competes with private rivals. One of Katsoulacos' main assumptions is that existing public firms are usually highly inefficient relative to the newly established private firms. According to Estrin and Hare (1992), firms in transition economies go through three phases: first, pre-transition where firms have price and output targets and seek to minimise output subject to a profit constraint; second, commercialisation in which prices are liberalised and budget constraints harden; third, privatisation in which firms behave like profit maximising firms in a market economy.

However, these studies all assume that private firms – either new or privatised – are *per se* more efficient that the state-owned ones. This is a hypothesis to be confronted by the empirical evidence.

Few empirical works are available on the topic: Belka (1994), Brada, Singh and Török (1994), Čapek (1994), Dobrinsky (1994), Gomulka (1994), Pinto, Belka and Krajewski (1993), Schaffer (1992) and Sgard (1995). An overall survey is given in Carlin *et al.* (1994). But still the confrontation of data by theoretical assumptions is scarce.

192

Table 7.1. Macroeconomic indicators, 1985–94

	GDP	Consumption	Investment	Exports	Imports	Net foreign debt
	Annual percentage increase			(mn$US)		
1985	−0.3	1.7	−3.5	8,267	7,846	8,046
1986	1.5	2.4	8.6	8,850	9,263	10,668
1987	4.1	3.3	3.2	9,199	9,448	13,683
1988	−0.1	−2.8	−3.3	9,699	9,116	13,966
1989	0.7	0.8	1.2	9,605	8,819	14,900
1990	−3.5	−2.7	−4.2	9,588	8,647	15,938
1991	−11.9	−5.1	−21.1	10,187	11,382	14,554
1992	−3.1	0.6	−20.4	10,705	11,079	13,276
1993	−0.6	5.4	32.3	8,907	12,530	14,927
1994	2.9	−2.3	19.8	10,701	14,554	18,936

Sources: CSO, National Accounts Hungary 1991–1993 (Budapest, 1995); Year-books of National Bank of Hungary.

The objective of this chapter is to investigate the phases Hungarian exporting firms went through between 1985 and 1994, how they responded to different signals and if there was any change in their reaction. The scope of the chapter will be limited to the examination of profitability and of the production function.

1 General performance

Hungarian macroeconomic performance reflects the depth of the structural crisis. The very uneven economic growth of the late 1980s was followed by a steep decline of output, consumption and investment (see table 7.1). Trade reorientation from rouble to dollar was quite successful. The dollar value of exports increased until 1992, while imports – after a decline in 1989 and 1990 – increased rather quickly. In 1993 exports fell considerably, while imports continued to grow, provoking a massive increase in net foreign debt. The total domestic demand increased by 9.9 per cent – an average of a 5.4 per cent increase in consumption and a 32.3 per cent increase in gross capital formation – in 1993, suggesting that it might have caused the huge trade deficit. The structure of consumption and capital formation reveals that a large part of the increase was due to public consumption and to inventory accumulation, since private consumption grew only by 1.5 per cent, while gross fixed capital formation grew by 1.7 per cent. This structure reflects the role of

Table 7.2. Different profitability measures of the corporate sector, 1985–94 (per cent)

	Ratio of pre-tax profit		Ratio of after-tax profit	
	To sales	To equity	To sales	To equity
1985	5.1	11.9	2.8	6.6
1986	5.3	11.6	2.8	6.2
1987	5.8	13.0	3.0	6.8
1988	3.9	8.1	2.5	5.2
1989	4.1	8.7	2.8	5.9
1990	3.2	6.8	2.8	6.0
1991	0.4	0.6	0.7	1.1
1992	−4.6	−5.8	−5.3	−6.8
1993	−1.7	−2.2	−2.8	−3.5
1994	1.6	2.3	1.1	1.6

Source: Authors' computation.

the budget deficit – the imports of Russian MIG-29s as payments for the accumulated Soviet trade deficit excepted – but some statistical uncertainties in national accounts cannot be ruled out – namely, that some measurement inconsistencies between different GDP concepts might have been accounted for in inventory accumulation. In 1994, the total domestic demand increased at a lower pace (by 2.2 per cent), total consumption declined by 2.3 per cent, while gross capital formation increased by another 19.8 per cent. The trade deficit remained over $3.5billion, increasing the foreign debt significantly.

The state of the corporate sector mirrors the macroeconomic indicators: positive profit ratios dominated until 1991 and heavy losses came afterwards (see table 7.2). In 1991 after-tax profit was higher than pre-tax profit, because there were important tax reimbursements in 1991 on excessive advance profit tax payments in 1990. After two years of losses until 1994 positive profit rates have prevailed.

This double – microeconomic and macroeconomic – shock can be analysed in the context of Kornai's so-called 'transformational recession' (Kornai, 1993). In this chapter the analysis will concentrate on the explanation of profit variation across firms and on the estimation of production functions. The major question is how the new bankruptcy and accounting regulations and the foreign capital inflow changed the environment for firms. It is assumed that foreign ownership imposes profitability and growth as a major objective for firms, and might have had an effect on the overall environment.

2   Empirical model of profit

Let us try to look beyond general tendencies. The selected approach is rather simple and pragmatic. On the basis of the available data we tried to identify variables affecting the profit margin. We are fully aware that there is a large number of factors that influence profit, but their effect cannot be quantified, or even measured. Nevertheless, if we manage to estimate profit by plausible economic factors with a satisfactory model we may claim that part of the explanation of profitability differences among firms has been found.

2.1   Data issues

The data base for this exercise consists of the profit and loss account and balance sheet data of the main Hungarian exporting firms between 1985 and 1994.[1] A firm has been selected and defined as main exporter if it exported more than $US 1 million in any year between 1985 and 1994. We were able to identify these firms and follow their performance record. During this period thousands of new firms were established; some were new firms founded by domestic or foreign investors, but many were created from the assets of existing SOEs. Our main problem with the data set was to find the firms for which 'commercialisation' meant only a change of name. In other cases they were treated as totally new entities following the natural process of entry and exit.

There is quite a lot of criticism about any use of balance sheet and profit and loss account data in transition economies, especially concerning profit and assets (e.g. Carlin, van Reenen and Wolfe, 1994, criticising Pinto, Belka and Krajewski, 1993). A large part of this criticism is rightly placed, but one has to take into account that the necessary consequence is that the same treatment should also be applied to most macro indicators, since they are computed on the basis of enterprise information supplied by firms. The procedure of making consistent data from different statistical sources offers little consolation, because it can be used only on an aggregate level. We are in favour of extreme caution with respect to any interpretation of results obtained using these data, but we are also convinced that one should not disregard them. The ideal would be to combine balance sheet and survey-type information, but this is beyond the scope of the present study. We hope that our interpretation will contribute to the understanding of Hungarian firms' behaviour during transition.

2.2   Profit ratio equation

We used regression analysis as an exploratory tool for analysing profitability. Economic theory tells us very little about the determinants of profitability in an imperfect capital market. (In a perfect capital market, expected profit margins should reflect the capital:output ratio.) In our sample period the imperfections of the capital market as well as market conditions, economic regulations and behavioural rules changed, all affecting profitability. Between 1986 and 1994 one cannot find two years when firms could operate under similar conditions. So we decided to use statistical criteria for model selection.

The dependent variable of the estimated regressions is the after-tax profit margin, i.e. the after-tax profit divided by the total sales. Based on the historic cost concept there are two main widely used measures of firm profitability: the first relates profit to equity, the second to sales. We preferred the latter, because of the frequent revaluation of assets due to commercialisation and/or privatisation and to the rather unrealistic asset values in those cases where nothing comparable has happened and the asset values have only very limited economic meaning. It would be ideal to use both profitability measures; for the first indicator we would need to know the time of events influencing asset value, otherwise there is no way to separate increases in asset values caused by different reasons.

The first striking feature of our empirical results is the level of the average profit margin of Hungarian firms, compared to the level expected in a Western country. Since 1968, Hungarian firms were able to operate on markets with much greater freedom than earlier, or than in any other socialist economy. Central planners, however, did not want to lose their grip on investments. Profitability was kept at an artificially low level by price controls and by other means, to force companies to rely on centrally rationed investment funds and subsidised investment loans. Economic transition started from this situation, and few firms have been able substantially to change the inherited position ever since.

Economic transition was coupled with a permanent deterioration of the industrial sectors' financial position. Some of the components were external – the dissolution of the CMEA meant that many firms lost their safe markets. Most components were related to changes in economic policy, regulation and the market situation. Most subsidies and many tax reliefs were abolished; firms had to face a much higher interest burden on their debts than they could ever have anticipated; imports were liberalised, so the domestic market position became insecure, etc. Economic transition brought financial crisis for many firms.

'Profitability' had a special meaning in the socialist economy. As shortages were rampant central planners wanted to give an incentive to firms to deliver their products to the users as quickly as possible. Firms could claim financial results at delivery instead of on actual payment. In this way, firms effectively gave free credit to their buyers, but they got their rewards from the planners for quick fulfilment of orders. As bankruptcy was unknown in the centrally planned economy and payment was received sooner or later (it was implicitly guaranteed by the government), this accounting practice did not really matter. However, as the marketisation of the economy started and more and more firms defaulted on their payment, such free credit caused substantial financial strain both for firms and for the entire economy. Reported profits became highly questionable, as they were based on deliveries which might have never been paid for. In 1992, new accounting standards and bankruptcy regulations were introduced in conformity with the rules of the market economy (see chapters 1 and 8), and firms had to write off their bad loans. Since then, profitability has more and more reflected true market performance. Many firms went bankrupt in the second half of 1992, and this led to a severe deterioration of most firms' profitability.

Most explanatory variables (in the regressions) are ratios in table 7.3. The exception is negative assets which is a binary (dummy) variable, indicating that accumulated losses exceed the equity capital of the firm. The depreciation rate is the ratio of depreciation to net fixed asset value. Foreign ownership is the percentage share of the assets owned by foreign investors in the equity of the firm. It would have been very important to use other ownership variables, not only foreign ownership. However, these potential variables are very unreliable since a large part of non-state assets were of commercialised, joint stock companies owned by the state. That is why the distinction between 'private' and 'state-owned' was not used. All other variables are relative to the sales total, e.g. 'exports' stands for the exports divided by the sales of the firm. (L) indicates that the variable is lagged by one period.

One asterisk (*) indicates that the relevant test (t-test for the significance of the coefficient estimates or the diagnostic test) is significant at the 5 per cent level, while two asterisks (**) indicate that the test is significant at the 1 per cent level. In the Breusch–Pagan heteroscedasticity test (χ^2 form) the explanatory variables and the relevant squared variables were used. The *RESET*-test, proposed by Ramsey (1969) is a general diagnostic test for the functional form and other cross-sectional characteristics of the model, cf: Körösi, Matyás and Székely (1992). The *LM*-test for sector is the joint test of the binary variables indicating the one-digit sectoral classification (χ^2_{10}).

All estimated regressions have non-normally distributed, heteroscedastic

Table 7.3. Profit equations

Variable	1986	1987	1988	1989	1990	1991	1992	1993	1994
Profit margin (L)	0.787043**	1.07513**	0.318220*	0.267304**	0.703602**	0.660836**	0.354090	0.327470**	0.4449**
Exports	0.065924*					0.053276*	0.102574**	0.059297*	
Exports (L)	−0.056936*								
Rouble exports			−0.027309*		0.013470*				
Net capital	−0.015495**		−0.114943*		0.019664**	0.000743862*			
Net capital (L)			0.147133**	−0.188246**	−0.148760**	−0.222895**	−0.181492*		
Payables			−0.075165*	0.037257**		0.091793*			
Payables (L)			0.078129*	0.039012**	0.027096*	−0.211388**	−0.643380**	−0.306237**	−0.2858**
Receivables			0.045763**		−0.107282*				
Wage bill		−0.785072**	−0.363017**	−0.477893**	−0.642845**	−0.618123**	0.287311*	0.3471**	
Wage bill (L)		0.669567**	0.735576**		−0.484099*				
Bank cost							−0.1978**		
Bank cost (L)									
Inventories									
Inventories (L)		−0.028832*		−0.032348**			−0.128132*		
Depreciation	0.194555**		−0.844983**	−0.748284**	−1.37940**		−1.2054**		
Depreciation (L)			1.06570**	0.437834**	0.980456**		0.9197*		
Depreciation rate	−0.013586**		−0.269453**						
Depreciation rate (L)					−0.112475**				
Negative assets				0.293836**	0.586311**	−0.228985**	−0.294519**	−0.2560**	
Foreign ownership					0.064168**	0.058880**	0.0017557*		
Foreign ownership (L)									
Taxes, etc.		−0.211594**		0.011958**					
Taxes, etc. (L)		0.211382**							
Constant	0.00585777	0.00665217	0.015857*	0.052911**	0.033898**	0.021585	0.025870	0.072035**	0.0370**

	659	672	661	686	731	990	945	826	1280
Nob									
Mean of dep. var.	0.039195	0.038858	0.024932	0.019283	0.0033892	−0.024096	−0.097265	−0.075194	−0.02545
Std dev. of dep. var.	0.038454	0.053531	0.078273	0.055125	0.076599	0.158166	0.269238	0.276492	0.22384
SEE	0.023058	0.032701	0.041629	0.044361	0.058257	0.125044	0.209569	0.192974	0.16454
R^2	0.643743	0.630171	0.720564	0.359965	0.431871	0.381297	0.399903	0.517020	0.46259
$\bar{R}^2$	0.640464	0.626834	0.717135	0.352402	0.421570	0.374977	0.394127	0.512887	0.45963
BP-heteroscedasticity	44*	113**	111**	119**	211**	200**	320**	333**	510**
JB-normality	48069**	645313**	70175**	136517**	2724**	54762**	8115**	7682**	24889**
$RESET\ y^2$	2.62	34.55**	0.27	0.15	0.11	0.55	2.58	1.03	1.57
$RESET\ y^2, y^3$	1.62	896.99**	1.20	0.13	0.06	2.24	2.05	1.01	4.85**
LM-test for sectors	15.15	17.53	14.92	16.73	11.32	12.81	17.18	20.57*	13.42

residuals (see table 7.3). Non-normality should not be surprising, as we used a highly truncated sample in all cases. Heteroscedasticity most probably reflects heterogeneity of firms left unexplained by those models, explored later. It is very encouraging that the *RESET*-test indicates severe specification problems in one year – 1987 – only. The Chow-test for structural break was significant at the 1 per cent level for all consecutive years – i.e. the determinants of profitability had different effects in different years. This makes the pooled estimation highly questionable, which is why the results are not presented. We prefer to treat our panel as repeated cross-sections. The explanatory power of variables is quite high, it varies between 35 and 72 per cent. The regressions had a much better fit in the pre-transition period than afterwards.

As we used regression as an exploratory tool, we do not attach economic significance to all coefficients. However, some interesting tendencies are apparent in the sequence of estimated regressions. It is clear that the most important factors influencing profitability changed substantially during our sample period. Some of these changes are institutional, e.g. rouble exports ceased to exist, many subsidies were abolished, taxation rules changed; others reflect changing economic conditions.

We use the lagged profit margin as an indicator for the change in the effect of other, ignored variables. The closer this coefficient to 1, the less these relationships changed. Clearly, there were substantial changes in all years after 1987, especially in the period 1988–9, when the transition started, and in 1992–3, when the new accounting standards were introduced and bankruptcy became a real threat.

As Hungary is a small open economy, foreign trade is very important. Many firms are simply too big for the Hungarian market, they could not survive without exports. Large export shares almost always improved company profitability, especially after 1991. However, this was true only for exports to real markets: rouble exports had negative effects on profitability in 1988. The coefficient was insignificant in other years, but negative throughout the 1980s. The shrinking CMEA market proved to be a costly trap for many firms. This result is against common sense, it was – and perhaps still is – thought that the different government guarantee schemes and other discretionary treatment accompanying rouble exports ensured higher profitability in the second half of the 1980s.

The capital:output ratio has only a limited effect on the profit margin which is a clear indication of capital market imperfections; it suggests that standard microeconomic analysis of the Hungarian economy is hardly feasible. Profitability is increasingly more sensitive to some cost components, such as wages and bank costs, and the effect of high interest rates becomes important.

Foreign ownership had controversial effects. Initially, when larger-scale foreign investment started in 1989, it had a very strong positive effect on firms' profitability. Obviously, the first foreign investors had the best opportunity to pick those firms where they could expect the highest return on their investment. The first investors also received substantial incentives from the government, e.g. tax holidays. However, as the economic situation became more difficult and firms learned to operate in a more market oriented economy, this advantage largely disappeared. Foreign investment may have influenced the factors determining firms' profitability (e.g. export potential), but mostly lost their special positive effect on profitability. This probably reflects the fact that foreign investment had become a 'normal' feature of the Hungarian corporate sector. It certainly shows that firms where there is no foreign ownership learned to operate similarly. Many of these firms were still owned by the state in 1994. As there does not seem to be much difference in profitability due to foreign private ownership, it also casts some doubt on the relevance of theoretical papers assuming this. However, foreign firms may outperform domestic firms in other aspects of their performance or in skill in transferring the profit, but the analysis of these possibilities is beyond the scope of this chapter.

In 1990 it was quite 'profitable' to have negative equity capital as the negative asset dummy had a high positive coefficient. This might have been linked to the specific situation of Hungarian corporate transformation – that is, a large number of firms was set up with very low minimum equity requirements, and after the first year of unprofitable functioning they became highly profitable. Since 1992 the coefficient has been negative, reflecting the expected effect of negative assets on profitability and indicating some normalisation of corporate behaviour.

Payables and receivables have been significant factors in explaining profit margins since 1988. The fact that these variables ceased to affect profit in 1993 proves that inter-enterprise credit has practically disappeared in Hungary.

The wage bill had a negative effect on profitability between 1990 and 1993, and this persisted in 1994 for the instantaneous variable, but if the lagged wage bill is taken into account then the overall effect becomes positive. This offers a possibility to ascribe increasing marginal labour productivity to the deep restructuring of the labour market. The result of one year is not enough to draw such a conclusion, however.

We used the estimated regressions as starting points for further analysis.

We tried to identify important groups of companies which had unusual behaviour. We analysed three aspects: if the industrial sector had an effect, if monopolisation mattered, and if the size of the firm had any impact on the relationship.

2.3 Sectoral effects

The first, and probably most obvious question was if the sectoral breakdown of the economy had any discernible effect on the behaviour of firms. We tested if the sectoral indicators had significant effect and the results were that sectors usually do not have any effect. We also tested if different sectors had different behavioural rules: in most years, the computed Chow-test was insignificant. Sector is not a relevant indicator for the heterogeneity of corporate behaviour.[2]

2.4 Market power effects

Monopolists had special treatment in the socialist economy. They had regular and intensive contacts with policy makers, and could rely on discretionary treatment. Frequently, these firms were artificially created. Central planners preferred to deal with a small number of large firms; they wanted to create firms which were responsible for the entire supply of a specific product which made planning much simpler. In the early years of socialism many potential competitors were forced into conglomerates. The new firms became (quasi-) monopolists, but they could hardly operate as a single entity. Frequently, productivity decreased and costs increased after amalgamation.

Few monopolists were created after 1968, but the structure of firms has hardly changed. The large conglomerates, created in the early stages of socialism, could regularly rely on a special treatment from the government: they could get special subsidies, frequent subsidised loans, firm-specific financial regulation, etc. Profitability was less important for them than for other firms. However, as economic transition started, they were no longer treated preferentially.

In our model, a firm was considered a monopolist when its share in the total sales of the sector was greater than the given threshold – 25 or 40 per cent – or if there were fewer firms in the sector than the given limit – 3 or 4.[3] Sectors were determined according to the four-digit classification. Unfortunately, industrial classification was changed in 1992. The former classification was very different from the UN standard, while the new classification is the ISIC code. The two are incompatible even at the two-digit level, thus we were unable to create a uniform classification for the entire sample period. The change in classification influences the outcome in the tests for the effect of monopolisation.

Chow-tests clearly indicate that before the economic transition started in 1989 monopolists' profitability was determined in a different way from that of other firms (see table 7.4). It is not evident if the reappearance of distinctive behaviour in 1992 was due to changes in the industrial classification (which clearly had a strong influence on the selection of monopolists), or reflects the impact of the new accounting standards and bankruptcy rules on monopolists. In late 1992, the government, worried about the possibility of a highly destructive wave of bankruptcies, guaranteed many bad loans in the framework of a corporate restructuring programme (see chapter 8). The scheme was also repeated in 1993. Both programmes clearly favoured large firms – monopolists. In 1993, the government even singled out several well known troubled monopolists for special financial treatment. According to another explanation large firms needed time – 2–3 years – to be able to cope with the increased import competition or achieve some form of government protection.

The average profitability of monopolists was lower than that of other firms before the transition period, reflecting the relative unimportance of profitability as well as their inefficiencies. However, after the economic transition monopolists were better able to maintain their profit margins. Whether this was due to their capability to restructure or to their large market power needs further investigation.

2.5 Size effects

We tried to measure the importance of firm size. This is a different classification from the previous one: not all the monopolists are large firms.

The size of firms was measured by four variables: capital (net and gross), sales and the wage bill. In the years 1986–91, a firm is defined as 'large' if any of these four variables is greater than the annual average *plus* the standard error of the variable. Between 1992 and 1994, a firm is defined as 'large' if any of these four variables is greater than the annual average *plus* 0.75 times the standard error of the variable. (The average and the standard error is computed for the sample used in the regressions. Relative errors were much greater in 1992–4.) A firm is defined as 'small' if any of the four variables is smaller than its annual average *minus* a constant share of the standard error. The constant share was 0.20 until 1991, 0.15 afterwards. Here we have to emphasise that the small firms within our sample cover important exporters only; there are very few really small family firms among them.

Table 7.4. Results for the monopoly effect, 1986–94

A Number of observations

Period	Total	Number<3	Number<4	Share>0.4	Share>0.25
1986	659	55	88	60	106
1987	672	57	86	62	99
1988	661	52	77	60	98
1989	686	46	74	58	95
1990	731	25	47	51	84
1991	990	35	57	59	96
1992	944	57	93	103	157
1993	824	68	118	119	167
1994	1,280	59	99	101	161
1986–94	7,447	454	739	673	1063

B Mean profit margin (per cent)

Period	Total	Number<3	Number<4	Share>0.4	Share>0.25
1986	3.92	2.68	2.93	2.83	3.26
1987	3.89	1.76	2.44	2.88	3.20
1988	2.49	3.39	3.19	3.09	2.96
1989	1.93	3.54	1.67	3.22	2.17
1990	0.34	2.26	3.38	3.17	2.45
1991	−2.41	1.88	3.85	1.80	1.82
1992	−9.73	6.84	−9.62	−8.05	−8.87
1993	−7.23	−11.31	−8.40	−5.86	−5.33
1994	−2.55	−11.90	−9.58	−6.11	−2.85
1986–94	−1.66	−2.54	−2.46	−1.72	−1.13

C Weighted mean of profit margin

Period	Total	Number<3	Number<4	Share>0.4	Share>0.25
1986	2.81	2.49	2.60	1.99	2.47
1987	2.85	2.47	2.72	2.13	2.41
1988	2.23	2.52	3.05	2.14	2.36
1989	2.46	4.22	3.62	3.47	3.20
1990	1.96	1.46	6.48	4.24	3.37
1991	0.21	1.77	2.74	2.57	2.36
1992	−4.92	−2.58	−3.25	−4.67	−4.96
1993	−1.59	−2.70	−1.90	−2.55	−1.86
1994	1.11	−0.09	0.08	0.42	0.97
1986–94	0.90	0.55	1.30	0.76	1.01

D Chow-test for structural break

Period	Number<3	Number<4	Share>0.4	Share>0.25
1986	13.85**	10.45**	4.44**	3.05**
1987	48.43**	37.51**	2.50*	3.66**
1988	13.99**	16.25**	1.94*	2.27*
1989	1.51	10.40	1.84	8.70
1990	0.21	0.74	0.68	0.87
1991	0.43	0.81	0.50	0.51
1992	4.72**	2.23*	5.05**	3.87**
1993	2.63**	2.35*	1.20	1.53
1994	9.95**	12.54**	4.65**	4.59**

The size of firms revealed an interesting feature: the behaviour of the large and medium-sized firms was similar, while small firms behaved differently (see table 7.5). Small firms had to be more flexible, more market oriented in socialism, as they could not rely on special treatment. Their average profitability was higher than that of the other firms. However, they were the real losers in the economic transition. They had few resources and very few reserves. Higher risks and more difficult market conditions destroyed their opportunities and made them much more vulnerable to increased import competition. They had very little access to capital markets: foreign investors were interested in larger firms, while the domestic capital market remained under-developed. Thus they could not restructure, modernise their production or adopt new behaviour, and were locked into a deteriorating market situation. They also had to compete against a great number of newly established upcoming even smaller private firms which did not export much and so are not included in our sample. They lost their profitability faster, and, on the average, went much further into the red than the larger firms. It clearly indicates the biggest problem of the economic transition in Hungary: it was advantageous for too few, and destroyed too many.

3 Cobb–Douglas production functions

It is clear that profitability cannot be regarded as the only performance indicator of a firm. To complete the analysis, other performance indicators have to be considered. Here we will provide the results of a very simple exercise, the estimation of production functions.

Cobb–Douglas production functions were estimated for each year in our sample. The sample consists of the 'productive' sectors only, excluding trade and most other services. The output variable is the value

Table 7.5. Results for the size effect, 1986–94

A Number of observations				
Period	Total	Small	Medium	Large
1986	659	465	144	50
1987	672	470	148	54
1988	661	456	160	45
1989	686	457	180	49
1990	731	430	265	36
1991	990	582	351	57
1992	944	563	343	38
1993	824	516	276	32
1994	1,280	839	386	55
1986–94	7,447	4,778	2,253	416

B Mean profit margins (per cent)				
Year	Total	Small	Medium	Large
1986	2.81	4.18	3.75	2.06
1987	2.85	4.13	3.75	2.15
1988	2.23	2.66	1.98	2.70
1989	2.46	1.71	2.17	3.07
1990	1.96	−0.17	0.82	2.83
1991	0.21	−3.49	−0.63	−2.45
1992	−4.92	−12.48	−5.34	−8.63
1993	−1.59	−10.77	−1.61	1.44
1994	1.11	−4.21	0.48	1.53
1986–94	0.90	−2.61	−0.09	0.61

C Weighted mean of profit margins (per cent)				
Year	Total	Small	Medium	Large
1986	2.81	3.44	3.58	2.00
1987	2.85	3.50	3.62	2.02
1988	2.23	2.55	2.22	2.06
1989	2.46	1.69	2.15	3.04
1990	1.96	0.28	1.16	3.41
1991	0.21	−2.11	−.14	1.37
1992	−4.92	−13.39	−4.03	−3.36
1993	−1.59	−7.37	−1.11	−0.40
1994	1.11	−0.84	0.93	1.74
1986–94	0.90	−0.02	0.72	1.42

D Chow-test for structural break

Year	Small	Medium	Large
1986	1.15	1.93	0.99
1987	2.88**	2.71**	0.57
1988	8.50**	8.97**	1.41
1989	2.20*	1.24	1.70
1990	1.11	1.08	0.95
1991	1.55	1.08	1.82*
1992	2.65**	3.20**	1.17
1993	4.00**	3.74**	0.48
1994	4.99**	3.85**	0.91

added of the firm at 1991 prices. Explanatory variables are the capital stock of the firm and the wage[4] bill, both at 1991 prices. Linearised functions were estimated: the so-called log-log specification.

Errors were expected to be heteroscedastic, as the size of firms varies substantially. Thus the figures in parentheses under the estimated coefficients are the heteroscedasticity consistent standard errors (see table 7.6). The non-normality of the errors is not very surprising either: it is partly due to the size effect discussed above, but the characteristics of the sample may also contribute, as our sample is not representative of all firms.

One asterisk (*) indicates that the relevant test (diagnostic tests or t-test for the significance of the coefficient estimates; for the returns to scale $(r) H_0 : r = 1$) is significant at the 5 per cent level, while two asterisks (**) indicate that the test is significant at the 1 per cent level. The χ^2 version was used both for White's heteroscedasticity-test and for the LM-test for sector – the joint test of the binary variables indicating the one-digit sectoral classification.

As sectoral differences are always significant, the same production function was also estimated for each sector under consideration. Detailed results for the sectors are not presented here. The sectoral range summarises the coefficient estimates: these figures are the minimal and the maximal values of the sectoral estimates. Clearly, the ranges – almost always wide – indicate that there are very heterogeneous technologies in use in Hungarian industry.

Sectoral production functions frequently 'outperform' the aggregate ones. Except for 1993 the $RESET$-test is rarely significant. There are sectors where tests for homoscedasticity and normality are usually insignificant. The fit is usually better, frequently much better in the sectoral equations than in the aggregate ones, except for Food and

Table 7.6. Estimated Cobb–Douglas functions, 1985–94

Variable	1985	1986	1987	1988	1989	1990	1991	1992	1993	1994
Capital	0.394317	0.385246	0.442124	0.348389	0.416126	0.114860	0.087419	0.111399	0.111381	0.074300
Std err.	0.03776**	0.04581**	0.04173**	0.04620**	0.04842**	0.03104**	0.02611**	0.01677**	0.01693**	0.01774**
Sectoral range	0.183–0.404	0.017–0.520	0.251–0.544	0.093–0.686	0.226–0.491	0.051–0.201	−0.004–0.271	−0.004–0.287	0.083–0.228	0.053–0.160
Wage	0.550641	0.530851	0.507437	0.671520	0.571300	0.822680	0.777843	0.724594	0.648377	0.738699
Std err.	0.03998**	0.04822**	0.04539**	0.04825**	0.04880**	0.04708**	0.03886**	0.02864**	0.02761**	0.02555**
Sectoral range	0.493–0.833	0.529–0.950	0.592–0.728	0.414–0.915	0.394–0.734	0.761–0.946	0.654–1.040	0.610–0.925	0.613–0.871	0.716–0.909
Constant	0.689695	0.832330	0.625691	0.224266	0.316856	0.925299	1.15751	1.26661	1.64251	1.09800
Std err.	0.11480**	0.15136**	0.13051**	0.13872	0.15575*	0.11674**	0.09298**	0.08761**	0.09012**	0.08361**
Returns to scale	0.944959	0.916097	0.949561	1.01991	0.987426	0.937539	0.865262	0.835993	0.759758	0.812999
Std err.	0.02025**	0.02597**	0.02251**	0.02267	0.02386	0.02656*	0.021615**	0.01945**	0.01888**	0.01511**
Sectoral range	0.874–1.058	0.863–1.049	0.897–1.136	0.908–1.100	0.731–1.034	0.859–1.072	0.888–1.062	0.868–0.979	0.737–0.967	0.815–0.962
Nob	627	622	605	637	695	999	1164	1330	1208	1793
Mean of dep. var	5.65081	5.67697	5.75062	5.66080	5.68900	5.21735	4.92744	4.86175	5.16592	5.28281
S. dev of dep. var	1.09094	1.10227	1.13942	1.20634	1.24227	1.49576	1.46768	1.47016	1.37556	1.50168
SEE	0.48394	0.54295	0.53728	0.58391	0.65004	.707661	0.76719	0.79810	0.75258	0.73957
R^2	0.80384	0.75814	0.77838	0.76644	0.72698	.776614	0.72722	0.70573	0.70116	0.75771
Adj. R^2	0.80321	0.75736	0.77765	0.76570	0.72619	.776165	0.72675	0.70529	0.70066	0.75744
White-hetero	21**	18**	10	14**	8	76**	61**	146**	52**	198**
JB-normality	3286**	4442**	1491**	9170**	7133**	5163**	1427**	747**	1231**	1494**
RESET y^2	1.13**	0.97	0.02	0.74	9.57**	6.91**	72.15**	34.77**	42.27**	16.84**
RESET y^2, y^3	1.16**	3.02	0.71	0.44	13.63**	8.27**	40.30**	22.00**	21.52**	30.95**
LM-test for sector	84.9**	90.0**	109.**	73.8**	72.6**	83.9**	63.1**	63.5**	59.6**	75.5**

agriculture, where the fit is poor before 1990, but much better afterwards. In some industrial sectors these simple Cobb–Douglas functions perform surprisingly well.

This heterogeneity certainly influenced the estimated coefficients presented in table 7.6. However, the overall tendencies apparent in the table are largely supported by sectoral evidence. One can make two important observations. First, decreasing returns to scale characterised the Hungarian economy in all years except 1988 and 1989, i.e. small firms use resources more efficiently than large ones on the average. Second, there is a notable shift from capital to labour. In the 1980s the elasticity of capital was unusually high for most Hungarian industries. After 1989 the situation quickly turned into a more familiar one, where the contribution of labour becomes much more important.

4   Conclusions

In the early 1990s the environment for firms was mainly influenced by the effect of price and foreign trade liberalisation in Hungary. These changes, combined with the collapse of the CMEA, put enormous pressure on the society. Large output loss and massive unemployment followed. Consequently, profitability fell dramatically worsened by the new bankruptcy regulation and by the new accounting rules. These measures proved to be too harsh. The legal system was unable to cope with the sudden flood of bankruptcy or liquidation cases. These serious problems notwithstanding, there was a substantial overall change in the business climate, enhanced by the establishment of prudential banking and by the more or less continuous inflow of foreign capital, which was only temporarily halted by the effect of government direct intervention. The case-by-case privatisation without any single spectacular shift in ownership structure created institutions which helped to establish a relatively clear corporate governance structure, despite being sometimes heavily burdened by the lack of transparency and by corruption charges.

Our results presented here demonstrate these substantial changes and can be interpreted as indicative of deep restructuring. By 1993–4 foreign trade and prices had been almost fully liberalised (with a few exceptions in certain public utilities and energy), privatisation had advanced in an irreversible way and foreign capital had steadily increased its presence in the Hungarian economy. The labour market was radically overhauled. Our results cast serious doubts on concerns about the loss of international competitiveness due to high labour costs: on the contrary, labour costs played a diminishing role in profitability. The overall environment has significantly shifted towards that of a market economy.

210   László Halpern and Gábor Kőrösi

Until 1989, returns to scale were constant or almost so, but significantly declined afterwards. This may explain why large firms were not obliged to change their way of functioning in contrast with small and medium-sized firms. On the other hand, firms in a monopoly position were significantly different before 1989 and after 1991. One can assume that these firms revealed new patterns of behaviour and that the role of market structure determined their position in different ways – entry costs, investment indivisibilities, access to results of innovation, etc. – and the role of paternalistic behaviour, their bargaining power against regulators has largely diminished.

It is not very easy to interpret the decline of returns to scale; it may perhaps be attributed to two contradictory factors. According to new international trade theory, the major motivation of the international mobility of capital is the quest for increasing returns. Since foreign direct investment in Hungary was in an early phase in the early 1990s it is reasonable that it has not brought all the expected results as yet. On the other hand, external and internal demand shocks had an effect not only on the profitability but also on the output loss with a fixed asset stock adjustment lagging behind. The adjustment of labour was much faster, with some devastating regional and social effects. The necessary external financing of new investment was not available, since banks were reluctant to extend credit to firms with uncertain future profit perspectives, and the budget deficit crowded out good firms, forcing them to rely on foreign finance. The March 1995 austerity measures modified the position of the corporate sector and put them in a better position on the basis of partly achieved microeconomic restructuring.

NOTES

The financial support of EU PHARE ACE programme No. 94–0590–R is gratefully acknowledged.
1   An alternative would be to model on sectoral level, as in Commander and Ugaz (1993) and Commander *et al.* (1993). It can only be accepted as a compromise due to data constraints, since the within-sector variation exceeds that of between-sector, as will be shown later.
2   Kambhampati (1995) found persistent sectoral differences in profit rates for Indian firms between 1970 and 1985, which can be explained by the concentration ratio, ratio of advertisement costs to sales, output growth, cost disadvantage ratio and public sector dummy. The hypothesis was that industries in which advertisement costs are high are those which are likely to have succeeded in creating brand loyalty. They are therefore able to increase the costs that new entrants have to meet to operate in the industry. This sets up a barrier to entry, so high profit differentials can be maintained over time.

A high cost disadvantage ratio implies that low-scale entry into the industry is unprofitable.

3 The solution is rather rudimentary, reflecting the stage of our preliminary estimations. A Herfindahl index or other sophisticated approach can be used to assess the aggregate degree of monopolistic behaviour of an industry (see, for example, Aiginger, Brandner and Wügel, 1995 for some industrial sectors in Austria). The other caveat is the neglect of the effect of import competition: growing imports may weaken a firm's monopoly position. In static terms the industry dummy incorporates the effect of import liberalisation.

4 It would have been better to use the number of employees, instead of wages. In certain years, however, employee data are very unreliable.

REFERENCES

Aghion, P., O. Blanchard and R. Burgess (1994) 'The behaviour of state firms in Eastern Europe, pre-privatisation', *European Economic Review*, **38**, 1327–49

Aiginger, K., P. Brandner and M. Wüger (1995) 'Measuring market power for some industrial sectors in Austria', *Applied Economics*, **27**, 369–76

Belka, M. (1994) 'Financial restructuring of banks and enterprises in Poland', *Most*, **4**, 71–84

Brada, J., I. Singh and Á. Török (1994) *Firms Afloat and Firms Adrift: Hungarian Industry and the Economic Transition*, Armonk, NY: M.E. Sharpe: 104

Čapek, A. (1994) 'The bad debts problem in the Czech economy', *Most*, **4**, 59–70

Carlin, W., J. Van Reenen and T. Wolfe (1994) 'Enterprise restructuring in the transition: an analytical survey of the case study evidence from central and eastern Europe', *EBRD Working Paper*, **14**, 85

Commander, S. and C. Ugaz (1993) 'Hungary country study. Employment, output and wages in the state sector: some preliminary analysis', Research Project on Labour Markets in Transitional Socialist Economies (16–17 April), Stirin, 14

Commander, S., J. Köllő, C. Ugaz and B. Világi (1993) 'Hungary. Unemployment, restructuring and the labor market in East Europe and Russia', *IBRD*, **7–8** (October), 31

Dobrinsky, R. (1994) 'The problem of bad loans and enterprise indebtedness in Bulgaria', *Most*, **4**, 37–58

Estrin, S. and P. Hare (1992) 'Firms in transition: modelling enterprise adjustment', Centre for Economic Performance, LSE, *Discussion Paper*, **89**, 42

Gomulka, S. (1994) 'The financial situation of enterprises and its impact on monetary and fiscal policies, Poland 1992–93', *Economics of Transition*, **2**, 189–208

Halpern, L. (1993) 'Factors and effects of trade reorientation in Hungary', Centre for Economic Policy Research, *Discussion Paper*, **772**, 63, and in J. Gács and G. Winckler (eds.), *International Trade and Restructuring in Eastern Europe*, Heidelberg: Physica Verlag (1994), 265–92

Kambhampati, U.S. (1995) 'The persistence of profit differentials in Indian industry', *Applied Economics*, **27**, 353–61

Katsoulacos, Y. (1994) 'Firms' objectives in transition economies', *Journal of Comparative Economics*, **19**, 392–409

Kornai, J. (1993) 'Transformational recession: general phenomenon examined through the example of Hungary's development', *Economie Appliquée*, **46**, 181–227

Kőrösi, G., L. Mátyás and I.P. Székely (1992) *Practical Econometrics*, Aldershot:Avebury, 319

Pinto, B., M. Belka and S. Krajewski, S. (1993) 'Transforming state enterprises in Poland: microeconomic evidence on adjustment', *Brookings Papers on Economic Activity*, **1**, 213

Ramsey, J.B. (1969) 'Tests for specification errors in classical linear least squares regression analysis', *Journal of the Royal Statistical Society*, Series B, **31** (2)

Schaffer, M. (1992) 'The enterprise sector and emergence of the Polish fiscal crisis 1990–91', IBRD Transition and Macro-Adjustment Division, Country Economics Department, *Research Paper Series*, **31**, 34

Sgard, J. (1995) 'Le financement de la transition en Europe centrale et balkanique', *Economie Internationale*, **62**, 61–103

Discussion

JAN SVEJNAR

In their chapter 7, László Halpern and Gábor Kőrösi present a very interesting analysis of profitability and production in export-oriented Hungarian firms. In particular, they use an unbalanced annual panel of data on 650–1,800 firms that each exported at least US$1 million in any year during the 1985–94 period. With these data, the authors estimate first-order distributed lag profit functions and static Cobb–Douglas production functions. Since Chow tests reject the hypothesis of equal coefficients over time, the authors base their estimates on two-year, contiguous panels of data.

In several respects, the chapter constitutes a pioneering piece of empirical research. Let me mention the two most important aspects. First, the chapter provides one of the first empirical studies of corporate profitability in a large sample of firms during the transition from plan to market. The transition has been a complex process and an understanding of the determinants of enterprise profitability is therefore of major policy importance. The study is hence a welcome addition to the limited body of empirical research in this area. Second, the chapter provides estimates of production function parameters and their changes over time. As such, it generates a useful understanding of the production technology and its dynamics at the firm level.

There are also obvious limitations to this type of analysis. A study of corporate profitability in a transition economy clearly represents one of the most controversial inquiries. Governments in the transition economies have been forced to impose high taxes and thus have provided firms with strong incentives to disguise profits. At the same time, governments have been much less able to implement an effective accounting and tax enforcement system that would prevent firms from disguising profits. A plethora of problems thus arise in the context of measurement of profits, and this caveat needs to be borne in mind when assessing the findings of this study. The second drawback is that the specification of the profit equation is not rooted in theory. The estimating equation is hence neither structural nor reduced form and, as I discuss below, it is difficult to interpret the estimated coefficients. Yet, one should turn this weakness into strength and join the authors in treating the estimation as an exploration of new systematic relationships in a large set of variables.

As mentioned above, the analysis is based on an enterprise sample that spans the period 1985–94. The authors are hence able to observe firms both before and during the transition, which in Hungary started earlier than in the other Central and East European (CEE) economies. Indeed, the exact starting point is hard to determine and the authors place it around 1988–9. This appears reasonable and it splits the sample roughly half and half in terms of the pre-transition and transition observations. There are also important legal–institutional developments during the transition period, as new accounting standards and bankruptcy regulations came into effect in 1992.

The raw profit/sales data suggest that the pre-tax (after tax) profit rate was maintained by the planners at a modest level of about 5–6 per cent (3 per cent) in the mid-1980s. It started declining in 1988, as the transition set in, and it turned into losses in the 1993 period before recovering modestly in 1994. This behaviour is consistent with a number of explanations – e.g. a transition shock that brought about subsequent restructuring of firms, as well as losses that were induced by a combination of the new accounting system (firms could no longer calculate profit using revenues on unpaid deliveries) and greater tax evasion. All these factors were probably present. It is notable, however, that many firms went bankrupt in the second half of 1992, indicating that accounting losses had real-world repercussions.

The profit regressions relate the after-tax profit rate to a large number of current and lagged variables. Most of these variables are quantity indicators, such as exports, the wage bill, payables and receivables. Many are endogenous and one can easily imagine reverse causality to that implied in the paper (e.g., profitability affecting the wage bill that the firm is able to pay worker-insiders, as compared to the implied hypothesis of the causality going from the wage bill to profits). It is hence not altogether clear how to interpret the estimated coefficients. Still, some relationships are interesting and interpretable. The share of enterprise capital owned by foreigners has a positive effect on profits in the first three years of the transition but the effect becomes insignificant thereafter. The authors interpret the significant coefficients as reflecting a selectivity bias (Western firms that came first could select and acquire the most profitable firms) rather than demonstrating that Western investors restructured firms and thus increased profits. They also interpret the loss of significance of this coefficient in 1992–4 as signifying that domestic firms caught up with the foreign owned ones, rather than the possibility that foreign firms started transfer pricing once tax holidays expired, and thus reported lower profit.

The authors also find that in terms of the profit equation there is no sectoral effect but that medium-sized and large firms behave differently than small firms. In particular, small firms are found to have been more profitable before the transition (receiving no subsidies) but to have been losers during the transition. Again, while the basic finding about the difference between the larger and smaller firms is useful, one can easily think of other plausible interpretations – e.g. the fact that smaller firms are usually better able to hide profits.

In the production function analysis, the authors find that with the exception of 1988 and 1989, the behaviour of firms was characterised by decreasing returns to scale. Their estimates also suggest that the coefficient of capital fell and that of labour rose in 1990 and that they basically remained at the new levels in the 1990s. These are important structural features that deserve further study. If confirmed, they would imply that smaller firms are on average more efficient than larger ones (decreasing returns) and that, given the levels of inputs and output, labour's marginal product has risen relative to that of capital. Since the authors essentially carry out a repeated cross-sectional analysis, the finding of decreasing returns may be consistent with increasing total factor productivity (TFP) over time, as suggested by the higher value of the estimated intercept term in the 1990s as compared to the 1980s. With cross-sectional data and a Cobb–Douglas production function, it is also difficult to disentangle returns to scale and technical progress (changes in TFP). Further research in this area is thus needed. The decline in the marginal product of capital and increase in that of labour may reflect technical changes (new technologies), as well as an increased capital:

labour ratio (brought about, for instance, by labour shedding and higher investment) with a given technology. Since the study does not provide the basic data on capital, labour and input, these hypotheses will have to be verified in future research.

There are also two special factors that may be creating the special production function findings. First, the authors do not have a complete set of observations on labour input and use the wage bill of each firm in its stead. Yet, the wage bill is a principal component of value added, which is used as the dependent variable in the regressions. The estimated coefficients may hence be biased as a result of the near identity of the two measures. Second, the shift of the estimated coefficient from capital to labour occurs in 1990, the same year in which the sample size jumps from 695 to 999. This is a large increase in sample size that may mean that there is a major shift in its composition. The shift in the relative input coefficients may in part be brought about by this change in the composition of the sample.

Overall, the econometric methodology used by Halpern and Kőrösi is sound, and the estimation seems to be carried out with care. The study represents an important addition to our limited stock of knowledge about the functioning of firms in Central and Eastern Europe.

8 Hungary's Ponzi game

LÁSZLÓ SZAKADÁT

In this chapter I will review the development of the Hungarian banking sector since the late 1980s. This process has not been at all smooth. A political decision about reforming the banking sector was made under the old regime in 1983, but it seems that the transition will be finally completed only at the end of 1997, with the privatisation of those commercial banks that are still left under state control. Privatisation of the former state-owned commercial banks (SOCBs) was nowhere on the agenda of the socialist government in the 1980s. Since then, private banks have become dominant and a significant part of the Hungarian credit market is now controlled by foreign banks. Here I will focus on the restructuring of state banks that eventually resulted in an almost fully-fledged private commercial banking sector, the first in Central Europe. I will sketch the development of the banking sector before 1992, discussing the evolution of the bad debt problem, and the various policy measures Hungarian governments have taken in order to stabilise domestic banks, and I will try to show the alternatives policy makers had to choose from. Although the process has been long and expensive, the SOCBs' portfolio has been cleaned; I will argue that this development was more or less determined by the liberalisation of the entry of foreign banks in 1989 and by the adoption of the Banking Act in December 1991. As a result of this process, a major part of the SOCBs has been transformed into private ownership. The controlling stakes of privatised banks have been mostly obtained by strategic investors and therefore the state has no longer any direct control over credit allocation in the Hungarian economy any more. All these facts suggest that Hungary could proceed furthest among the Central European economies in transforming the banking sector, which will help the development of the economy as a whole.

216

1   Reforming the Hungarian banking sector, 1987–91

In 1987, after a political decision, a two-tier banking system was artificially created by decrees. From the credit departments of the National Bank of Hungary (NBH) three big commercial banks were set up and gradually the central bank withdrew from direct financing of enterprises.[1] The primary goal of the reform was to create a competitive environment for credit allocation free from state intervention and to establish a proper structure for effective monetary policy. A good review of the early phase of transformation can be found in Estrin, Hare and Márta (1992), Spéder (1991) and Spéder and Várhegyi (1992); Nyers and Lutz (1992) provide a good source of data.

The newly established commercial banks – the Hungarian Credit Bank (MHB), the National Commercial and the Credit Bank (K&H) and Budapest Bank (BB) – inherited their portfolios and clienteles from the central bank. The equity base of these banks was inadequate when they were formed. In the early 1990s a significant part of their loan portfolios became non-performing due to the economic recession and political and economic changes, or misallocation. The problem was exacerbated by the fact that the management and personnel of these banks were not competent to manage their institutions, guarantee prudent operation, evaluate new loan applications, make risk assessments, or conduct work-outs, etc. Moreover, the banking sector did not operate in a political vacuum – banking regulation was poorly designed and effective super-vision did not exist.

1.1   Why did banks accumulate bad loans?

Bad debts can be either inherited from the past (and in this case the whole issue is a stock problem), and/or can be produced by banks themselves (which is a flow problem). Both can, and probably must, be treated differently (Bonin and Schaffer, 1995). Hungarian SOCBs both inherited and produced bad loans. For this reason a targeted and rapid state intervention would have been necessary in order to solve the stock problem in line with comprehensive changes in the regulatory framework to curb the flow problem. In fact, precisely the opposite happened. First, the state deserted the aggregate economy (type 1 desertion of the state) and then it also drew back from running the market infrastructure (type 2 desertion of the state) (Ábel and Bonin, 1994). This chapter is concerned with the second type of state desertion, which proved to be rather costly for Hungarian tax payers.

The switch to a two-tier banking system took place when the economy stagnated and inflation started to increase. This environment affected both sides of the credit market. On the supply side long-term financing became riskier because of the increasing rate of inflation and because in an inflationary period rational calculation is more difficult. All these facts induced banks to stop extending more investment credits and to behave more cautiously. Even if real interest rates did not explain this fully, the demand for loans by first-rate clients also decreased (see figure 8.1–8.3, pp. 219–21, and table 8.4 and 8.5, pp. 227–8). Although the demand by small businesses continuously increased as a consequence of the growing number of small private ventures, it could not counterbalance the decreasing demand of creditworthy clients. Moreover, lending to these new small businesses was rather risky. Nonetheless, even if to some extent both demand and supply were simultaneously constrained, this did not mean that the two effects could cancel each other out. The situation got worse, because good, creditworthy firms switched to equity and bond financing instead of borrowing expensive bank resources, while big loss maker state-owned enterprises (SOEs), which were struggling with heavy liquidity problems, wanted to maintain their borrowing, and were dependent on bank resources. The short-term credit supply did not meet the demand of financially distressed SOEs, and as a consequence, forced interfirm commercial crediting (queueing) started to evolve.

Firms having permanent liquidity problems but still being in a monopsonistic position responded to the shortage of bank credit by forcing their suppliers to provide commercial credit, and they also stopped paying their other liabilities. The major portion of the total arrears was concentrated in about 25–30 enterprises in engineering and light industry, mining and metallurgy, but this phenomenon spread over the whole economy. By the end of 1989 these arrears amounted to about HUF 127 bn (USD 2.1 bn), of which HUF 73 bn (USD 1.2 bn) was the accumulated debt of firms having arrears over HUF 25 mn. As a consequence of the deterioration of financial discipline, the value of these arrears simply increased further (see table 8.1). Because firms also owed banks, some people expected the solution to come from the financial institutions, but they were rather passive for several reasons: (1) approximately only one-third of the total amount was bank arrears, i.e. the major part of the debt concerned other parties (suppliers and state creditors); (2) banks had access to the accounts of their debtors and could automatically debit these accounts – even without the consent of firms – if an amount appeared on them; and banks usually demanded such a creditor seniority when enterprises opened an account; (3) had banks tried to collect these debts, even this one-third could have jeopardised their own existence.

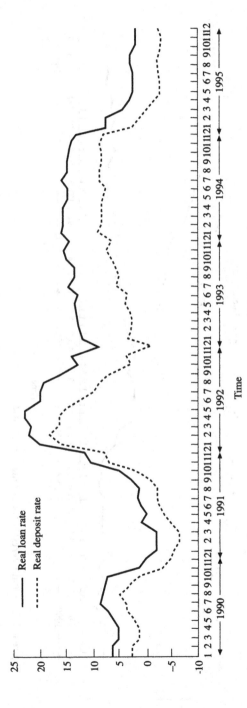

Figure 8.1 Real interest rates, 1990–5

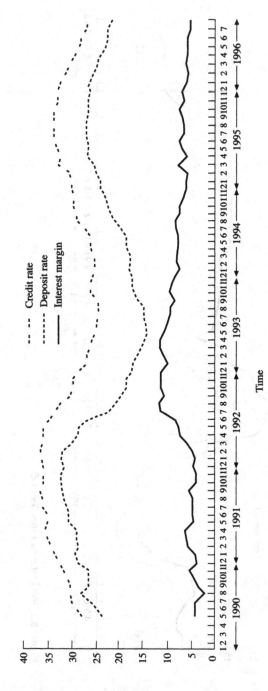

Figure 8.2 Nominal interest rates and margin, 1990–6

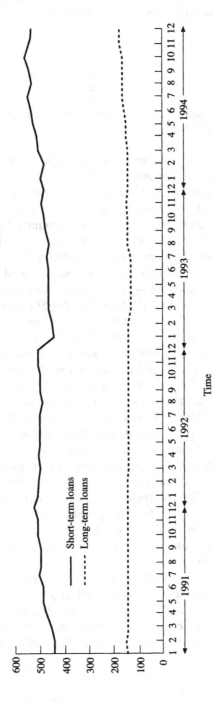

Figure 8.3 Corporate loans, 1991–4, HUF bn

Table 8.1. Arrears of larger firms, 1987–92

	Arrears (HUF bn)	No. of firms
1987	14	82
1988	46	208
1989	73	314
1990	90	432
1991	159	1,021
1992 April	197	1,097

Source: Marsi and Pap (1993).

Nonetheless, where it was possible banks sought to withdraw credits from less creditworthy enterprises, but in the case of big debtors this would have immediately pushed them into the red. SOCBs were not interested in filing their big debtors for liquidation because (1) again, banks usually had access to their clients' accounts; (2) due to the extended nature of indebtedness, a mass liquidation would have devalued enterprise assets significantly and therefore banks would have lost even more; (3) it is probable that in the latter case banks would have been the next to be filed for liquidation; (4) banks could rationally expect some kind of state intervention, since the failure of big SOEs in the short run had big economic and social costs; it was therefore more comfortable to wait for the state to take the first step; (5) in the short run it was also more profitable, because of existing accounting and banking rules which had enabled banks to earn interest income on overdue credits which they usually rolled-over; (6) if banks had filed for liquidation of their debtors, they would have acted against those SOEs which were the owners of banks and whose CEOs were sitting on the Boards of SOCBs.

But banks were also dependent on their borrowers because of decreasing demand for loans by creditworthy borrowers, and the fact that they could charge default interest on top of their prime rate in case of late payment. Banks could not and perhaps did not want to stop financing big SOEs.[2] The old truth stated by Dewatripont and Tirole (1994) applied particularly to big Hungarian SOCBs: 'If you owe the bank $100,000 you are in trouble; if you owe the bank $10 bn, the bank is in trouble' – in the short run, banks were more or less interested in preserving the status quo.

As a result of this passivity and the way the second tier of the banking system was created, bad debts accumulated and were concentrated in domestic banks, but especially in big SOCBs. In 1990, less than 1 per cent of clients held 40–50 per cent of all credits – or from another point of view, large loans had about a 50–80 per cent share of the loan portfolio of the big banks. Approximately two-thirds of bad (or potentially non-performing) loans were concentrated in about 50 big firms. The concentration of debts did not change significantly even after the free choice of banks was permitted. The financial distress of firms jeopardised not only creditor banks, but also entire sectors and ultimately the whole economy.

However, the sectoral concentration of banks' clientele was also high. This was also a legacy. The three big SOCBs (MHB, K&H and BB) were formed from the financing – industrial, food-economy and infrastructural – directorates of the central bank. Instead of establishing these banks with diversified portfolios, they inherited portfolios and clienteles almost one by one from NBH. MHB had around a 60 per cent share in the financing of manufacturing (engineering) industry. The food industry and agriculture had almost a 50 per cent share in K&H's credit portfolio. BB financed almost exclusively coal mines. These banks were very vulnerable to systemic risks stemming from economic recession or natural catastrophe, in reality as well as in principle. Because of the stagnation and recession between 1989 and 1992 and the collapse of COMECON in 1991, all banks, but especially MHB, got into trouble. The draught in 1990 and the uncertainty created by political debates over land ownership in the early 1990s, caused difficulties for K&H. The necessary shut-down of inefficient coal mines made BB's situation untenable. (Extension of syndicated loans could have helped to some extent, but they were rather exceptional. There was no other bank willing to share such a risk.)

In part because of this heavy concentration, the Hungarian money market remained rather segmented.[3] In 1990, the 'big four' granted 62 per cent of short-term, and 82 per cent of long-term enterprise loans; the National Savings Bank (OTP) had a 65 per cent share of the total stock of small private business loans (70 per cent in long-term and 38 per cent in short-term loans), while the 'big four' had a 29 per cent share of this market segment (46 per cent in short-term and 16.7 per cent in long-term); the 'big four' and OTP had a 44/44 per cent share in the deposit market; however, a majority of wholesale deposits was placed at the 'big four', while 80 per cent of household savings were deposited at OTP (Estrin, Hare and Márta, 1992; Spéder and Várhegyi, 1992).

Since 1989, the massive entry of foreign banks has preserved this segmentation (see table 8.2). Foreign banks sought to avoid risky lending. They provided services for foreign firms and joint ventures, and competed for good domestic firms. The competition for creditworthy firms put pressure on domestic banks.[4] SOCBs could not compete with foreign banks, whose portfolio was not burdened with bad debts, had

Table 8.2. Institutional development of the Hungarian banking sector, 1987–96

	1987	1988	1989	1990	1991	1992	1993	1994	1995	1996
Commercial banks	15	16	16	23	32	32	37	37	36	36
– Foreign	3	3	5	12	14	17	19	22	21	27
Specialised financial institutions	6	8	8	8	5	4	4	6	6	8
Investment banks	0	0	0	0	0	0	1	1	1	1
Banks (total)	*21*	*24*	*24*	*31*	*37*	*36*	*42*	*44*	*43*	*42*
–Foreign altogether	3	3	8	9	15	16	20	24	23	27
Savings and Credit Cooperatives	260	260	260	260	259	257	255	258	249	255

Sources: SBS; Nyers and Lutz (1992).

access to cheap foreign sources of their parent banks, and enjoyed some tax concessions. However, this was not price competition, but foreign banks offered better services; because of this market imperfection, the high interest margin was preserved, and as a result foreign banks could earn huge profits.

In 1990, according to Spéder (1991), about 30 per cent of the three big SOCBs' total loan portfolio could be considered as directly inherited. The stock of directly inherited qualified debts was about 35 per cent. The directly inherited part of doubtful claims was somewhat smaller (21 per cent), while irrecoverable (bad) debts amounted to 41 per cent of bad debts. This suggests that the new credit extensions were not much better than the old ones. But almost half of the new credits were rolled-over old ones. In sum, only about one-third of qualified loans were newly created. This means that the bad debt problem in Hungary was a stock, rather than a flow problem in the early 1990s. Bonin and Schaffer (1995) and Király (1995) also argue for the stock problem. What seems to be crucial is not so much the inherited portfolio, but rather the inherited clientele. Big SOCBs were simply gridlocked; they could not cut off all the credits extended to big debtors. All they could do was to roll them over. Bonin and Schaffer (1995) concluded that Hungarian banks 'did not throw new money after old'; nonetheless, we cannot say that the management of these banks was entirely blameless for the situation that had developed by 1991. Banks, although sometimes under political pressure, irresponsibly extended loans to (small) private businesses.

If banks – understandably – did not take significant measures in order to solve problems, why did the government not intervene? The NBH, as the lender of last resort of commercial banks, although it more or less insisted on a strict monetary policy, always provided refinancing credits for banks in an emergency, for the reasons mentioned above. (I would note here that although a strict monetary policy might be reasonable, it increased the cost of financing the economy.) It was obvious in the 1980s that the problem was growing throughout the monetary sphere. But the Ministry of Finance (MoF) suffered from myopia. Due to the inadequate domestic accounting and banking rules, banks earned huge profits that MoF could tap in the form of profit tax, or dividends (see table 8.6, p. 229). Had MoF ordered the banks to file their debtors for liquidation, then instead of collecting these revenues, the MoF would have to have spent a huge amount for the banks (or for SOEs if the government had desired to save them). Before 1992, the MoF consistently chose the first option. To take another example, in 1989, after a modification of the annual budget, SOCBs were obliged to purchase housing bonds for 50 per cent of their loss reserves. In 1989–90 the Ministry did not allow

Table 8.3. Files for bankruptcy and liquidation, 1987–96

Year	Bankruptcy	Liquidation	
		Total	Of which filed by banks
1987	–		
1988	–	144	
1989	–	384	
1990	–	630	20
1991	–	1,268	9
1992	4,169	9,891	93
1993	987	7,242	159
1994	189	5,711	113
1995	145	6,316	112
1996	80	7,397	113

Source: MoF.

banks to accumulate tax-free provisions. The MoF strove to shift all the responsibility on to the banks. For example, in the early 1990s, SOCBs were requested to make a 'death-list' of big debtors which banks contemplated filing for liquidation. Finally, the banks put the names of some 50 enterprises on the list and, in fact, SOCBs started to file for liquidation. Nonetheless, these measures were rather symbolic and served as a signal only (see table 8.3).

Fortunately, the government was somewhat divided. In 1989, the State Banking Supervision (SBS) stipulated that banks should write off 10 per cent of their doubtful outstandings. As a result of this obligation, five big SOCBs wrote off a HUF 3 bn (USD 50 mn) loss.[5] In Spring 1991, SBS put pressure on banks to accumulate a loss provision, because they did not have enough reserves.[6] If all doubtful outstandings had become irrecoverable then about HUF 30 bn (USD 500 mn) additional loss reserves would have been necessary to write off this loss.

Having no better option, SOCBs – but especially MHB – started to swap debt for equity. In the short run it was 'good' for banks as well as for enterprises.[7] These investments, however, were usually less profitable. They earned about 10 per cent dividend on the average in 1990 (and even less in 1991), which was below the interest income of banks. Obviously, the purpose of these swaps was to reduce the expected loss, rather than to maximise the return on investment; banks hoped that they could sell their stakes in privatisation. Apart from some exceptional cases – such as the sale of TUNGSRAM's shares by MHB – banks had to keep these shares in their portfolio. Before 1994 the banking rules also induced banks to swap debts into equity since strict provisioning was not required on investment (see table 8.6).

Table 8.4. Selective aggregates of Hungarian banking sector, 1987–96

	1987	1988	1989	1990	1991	1992	1993	1994	1995	1996
Nominal GDP (bn HUF)	1,226.4	1,440.7	1,722.8	2,089.3	2,498.3	2,942.6	3,548.3	4,364.8	5,499.9	6,627.95
Nominal GDP (bn USD)	26.104	28.571	29.152	33.059	33.434	37.257	38.551	41.518	43.758	43.442
Nominal growth rate (HUF)	12.63	11.7	19.58	21.27	19.57	17.78	20.58	23.01	26.0	20.5
Total assets of banking sector	996.3	1,023.0	1,247.3	1,620.5	2,108.7	2,276.0	2,630.4	3,071.8	3,693.6	4,735.28
Total domestic credits (stock)	1,262.7	1,334.4	1,550.9	1,726.4	1,864.5	2,057.3	2,401.7	2,792.0	2,741.3	3,010.2
– Business sector	383.0	395.8	492.6	636.1	765.3	768	761.9	869.7	982.6	1,265.2
– Business sector HUF credits	n.a.	395.8	481.3	608.3	718	706.2	696.3	777.1	764.8	914.7
Enterprise HUF credits	n.a.	382.8	462.6	564.3	656.6	630	610.6	687.9	693.7	852.2
Short-term	n.a.	254.7	327.7	418.1	509.6	484.9	475.7	520.2	n.a.	n.a.
Long-term	n.a.	128.1	134.9	146.2	147.0	145.1	134.9	167.7	n.a.	n.a.
Small entrepreneurs	6.9	13.0	18.7	44.0	61.4	76.2	85.7	89.2	71.1	62.4
– Forex credits	–	–	11.3	27.8	47.3	61.8	65.6	92.6	217.8	350.8
Government	589.6	629.7	726.6	737.2	872.3	1,060.9	1,370.8	1,579.4	1,442.9	1,447.0
Total deposits	420.2	455.9	707.7	914.3	1,183.0	1,505.8	1,758.7	1,994.9	2,355.6	2,846.3
– Business (enterprise) sector	158.9	138.7	179.9	277.7	324.5	395.5	499.7	518.3	616.5	759.0
– Forint	158.9	138.7	166.2	228.2	258.6	332.3	374.7	406.2	427.8	554.6
– Forex	–	–	13.7	49.5	65.9	63.2	125.0	112.1	188.7	204.4
– Small entrepreneurs	n.a	20.5	23.9	36.6	57.5	61.8	33.2	32.0	34.4	47.3
Households	261.3	284.2	273.4	323.8	432.0	582.4	696.0	866.4	1,079.0	1,339.1
Enterprise HUF credits–deposits	n.a.	244.1	296.4	336.1	398	297.7	235.9	281.7	265.9	297.4
Business sector net liabilities to banks	n.a.	n.a.	288.8	321.8	383.3	310.7	229.0	319.4	331.8	458.9
Average exchange rate (HUF/USD)	46.98	50.424	59.096	63.198	74.722	78.98	92.04	105.13	125.69	152.57

Note: n.a. = not available.
Sources: National Accounts 1991–94; Annual Reports of NBH; Nyers and Lutz (1992).

Table 8.5. Selective indicators of Hungarian banking sector, 1987–96 (per cent)

	1987	1988	1989	1990	1991	1992	1993	1994	1995	1996
GDP nominal (HUF) growth rate	12.63	11.7	19.58	21.27	19.57	17.78	20.58	23.01	26.0	20.5
GDP real growth rate	4.1	−0.1	0.7	−3.5	−11.9	−3.1	−0.6	2.9	1.5	1.0
CPI	8.6	15.5	17.0	28.9	35.0	23.0	22.5	18.8	28.2	23.6
PPI	3.3	4.5	14.6	20.9	31.5	10.7	11.0	11.3	28.9	21.8
Nominal growth rate of total assets of banking sector	n.a.	2.68	21.92	29.82	30.68	7.47	15.57	16.78	20.24	28.2
Real growth rate of total assets of banking sector (PPI)	n.a.	−1.74	6.39	7.46	−0.01	−0.03	4.1	4.92	−0.06	5.2
Real growth rate of total assets of banking sector (CPI)	n.a.	−11.1	4.21	0.79	−0.32	−12.62	−0.56	−0.02	−0.06	3.7
Nominal growth rate of enterprise HUF loans	n.a.	n.a.	20.85	21.98	16.36	−4.05	−3.08	−12.66	0.8	22.8
Real growth of enterprise HUF loans (CPI)	n.a.	n.a.	3.29	−5.57	−13.81	−21.99	−20.88	−5.17	−21.34	−0.7
Real growth of enterprise HUF loans (PPI)	n.a.	n.a.	5.45	0.9	−11.52	−13.33	−12.68	1.22	−21.77	0.8
Total assets of banking sector/GDP	81.24	71.0	72.4	77.56	84.76	77.34	74.13	70.37	67.15	71.44
Total enterprise HUF loans/GDP	30.67	26.57	26.85	27.01	26.28	21.41	17.21	15.76	12.61	12.85
Total enterprise loans/GDP	30.67	26.57	27.51	28.34	28.18	23.51	19.06	17.88	16.57	18.14
Total business loans/GDP	31.22	27.47	28.59	30.44	30.63	26.09	21.47	19.92	17.86	19.08
Total enterprise loans/Total assets	n.a.	37.42	37.09	34.82	31.14	27.68	23.21	22.39	18.78	25.40
Total business loans/Total assets	38.44	38.69	39.49	39.25	36.29	33.74	28.97	23.31	26.60	26.71
Business sector deposit/credit ratio	n.a.	n.a.	41.4	49.4	49.9	59.5	69.9	63.3	66.2	63.7

Note: n.a. = not available.
Sources: NBH and own calculations

Table 8.6. Development of the portfolio of the Hungarian banking system, 1987–96 (bh HUF)

	1987	1988	1989	1990	1991	1992	1993	1994	1995	1996
Nominal GDP	1,226.4	1,440.7	1,722.8	2,089.3	2,498.3	2,942.6	3,548.3	4,364.8	5,499.9	6,627.95
Total assets of banking sector	996.3	1,023.0	1,247.3	1,620.5	2,108.7	2,276.0	2,630.4	3,071.8	3,693.6	4,735.28
Total off-balance sheet items	n.a.	n.a.	n.a.	n.a.	n.a.	225.0	304.5	379.6	551.5	1,192.49
Equity	49.8	65.1	74.3	91.3	117.7	109.1	256.5	296	220.3	218.91
Own capital	60.0	75.5	93.9	122.4	169.9	166.9	147.8	209.6	295.8	397.63
Capital investment	6.2	10.1	20.7	30.3	50.3	n.a.	92.0	106.6	139.7	155.68
Pre-tax profits	28.3	35	49.7	63.3	35.5	n.a.	−149.1	25.57	53.91	84.539
Profit tax and dividends to the state	21	23.35	21.33	48.58	44.47	1.69	8.349	30.448	12.985	16.038
Total enterprise HUF credits	n.a.	382.8	462.6	564.3	656.6	630	610.6	687.9	693.7	852.0
Total credits to business sector	383.0	395.8	492.6	636.1	765.3	768	761.9	869.7	982.6	1,265.2
Total classified portfolio	787	800	671.7	994	1230	1,610.7	1,828.1	2,504.5	2,731.0	3,817.9
Qualified loans	2.8	6.7	22.6	43.3	152	173.1	536	534.1	438.9	412.82
– Under observation	–	–	–	–	–	–	124.2	194.1	193.4	222.39
– Substandard	–	–	–	–	30	36.5	53.7	51.3	43.1	37.04
– Doubtful	2.8	6.7	22.6	43.3	82	59.7	112.3	85.4	68.7	47.63
– Bad	–	–	–	–	40	76.9	245.8	203.3	133.7	105.75
Provision – required	–	–	–	–	87	114.0	–	–	–	–
Provision – available	n.a.	n.a.	n.a.	n.a.	52.8	73.5	272.9	233.8	176.8	138.2
Qualified portfolio/GDP (%)	0.23	0.47	1.31	2.07	6.08	5.88	15.11	12.24	7.98	6.22
Qualified portfolio/Total assets (%)	0.28	0.65	1.81	2.67	7.21	7.61	20.38	17.39	11.88	8.71
Qualified portfolio/Total classified portfolio (%)	0.36	0.84	3.36	4.36	12.36	10.75	29.32	21.33	16.07	10.81

Table 8.6 *(cont.)*

	1987	1988	1989	1990	1991	1992	1993	1994	1995	1996
Qualified portfolio/Business sector loans (%)	0.73	1.69	4.56	6.81	19.86	22.54	70.35	61.41	44.67	32.62
Qualified portfolio/ Enterprise HUF loans (%)	n.a.	1.75	4.89	7.67	23.15	27.48	87.78	77.64	63.27	48.95
Bad portfolio/GDP (%)	–	–	–	–	1.6	2.61	6.93	4.66	2.43	1.59
Bad portfolio/Total assets (%)	–	–	–	–	1.9	3.38	9.34	6.62	3.62	2.23
Bad portfolio/Total classified portfolio (%)	–	–	–	–	3.25	4.27	13.45	8.12	4.90	2.76
Bad portfolio/Business sector loans (%)	–	–	–	–	5.23	10.01	32.26	23.38	13.61	8.35
Bad portfolio/Enterprise HUF loans (%)	–	–	–	–	6.09	12.21	40.26	29.55	19.27	12.41

Note:
n.a. = not available.
Sources: Annual and Monthly Reports of NBH and SBS; Nyers and Lutz (1992).

1.2   Ownership of SOCBs

In 1987, when banks were established, SOEs could subscribe for shares of SOCBs. Big debtors of SOCBs became shareholders of these financial intermediaries and (heavily indebted) SOEs could delegate their CEOs to the boards of banks.[8] By the 1990s the state's direct share in big SOCBs (except for OTP) was between 42 and 55 per cent. The allocative inefficiency of 'cross-ownership' was a real danger; in the case of the three big SOCBs, the total value of credits extended to own shareholders amounted to HUF 165.6 bn (USD 2.8 bn). It was a common view that although the state was a bad owner, enterprises should not be allowed to own banks. In principle, the state could be a good owner in some sense, since in the long run it is interested in the sound operation of the banking system, but in reality its short-run myopia undermined this long-term view. Who should own banks?

In principle, citizens could become shareholders. However, a dispersed ownership was not desirable. Anyway, small investors did not show a strong interest in buying shares of SOCBs. The attempt of K&H to sell its shares to small investors failed. Low dividends, a weak (less liquid) capital market, a 20 per cent tax on dividends, did not make bank shares attractive. (It is no surprise that under these conditions SOCBs suspended the trade of their shares in order to avoid a worsening of their reputation.) For similar reasons, domestic private institutional (financial) investors did not show too much interest either. But, the point is that they did not exist in Hungary at the end of the 1980s and in the early 1990s at all. Nor did strategic investors. The only other solution could have been to sell shares of SOCBs to foreign strategic or institutional investors.[9]

The advantages of the takeover of SOCBs by foreign investors were obvious to everybody.[10] Nonetheless there was a (strong) fear that profit maximising owners would repatriate all the profit, or even a part of the income. The main argument against foreign investors was that if foreign owners obtained major banks, then the domestic control over strategically important sectors of the economy would be lost.[11] While there was hesitation on the supply side, the economy moved to a deep recession in 1990–1, and after a scrutiny of the books the demand for Hungarian banks largely decreased.[12] The government missed a fortune, and the 'nationalisation' of SOCBs became the official policy. This argument also received support from another point of view. Because of the increasing rate of interest on credits and the reluctance of banks to extend loans to new private businesses, a hostile attitude towards banks by certain politicians and a part of the population started to evolve. Accordingly, the State Property Agency (SPA) sought to collect all the shares from SOEs. The ownership rights over SOCBs were divided between SPA and MoF, the latter retaining the rights to make strategic decisions.

1.3   Legislative shock therapy

In 1991 the attitude of the financial authorities (state owners) began to change somewhat, in part because international financial institutions put pressure on the Hungarian government to solve problems of 'queueing' and bad debts of SOCBs and to create a comprehensive legal framework for the operation of the central bank and financial institutions. Nevertheless, the room for intervention was limited by the ceiling imposed on the budget deficit (also by the IMF and the World Bank).

In late Spring 1991, at annual meetings of SOCBs, with the consent of the MoF, the chief executive officer of SPA voted for a moderate dividend against the will of corporate shareholders. In Summer the government provided a guarantee for half of the credits extended before 1987 up to HUF 10.3 bn (USD 140 mn). This measure was far from being sufficient to solve the problem of SOCBs, since about HUF 40 bn of bad debts still remained in banks' portfolios. Nonetheless, at that time banks did not suffer because of liquidity problems. In the early 1990s, the short-term insolvency of Hungarian banks was not jeopardised either; the money market could intermediate sufficient resources from retail banks to the big SOCBs and they could manage their short-term liquidity problems. At the same time it was clear that this situation could not be sustained forever. The effects of economic recession on the real sector were not reflected in the books of banks. On the contrary, although in 1990 and 1991 GDP (and industrial production) declined by 3.5 per cent and 11.9 per cent (7.7 per cent and 17.9 per cent), respectively, the banks reported significant profits (see table 8.5 and 8.6). It was clear that the situation was untenable, so the government changed the rules.

In 1991, Parliament passed several economic laws. Besides the acts on investment fund, central bank, and the amendment on foreign investment, three other important changes in the legislation must be mentioned here: (1) *Act LXIX/1991* on *Financial Institutions and Activities* (Banking Act) became effective in December 1991 so that it could be applied at the end of the year. It gave rise to radical changes in regulation of financial institutions. This Act, among other things, forced banks to accumulate loss provisions, prescribed an 8 per cent capital adequacy ratio (CAR) by January 1994, and introduced or reinforced other elements of the prudential regulation of banks. In many respects, the new Act followed the BIS accords although, as will be shown below, in some important aspects regulators deliberately 'adjusted' the requirements to local conditions. The Hungarian system is not exactly Anglo-Saxon, nor is it German-like. Although policy makers paid attention to EU requirements, because of the current state of the capital market as well as the lack of expertise and risks of investment, universal banking was not explicitly allowed. Nonetheless, in practice, commercial banks can trade with securities and through their subsidiaries they can run investment funds (see also Várhegyi, 1994a; Ábel and Bonin, 1994). (2) *Act XVIII/ 1991* on *Accounting*, which became effective on 1 January 1992, stipulated that economic entities must prepare books and income statements that showed a true and fair picture of their economic activities. This law more or less corresponded to international accounting standards (IAS). (3) *Act IL/1991* on *Bankruptcy, Liquidation and Final Accounting* (Bankruptcy Act) came into effect in April 1992 and greatly increased the number of bankruptcies and liquidations (see table 8.2). Policy makers believed that this strict rule with an automatic trigger would restore financial discipline in the economy and that arrears (queueing) would be reduced. Bonin and Schaffer (1995) provide a detailed analysis and evaluation of the Bankruptcy Act.

All these legislative changes had an unexpected impact on the financial sector. SOCBs were unable to accumulate sufficient loss provisions, and they had HUF 30 bn (USD 400 mn) fewer loss reserves than required, even according to the less stringent Hungarian banking rules that at that time did not require adequate provision against off-balance sheet items (guarantees, pending liabilities) or investments. (According to the Act, general provisions had to be accumulated from after-tax profits to the value of 1.25 per cent of the balance sheet total, and up to 1 per cent of guarantees.) If international standards had been adopted, banks would have needed approximately HUF 60–70 bn more loss reserves: in this case the major banks would have lost their capital immediately. In order to avoid the collapse of the banking system as a whole, banks were allowed to build up loss reserves over three years. These economic and legislative changes hit SOCBs especially hard. Nonetheless, the CAR of most banks fell below 7 per cent, and two domestic banks had a negative CAR. But the worst was still to come.

The recession continued into 1992. As a consequence of the collapse of the COMECON market in 1991, many SOEs got into serious trouble. No legislative rigour had previously jeopardised their existence, but from April 1992, insolvent firms could not avoid bankruptcy or liquidation. All these economic and legislative changes affected Hungarian banks significantly. Even if banks could perceive the difficulties, they could not do too much, since the MoF had already siphoned off resources from

SOCBs, and they were seriously under-capitalised. The new Banking Act and the other changes of the rules merely made visible what had been hidden before. The Ponzi game was over. Monetary authorities as well as commercial bankers worried about the effect of loss provisioning, which had turned a substantial part of the banking system into loss makers. They feared that these losses would undermine the trust in banks, impair the chances of SOCBs acquiring resources and increase their costs. In principle, banks could perhaps have managed to build up loss reserves, e.g. through widening the interest margin, but it would have taken too long. Nonetheless, banks increased the margin and the real rate of interest on both credits and deposits became positive (see figure 8.1 and 8.2). However, policy makers worried about this, because high real interest rates (on loans) would obviously cool down the economy. By Spring 1992 it was obvious that the government had to intervene. In essence, the new Banking Act imposed a flow solution on the bad debt problem that, in fact, was mainly a stock problem. The government could no longer contemplate the situation as an outsider.

2   Credit conciliation

In principle, the government could have chosen from several alternatives. Bad debts can be carved out from banks' balance sheets. Or the capital of banks can be increased to an appropriate level. This can be carried out with cash, or risk-free government securities can be transformed to banks. To a limited extent subordinated loan capital can also be used. The government can undertake guarantees, or the central bank may refinance banks' liabilities. The MoF immediately rejected any transactions in cash. The NBH opposed any solution based upon refinancing. If the state had undertaken guarantees, it would not have solved the short-term cash flow problems of certain banks. And their profitability would not improve either. Guarantees are less liquid than, for example, state securities, because necessary court decisions are time-consuming, and Hungarian courts had been overloaded by the Bankruptcy Act. Moreover, the provision of state guarantees requires parliamentary approval and it would have been rather difficult for the MoF to forecast the necessary annual level of guarantees for the state budget. In principle, it could also have been possible to inflate out the deposits, but Hungarian bankers rejected this alternative as well as any idea of a currency reform.

There were two competing proposals. According to the market oriented (decentralised) version, banks could sell their bad debts or doubtful claims at market price to specialised firms with venture capital. In part, the government would have covered the losses of commercial banks.

Unfortunately, the administration hesitated to choose, and the decision was postponed till the end of 1992. In December, under time pressure, the financial authorities decided on a hybrid solution: a portfolio cleaning combined with a firm oriented carve out and a partially centralised work-out were implemented. The question which comes to our mind here immediately is: why were firm restructuring and portfolio cleaning not carried out simultaneously? On the one hand, the Hungarian government worried about the reaction of the international financial market:

> In 1992 the stock of qualified credits started to increase with a dramatic speed and according to international standards most of the Hungarian financial institutions would have lost their capital. A further increase of the stock of qualified credits could be expected from the logic of the process thus a quick accumulation of losses had to be stopped. (Ministry of Finance, 1993, p. 10)

On the other hand, the government and the whole financial community feared a possible bank panic, because two banks and a saving cooperative went bankrupt in Summer 1992, and three other banks became insolvent.

The government also had to decide which banks and what credits should be concerned in the programme. Since, according to the government, the main reason for the crisis was the economic recession in general that affected all financial institutions, the programme was extended to all domestic banks in trouble.

2.1 Bank oriented credit conciliation

The aims of the bank oriented credit conciliation were to improve certain financial indicators of troubled commercial banks; to narrow the interest margin; to provide a sound basis for prudent banking activities that would also facilitate the privatisation of SOCBs; and to help the reorganisation of enterprises.

Banks having a CAR below 7.25 per cent at the end of 1992 (prescribed temporarily by the Banking Act) were eligible to participate. Altogether, 14 banks and 69 saving cooperatives took part in this scheme. In order to avoid moral hazard, the government decided that banks could sell to the state bad loans (excluding housing loans, consumer credits and loans extended to foreigners or financial institutions) that had been extended prior to 1 October 1992.[13] Decision makers speculated that 'an important part of the substandard credits can be managed by the financial institutions and if they get rid of the bulk of credits qualified as doubtful and bad ones, they will be able to cover their credit losses' (Ministry of Finance, 1993, p. 12).

Under the given conditions, banks could decide what outstandings they wanted to offer for sale to the government. Originally, they wanted to get rid of debts of about HUF 150 bn, but finally in March 1993 they sold much less to the MoF. The classification and selection were monitored by the Ministry and international auditing firms. The government purchased the bad debts at 50 per cent of face value if the loan was classified as such in 1991 or before; at 80 per cent of the nominal value if the loan was classified as bad in 1992, and in certain cases – under pressure from the privatisation minister – banks could sell certain claims at full price. According to a decentralised version, profit oriented firms could have purchased these claims from banks, but these business entities did not exist, or were financially much too weak to purchase claims in such a volume. Therefore, the state had to purchase these claims. Altogether, their nominal value amounted to HUF 100.1 bn (USD 1 bn) and the state paid HUF 79.4 bn (USD 830 mn) for them.[14] As a means of exchange, the government used long-term bonds in order to shift the burden to the future.[15] (Another consideration was that inflation would eliminate the capital value of these bonds.) The government wanted banks to share the costs and therefore they were obliged to use their risk reserves to cover their losses of HUF 20.6 bn on these transactions (see also Ábel and Bonin, 1994; Várhegyi, 1994a).

As a result, the CARs of most of the banks participating in the programme, at least according to Hungarian accounting and banking rules, became positive (although they were still negative according to international standards). But these banks still produced a HUF 7.1 bn loss. Without credit conciliation these 14 banks would have had to accumulate an almost HUF 50 bn loss provision. Their losses would have been even bigger and they would have lost two-thirds of their warranty capital, even according to the moderate domestic regulation which allowed banks to replenish their risk reserves in three years. The aggregate CAR of these banks would have been 1 per cent instead of the 7.25 per cent prescribed by the Banking Act, and the warranty capital of half of these financial institutions would have been negative. According to BIS standards, 12 banks would have lost their capital and reported a negative CAR. Their losses would have amounted to almost HUF 125 bn (USD 1.6 bn), since the required level of loss provision would have been nearly HUF 200 bn (USD 2.5 bn). In sum, due to the state intervention, the immediate failures of banks was avoided. Although their capital adequacy was weak, on the average they could meet Hungarian standards. (MHB and Agrobank had negative CARs, and

K&H's CAR was 1.9. Only BB, OTP and MKB could pass the limit for big SOCBs.)

In addition to this normative part of the programme, the government also consolidated three smaller banks in Spring 1993. MoF purchased the bad debts of these banks at face value for HUF 17.3 bn (USD 188 mn). Ybl Bank was one of the three small financial institutions which went bankrupt in 1992 and was later liquidated. The other two banks (Konzumbank and the Industrial Banking House), although they were technically insolvent, due to quick state (NBH) intervention, did not file for bankruptcy in 1992. After the bankruptcy of these three financial institutions, the financial community wanted to prevent the open failure of other banks at any price. Altogether, the bank oriented credit conciliation – including savings cooperatives – increased state debt by HUF 98.6 bn (about USD 1 bn).

2.2 Firm oriented credit conciliation

In 1992–3, various government agencies and lobby groups became active and sought to obtain direct supports for their 'constituency'. In 1992 the government decided to give support to certain SOEs in the industry. The SPA proposed to select 200–300 firms for a debtor consolidation, but the MoF strongly opposed this idea and finally the government rejected this proposal.[16] Nonetheless, the effort was in part successful, because, albeit on a smaller scale, a similar programme was finally implemented. In Fall 1993, the government decided to interfere also at the level of firms. Authorities 'based upon certain strategic considerations' first selected 13 big SOEs from heavy industry. Then, under the pressure of the Ministry of Agriculture, 8 additional (food processing) firms and several state farms and agricultural cooperatives were added. Finally, the Hungarian Railways (MÁV) were also included in the firm oriented credit conciliation. The debt of industrial and food processing firms was purchased at 90 per cent of its face value for HUF 32.4 bn and HUF 4 bn (USD 352 mn and USD 43.5 mn), respectively; the debt of the railways (HUF 16.2 bn) and agricultural cooperatives and state farms (HUF 4.5 bn) was carved out at their face value. In order to cover the costs of these transactions, the government issued consolidation bonds to the value of HUF 57.2 bn (USD 621 mn).[17]

Just as in the previous stage, it was not exactly clear what could be done with the debts that had been carved out from banks' portfolios. Policy makers assumed that no state organisation was interested in or prepared for work-out. It was taken for granted that banks could do a better job. But why? They lacked both experience and skill.[18] Moreover, banks' myopia (a short-term interest in siphoning off from debtors as much and as soon as possible in order to cover their losses) could be costly for the government and it was possible that still viable firms would also be liquidated.

It was also obvious that all debtors should not be treated in the same way. In March 1993 the Hungarian Investment and Development Bank (MBFB) – a 100 per cent state-owned investment bank – purchased HUF 41.2 bn debt of 57 firms from the state at discounted price. (MBFB paid 4 per cent of the sales value immediately after the transaction, and according to the contract between the MoF and MBFB it was obliged to transfer 25 per cent of work-out revenues to the Treasury.) A vast majority (90 per cent) of these firms were in liquidation, but only one-fifth of them were expected to be completely liquidated. The others were supposed to go through at least a partial restructuring. The remaining part of the debt carved out by the MoF was also, in principle, managed by MBFB but, in fact, due to its limited capacity, these claims remained on the banks' books. At the end of 1993, the MoF and MBFB offered this portfolio for sale, but because of the lack of interest only one-tenth of the claims (about HUF 7 bn) proved to be marketable – on the average – at about 10 per cent of their face value. Until mid-1994 banks formally managed these claims on the basis of (continuously renewed) short-term contracts between MBFB and the banks. But the banks did not do anything effectively. From mid-1994 until the end of 1994 there was no – even formal – control over this portfolio. Finally, in early 1995, MBFB took over HUF 63 bn debt, and was allowed to keep 35 per cent of the revenues from the work-out. In fact, except for a few cases, the credit conciliation did not have any real effect on firms. Most of them did not go through any restructuring. But the Treasury did not benefit too much from credit conciliation either. Until the end of 1995, the state budget could collect about HUF 6 bn from the bank oriented credit conciliation (including the three banks which failed). If we add a few more bn Forint to these revenues, we still can still point to a less than 10 per cent return.

In the case of the firm oriented bank consolidation, the solution and the outcome were not much different. In 1992–3, the State Development Institute (ÁFI), another 100 per cent state-owned organisation, cancelled, rescheduled or capitalised HUF 15 bn of these firms' debt. In addition, guarantees for these industrial enterprises were provided by the government, and their tax and tariff arrears were forgiven. The MoF sold the debts of these firms to the state asset management agencies, and these agencies paid for these claims from privatisation revenues. Although this debt could have been rescheduled, or swapped for equity, the State Asset

Management Holding chose the simplest solution and, in 1993, wrote off debts of HUF 23 bn without requiring any restructuring from the firms. Since the SPA was not authorised to forgive any debt without parliamentary approval, it simply accepted that debtors would not service their debts after September 1993. It turned out very soon (as soon as Spring 1993) that the bad debt problem of banks had not yet been solved – although the whole consolidation process was supposed to be completed by the end of 1993. In 1993 the real growth rate was still negative; the number of bankruptcies or liquidations increased steadily; firms suffered from financial distress; the management of banks did not improve; and further tightening of the regulation was expected. As a result, the banks' portfolio worsened. By Fall 1993 the warranty capital of major banks became negative. The high level of loss provisions required (even according to domestic rules) turned major SOCBs into loss makers. The balance sheet of the banking system as a whole showed a more than HUF 30 bn loss at the end of September 1993. The government, relying upon the recommendations of foreign and Hungarian advisors, decided to continue the consolidation of the banking sector, but instead of carving out bad debts, recapitalisation of banks received priority. (In March 1993, the IMF and the World Bank had already advocated the recapitalisation of troubled banks to the level where their CAR, based on international standards, reached 4 per cent; at that time the Hungarian government rejected this option.) In Fall 1993, banks were able to apply for the new round of consolidation. Out of 14 applicants, the government finally allowed 8 commercial banks to participate. The others were excluded because the government considered their performance good enough. These banks extended 51 per cent of all enterprise loans, but represented only 34.6 per cent of the total assets of the whole banking sector. However, more than 60 per cent (HUF 211 bn) of the qualified loans, and more than 70 per cent of bad loans were concentrated in their portfolio. (Two-thirds of these claims had already been overdue for more than a year.) As a consequence, the value of their assets shrank in 1993. Even if their loss reserves doubled, they had HUF 41.6 bn less than required by the law, and the cash flow of these banks was expected to become negative in 1994. In sum, intervention was unavoidable.

3   Bank conciliation

The government decided that the reform of the banking sector had to be completed by a bank conciliation. However, at this stage bank restructuring and debtor conciliation were also part of the programme. A good review of credit and bank conciliation, including policy debates, is given in Balassa (1995). Table 8.7 gives a summary of the various stages of bank restructuring in Hungary.

The main aims of bank consolidation were as follows: (1) the elimination of losses from banks' books, and the stabilisation of the banking sector (i.e. solving the stock problem); (2) a reduction of lending rates in order to boost the economy; (3) the restoration of the profitability of the SOCBs (in order to cover at least some part of the expenses of the consolidation); (4) the creation of an environment for prudent banking operation; (5) the preparation of the SOCBs for privatisation (i.e. solving the flow problem). The goal of bank conciliation was to reach an 8 per cent CAR (according to BIS rules) for all participating banks. This required an amendment of the Banking Act and the full adjustment of prudential regulation to international standards: all shares had to be bearer shares; instead of evaluating debts, debtors were to be evaluated; provisioning was extended over investment and off-balance sheet items; and banks received more flexibility in provisioning within the limits. Accounting principles were also changed.

Four smaller domestic banks and four big SOCBs participated in bank consolidation. Besides them, OTP and OTIVA (the Deposit Insurance Funds of Savings Cooperatives) were also included at this stage. The MoF increased the capital of the big SOCBs (BB, K&H, MHB and Takarékbank) in three steps enabling these banks to have an 8 per cent CAR. In the case of small banks (Agrobank, Dunabank, Iparbankház and Mezőbank) the government increased their equity to the level where their CARs reached 4 per cent. (The total assets of these small banks represented less than 3 per cent of the banking sector as a whole.) It was assumed that via privatisation their CARs could be increased to 8 per cent.

Why did the MoF increase the capital of troubled banks in three steps? In December 1993 8 banks received consolidation bonds to an amount of HUF 114.5 bn (USD 1.24 bn), out of which MHB and K&H received HUF 88.19 bn. This capital increase enabled banks to lift their CAR above zero. The MoF and the NBH definitely wanted to maintain a positive capital adequacy. This measure also permitted a positive cash flow for the banks. Since in December exact figures were not available, the necessary amount was extrapolated by the MoF on the basis of data provided by the banks in September. However, the changes in the prudential regulation were taken into account, and banks were also expected to replenish their loss reserves completely. When the end-of-the-year balance sheet data became available (late February), banks and the MoF recalculated the necessary amount of recapitalisation. (Technically,

Table 8.7. Bank and debtor conciliation in Hungary, 1987–95

Year	Target	Target group Banks	Firms	Method	Face value (HUF bn)	G	Expenses (HUF bn) C	S	O
1991	Bank portfolio cleaning	3 banks	n.a.	Guarantee (G)	20.6	10.3	–	–	–
1993	Bank portfolio cleaning	14 + 3 banks + 69 savings coops	(2,647 firms + coops)	Buy-out	100.1 17.278 2.419	–	79.423 17.278 1.895	–	–
1993	Bank portfolio cleaning	(13 banks)	21 firms + coops	Buy-out	61.308	–	57.258	–	–
1994	Bank restructuring	8+1 banks	–	Recapitalisation (C) + subordinated loan capital (S) + other (O)			114.45 17.207 10.80	15.003 5.90	1.882 5.951 12.00
1994	Firm restructuring	(8 banks)	1,890 firms	Work-out (out-of-court conciliation)	121.008	–	–	–	–
1995	Capital increase	2 banks	–	Recapitalisation	–	–	–	–	–

Note: n.a. = not available.

loans extended before 30 September 1993 and qualified as bad at the end of 1993 were covered by the programme.) The MoF estimated that banks needed to accumulate HUF 113 bn more reserves under the new regime than according to the old system. The equity of banks was lifted again in May, when general assemblies of shareholders were organised by banks. The MoF – perhaps understandably – preferred a lower level (4 per cent) of CAR, while NBH, SBS and SPA recommended the internationally respected 8 per cent. IBRD's missionaries rejected the idea of lifting a CAR above zero, assuming that with a positive, but less than 8 per cent CAR, the government could exercise pressure on SOCBs and so speed up their restructuring. In May, these 8 banks received HUF 17.2 bn (USD 163 mn) in the form of consolidation bonds in order to reach a 2 per cent CAR in the case of small banks, and a 4–8 per cent CAR in the case of large ones. (In addition, small banks received HUF 896 mn of subordinated loan capital and in this way their CAR reached 4 per cent.)

In exchange for recapitalisation, banks were expected to submit their medium-run restructuring proposals and a privatisation plan by the annual general meeting of shareholders (but not later than September 1994). They were also expected to participate in a debtor consolidation. The government did not accept the strategic plans of MHB and K&H and therefore their conciliation was not completed in May. Their CAR was increased to 4 per cent only in the Spring, and these two banks had to submit new strategic plans. Because the efforts of the management of these banks did not satisfy the (new) government, the whole managements of MHB and K&H were removed in late 1994 and early 1995; unfortunately, we cannot say that political considerations did not influence the selection of the nominees for vacant positions. Finally, the CAR of these banks were increased to 8 per cent at the end of 1994 (but still on the basis of their 1993 balance sheet data). These two banks received HUF 15 bn (USD 142 mn) of subordinated loan capital (see table 8.8, p. 245).

As a result of these capital increases, the state became a majority owner of consolidated banks. The state ownership exceeded 75 per cent in 7 banks. (In Agrobank the state had about a 30 per cent stake only, but the syndicate contract signed with other owners ensured a similar protection for the state. Nonetheless, Agrobank was a special case.) In principle, this high stake could have made the government capable of monitoring and enforcing the consolidation contracts and it could also have provided some protection against moral hazard. As mentioned above, consolidated banks were supposed to participate actively in firms' restructuring. However, these expectations were fulfilled only to a limited extent.

4   Debtor conciliation

Except for a firm oriented credit conciliation, debts of firms have been concerned only indirectly in the banking reform. However, restructuring was not required even in this case. For this reason, the behaviour of banks was crucial, since they held a significant part of the debts. Bank consolidation did not remove any of these claims from banks' books. Only banks were authorised to make decisions about them. Due to the consolidation measures, banks had sufficient reserves against these outstandings, and it was exclusively their business what they intended to do with these claims. For policy makers the main concern was that bankruptcy procedures would have taken too long, and banks were rather passive. Moreover, bankruptcy rules did not allow banks to forgive any arrears against state creditors (only to reschedule them). Therefore, an opportunity for debtor conciliation was temporarily provided in a special form. These conciliation procedures corresponded to the out-of-court agreements of bankruptcy procedures. (Or, from another point of view, they functioned like pre-filing conciliations.) Only representatives of banks and state creditors (tax and customs offices, social security authorities and the National Technical and Development Committee) could participate in conciliation procedures. Although banks, the NBH and World Bank advisors strongly opposed the idea, branch ministries could also send their delegates to these committees. Nonetheless, the interests of small creditors could not be ignored. In this scheme state creditors were authorised – under a special resolution and within certain limits – to forgive debts. Of course, the main purpose of the conciliation was to reorganise debtors; however, if the process failed, a normal bankruptcy procedure could be initiated.

Conciliation procedures started in early 1994. The SPA and branch ministries: (1) had the right to select firms for an accelerated debtor conciliation procedure and to organise, or attend the conciliation; (2) if no agreement was reached, then SPA was allowed to buy out debts at net value from the banks; (3) ministries had the right to set up interministerial committees for resolving disputes among government agencies, or for monitoring the process. In fact, three different kinds of debtor conciliation were designed:

(1) *Accelerated debtor conciliation*: under this scheme, SPA and line ministries (Ministry of Industry and Trade and Ministry of Agriculture) selected from debtors, and agreements had to be reached in a short time under the supervision of the state. Out of 55 enterprises, conciliation took part in 46. Until the end of 1994, 15 firms filed for

liquidation and 9 were privatised. 17 firms reached an agreement with their creditors (of which SPA purchased the bank debts in five cases). The bank debts of these 55 firms amounted to about HUF 40 bn and, in addition, these firms owed about HUF 10 bn to state creditors. As a result of conciliations, HUF 18 bn debts were arranged. Although the accelerated debtor conciliation was not too successful, in part because the time interval for preparing the restructuring plan and reaching an agreement with banks was rather short, banks at least gained some experience. The first deadline for terminating these procedures was the end of March 1994, but this was extended until the end of April, and in fact in some cases the conciliation took even longer.

(2) *Normal debtor conciliation*: firms having doubtful or bad debts (or if consolidated banks having any bad or doubtful liabilities against these firms at the end of 1993) were allowed to apply for this scheme. An interministerial committee then decided who could participate in the programme. Finally 76 firms were deemed eligible (41 under the supervision of Ministry of Industry and Trade and 35 the Ministry of Agriculture). These firms had HUF 47.143 bn debts, of which HUF 28.4 bn were bank debts. These firms were also requested to submit a reorganisation plan. However, in most cases proposals were rejected or returned for refinement. Some banks were active, some not. Strict deadlines again proved to be a drawback. Procedures should have been completed by the end of 1994, but the deadline was later extended until the end of June 1995. The most striking fact in this scheme is that private firms were also selected by government agencies. It is rather hard to find any argument for such a policy.

(3) *Simplified debtor conciliation*: all other applicants, who did not take part in the previous two schemes, were eligible to participate in this one under the same conditions. At this stage, the authorities were not involved.

Table 8.8 provides a summary of debtor conciliation. Out of 13,069 debtors, 1,890 firms indicated their interest in debt conciliation. Creditors reached an agreement with their debtors in 354 cases only. The total value of bad and doubtful loans firms owed the banks amounted to HUF 227 bn, and the banks formed HUF 154 bn loss reserves against these outstandings. However, the debts of firms which finally applied for debtor conciliation were HUF 121 bn, against which banks had about HUF 80 bn loss reserves. State creditors were involved in debt arrangements in 149 cases, SPA in 31 cases. As can be seen, the arrears against various state creditors were also significant.

Table 8.8. Main characteristics of debtor conciliation, 31 December 1993

		Banks	State creditors	SPA	Social security
Potential applicants (31 December 1993)					
Number of cases		13,069	–	–	–
Debts	HUF mn	227,329	–	–	–
Applications (31 December 1993)					
Number of cases		1,890	708	–	655
Debts	HUF mn	121,008	25,506	–	n.a.
Unsettled cases (31 December 1993)					
Number of cases		1,536	559	–	754
Debts	HUF mn	77,039	15,909	–	–
Agreements					
Number of cases		354	149	31	81
Agreement with	– forgiving HUF mn	19,536	3,890	267	966
	rescheduling HUF mn	6,649	5,562	–	4,345
	– swap HUF mn	3,986	293	1,008	52
	mixed HUF mn	30,171	9,745	1,275	5,363

According to Balassa (1995) these agreements arranged 29 per cent of bank debt and almost 6 per cent of debt of state creditors. It seems that banks used only a portion of their loss reserves and a significant part of them could be freed up. However, as can be seen from table 8.8, the vast majority of debtors did not apply and therefore their debts had to be written off. Two major banks (MHB and K&H) followed the advice of IBRD and 'split' into a 'good' bank and a 'bad bank'. They transferred bad debts to subsidiaries specialised in work-out. Perhaps debtor conciliation did not meet their expectations, but banks could finally get rid of most of their non-performing loans. As can be seen in table 8.6 (pp. 229–30), the portfolio of banks improved significantly after 1995. This also paved the way for their privatisation.

5   Privatisation of state banks

The Banking Act of 1991 had already set some guidelines as well as a provisional deadline for the privatisation of SOCBs. The Act stipulated that direct and indirect ownership of any single owner – with the exception of financial institutions – might not exceed 25 per cent of the equity. Although this restriction did not apply to the state until the end of 1996, the Act put a ceiling on the voting rights of the state owner after 1 January 1995.

At the beginning of 1992, financial institutions were obliged to renew their licences by law, and bearer shares had to be transformed into registered shares. As mentioned above, state property agencies tried to collect the shares of SOCBs from SOEs. Although this effort was not fully successful, the ownership of banks became more transparent. This measure was one of the rare exceptions when the Hungarian government did not make an ad hoc decision, but thought strategically and made a correct choice. In part due to this policy, cross-ownership decreased significantly.

As mentioned above, before 1991 the effective privatisation of SOCBs was nowhere on the agenda. Between 1991 and 1994 the economic situation did not favour the sale of SOCBs. The net value of the major Hungarian SOCBs was negative, and the Hungarian government decided to clean up the banks' portfolio, and to restructure troubled banks so as to make them marketable. It was rather straightforward – as I showed above – since except for foreign ownership no other form of ownership was really viable. However, bank privatisation is a politically sensitive issue, and not only in transition economies. The authorities first envisaged a sequential privatisation: strategic investors could obtain control via a capital increase followed by an open sale of the remaining shares of the state. The logic behind this option was that dispersed ownership would not jeopardise the interest of strategic investors and the Treasury can also collect higher revenues from such transactions. However, the budgetary consideration overrode this idea. Before individual privatisation deals are dealt with, let us pause for a moment.

As mentioned above, not everybody supported the sale of SOCBs to foreigners. However, could foreign ownership have been avoided? I do not think so. The moment foreign banks entered the Hungarian credit market, they immediately enjoyed such a significant comparative advantage over domestic banks that the latter were never able to catch up. Foreign and joint venture banks had a clean portfolio. In the early years they enjoyed certain tax concessions. They were run by qualified commercial bankers. They had easy access to cheap foreign sources, and they could also take advantage of market imperfections. Not surprisingly, these banks were highly profitable. Under these conditions and due to the government's budget constraint, in my opinion, there was no real alternative to selling the big SOCBs to foreigners. There was only one question: were they marketable at all?

Of the five big SOCBs, MKB was the first the government offered for sale. The German Bayerische Landesbank and EBRD obtained a 25 and 16 per cent stake altogether for DM 57 mn in late 1994 and mid-1995. These two investors first purchased existing shares and then subscribed to newly issued shares. Another foreign investor owns 8 per cent of shares, and the remaining shares are in domestic hands or in the bank's portfolio. After these transactions the state ownership had by 1995 decreased to 27 per cent.

In 1994, 19.5 per cent of OTP's equity was offered for sale to Hungarian investors. A year later, another 21 per cent of the shares were transferred to Social Security and Pension Funds, and municipalities, while 20 per cent were sold directly to foreign institutional investors and employees purchased 5 per cent. In 1995, domestic small investors purchased another 8 per cent. These transactions resulted in revenues of HUF 10 bn (about USD 90 mn) for the government. (According to privatisation laws the state wants to retain 25 per cent + 1 vote in this bank in the long run.) This bank was not offered to foreign strategic investors because of its dominant position in retail banking. In fact, the bank operates under the control of management. Therefore, it can be expected that OTP will rapidly lose its market share – perhaps in the very near future.

In December 1995, the American General Electric Capital and EBRD purchased 27.5 per cent and 32.5 per cent of shares, respectively, of BB for HUF 12 bn (USD 87 mn).[19] However, it was probably a bad deal. At first glance the government could count on 60 dollars of net revenues (!)

from this deal, but because of some special provisions of the contract this sale actually turned out to be a net loss. The Hungarian State had to buy back Polgári Bank (a retail banking subsidiary of BB) from the new owners for HUF 1.1 bn (USD 7.3 mn). Because there was some foreign interest in purchasing this small bank, we still await the final result of this deal. It is obvious that the sale of BB was politically motivated, and the strategic behaviour of buyers also weakened the position of the Hungarian government in this transaction. GE Capital and EBRD knew that if the privatisation transaction had not been realised, then BB would have had to pay back to the state the temporarily transferred capital reserves. In addition, at that time the risk rating of the country was worse than a year later, when MHB was successfully sold.

It was the general opinion that MHB and K&H were the 'worst' big SOCBs in Hungary. Therefore it was rather surprising when the Dutch ABN–AMRO purchased 89.23 per cent of MHB's equity for about HUF 14 bn (USD 89.23 mn) at 222 per cent of the face value. (MKB's shares were sold approximately at similar margin, while OTP's shares were distributed at 120 per cent. The margin of BB's shares is not clear, but in the first round it was roughly about 100 per cent.) Shortly after the privatisation, the Dutch investors increased the equity of the bank, and MHB became a big bank again. In the privatisation contract the new owners committed themselves to raise the equity by USD 100 mn by the end of 1997. It seems that MHB will become one of the major banks in the Hungarian market – as it was in 1987.

The privatisation of K&H has not yet been completed. It seems that the management would like to obtain the control over the bank, and the chief executive officers of K&H will try to follow the strategy of OTP's management. The government declared that this transaction would be completed by the end of 1997.

In Hungary the first big SOCBs were sold, with the order of their privatisation related to their performance and financial position. Marketable ones were privatised first, and then the others. MKB did not have too much bad debt, but its market share was smaller than that of the rest. OTP was the biggest and it was also in relatively good shape, but because of its special position in the Hungarian financial market, the government was more cautious. Perhaps BB was in somewhat better shape than MHB or K&H (at least in 1995), but it was much less attractive than MKB or OTP, and was the smallest of the group.

Some interesting lessons can be learned for other countries still facing the problem of privatisation of big SOCBs. On the experience of the successful sale of MHB, the scandalous sale of BB, and the privatisation of MKB or OTP we can conclude that: (1) the state should not desert and must participate actively in privatisation of SOCBs; (2) the better the banks are prepared for privatisation and the more thoroughly the tender is organised, the more the state as well as the banks can benefit; (3) competition should not be excluded even in the last round of sales procedures; (4) after portfolio cleaning, recapitalisation, and restructuring, SOCBs must be privatised as quickly as possible; (5) if there is just one buyer to be bargained with, some flexibility must always be provided in privatisation in order to avoid detrimental strategic behaviour by the buyers; (6) the government must resist pressures from political or interest groups. In the case of MHB's privatisation, private banks (including already privatised SOCBs) lobbied heavily against the deal, because they did not want to see another strong competitor on the market (Bede, 1996).

6   Assessment and policy recommendations

As can be seen, in many respects Hungarian bank restructuring met its aims. Although at a high cost, the bad debts of SOCBs have been carved out. As a result of various credit and bank consolidation schemes the portfolio of SOCBs has improved significantly (see table 8.6, pp. 229–30). The elimination of bad loans from the balance sheets of SOCBs resulted in decreasing lending rates in real terms and a narrower margin (see figure 8.1 and 8.2, pp. 219–20). In 1994, consolidated banks had a positive cash flow, and produced small profits, i.e. the profitability of banks had improved (see table 8.6). This could also have contributed to the fact that four out of five SOCBs have already been privatised. In order to cover at least partially the expenses of various schemes, the Treasury could collect some revenues from the privatisation of SOCBs as well as increasing profit taxes. Since major banks are in foreign hands, the state has no direct control over the credit allocation. For Hungary, as a small country with an open economy, the free flow of resources may substantially assist the improvement of the allocative efficiency of the market as a whole.

As is well known, the restructuring of the banking sector took place gradually. The whole process involved 18 banks altogether; three big ones participated in all stages, seven in two, and eight banks in one phase only. This gradualism corresponds, more or less, to the Hungarian tradition. Nevertheless, in this special case gradualism is more questionable. If banks had started their restructuring in 1992–3, the transformation of the banking sector would perhaps have been cheaper. Many authors argue that the stock problem was dominant, and the deterioration of banks' portfolio was a consequence of external economic or political factors, or can be explained by changes in the regulations.

According to Balassa (1995), the cost of the credit and bank conciliation could have been, in an optimal case, 20–25 per cent lower. However, the lengthy multi-stage procedure is also considered a main reason for the high expense. Without the consecutive stages, the moral hazard of various agents, especially commercial bankers and firm managers, could have been avoided. For example, when some details of the debtor consolidation programme for businesses became known in Fall 1993, firms stopped servicing their debts. By the end of the year the interest payment and bank fee arrears of debtors in MHB had increased by 50 per cent compared with the end of 1992. According to some anecdotal evidence fraud at banks could not be excluded either. According to a report of a big SOCB prepared in early 1994, the loss in the whole banking sector due to fraud could have amounted to HUF 20 bn, and this sum is probably a modest estimate. These costs also had to be covered by the programmes, although some people may say that once these losses had occurred they had to be covered in one way or another.

Perhaps bond financing of these schemes was not the best choice either. Probably for political reasons the interest payments on consolidation bonds started only in Spring 1994 (when the mandate of the conservative government expired). Between 1994 and 1996 MoF paid out interest of HUF 54.47 bn, HUF 96.61 bn and HUF 78.04 bn, respectively, on consolidation bonds.

As the Hungarian experience also proved, the rules of the game matter a great deal. In the banking sector, regulation plays an important role. Here I want to emphasise only one point. Most of the decisions were made by the MoF, and fiscal considerations dominated the whole process. From this point of view, I think the separation of state banking supervision from the MoF and from the NBH was a good decision. As Tirole (1994) and Dixit (1996) point out, in the case of multi-task agency problems, the control of public enterprises (in our case, SOCBs) can best be performed if multiple principals with different objectives are created. In this situation, as was shown, external discipline, competition or transparency may also help to overcome difficulties. When, under external pressure, the Banking Act and various elements of prudential regulation were introduced, SBS gained more ground and could at least to some extent counterbalance the interest of other government agencies, even if SBS did not perform perfectly.

On the other hand, it was in my opinion a mistake to adopt BIS rules gradually. Moreover, the 8 per cent CAR for banks as a criterion for prudential operation became a fetish. Of course, for the government, especially the MoF, this view could simplify bank restructuring to a one-dimensional issue which was relatively easy to handle. Nonetheless the failure of small banks after their recapitalisation clearly shows that it is not true that below the 8 per cent CAR everything is wrong and over the 8 per cent CAR everything is fine. Dewatripont and Tirole (1994) comprehensively treat the problem of banking regulation, although in a different set-up, although from another viewpoint the practice of the Hungarian government corresponded to one of their findings. In a macroeconomic recession, aggregate shocks may hit every bank simultaneously and therefore temporary rejection of the 8 per cent CAR can be advantageous.

As it was shown in this chapter, the Hungarian banking sector went through significant changes. In many respects, success was achieved, but the bill was also high. The costs of these programmes are already sunk, but what should be worrying the monetary authorities and commercial banks is that Hungarian firms use less bank credit than their counterparts in other countries. This clearly shows that inflation should have been and still must be taken more seriously. Nonetheless banks are supposed to be, and hopefully, as the result of consolidation measures will be, taking an active part in financing the economy in the future.

NOTES

1 However, indirect control through central bank refinancing has temporarily played an important role in short-term borrowing of enterprises and is still significant in long-term financing. At the beginning of 1987 the gap between the assets, equity and deposit stocks of the newly created SOCBs was entirely filled by refinancing the credits of the NBH. This stock amounted to 70 per cent of the total liabilities of the big banks. Due to increases in their deposits, equity, and the development of an interbank money market, banks became more independent from central bank refinancing, but in 1990 these sources still accounted for 15 per cent of the banking sector's total liabilities.

2 Perotti (1993) develops a model in which he shows a certain bias to allocate excessively scarce bank resources to (indebted) SOEs instead of more profitable private borrowers which could have slowed down the transition and resulted in a potential concentration of risk in banks even after bank privatisation. This finding may apply to these big SOEs. But as indicated, in certain cases banks tried to withdraw from lending to risky firms. Moreover, private firms, as pointed out, were at least as risky as their state-owned counterparts.

3 Nonetheless, some development did take place. In 1987, out of 21 financial institutions, only five big commercial banks were authorised to keep accounts of business entities. Except for the Hungarian Foreign Trade Bank (MKB) – which was established under the socialist era in 1950 and specialised in financing foreign trade – and three other banks with foreign participation, domestic banks were not allowed to transact in foreign exchange. Nor could they collect household deposits. OTP and the saving cooperatives had an exclusive licence in retail banking (financing of households, small entrepre-

neurs and municipalities). These restrictions were gradually abolished. After July 1989 commercial banks were authorised to extend credits in foreign exchange to domestic firms out of their own foreign currency deposits at their own risk. In the first quarter of 1990, certain banks received a licence to carry out trade-related transactions for their clients as well as international services and transactions when the money was transferred from their clients' forex accounts. (In March 1989, related to the gradual liberalisation of convertible imports, a limited foreign exchange market was opened. The Central Bank made foreign exchange available to economic entities, or private persons authorised to trade in convertible currency.) In the middle of 1988 the Post Bank and Savings Bank Corporation Ltd (Postabank) was established in order to break the monopoly position of OTP in retail banking. Since 1 January 1989, other commercial banks have also been authorised to provide services for households. At the same time OTP and Postabank also received a full licence for commercial banking. (In order to enable banks to pay the market rate of interest on household deposits, the interest rate on housing loans from the beginning of 1989 was adjusted to the market rate.)

4 Hungarian SOCBs frequently established joint ventures with foreign capital, or purchased shares of such financial institutions which, in many cases, operated in the same segment of the market. They therefore created competitors for themselves.

5 As has happened both before and since, financial authorities, but especially line ministries, or state asset management agencies, assume that it is sufficient to write off the debts of SOEs and then everything will continue smoothly. Firms' restructuring and loan conciliation have not been interlinked.

6 There was only one bank (BB) which followed SBS' instruction, all the other banks paid more attention to the MoF's tax motive. The Ministry heavily criticised and blamed the management of BB because – according to MoF – the management wanted to hide the profit from the Treasury.

7 Although in 1989 banks still invested more in other financial institutions (HUF 4.2 bn), swap transactions increased rapidly. At the end of 1989 the stock of investment in the real sector by banks amounted to HUF 4.7 bn. The share of the big five SOCBs on these investments comprised about 70–80 per cent. On the basis of non-consolidated balance sheet data, Spéder (1991) estimated that the MHB concentrated 46 per cent of all investment of the banking sector, while K&H had a 15 per cent share, MKB's portion was 13 per cent, and BB's share was only 6 per cent.

8 SOCBs frequently tried to persuade their clients to subscribe to their shares and sometimes banks themselves granted loans to SOEs in order to reduce the dominance of direct state ownership. Firms probably subscribed to bank shares because they assumed that they could have better access to bank resources.

9 Spéder and Várhegyi (1992) mention another alternative. In principle, SOCBs could also have been privatised indirectly in the medium run. Privatisation of SOEs holding shares of SOCBs would have eventually resulted in the privatisation of these banks. Moreover, if these SOEs had been decentralised, such a downsizing would have reduced the vulnerability of banks to their dependence on big debtors.

10 Beside the usual benefits (such as fresh capital, technology, know-how, markets, etc.) the NBH and MoF supported the sales of banks, since these

transactions could have resulted in hard currency revenues, additional credit lines and export financing capacity for the country. And the strong profit motive of new owners could have had some positive spillover effect on borrowers as well. Nonetheless, the tax allowances that, presumably would have been necessary could have reduced the stream of future revenues, and the necessary liberalisation of foreign exchange would have immediately reduced the discretionary power of the central bank.

11 Interestingly enough, the strongest opponent of the sale of SOCBs to foreigners was Lajos Bokros, who first became the CEO of BB and afterwards was appointed Minister of Finance in Spring 1995, and sold BB to foreign investors at the end of the year (Bokros, 1990).

12 Sándor Demján, the CEO of MHB, found a German buyer for his bank but the deal was torpedoed officially and he was removed from his position.

13 'The main cause, the portfolio-deteriorating effect of the shrinking economy, still asserts itself. On this basis it may be questioned if the consolidation should also be extended to credits granted now and becoming 'qualified' later. This would, however, stimulate the banks to irresponsible lending. We have, therefore, chosen the solution (as a compromise) that *credits granted prior to 1 October 1992 may be included into the system.* (At that time the banks hardly knew the system of credit conciliation would be expected, therefore it could not influence them when taking decisions on extending credits.)' (Ministry of Finance, 1993, pp. 11–12, emphasis in the original)

14 Of course, these claims were concentrated mostly in large banks. Big SOCBs transferred the credit stock of HUF 85.2 bn to the government and received bonds of HUF 66.7 bn in exchange. But the debts of 2,647 firms were also concentrated in a smaller group: HUF 77.5 bn (75.6 per cent of all claims) were debts of 709 firms in bankruptcy or liquidation. At the end of 1992 banks got rid of 95 per cent of debts of those firms that were in bankruptcy or liquidation. The debts of firms in liquidation amounted to HUF 63.6 bn, and of those in bankruptcy to HUF 13.9 bn. This high concentration is shown by the fact that 337 firms, out of 709 enterprises in bankruptcy or liquidation, were clients of the big four SOCBs and owed the banks HUF 64.4 bn (Marsi and Pap, 1993).

15 Banks received 'A' series consolidation bonds, which bear interest similar to the market rate of interest and they received 'B' series consolidation bonds for their outstanding interest payments. Although according to the original plan the Treasury would have taken back 50 per cent of the interest payment on bonds in the form of a consolidation fee, it was later cancelled, and 'B' series bonds were exchanged for 'A' series ones.

16 The NBH, the MoF and SBS did not support the idea of centralised portfolio cleaning, because they did not want to see another top state asset management organisation responsible for SOEs besides the existing ones. They also argued that it would be difficult to recruit staff for this new agency, and the decisions of this agency probably would be rather discretionary which would have induced moral hazard.

17 Because the debts of these insolvent firms remained on the books of their creditors after the bank oriented credit conciliation, which means that they were not classified as bad at that time, we may suppose that banks probably behaved strategically. They might assume that it was better to sell the debt of big SOEs at face value to the state than to include them in the consolidation

254   László Szakadát

scheme. Needless to say, this fact already foreshadowed the necessity of another phase of consolidation, since the credit stock of these enterprises was significant and these debtors were really in bad shape.

18 For the same reasons Dittus and Prowse (1996) argue that East European commercial banks could not be successful in active monitoring of their borrowers (like the Japanese) or investment (like the Germans). They lack human resources, therefore financial institutions themselves are not too much interested in investment banking activity. In the short run, credit allocation alone was already too big a challenge for them. Nonetheless, they also admitted that work-out of default firms might be a useful 'exercise' for a bank to gain experience in restructuring of firms.

19 In 1995 the SPA transferred to BB capital reserves of HUF 12 bn in order to increase the warranty capital of the bank. Decision makers expected in this way to reach a better price.

REFERENCES

Ábel, I. and J. Bonin (1994) 'State desertion and credit market failure in the Hungarian transition', *Acta Oeconomica*, **46**, 97–112

Baer, H.L. and C.W. Gray (1996) 'Debt as a control device in transitional economies: the experiences of Hungary and Poland', in R. Frydman, C. Gray and A. Rapaczynski (eds.), *Corporate Governance in Central Europe and Russia*, Budapest: Central European University Press, 68–110

Balassa, B. (1995) 'A magyar bankrendszer konszolidációja (1992–94) és jelenlegi helyzete' (The consolidation of the Hungarian banking sector (1992–94) and its current state), Budapest, manuscript

Bede, R. (1996) 'Az ÁPV Rt. jó árat akar' (SPA wants a good price), Hitelvilág, **4**, 3–4

Bokros, L. (1990) 'Gondolatok a pénzintézetek tulajdonviszonyainak reformjához' (Remarks on the ownership reform of financial institutions), *Bankszemle*, **34**, 1–7

Bonin, J. and M. Schaffer (1995) 'Banks, firms, bad debts and bankruptcy in Hungary 1991–1994', Centre for Economic Performance, LSE, *Working Paper*, **657**

Bonin, J. and I. Székely (1994) *The Development and Reform of Financial Systems in Central and Eastern Europe*, Aldershot: Edward Elgar

Borish, M., W. Ding and N. Michel (1996) 'On the road to EU accession', World Bank, *Discussion Paper*, **345**

Dewatripont, M. and J. Tirole (1994) *The Prudential Regulation of Banks*, Cambridge, MA: MIT Press

Dittus, P. and S. Prowse (1996) 'Corporate control in Central Europe and Russia: should banks own shares?', in R. Frydman, C. Gray and A. Rapaczynski (eds.), *Corporate Governance in Central Europe and Russia*, Budapest: Central European University Press, 20–67

Dixit, A. (1996) *The Making of Economic Policy*, Cambridge, MA: MIT Press

Estrin, S., P. Hare and S. Márta (1992) 'Banking in transition: development and current problems in Hungary', *Soviet Studies*, **44**, 785–808

Frydman, R., C. Gray and A. Rapaczynski (eds.) (1996) *Corporate Governance in Central Europe and Russia*, Budapest: Central European University Press

Király, J. (1995) 'The Hungarian Fisher-cycle or the possible interpretation of the capital loss of Hungarian banks', *Acta Oeconomica*, **47**, 323–42

Marsi, E. and J. Pap (1993), 'A csődtörvény hatása a pénzintézetekre' (The impact of the Bankruptcy Law on financial institutions), *Bankszemle*, **32**, 27–39

Ministry of Finance (1993) 'The Hungarian credit conciliation (1992)', *Public Finance in Hungary*, **118**, Budapest: Perfect

(1994a) 'Necessity and realization of the credit (bank) consolidation in Hungary', *Public Finance in Hungary*, **132**, Budapest: Perfect

(1994b) 'Activity and position of the Hungarian banks in 1992', *Public Finance in Hungary*, **135**, Budapest: Perfect

Nyers, R. and G. Lutz (1992) 'A Bankrendszer főbb jellemzői az 1987–1991 évi mérlegbeszámolók alapján' (Main characteristics of the banking sector 1987–1991 on the basis of balance sheet data), *Bankszemle*, **36**, 9–34

Perotti, E. (1993) 'Bank lending in transition economies', *Journal of Banking and Finance*, **17**, 1021–32

Spéder, Z. (1991) 'The characteristic behaviour of Hungarian commercial banks', *Acta Oeconomica*, **43**, 131–48

Spéder, Z. and E. Várhegyi (1992) 'On the eve of the second bank reform', *Acta Oeconomica*, **43**, 53–76

Tirole, J. (1994) 'The internal organization of government', *Oxford Economic Papers*, **46**, 1–29

Várhegyi, E. (1994a) 'The "second" reform of the Hungarian banking system', in J. Bonin and I. Székely, *The Development and Reform of Financial Systems in Central and Eastern Europe*, Aldershot: Edward Elgar, 293–308

(1994b) 'Monetary and banking policy during the period of the Antall government', *Acta Oeconomica*, **46**, 113–132

Discussion

JÉRÔME SGARD

Chapter 8 by László Szakadát presents a detailed overview of the evolution of the Hungarian commercial banking sector since the break-up of the old monobank system in 1987. Three main periods can be identified. The first one ran until 1992 and was characterised by piecemeal reforms, increasing difficulties in the real sector and a high level of taxation which clearly had adverse consequences on the future adjustment of banks. From 1992 until late 1995, a series of recapitalisations and restructuring programmes was implemented, most of the time in a context of financial distress in both the real and the banking sectors: falling levels of solvency, recession and increasing macroeconomic imbalances explain the underlying fear by public authorities that a low level confidence crisis might develop into an open systemic crisis. A third period, from 1995 onwards, witnessed a gradual stabilisation of the sector like that in the credit market (lower real interest rates, reduced intermediation margins, etc.). This was made possible, *inter alia*, thanks to a rapid privatisation drive, which put most of the large commercial banks under foreign control; by the end of 1996, more than 40 per cent of the sector, in asset terms, was foreign-controlled.

On an *ex post*, comparative basis, the restructuring of the Hungarian banking sector appears as a very long, painful and costly process. Its direct, total cost was over 9 per cent of GDP, against less than 3 per cent for comparable programmes in Poland or Slovenia. Servicing costs represented around 1 per cent of GDP in 1996, close to 4 per cent of (central government) fiscal revenue. Moreover, the recovery of the Hungarian credit market proved at best gradual: in real terms, the stock of enterprise credit decreased continuously after 1992, due both to a slow growth in new credits and to continuing high levels of credit write-offs. Indeed, from the beginning of 1994 until September 1996, the latter represented more than 15 per cent of the flow of new enterprise credits, more than enough to explain the slow growth in the sector's capital base.

This painful experiment with financial reforms contrasts with initial conditions which were generally considered as rather promising; the trends in the real sector (productivity gains, export growth, etc.) proved no more adverse than in the rest of Central Europe. This raises three sets of questions, on which Szakadát's chapter provides much information and analysis: What were the main causes of the 1992 banking crisis starting in spring 1992? What went wrong during the restructuring process? What might the consequences of this episode be for the long-term development of the Hungarian financial sector?

1   The causes of the banking crisis

Szakadát first identifies a series of crisis factors which have been observed in most, if not all transition economies: the inherited stock of enterprise credit was of course of a dismal quality, recession made things worse, and banks were grossly under-capitalised from the onset, which exposed them directly to attempts at capture by large, over-indebted industrial concerns. Other, more specific elements were then added. First, bad loans were concentrated in a very limited number of enterprises: in Hungary, in 1990, 50 firms owned more than two-thirds of the total stock of non-performing loans. Things were only made worse when, after 1987, the directors of these enterprises were invited in large numbers to join the Boards of the newly created, state-owned commercial banks; moreover, the asset portfolio of these new institutions showed very strong sectoral specialisation, which also increased pressure by hard-core, industrial lobbies, including the older 'technical ministries'.

Although, from experience, these various micro level and institutional factors have often proved decisive in the success of transition reforms, there also remains a strong case for a macroeconomic argument. This originates in the extreme pressure exerted on the domestic economy by the large budget deficit in a context of tight monetary policy: starting from a roughly balanced position in 1990 and 1991, public borrowing requirements increased sharply from the second quarter of 1992, a trend which was not reversed until 1995. While the state had absorbed 19 per cent of the nominal increase in domestic credit in 1991, its relative share rose to 80 per cent over the last three quarters of 1992. At the same time, the intake of new credits by the enterprise sector was reduced, in relative terms, from 45 per cent to 22 per cent, with the consequence that its total stock, in real terms, actually fell in 1992 by around 7 per cent.[1] With real, *ex post* interest rates between 18 and 21 per cent, enterprises were subject to a sudden, massive drain of liquidity at a time when production levels were at their lowest. Figure D8.1 compares the quarterly increase in gross enterprise credit with an estimate of interest payments due on the outstanding stock, which gives a measure of the collapse in the credit market in 1992–3.[2]

The conjunction of a large public deficit, hard constraints on foreign payments, a tight monetary policy and a weak banking sector provides the background for the 'legislative shock' of spring 1992, as described by Szakadát, which directly hit the bank–enterprise relationship (new bankruptcy law, new supervisory and accounting rules; see Bonin and Schaffer, 1995; Sgard, 1995). At that time, two regulatory aspects proved especially damaging: the new law provided that banks had to file for bankruptcy any enterprise showing arrears with only *one* credit line; all the creditor banks of this firm should then classify as non-performing *all* debts owed to it, whatever their own capital base and loan loss reserves. By the end of 1992, under BIS accounting standards, 12 of the 14 largest commercial banks had a negative net value, with the implication that they were technically bankrupt.

The consequences were threefold: the courts were swamped with cases; banks had to write-down a large part of their assets without having the necessary capital base in order to remain solvent themselves; a chain reaction in the banking and enterprise sectors then further disrupted

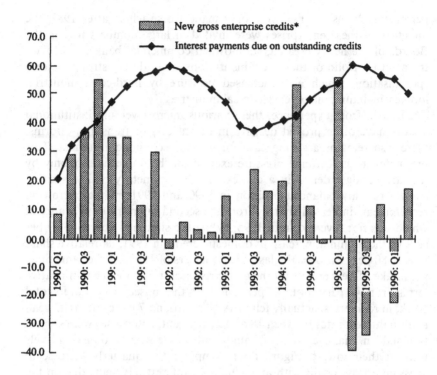

Figure D8.1 Estimates of bank enterprises' credit flows, 1990–6
* Change in stock over period: after 1994 case-by-case write-offs make
interpretation of the figures difficult.

flows of payments and probably played a substantial role in the extension
of the crisis throughout the economy (see Király, 1995). The usual
indices of a banking crisis can be observed during this period: interest
spread between the banks' lending rate and the benchmark money rate
increased widely, reflecting liquidity problems in the banking sector, with
the internal spread (average lending rates *minus* average deposit rates)
decreasing only slowly, due to ongoing solvency problems (see figure
D8.2; Goldstein and Turner, 1996; Honohan, 1997).

The difficult situation in 1992 and early 1993 was also reflected in the
chaotic conditions under which the interbank market operated: only the
largest banks had regular access to the money market, which meant that
the counterpart risk was considered very large by major participants.
This also explains why the risk of a systemic crisis was also considered
critical by the public authorities, and why the first recapitalisation
programme, decided upon at the end of 1992, had a distinct, although

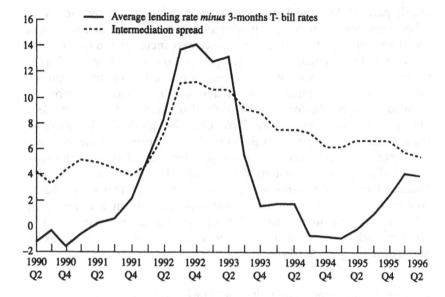

Figure D8.2 Interest spreads, 1990–6

extensive, stop-gap character. However, a large-scale confidence crisis did not erupt and there were no large liquidity injections by the Central Bank. In other words, even at a time of extreme tension on the micro level, the crisis was not allowed to spill over into the macroeconomy.

A key factor, bearing in mind this background, accounts for the destructive pressure exerted by fiscal deficits on the domestic financial sector: foreign debt, which had remained at an extremely high level since the early 1980s. Foreign public interest payments, as derived from the balance of payments, averaged 89 per cent of the increase in state liabilities to commercial banks over the 1992–4 period, at a time when the primary fiscal account showed either a very limited deficit or a substantial surplus. Foreign interest payments thus appear to have played a strong though indirect role in crowding enterprises out of the credit market, as well as in the ensuing disruptions in the bank–enterprise credit relationship.

This reflects the more general lesson that, during a transition, the management of inherited debts, both domestic and foreign, bears heavily on the adjustment in the financial sector as, presumably, also on restructuring and growth patterns in the real economy. In this respect, the oft-cited refusal by Hungarian policy makers, before and after the political transition, to opt for any kind of write-off or partial default, was clearly paralleled on the domestic scene: contrary to the experience of *all* other transition economies, only a small volume of inflationary tax was levied upon deposit holders, and no losses were incurred as a result of the banking crisis. Hungary's strategic priority on internal and external financial reputation was thus the polar opposite to Poland's response: after the stock of domestic assets and liabilities had been strongly deflated by high inflation in 1989, Poland obtained a 50 per cent debt reduction on both London and Paris Club foreign debt.[3] Although, in the latter case, the 'choice' for policy makers was extremely constrained, this experience highlighted the advantages of an early default on the dead weight of inherited, low-quality debt, which otherwise would have to be financed from future, hard-earned resources. On the other hand, the *ex post* costs of default have apparently been limited: on average, since 1992, the increase in real bank deposits was higher in Poland than in Hungary, while both countries gained access on comparable terms to international capital markets.

2   What went wrong during the restructuring process?

While international evidence shows that rapid, once-for-all recapitalisation is decisive in order to limit the impact of a banking crisis, there are reasons to believe that policy reactions in Hungary have had some adverse consequences.

One point, mentioned only in passing by Szakadát, is that the failure of the first (late 1992) bank recapitalisation was apparently linked to a large-scale dynamic of moral hazard. Indeed, at the beginning of 1993, agents seem to have rapidly come to the conclusion that the new resources brought to the banks would prove insufficient and that a second recapitalisation would sooner or later take place. Consequently, many of them seem to have stopped servicing their bank debt, probably also encouraged by the poor performance of the commercial courts in enforcing contractual discipline. Szakadát mentions that although 50 enterprises concentrated two-thirds of total non-performing loans in 1990, 1,890 were eventually included in the final (1994–5) out-of-court 'conciliation' procedure. While the first figure should not necessarily be considered as an estimate of the extent of restructuring needed at that time, the change in magnitude over four years is amazing. Poland's own successful out-of-court programme, started in March 1993, on which Hungary's drew in some respects, was limited to 200 enterprises (van Wijnbergen, 1997).

Conversely, the experience with centralised bank restructuring (where bad loans are carved out and transferred to a specialised public financial institution) proved disappointing in both countries: both the Hungarian December 1992 programme and the long restructuring process of the large Polish specialised banks (BGZ and PKO, most notably, which were not included in the out-of-court procedure) gave disappointing results. Another common experience is that large amounts of long-term recapitalisation bonds with poor liquidity can make more difficult the management of the banks' balance sheets: if the interest rate curve becomes less flexible, other things being equal, the transmission mechanisms of monetary policy will be less efficient.

A second characteristic of the Hungarian experience noted by Szakadát is the high level of state intervention in microeconomic decisions while trying to sort out the banks. In the first (late 1992) recapitalisation, public bonds were given to banks in a highly discretionary way, without substantial conditions or commitments being imposed upon bank managers. The direct, 'firm oriented' recapitalisation, as well as the 'conciliation procedures' (both in 1994–5), also failed to put the state at arm's-length from micro level interests. It is indeed highly significant that out-of-court negotiations between enterprises and their debtors included only the banks and state bodies (and the old 'technical ministries'), with an inter-ministerial committee monitoring the process. In the Polish case, by contrast, public liabilities were also included in the financial restructuring, but the state as an agent was excluded from negotiations and even had no right of veto on the final outcome. Thus negotiations started, and remained, on a purely microeconomic level, while the Hungarian procedure was apparently exposed to heavier pressures by vested interests. Szakadát mentions this point; Borish et al. (1996) also underline it, as well as the delayed reaction against asset-stripping by SOE managers.

Having read Szakadát's detailed description of the successive restructuring programmes, one thus comes to the conclusion that two factors have considerably increased Hungary's difficulties with reforming its banking system:

(a) under-estimation of the impact of foreign over-indebtedness on a reforming, fragile microeconomy with weak financial discipline;
(b) inadequate state policies towards micro level transactions and interests, which eventually left it with limited credibility towards the most entrenched agents. In this respect, selling off the largest banks to foreign shareholders was perhaps the best response to the high costs of rebuilding a sound banking sector, but also the difficulty of curtailing these multifarious, untransparent relationships so damaging to reform.

3   What might the future consequences of the banking crisis be?

Many variables and events will bear on the future development of the
Hungarian financial sector, which may deepen or palliate the consequences of the past crisis: the evolution of the capital market and its
capacity to mobilise local resources, the recovery in the domestic
enterprise sector, the medium-term strategy of the new players in the
banking sector, etc.

In this respect, the strong dualistic structure of the Hungarian economy
will probably remain one of its most enduring characteristics, one which
indeed developed very early during the transition. Arguably, the prime
element was the choice to give a leading role to foreign direct investment
(FDI) in the restructuring and development of the export sector;
conversely, the domestic sector (except utilities) has relied comparatively
heavily on scarce domestic resources and has shown much less dyna-
mism. As a complementary factor, developments in the financial sector
may also bear on this trend, in two different ways. First, drawing *inter
alia* on Bonin and Schaffer (1995), there are indications that the credit
squeeze and the banking crisis of 1992 may have destroyed a substantial
layer of small and medium-sized enterprises, especially in the emerging
private sector. This shock on the supply side of the real economy could
have reduced the basis for the emerging recovery, as for future
enterprise-to-enterprise privatisations.

The transfer of the largest part of the domestic banking sector under
foreign control could also have adverse long-term consequences if these
new players continue to develop along the lines generally adopted by
foreign banks in Hungary since the early 1990s: i.e. a specialisation on
servicing the exporting sector, with possible extensions towards a limited
number of potentially highly beneficial market segments (consumer
credit, property and capital markets). The development of small-sized,
domestically oriented enterprises could then suffer from insufficient
supply of intermediated finance, due to the high costs of monitoring this
sector. Indeed, when considering the emerging economies, the large
number of international banks which invest in retail banking outside
their domestic base is probably still less than 10. The fact that one of the
major Hungarian banks (Budapest Bank, BB) has been bought by a non-
bank financial institution which focuses on specialised services (General
Electric's financial arm) may be of some concern in this respect.

A low capacity to mobilise domestic savings could thus increase the
vulnerability of a growth regime based upon imported capital, attracted
by cheap, highly qualified labour. Of course, many countries in the world
present comparable features and have proved able to increase their

populations' income level over the medium term (for example, Ireland since the mid-1980s). But such regimes can also translate into weak or unstable growth, associated with large inequalities in revenue levels.

NOTES

1 Deflated by the index of production prices, yearly average figures. Partial transfers of housing debt, from households to the state, and anticipated amortisation by the former in 1991, means that the direct comparison of domestic credit figures with those of 1992 requires caution. The demand for public bonds by non-financial agents was negligible over the whole period.
2 Figures for the years 1994–6 should be interpreted with caution as a substantial part of outstanding credits has been written-off gradually, on a case-by-case basis, and should hence not be fully interpreted as any kind of 'outflow' of enterprise resources towards the banks.
3 Both types of agreements were finalised in 1994–5, but interest on amortisation payments have been sharply reduced, voluntarily or not, since late 1989 (see Sgard, 1997).

REFERENCES

Bonin, J. and M. Schaffer (1994) *The Development and Reform of Financial Systems in Central and Eastern Europe*, Aldershot: Edward Elgar
(1995) 'Banks, firms, bad debts and bankruptcy in Hungary, 1991–1994', Centre for Economic Performance, LSE, *Discussion Paper*, **234**
Borish, M., W. Ding and M. Noel (1996) 'On the road to EU accession: financial sector development in Central Europe', Washington, DC: World Bank
Goldstein, M. and P. Turner (1996) 'Banking crisis in emerging economies: origins and policy options', *Economic Papers*, **46**, Basle: BIS
Honohan, P. (1997) 'Banking system failures in developing and transition economies: diagnosis and prediction', *Working Paper*, **39**. Basle: BIS
Király, J. (1995) 'The Hungarian Fisher-cycle or the possible interpretation of the capital loss of Hungarian banks', *Acta Oeconomica*, **47**
Sgard, J. (1995) 'Recapitalisation bancaire et aléa moral en Hongrie et en Pologne', *Revue Economique*, **46**
(1997) 'Foreign debt settlements in Bulgaria, Hungary and Poland, 1989–1996', forthcoming in C. Helmenstein (ed.), *Capital Markets in Transition Economies*, Aldershot: Edward Elgar
van Wijnbergen, S. (1997) 'On the role of banks in enterprise restructuring: the Polish example', *Journal of Comparative Economics*, **24**

Part Three
Labour markets

9 The minimum wage in Hungary: subsistence minimum and/or bargaining tool?

JENŐ KOLTAY

In this chapter, we will discuss minimum wage fixing in the general context of the wage determination process after the abandonment of a Tax-based Incomes Policy (TIP)-type central wage control. The antecedents, role and functions of the Hungarian minimum wage as well as its enforcement and early fragmentation will be examined in order to assess the case for a statutory minimum wage in the present circumstances compared to market economies and other economies in transition.

A guaranteed minimum wage comparable to its Western counterparts was introduced in 1989 when the newly created macro level, tripartite institution (the National Interest Reconciliation Council, OÉT, renamed the Interest Reconciliation Council, ÉT, in 1990 after the regime change) was given the right to negotiate and fix an economy-wide, uniform, statutory minimum wage. The amount agreed and announced subsequently in a government decree is a monthly or hourly basic wage or salary for a full-time employment.

1 Minimum wages in market economies

In industrialised market economies wages are determined through collective bargaining (except in the USA, where only 30 per cent of workers are covered by collective agreements). Wage rates fixed in the agreements are binding minima for categories of employees and grades along the wage scale. Rates at the bottom of wage scales correspond to a whole set of minimum wages, differing from branch to branch and even more from firm to firm.

In addition or complementary to this many countries introduced a national minimum wage, long ago (as in Europe and the USA) or more recently (as in Taiwan and Korea). Minimum wages are fixed by legislation or by collective agreements; in certain countries coverage is somewhat limited or rates somewhat differentiated, mostly for young workers. The original and still primary objective of the minimum wage (set as a norm in ILO Convention 26, 1930) is to protect the lowest paid, but it gained a role of varying importance in the whole bargaining process, influencing increases all the way along the wage hierarchy.

2   Economic effects of minimum wages

The economic impact of minimum wages, especially on employment, remains a controversial issue. In the textbook approach, a wage floor, pushing at least some wages above market clearing level, has an adverse effect on employment (except for a monopsony situation, where it could even increase employment). In reality, much depends on its level relative to the average wage and other costs, on the proportion of employees affected and on the size of the non-protected, informal sector (Bazen and Benhayoun, 1995). A synthetic indicator of its level and potential impact is the minimum wage average wage ratio, measured in terms of after-tax take-home pay if redistribution aspects are concerned or in terms of total costs if labour market effects are concerned.

Towards the end of the 1970s, minimum wages were cited as a possible major cause of the unemployment then at its peak in developed countries, and in the 1980s measures were taken to lower its level relative to average earnings (by moderating indexation from 1986 in France) or to freeze its increase (1981-9 in the USA and 1984-9 in the Netherlands); the subminimum for young employees was reduced (in the Netherlands) or abolished (under the age of 21 in the UK).

Abundant American research evidence (reviewed in Freeman, 1994) identified a modest adverse effect on employment for the pre-1980 period (finding that a 10 per cent rise in the federal minimum reduced employment by 1-2 per cent, mostly for young workers). In the 1980s, the relative fall in the minimum wage had no significant positive employment impact. According to recent research the more than 25 per cent increase after the long freeze had no significant negative impact on employment and some studies (Katz and Krueger, 1992) find that it may actually have increased employment (the long-run adverse effect may contradict a precarious explanation by monopsony in local labour markets).

Research results, drawn on a smaller number of available time series data sets in Europe (reviewed in Bazen and Benhayoun, 1995) are meagre. Studies for the 1980s in France, when subsequent upratings substantially increased the minimum wage relative to average earnings, also found a modest adverse effect (suggesting a 1-2 per cent employment-reducing effect for a 10 per cent minimum wage increase in the case of workers under 25). (Recently revised French data series suggest an even smaller impact.) Abolition of the minimum wage in the UK has not found solid justification in research evidence; doubts concerning the existence of minimum wage effects on employment have been raised for other countries, too.

3   Wage control and minimum wage in Hungary before 1989

The antecedents of the current minimum wage can be quickly dealt with. In the command economy with administrative wage control, paternalist social protection and no open inflation or unemployment, there was no room for a minimum wage. Although after the 1968 economic reform the government declared a sort of official wage minimum, it was much more a by-product than an instrument of the tax-based wage control.

Between 1971 and 1988 this official minimum was adjusted only four times. In 1971, at HUF 960, it was equal to the lowest wage actually paid. In 1976, 1982 and 1983, at HUF 1,320, 1,640 and 2,290, it lagged behind the lowest wage actually paid (HUF 1,210, 1,350 and 2,000, respectively). While wage and pension rises followed inflation (rising from 1–2 per cent to around 7 per cent), the government-announced wage minimum tended to fall from about 44 per cent of the average wage in 1971 to around 30 per cent in 1976 and 1982, climbing again to 42 per cent in 1983. Then the government left the wage minimum unchanged, and let it fall again to less then 30 per cent of the average wage in 1987, despite accelerating consumer price inflation. Voices supporting the case for a regularly adjusted guaranteed minimum wage became stronger.

In 1988, a comprehensive tax reform implementing the major taxes of market economies (Personal Income Tax (PIT), Value Added Tax, Corporate Income Tax) gave a cost-push impetus to inflation, almost twice as high as the previous year (see chapter 4). Nominal wages (including a 'technical' increase of before-tax wages) went up by around 30 per cent and the wage minimum was raised by 50 per cent to regain its one-time level compared to the average wage after tax (see table 9.1).

4   Wage guidelines and minimum wage fixing after 1989

While inflation kept growing, government control on wages became even stricter in 1989 and held the nominal wage increase below the rise in

Table 9.1. Changes in wage determination and minimum wage evolution in Hungary, 1945–96

Year–month	Wage determination		Minimum wage
	General	Minimum	(HUF)
1945	Collective bargaining	Collective bargaining	..
1950	Central planning	Central planning	–
1968	Parametric wage control	Government	
1971			960[a]
1976			1,210[a]
1982			1,350[a]
1983			2,000[a]
1988–01	(PIT)		3,000[b]
1989–03		Tripartite negotiations	3 700[b]
–10		(OÉT)	4,000[b]
1990–02			4,800[b]
–09		(ÉT)	5,600[c]
–11			5,800[c]
1991–03			7,000[c]
1992–01	Wage control relaxed		8,000[c]
1993–02	Wage control abandoned		9,000[b]
1994–02			10,500[b]
1995–02			12,200
1996–02			14,400

Notes:
[a] At that time there was no PIT; only a social security contribution, with a strange progressivity, was to be paid by employees on the whole amount of all wages.
[b] Exempt from PIT.
[c] Before PIT.
Sources: OÉT; ÉT.

consumer prices. As a concession of the outgoing regime, tripartite negotiations were institutionalised and allowed to fix a new statutory minimum wage. It was raised twice that year and amounted to about half the after-tax average wage. The freedom of wage determination was still constrained, putting a more or less strict upper limit on wage increases

Table 9.2. Average wage, real wage and minimum wage growth in Hungary, 1971–95

Year–month	Average wage		Real wage (in % of previous year)	Average wage (in % of SM)	Minimum wage (in % of AW)
	(net[a] in HUF)	(in % of previous year)			
1971	2,182[b]	..	102.3	165	44
1976	4,150[c]	..	100.1	268	29
1982	4,542	100	99.3	236	30
1983	4,761	104.8	96.8	231	42
1984	5,342	112.2	97.6	243	37
1985	5,866	109.3	100.6	245	34
1986	6,291	107.7	101.9	252	32
1987	6,808	108.2	99.4	244	29
1988	7,015	103.0	98.7	220	42
1989–10/12	8,260	117.7	100.9	220	48
1990–11/12	10,108	122.3	94.9	180	57
1991–03/12	11,836	117.4	92.0	150	59
1992–08	13,617	115.0	97.0	124	59
1993–08	16,280[d]	119.5		137	55
1994–01/07	21,715[d]	125.3	106.3		48
1995–01/07	25,128[d]	115.7	90.5		49

Notes:
[a] From 1988 after-tax wages (gross average wages: 1986 6,291 HUF, 1987 6,808 HUF, 1988 8,817 HUF, 1989 10,018 HUF, 1990 12,664 HUF, 1991 16,932 HUF, 1992 22,365 HUF, 1993 24,710 HUF).
[b] 1970.
[c] 1980.
[d] Average of net total earnings (average of gross total earnings 1994–01/07 31,063 HUF, 1995–01/07 37,509 HUF.
Sources: Calculations based on CSO; OMK data collected by Z. Orolin.

without setting a lower limit. Tripartite negotiations loosened the wage ceiling and brought in a general wage floor with the minimum wage (see table 9.2).

In 1990–3, with further accelerating inflation, the government shared wage determination responsibilities with the tripartite ÉT, parallel to a growing *de facto* wage setting autonomy of employers in the private sector. The ÉT began to negotiate guidelines for average, minimum and maximum wage increases and on the scope of tax-free wage increases (for joint ventures, small firms, railways, agriculture and enterprises where wage growth remained below the increase in value added). Then came the conditional removal of the tax threat dependent on the moderate wage behaviour of the social partners. Wage cost increasing levies (44 per cent employers' social security contribution, 5 per cent employers' unemployment insurance contribution above the then 20–44 per cent PIT, 10 per cent employees' social security contribution and 1.5 per cent employees' unemployment insurance contribution to be paid from wages) and hardening market constraints limited employers' willingness to raise wages. Notwithstanding economic recession, subsequent ÉT agreements undermined the minimum wage more than the rise in consumer prices and increased further its level against the after-tax average wage (of course, this increase was less important if compared to before-tax wages or taking into account the PIT descending to minimum wages in these years). The union demand for a tax exempt minimum wage was achieved in 1993.

Encouraged by the decelerating trend of general wage increases, the government restored the freedom of wage determination and took the risk of relying exclusively on negotiated wage guidelines from 1993 onwards. In the meantime, the unprecedented deterioration of living conditions accompanying the transformation process upgraded the minimum wage. Once a matter of secondary importance, it became a primary bargaining issue and an important social protection matter. Regular adjustments increased the minimum wage each year and in 1995, when negotiations on wage increase guidelines broke down, it was the only wage-related issue on which the ÉT reached agreement. Returning to the bargaining table in 1996 an agreement was reached not only on minimum wage adjustment but on wage guidelines for the whole year.

5　Subsistence minimum and minimum wage

In an economy where labour force participation of both men and women is high, the ratio of wage earners in the population among the highest in the world, the state sector overwhelming, prices and wages controlled and the wage scale compressed, no or low inflation, no open unemployment and officially non-existent poverty, no need was felt for a separate protection of the low-paid by a minimum wage or other means. Only researchers were concerned about low income and poverty; they used unpublished Central Statistical Office (CSO) calculations expressing subsistence minimum as a percentage of average/median income.

General wage-increase rounds and intermittent corrective wage measures and in-kind benefits fulfilled the role of wage and incomes policies. Changes began towards the end of the 1970s, price control was loosened, inflation rose and greater efforts were made to curb purchasing power. Real wages stagnated or tended to fall but transfer payments, social benefits and incomes from sources outside the scope of direct state

Table 9.3. Minimum wage, average wage and subsistence minimum[a] in Hungary, 1989–94 (yearly average figures)

	1989	1990	1991	1992	1993	1994
GAE	10,572	13,450	17,914	22,284	27,186	33,173
NAE	8,235	10,192	12,935	15,618	18,377	23,003
GMW	3,658	5,017	6,700	8,000	8,917	10,375
NMW	3,294	4,515	5,989	7,122	7,847	9,178
SM	3,760	5,349	7,147	8,162	11,183	13,306
GMW/GAE	34.6	37.3	37.4	35.9	32.8	31.2
NMW/NAE	40.3	44.7	46.3	45.6	42.7	39.9
GMW/SM	97.3	93.8	93.7	98.0	79.7	78.0
NMW/SM	87.6	84.4	83.8	82.7	70.2	69.0

Notes: [a] Per head, for an urban couple with two children.
GAE = Gross average earnings.
NAE = Net average earnings.
GMW = Gross min. wage HUF/month.
NMW = Net min. wage HUF/month.
SM = Subsistence min. HUF/month.
Source: MÜM Bérmegállapodások főosztálya: A minimálbér szerepe kormányzati megközelítésben. 1851–1/1995. IV/3 (Ministry of Labour, Department of Wage Agreements: The role of the minimum wage – from the government's point of view) (June 1995, CSO data).

control continued to rise. The shrinking proportion of wage earnings in total incomes, especially for low-paid groups, both reflected and explained the lack of interest in a minimum wage from a social protection point of view (see table 9.3 and figure 9.1).

However, unlike some other countries of the region Hungarian minimum subsistence calculations became more sophisticated and the subject of ever-wider interest, but it was only in 1985 that the CSO was allowed to publish subsistence minima figures for the first time in the post-war period. These figures showed a HUF 2,500 minimum subsistence level (and a HUF 3,050 social minimum) per head for economically active families against a HUF 2,000 minimum wage for 1984. Neither politicians nor experts took a firm position regarding the extent to which the minimum subsistence level should be covered by wages and/ or social benefits. While minimum subsistence figures continued to rise, the minimum wage remained at its 1983 level for five years. From 1988 it gradually approached the CSO minimum subsistence figures and in 1990, uprated three times, it rose above that level, although remaining below the alternative minimum subsistence level calculated for a Budapest district. After 1990, the year of the regime change and the best year of the

274 Jenő Koltay

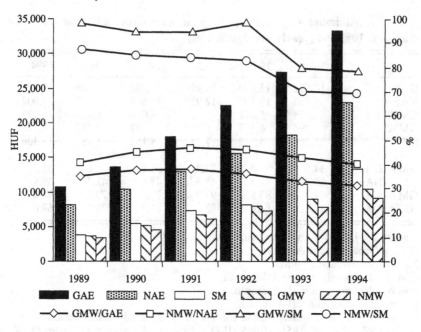

Notes:
GAE = Gross average earnings
NAE = Net average earnings
SM = Subsistence minimum HUF/month
GMW = Gross minimum wage HUF/month
NMW = Net minimum wage HUF/month

Source:
MÜM Bérmegállapodások föösztálya: A minimálbér szerepe kormányzati megközelítésben.
1851–1/1995. IV/3 (Ministry of Labour, Department of Wage Agreements: The role of the
minimum wage – from the government's point of view) (June 1995).

Figure 9.1 Proportion of wage earnings in total income, 1989–94

new minimum wage, it again began to fall below the minimum
subsistence level.

Heated debates continued and a kind of tripartite minimum subsistence
commission, formed in 1989 by Parliament, agreed on the primary
importance of minimum subsistence level calculations in orienting the
wage, tax and social security policies and called for an objective, but
socially determined minimum subsistence with solid foundations, to
serve as a reference point but not a subject for bargaining. The CSO
published quarterly new and already official figures, based on the 1991
household panel survey.

A consensus was beginning to form not only on the introduction of a statutory minimum wage but also on its regular adjustment taking into account the evolution of minimum subsistence level. Policy makers, social partners and experts were less unanimous on how closely the minimum wage should follow the minimum subsistence level and which subsistence minimum should serve as a reference point: should it equal the minimum subsistence level of a single wage earner, as defended by the unions (mainly the still dominant MSZOSZ), or should it fill the income gap left by an average wage *plus* children benefits in a two-adult, two-child household, up to the family minimum subsistence level, as advocated by some experts? The first figure is much higher (e.g. HUF 19,200 for an urban single person against HUF 13,750 per head for an urban family with two children in September 1994).

These questions, pertinent or not, were still open when the CSO in 1995, facing substantial changes in consumption levels and patterns, a deterioration in the quality of statistical data and contradictory judgements on minimum subsistence figures, put an end to minimum subsistence calculations and publication. Not only the link, but also the difference between minimum wage and minimum subsistence then became evident. Minimum subsistence is a social category to be covered at household level partly by wages, partly by other incomes (social benefits). Responsibility for it, shared by employers, government and local governments, is in redistribution, with a tendency to shift the burden from enterprises to government and from central government to local governments, along with much confusion around a safety net and needing to harmonise legitimate demands and scarce resources.

Since 1993, the part of total incomes composed of wage earnings in general and of state sector wages in particular, further diminished because of the dramatic fall in production and employment and the shift to unemployment, inactivity or work in the private sector was responsible for a complementary rise in the volume and share of transfer payments (unemployment benefits, social assistance payments), capital and other non-wage incomes. Open and increasing inequalities in wages, incomes and wealth, and poverty and deprivation at the bottom of the wage and income scale presented a strong argument for a statutory minimum wage and its regular adjustment to protect the low-paid, particularly those in the shrinking state or the expanding private sector not covered by collective agreements or public servants' statutes. Of course, low wages do not always mean low income; minimum wage earners belong to two different types of household: a less wage dependent, with substantial non-wage income, and a wage dependent, with negligible non-wage income, living in many cases below minimum subsistence level. School leavers earning the minimum but living in families with higher incomes

Table 9.4. Subsistence minimum, consumer price and minimum wage growth in Hungary, 1971–95

Year–month	Subsistence minimum		Consumer prices	Minimum wage	
	(in HUF per head[a])	(in % of previous year)	(in % of previous year)	(in %)	(in % of SM)
1971	1,320	..	102.0	..	72.7
1976	1,550	..	105.0	126	78.0
1982	1,920	124	106.9	112	70.3
1983	2,060	107	107.3	148	97.0
1984	2,200 (published)	107	108.3	100	90.9
1985	2,390	109	107.0	100	83.7
1986	2,500	105	105.3	100	80.0
1987	2,790	112	108.6	100	71.7
1988	3,180	114	115.7	150	94.3
1989–03	3,760	118		123	98.4
–10	..	..	117.0	133	..
1990–02	..	..		120	..
–09	4,990 (official)	133		140	112.2
–11	5,600		128.9	145	103.5
1991–01	6,450	115		100	89.9
–03	7,848		135.0	121	89.2
1992–01	8,870	113		114	90.2
–08	10,980		123.0	114	72.9
1993–02	..	..		113	..
–08	11,830	108	122.5	113	76.0
1994–02			118.8	107	
1995–02				116.2	

Note: [a] Calculated from CSO data, taking the average of different types of households
Sources: Calculations based on CSO; OMK data collected by Z. Orolin

form a special group (Freeman, 1994). We do not know much about the relative weight of these groups, the majority and probably most family-head minimum wage earners are to be found in the second group, although those working in the private sector are often under-reported for tax purposes but have a fair remuneration (see below for a trade union proposed remedy).

Even if the regular adjustment of the minimum wage to the evolution of the minimum subsistence level or to average wages is socially indicated and strongly supported on the employee side, it remains controversial – among other reasons – because of its presumed but unclarified impact on employment and wages above the minimum level (see table 9.4).

Employers are already aware of the social implications of the minimum wage, but they are also becoming more and more sensible of the impact of minimum wage increases on wage costs. After the extraordinary employment fall and with a low number of vacancies, jobs paid at a not fully adjusted minimum wage level or even below it, could be more attractive for job seekers. Much depends of course on the level and availability of unemployment compensation and social assistance.

6   Wage bargaining and/or minimum wage bargaining

State controls on wage determination and employer–employee relations had already been somewhat loosened in the 1980s (the lessons and limits of enterprise reforms are analysed in Koltay, 1986), but the transition to a market economy, implementing parliamentary democracy and redistributing property rights, opened up the perspective of collective bargaining and social partnership. The relevant legal frameworks – from trade union freedom and strike law to employers' autonomy – are in place, but problems of ongoing economic transformation and the asymmetry in industrial relations – with a still over-powerful state, weak or only emerging employers' associations and unions – do not favour collective bargaining.

The logic of collective bargaining, with the need to set a strict floor on wages and wage increases, first appeared with the negotiations on the minimum wage and then on wage guidelines representing the negotiated minima for wage increases, even if not always effectively. Central wage regulation before transition had been concerned only to fix a wage ceiling and shop floor level bargaining was only informal. As shown above, macro level negotiations in the tripartite ÉT are more or less active, but branch and enterprise level collective bargaining remains weak and sporadic. The employees' side is fragmented, the employers' side even more so. Union membership and coverage is shrinking, employers' federations do not have the necessary branch organisation structure to conduct negotiations and the authority to conclude and enforce agreements in the expanding private sector. Bargaining know-how and institutions at more decentralised levels, such as joint committees with equal representation of both sides, are still lacking.

The largest number of branch level collective agreements on wages was concluded in 1992. Most of the 24 agreements concerned only groups of enterprises, not whole branches and 21 of them (covering only 790,000 – that is, 40 per cent of employees in industry) contained at least a figure on average wage increase minima; in most cases these were only

Table 9.5. Collective agreements on wages in Hungary, 1992–6

	Branch level					Enterprise level		
	1992	1993	1994	1995	1996 I–VI	1992	1993	1994
Wage agreements (no.)	24	12	12	8	9	391	394	490
Firms concerned (no.)						950	712	622
Employees covered (in %)	40	12	11	5	7	25	32	21
from this								
Agreements								
on wage tariffs (no.)	12	10	10			118	177	219
on average wage incr. (no.)	17	6	6			292	291	293
highest min. incr. agreed (%)	14	14	18					
min. incr. recommended by ÉT (%)	13	10–13	13–15	12^a				
highest max, incr. agreed (%)	28	25	23					
max. incr. recommended by ÉT (%)	28	25	21–23	23^a				
on basic wage inc. (no.)	..	3	2			255	388	419
on wage minimum (no.)	6	7	7			71	198	183
highest figure agreed (HUF)	9,600	11,000	15,000	..	..		16	582
minimum wage fixed in ÉT (HUF)	8,000	9,000	10,500	12,200				

Note: ^{a} No ÉT agreement on wage guidelines for 1995, figures are recommendations of the employers' side.
Sources: OMK; Tóth (1995).

recommendations, not binding employers to give a corresponding rise for each employee concerned. At firm level about 400 agreements (covering 570,000 employees) were registered in the same year, containing more concrete (in some cases binding) wage increase figures. Instead of widening the scope and improving the wage setting capacity of collective agreements, however, a fall-off in new negotiations and renewal of outgoing agreements has been observed. By the end of 1994 12 branch level wage agreements were in force, in the first half of 1995 only 8 remained, covering about 10 per cent of all employees. The number of enterprise agreements on wages was increasing somewhat, but their coverage was shrinking (see table 9.5).

The total number of collective agreements readjusted from the past or concluded recently, including those detailing workplace labour relations, working conditions and some fringe benefits, is certainly higher. According to National Labour Centre (OMK) survey estimates, in 1993 there was some kind of collective agreement in about 38 per cent of enterprises, while the number of enterprise wage agreements (known from mandatory registration) was only 394. The statement that in transition economies a high proportion of at least state sector workers is covered by collective bargaining and their wages set this way (Jackman, 1994) does not hold for Hungary, if both coverage and contents of collective agreements is taken into account; it may be true if only the legal framework is considered.

Intermediate level tripartism failed to establish itself. At the macro level, government, unions and even employers have found it easier and cheaper to agree on minimum wage increases than on overall wage increases or overall wage increase limits. They accepted that minimum wage negotiations should be at the forefront of the bargaining scene, but had diverging views on the extent and frequency of minimum wage adjustments. Employers' positions were formed under increasing wage cost constraints; this holds also for the state, as a still dominant employer in public services, administration and the rest of the state sector. None of them had crystallised ideas on the role and functions of a guaranteed minimum wage in a transforming economy, but all of them were eager to demonstrate some positive results of interminable negotiations. Government and unions badly needed any success to help consolidate their position in the ever more painful transition process.

From the start of tripartite negotiations, the unions, old and new, were united in pushing the minimum wage increase before other bargaining issues and the majority of the fragmented union side followed the one-dimensional social approach of the largest MSZOSZ confederation in demanding minimum wages in line with or higher than the minimum subsistence calculated by the CSO. Only the new and small LIGA confederation expressed some reservation on possible negative consequences for prices and employment.

The ÉT partners consented to negotiate in terms of the (revised) minimum subsistence level, reflecting the continuously deteriorating living conditions, and agreed to corresponding minimum wage increases for 1990 and 1991. There was more sympathy on the government side, employers' representatives were becoming more reluctant because of the direct, indirect and potential impact of minimum wage increases on wage costs, with particular regard to increases in wage related levies and their propagation effect along the whole wage scale (Orolin, 1992).

Employers were told by the government that what the public sector, as the poorest employer, could afford should be reasonable for all other employers. The strongly divided employers were unanimous on this issue: minimum wage increases should remain in line with the ability to pay of the employers in the worst economic position – if not, numerous low-paid jobs would disappear. As a second best solution they (in vain) proposed lower taxes in compensation for higher wage costs; their next step was to demand (temporary) relief from the minimum wage increase. The agreement reached on this point raised the delicate problem of differentiated minimum wage fixing for agriculture, but also for other branches where the average wage was close to the minimum wage level (see below).

For most employees, the minimum wage represents the only guaranteed wage increase, agreements containing binding figures on a minimum obligatory increase of wage rates along the whole wage scale being rare. By demanding higher minimum wages trade unions aimed for increases in other wages, too. This familiar 'abuse' is rather strong in Hungary today, when real wages are falling, but the room for wage increases is rather limited; the social partners should take over the government's role in wage determination, but institutions and routines of collective bargaining are lacking. In such circumstances minimum wage negotiations using social arguments addressed to a government still deeply involved, serve partly as ersatz general wage negotiations based on market position and bargaining power of employers and unions.

It is undeniable that minimum wage increases create pressure for wage increases at higher levels, too, and have probably influenced wage decisions of employers cautious to preserve or widen hierarchical wage differences for incentive purposes. But the success of such efforts is compromised by the same circumstances which converted the minimum wage into a general bargaining tool. In the very large public service sector the new statutory wage scale was originally built directly onto the minimum wage, but was disconnected even in the implementation period in order to attenuate the budgetary impact and indirect demonstrative effect for other sectors. Another example is the confusion surrounding the 1992 complementary 'agreement' on economy-wide wage minima for different levels of the wage scale, taking the minimum wage as a starting point, on which the ÉT partners agreed, but were reluctant to decide if these wage rates were binding for employers or only a recommendation.

Looking at the few branch level agreements containing provisions for wage minima, the amount negotiated is in several cases above the statutory minimum wage fixed in the ÉT; these provisions are intended to be binding, while negotiated average wage increase figures are only recommendations. Usually the agreements take the statutory minimum wage as a starting point, complemented by a negotiated minimum for the average wage increase (the 1992 bakery branch agreement, for example, set the latter at 13 per cent but resulted in only a 4.5 per cent increase in terms of wage level, Ladó and Tóth,1995).

Table 9.6. The evolution of wages and prices in Hungary, 1992–6

	1992	1993	1994	1995	1996
ÉT wage guidelines in terms of average incr. of AW (%)	23	18	17–19	17[a]	19.5
in terms of minimum incr. of AW (%)	13	10–13	13–15	–	13
in terms of maximum incr. of AW (%)	28	25	21–23	–	24
Inflation forecasted (%)	20–25	14–17	16–22	26–28	20
Gross AW inc. in the enterprise sector (%)	26.6	25.1	23.6	19.7	
inflation (%)	23.0	22.5	18.8	28.2	

Notes:
AW = Average wage.
[a] No ÉT agreement on wage guidelines for 1995, figure is a recommendation of the employers' side.
Sources: OMK; CSO.

As figures of general wages evolution show (see table 9.6), wage increases were slowing down even as central wage controls were being abandoned and remaining more or less in line with negotiated wage guidelines; average recorded wages lagged behind price increases, except for the 'political' wage upswing in 1994 (a parliamentary election year), corrected the following year by a roughly 10 per cent drop in real wages.

The contents of wage agreements and the general evolution of wages show that minimum wage-centred bargaining could not do much for wages above the minimum level and guarantee an overall rise in individual wage rates, today the room for wage increases cannot be substantially enlarged in this way. On the other hand, the dangers associated with a 'free' rise of wages – which are real while macro-economic imbalances and precarious enterprises prevail (cf. Köllő, 1993 on doubts if changes in enterprises' wage increase-moderating behaviour were definitive) – have not materialised.

The present arrangement, especially the role of the ÉT and its future as the main institution of a wide-ranging and loosely defined tripartism, is at the centre of political debates (Héthy,1995). Discussed here in the context of wage determination only, it is developing into an appropriate institution to negotiate minimum wages and (while it is necessary) wage guidelines, but in a market economy it cannot assume the wage determining functions of bilateral collective agreements.

It is not yet clear if tendencies keeping wage decisions centralised will strengthen, or if wage setting responsibilities will be shifted to more decentralised levels. It is too early, and may even be misleading, to judge as yet how corporatist Hungary is, measured by such criteria as centralisation in wage negotiations, government role and weight, union density and wage dispersion (on which Cörvers and van Veen, 1995, give a recent review).

Under the specific circumstances of a transition period, the combination of minimum wage and wage guideline negotiations on a macro level, and more market-based unilateral employers' decisions, associated with some wage bargaining on a micro level seems to work, probably better than shifting wage setting to under-developed and inefficient institutions of branch level bargaining. Perhaps it fits the hypothesis (Calmfors and Drifill, 1988) that both highly centralised and highly decentralised systems are likely to do better from the point of view of macroeconomic performance than intermediate ones as it is by no means a system somewhere in between, but much more a mix of both extremes.

7 Protection of the low-paid and the minimum wage

The minimum wage in Hungary has moved far away from the role of a simple redistributive tool. Frequent social arguments used in minimum wage bargaining still evoke its original dimension and it has a stake in social policies, even if the outcome of the ongoing redistribution of social responsibilities between government and employers is not at all clear. When inflation is kept under control, there are no shortage phenomena and the minimum wage still stands comparison with the average wage, the minimum wage can protect the low-paid. In some other countries of the region, facing hyperinflation and shortages coupled with a sharply dichotomous double price system (e.g. in Russia or Moldova, where the minimum wage represents only 5 per cent of the minimum subsistence level), a completely eroded minimum wage cannot assume such a role, either in the protection of the low-paid or in the determination of wages.

Without attempting a comparative evaluation here, several things suggest that it is perhaps no more biased and no less efficient than other instruments blamed for similar deficiencies in the far from textbook Hungarian context. First of all, it is simple, transparent and relatively cheap from an administrative point of view, even if in addition to the single rate there is a subminimum below a certain age. Its fixing is in the right place from an institutional and procedural point of view, which is not the case with other redistributive tools; this should be appreciated in Hungary, where tax and transfer schemes are subject to interminable negotiations and constant modifications, becoming more and more complicated and less and less efficient. Further, it does not increase the high GDP:tax ratio and the budgetary deficit as opposed to subsidies and transfer payments which would be a better option if taxes were lower. It escapes targeting problems and does not interfere with market economy reforms in the budgetary sphere. The fact that it is associated with work can be a supplementary argument in economic policy debates.

An important point to be added (Freeman, 1994), is that it increases the incentive to work, unlike transfer payments, consumer subsidies and in-kind benefits. The latter certainly reduce incentives to work, but it is difficult to foresee how a higher wage floor, a positive incentive for workers but a higher entry cost for enterprises could shape the labour market and improve the chances of low-paid workers and low-paying employers. According to Freeman, it might promise easier enforcement and control, if affected workers complained about non-compliance. This does not seem to work in Hungary (see discussion below) but can help to keep associated costs at a reasonable level. One should not trust the minimum wage alone to protect the low-paid, whose relative position depends much more on the general state of the economy and on specific employment policy measures such as training and retraining schemes.

8   Enforcement and fragmentation of the minimum wage

The guaranteed minimum wage was introduced in a period when market economy institutions were being implemented and the economy was in deep recession. Changes in ownership and corporate governance, rising costs and taxes and evolution of the labour market tended to enlarge the scope of the minimum wage.

There were signs at the end of the 1980s that much larger groups than the young and the unskilled were being paid around the minimum wage level. The deepening of the economic crisis widened the pool of enterprises and branches paying low wages to employees ranging from the long-time disadvantaged to those who had recently lost their government-protected wage position, including traditional small enterprises, craftsmen, workers in cooperatives, communal services, light industries, agriculture and more and more public services like education, health and some heavy industries. It was no secret that branches in the worst position lagged years behind the minimum wage increases. Enterprises in difficulties often 'forgot' or were unable to pay the official minimum to their workers, as they did not pay social security contributions to the budget, for example. Others in better shape were paying more than the minimum wage but under-reporting for tax purposes (see table 9.7). A flashback to 1988, the year when the minimum wage was

Table 9.7. Estimated number and proportion of employees paid at minimum wage level or close to it in Hungary, 1991–3

Year	Basis of calculations of employees	Enterprise sector Number	(%)	Public services Number of employees	(%)
1991–7	7,100 HUF (minimum wage:7,000 HUF)	261,429	10.3	no data	no data
1992–1	8,000 HUF (minimum wage:8,000 HUF)	..	..	80,907	9.2
1992–11	8,200 HUF (minimum wage:8,000 HUF)	122,538	5.7	9,555	1.5
1993–10	9,200 HUF (minimum wage:9,000 HUF)	94,329	5.8	64	0

Sources: Ministry of Labour; Personal earnings survey.

conceived, shows that according to the rather approximate figures 28 per cent of those employed in agriculture, 27 per cent in retail, 15 per cent in craftsmanship and 13 per cent in light industries earned less than the HUF 3,700 minimum wage envisaged for the following year. In 1990, about one-quarter of all wage earners were, at least temporarily, below the minimum wage (raised in two steps to HUF 5,600), half of them worked in agriculture, the rest in textiles, trade, transport and construction. Even in public services one-fifth were affected by the minimum wage increase.

According to ÉT figures, in 1992, for example, 27 per cent of all employees (585,000, excluding public service) – 52 per cent of those working in agriculture, 41 per cent in light industries, 32 per cent in trade, 22 per cent in food processing, 9 per cent in electrical energy production and 6 per cent in chemical industries – were paid below HUF 9,000, the minimum wage amount negotiated for the next year (*Magyar Hírlap*, 1 December 1992). A Ministry of Labour survey gives lower figures, around 300,000 in May 1992, for the total number of those affected by the minimum wage increase – 24 per cent in agriculture and 16 per cent in light industries, etc. (*Figyelő*, 3 December 1992).

Statistical data and estimates on the number and characteristics of wage earners affected by the minimum wage are often too rough and sometimes more contradictory than in countries having a long experience with minimum wages (cf. Freeman, 1994). In Hungary, problems begin with the quantity of available information and continue with its reliability, therefore it is unwise to compare figures in table 9.7 with estimates showing a similar scope for the minimum wage in France or the USA in the 1980s.

Table 9.8. Distribution of under-payment, by branch and sector in Hungary, 1994

	% of employers concerned	% of employees concerned
Construction	17.8	1.4
Industry	19.5	1.5
Trade	21.0	2.6
Catering trade	3.7	10.0
Transport	10.1	0.2
Health and social care	9.1	0.2
Agriculture, Forestry, fishing	22.4	0.9
Post, tele- communication	7.7	0.4
Education	0	0
Other	24.2	1.6
Grand total	16.3	1.6
State enterprise	12.0	0.2
Corporation[a]	17.6	1.4
Cooperative	26.7	1.5
Public service	7.0	0.2
Other (entrepreneurs, associations, etc.)	34.9	9.9

Note: [a] In private, state or mixed ownership.
Source: Calculations based on data collected by the Hungarian Labour Inspectorate (OMMF).

The first, and up until now only, economy-wide campaign in May 1994 surveyed 1,845 employers and 104,033 employees in all sectors, branches and professional categories in proportion to their respective weights (without being statistically representative). Cases of payment below the minimum wage due were revealed in 22 per cent of the enterprises surveyed affecting 1.6 per cent of the total number of employees on average, but much more in branches with a higher proportion of low-wage earners (around 10 per cent of the total number of employees in catering, for example). The results confirm the tendencies of recent years for branch and sectoral distribution of under-payment (see tables 9.8 and 9.9); it was most frequent in small private enterprises and entrepreneurs (34.8 per cent) and least frequent in public service employers (7 per cent).

Table 9.9 shows that manual workers are affected proportionally 8 times more than other groups, unskilled workers 2.7 times more than skilled workers, part-time employed 2.5 times more than full-timers and

Table 9.9. The size distribution of under-payment for different categories in Hungary, 1994

	Total no. of employees	<1,000 HUF	1,000–2,000 HUF (no. of employees concerned)	>2,000 HUF
Manual	26,085	904	414	239
Non-manual	77,948	41	13	4
Unskilled	70,771	504	239	157
Skilled	33,262	449	186	80
Woman	42,420	404	170	89
>18 years	778	9	6	4
Part-timer	2,281	63	23	2
Pensioner	2,798	65	37	42

Source: Calculations based on data collected by the Hungarian Labour Inspectorate (OMMF)

working pensioners 3.3 times more than other groups. The only significant change is the gradual disappearance of gender differences – women were previously 3 times worse off than men in this respect. Unfortunately, no conclusions could be drawn on the age group under 18, because of their low number in the sample. As for the size of under-payment, survey results show that in the majority of cases it is around 10 per cent, but it can reach 20 per cent or more.

In the enterprises surveyed, typical cases of employers' 'negligence' were: not keeping up with changes in the minimum wage if they occurred within a year (which was usual that time); failing to calculate the proper minimum wage of employees working more or less than standard working time; paying disproportionately less to part-time workers and not paying more for longer working time, arguing that they were simply honouring the official minimum wage. If there is no written contract or record of the wage actually paid, frequent in small and medium-size enterprises, it may readily be supposed, but is difficult to prove, that under-payment has taken place. A similar problem frequently met in such enterprises is 'payment by results' without fixing the wage rate for a 100 per cent performance.

Departing from information gathered in enterprises surveyed, the typical delay in honouring minimum wage adjustments in deviant branches and enterprises is about one year. Tripartite negotiations in 1989 had accepted a couple of months' delay in adjusting the minimum wage to its statutory level in agriculture and in the non-agricultural cooperative sector. At the end of 1991 the same sectors were allowed to agree later on the date when the last increase should enter into force. In

1992 textile and food processing industries obtained unconditional relief from paying the actual minimum wage.

Disparities in wage paying capacities and tax compliance gradually led to a kind of branch level minimum wage bargaining in a non-negligible part of the economy with the outspoken or tacit approval of the ÉT, including the government. Repeated declarations and limited checks trying to enforce the minimum wage increases throughout the economy could not hamper the early fragmentation of the national minimum wage. Perhaps this gave the idea to the major trade union (MSZOSZ) to create another dimension of fragmentation with a proposal on hierarchically differentiated minimum wages. The three-stage structure would add to the present minimum wage a second for skilled workers and a third for those with a higher education. The arguments justifying this are twofold: first, it is only fair to exclude remuneration below qualification level; second, this would represent an effective measure to combat payment according to qualification level but under-reported.

Employers disapproved of the idea and the MSZOSZ-influenced government has so far expressed no official opinion, although the proposal remains on the bargaining table despite the failure of negotiations on a global economic and social agreement (Héthy, 1995) envisaged by the government and later replaced by a wage and price agreement not yet rejected or definitively concluded. In the context of the present analysis, this multiple rate proposal means not only potential further fragmentation, but also the most recent sign of using the minimum wage as a universal bargaining tool.

9 Minimum wage prospects and possible changes

The above proposal is certainly not the proper way to compensate for labour market and industrial relations' deficiencies and to develop minimum wage-fixing in the right direction. In countries with much longer experience a differentiation of the minimum wage by category and grade is an extreme case diluting the entire minimum wage concept (Italy being the only example). Some other countries are aiming at either limited changes preserving the scheme's basic characteristics or a total withdrawal. For the latter the UK is the only example (where a minimum wage of limited scope disappeared with the abolition of the Wage Councils in 1993). Elsewhere, recent changes have tended to erode its value relative to average wages and make it less binding by loosening or suppressing indexation to prices or wages (in Belgium, Italy, the Netherlands; and also in Greece, where the automatic indexation caused a substantial reduction in wage differentials) and by creating a subminimum for young workers (in Belgium, the Netherlands, France, Spain, Portugal and the USA).

International experience shows that times when minimum wage adjustments raised the wage of the lowest paid faster than the general wage rise are over, even in countries where a higher minimum wage, coupled with lower fringe benefits, taxes and other cost increasing levies is more acceptable than in Hungary, where these items are rather high.

If efforts to increase systematically the relative level of the minimum wage by automatic indexation or some other means were successful in a country with high inflation and unemployment, it would only aggravate the inflationary pressure and tensions on the labour market. And it would certainly call for a restructuring of the present wage determination system. Occasional attempts to raise the wage floor relative to average wages would only lead to further fragmentation of the minimum wage.

If indexation to productivity or some other macroeconomic indicator of productive efficiency is not compatible with a negotiated system, macroeconomic performance in general and productivity gains in particular should orient minimum wage negotiations. Hungary can cope with moderate yearly adjustments and preserve the single rate of the minimum wage. This does not exclude a subminimum for young workers aged under 18 or 19 or a temporary 6-months' subminimum for school leavers, though the full dimensions of this problem are not known and international experience is not unanimous on the positive employment effect of subminimum wages, although it suggests that they should be kept under the umbrella of minimum wage fixing.

10   Concluding remarks

In market economies, minimum wages have long been a fixture in the bargaining process, with greater or lesser government intervention, by legislation or by collective agreements. The original and still primary objective is to improve the position of the lowest-paid employees, but it gained a role of varying importance in the whole wage bargaining process, influencing increases along the whole wage scale with an impact on wage differentials and on employment.

With positive growth rate, low inflation and a balanced budget, minimum wages are regularly adjusted and generally enforced and their impact on other wages and wage costs does not compromise macroeconomic policy goals. Minimum wage increases remain in line with average wage growth and the number of workers paid at the minimum wage level does not increase, or even tends to decrease.

In Hungary, with a mix of macro level negotiations and enterprise level wage decisions, the bargaining function of the minimum wage may prevail over its social function. Under-developed bargaining institutions and deficient bargaining skills on the one hand, falling employment, high inflation and a budgetary deficit on the other, make it difficult or impossible to harmonise the social and bargaining functions of the minimum wage.

In such circumstances with sharply increasing wage differentiation, shrinking average wages in real terms and more workers paid around the minimum level or below, intensifying minimum wage demands and agreed increases can hardly assure effective protection for the low-paid and do much for the wages above the minimum level, aimed by the pressure for higher minimum wages.

Despite its bargaining 'abuse', a guaranteed minimum wage may remain an appropriate means to protect the low-paid in an economy in transition. Of course it cannot assure the subsistence minimum even in an economy where inflation is kept under control and there are no shortage phenomena. It could share this task with other benefits financed by enterprises, central and local governments according to a pattern of wage structure reshaping.

For the emerging social partners, especially for weak trade unions and governments in trouble, the minimum wage has a special legitimacy function. An agreement on a minimum wage increase can be one of the rare success indicators, relatively easy to get and demonstrating social sensibility and a willingness to cooperate in difficult times. The high level and the persistence of unemployment raises the question of the disregarded and unclarified impact of minimum wage increases on employment in the specific circumstances of Hungarian economic transformation.

NOTE

I am grateful to György Kopits (IMF, Budapest), Jean-Jacques Silvestre (LEST–CNRS, Aix-en-Provence), Daniel Vaughan-Whitehead (ILO–CEET, Budapest) and Charles Wyplosz (CEPR) for their comments on earlier versions of this chapter as well as to Zsuzsa Orolin (MKI – Labour Research Institute, Budapest) for her help in collecting data and István Ónodi Szabó (OMMF – Hungarian Labour Inspectorate, Budapest) for providing data.

REFERENCES

Bazen, S. and G. Benhayoun (1995) 'Minimum wage protection in Western industrialised economies', in G. Standing and D. Vaughan-Whitehead,

Minimum Wages in Central and Eastern Europe: From Protection to Destitution, Budapest, London and New York: Central European University Press

Calmfors, L. and J. Drifill (1988) 'Bargaining structure, corporatism and macroeconomic performance', *Economic Policy*, 6

Cörvers, F. and T. van Veen (1995) 'On the measurement of corporatism', *Labour*, 9

Freeman, R. (1994) 'Minimum wages again', *International Journal of Manpower*, 15

Héthy, L. (1995) 'Anatomy of a tripartite experiment: attempted social and economic agreement in Hungary', *International Labour Review*, 134

Jackman, R. (1994) 'Economic policy and employment in the transition economies of Central and Eastern Europe: what have we learned?', *International Labour Review*, 33

Katz, L. and A. Krueger (1992) 'The effects of the minimum wage on the fast-food industry', *Industrial and Labour Relations Review*, 46

Koltay, J. (1986) 'Réforme économique et démocratie industrielle en Hongrie', *Revue d'Etudes Comparatives Est–Ouest*, 17

(1995) 'The impact of the minimum wage on Hungarian wages and industrial relations', in G. Standing and D. Vaughan-Whitehead, *Minimum Wages in Central and Eastern Europe: From Protection to Destitution*, Budapest, London and New York: Central European University Press

Köllő, J. (1993) 'Megjegyzés a háromoldalú bérmegállapodások hatásosságáról' (Note on the effectiveness of tripartite wage agreements), *Közgazdasági Szemle*, 4

Ladó, M. and G. Tóth (1995) 'Helyzetkép az érdekegyeztetésről' (Report on the interest reconciliation), ÉT–PHARE, Budapest

Orolin, Z. (1992) 'Az 1991. évi minimálbéralku és tanulságai' (Minimum wage negotiations in 1991), *Kereskedelmi Szemle*, 3

Tóth, G. (1995) 'Bérmeghatározási rendszer' (System of wage determination 95), *Munkaügyi Szemle*, 5

Discussion

GEORGE KOPITS

Chapter 9 by Jenő Koltay contains a comprehensive account of the evolution of the minimum wage in Hungary since the early market oriented reforms. In particular, it explores the collective bargaining and social protection functions of the minimum wage. The author argues rather convincingly that, in recent years, the minimum wage has served

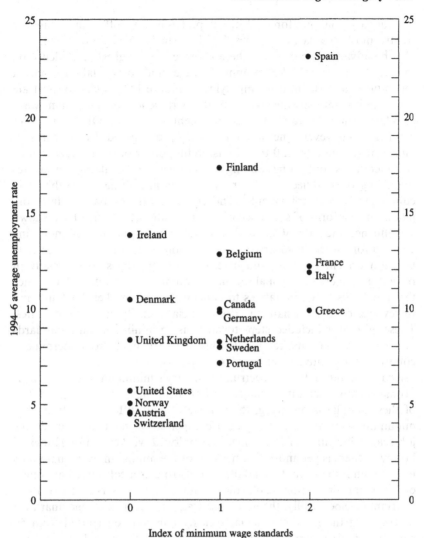

Figure D9.1 Relationship between unemployment rate and minimum wage standards, selected OECD countries, 1994–6

more as a bargaining tool for organised labour than as an anti-poverty instrument. Although the chapter recognises the possible effect of the minimum wage on unemployment – on the basis of a cursory review of the empirical literature on several advanced economies – this issue is left out of the scope of the investigation. In addition, the chapter fails to inquire about the influence of the minimum wage on the informalisation of Hungary's labour force. Without pretending to offer an exhaustive treatment of these last two issues, I wish to shed some light on them.

In the advanced economies, there is more than suggestive evidence on the contribution of the minimum wage and other labour market regulations to structural unemployment. Figure D9.1 seeks to illustrate the positive relationship between the stringency of minimum wage standards and the rate of unemployment for major OECD member countries. However, the minimum wage, quantified by a synthetic indicator (ranging from 0 to 2, in ascending order of stringency), can be considered as only one among a number of regulatory measures (including those reflected in increased hiring and firing costs) that may contribute to unemployment.[1] The effective rate of payroll taxation, mainly in the form of social security contributions, has also been shown to influence the rate of unemployment.[2] Indeed, because of mounting concern for the likely adverse effect of various regulations and of payroll taxation on employment and external competitiveness – especially in response to increased globalisation – a number of countries have since the mid-1980s taken initiatives to enhance labour market flexibility and to reverse, or at least halt, the rise in social security contribution rates. These initiatives included steps toward easing minimum wage standards and other labour market regulations that are likely to undermine a country's competitive position in external markets.

Across the international spectrum, Hungary's minimum wage standards probably rank at an intermediate level of stringency. The inhibiting effect of these standards on living, the relatively small difference between the minimum wage and unemployment compensation tends to dampen the job search incentive of low-skilled unemployed workers.[3] For Hungary, however, there is yet another dimension of the minimum wage that needs to be taken into account. In addition to its role as a collective bargaining or a social protection tool, the minimum wage serves as a fiscal instrument. Specifically, the minimum wage is used as the benchmark for determining the minimum social security contribution (raised from 60 per cent of the minimum wage in 1995), even if the actual wage of the employee falls below the minimum wage. (For this reason, occasionally, increments in the minimum wage were seen by the government as a benefit in disguise, inasmuch as they were expected to result in a much-needed revenue increase for the ailing social security system.) Thus, as the effective contribution rate (employee *plus* employer shares) exceeds one-third of the gross labour cost – a rather high rate by international standards – the adverse employment effect of the minimum wage is exacerbated.

Nonetheless, in Hungary, the actual unemployment effect of the minimum wage may be of secondary importance. More significant are perhaps the effects of the minimum wage in promoting the expansion of informal employment and the compression of declared money wages – the rest of the remuneration consisting of unrecorded cash payments and payments in kind – toward the minimum wage, so as to evade, or at least minimise, the social security contribution liability. The extent of these effects can be surmised from some surveys and estimates,[4] supported by ample anecdotal evidence.

Let me conclude by suggesting that future research on the minimum wage in Hungary be expanded to investigate, if possible empirically, its consequences for structural unemployment as well as the informalisation of the labour force. A likely implication of such research will be that efforts are needed to reduce prevailing rigidities in the labour market and to pursue a comprehensive social security reform that will allow for significant cuts in payroll contribution rates.[5]

NOTES

The views expressed do not necessarily reflect those of the International Monetary Fund.
1   See OECD (1994, chapter 4).
2   For recent international evidence, see Kopits (1997).
3   I am grateful to Gyula Pulay for bringing this point to my attention.
4   See Ékes (1993).
5   See Kopits (1995).

REFERENCES

Ékes, I. (1993)*Rejtett gazdaság – Láthatatlan jövedelmek, tegnap és ma* (The underground economy – invisible incomes, yesterday and today), Budapest: Oftech

Kopits, G. (1995) 'A foglalkoztatási és a szociálpolitika külgazdasági összefüggésben' (External implications of social and labour market policies), *Külgazdaság* (November), 65–73

(1997) '¿Contribuyen los impuestos sobre la nómina al desempleo? Análisis y evidencia internacional' (Do payroll taxes contribute to unemployment? Analysis and international evidence), paper presented at the Fifth Conference on Taxation of the Argentine Professional Council of Economic Sciences (Mar del Plata, 25–28 June)

Organisation for Economic Cooperation and Development (OECD) (1994) *Employment Outlook*, Paris: OECD (July)

10 Welfare institutions and the transition: in search of efficiency and equity

IVÁN CSABA AND ANDRÁS SEMJÉN

1 Introduction

In communism or state socialism an all-encompassing public sector played a major role in nearly every walk of life. It has generally been accepted that the transition to a market economy requires a strong emphasis on competition, and this makes change in the underlying ownership pattern necessary. The private sector (rapidly developing due to the privatisation of state-owned assets and a significant increase in the number of newly emerging private enterprises) must assume the lead from the public sector. However, there are certain areas of economic activity where the public sector is likely to keep a dominant role even in the longer run: it will justifiably remain a major producer of public goods and publicly provided private goods. There is a robust and clear economic rationale behind the public financing of public goods; nevertheless, economic theory does not provide a clear case for public provision or government production of public goods. It comes as no surprise, then, that institutional arrangements vary from country to country in this respect. In the case of impure public goods or mixed goods (such as education or health care) there is an even greater variety of possible institutional arrangements. However, the existence of market failure as well as some distributional concerns might provide a compelling rationale for government involvement in many areas. The border-lines of the public sector must be redefined in transitional economies: this redefinition will take place not only in sectors like primary industries or manufacturing but also in the field of public utilities and formerly government provided services.

In market economies the issue of efficiency within the public sector has aroused considerable interest for a long time and played an especially important role in determining government policies throughout the 1980s. Public sector efficiency became a top priority issue on the political

294

agenda in many countries (especially in the UK and the USA), and this factor undeniably led to interesting institutional arrangements (such as the emergence of quasi-markets in many fields of services). At the same time in communist economies efficiency in the 'traditional' public sector was largely neglected; these countries tended to favour bureaucratic provision across the board, running a high risk of X-inefficiency. Hungary was no exception: although the idea of simulating market forces was central throughout the history of economic reforms in Hungary, it hardly affected the realm of health care, education, or social services in the years of 'market socialism'. However, increasing budgetary pressures have put the issue of welfare reform on the agenda relatively early. Even in the mid-1980s the government had started to redefine its social welfare responsibilities, and started to move backwards, that is towards Bismarckian social insurance principles.[1] At the same time, some measures were also taken in local government finance that had an effect on locally provided public services.

Our goal is to analyse the situation in selected subsectors of the welfare system, and to show the policy responses to some economic problems related to 'traditional' public responsibilities during economic transition in Hungary. Due to limitations of space we cannot give a comprehensive picture here: we try, however, to give a proper background first by providing a concise overview of main trends in social welfare spending and institutional changes in the main welfare-related areas. Then we try to concentrate on two main policy fields: pensions and health care.

2 Some general trends

2.1 The inheritance

There is an interesting duality in the present welfare system: its main proportions and many of its institutional characteristics still reflect the remnants of the communist past. At the same time it already shows the effects of a new social paradigm responding to the needs of a market economy. The welfare system inherited from the communist period was common to a certain degree in all communist countries,[2] and though Hungary certainly developed a 'soft' version of state control and dominance, it was still no exception from the general rule. The communist state had subjects and not citizens, and while on the one hand it guaranteed a considerable level of security to its subjects (*inter alia*, a high level of job security and reasonable income security for old age and for some contingencies), on the other it deprived them of their ability to lead an independent life without relying on direct or indirect state assistance. Welfare policy was not a separate subsystem with identifiable social costs and benefits, instead it penetrated the economy as a whole. Needless to say, in such a system little if any role was played by voluntary non-governmental organisations and charities, however, family and kinship did retain a strong role in providing safety.

Many welfare functions – normally allocated to social policy in market economies – were left to employers, mainly in state-owned enterprises or cooperatives. However, the expanded social responsibility of employers was neither a beneficial consequence of competition on employment conditions nor was it due to union bargaining or a significant role given to social participation, as is often the case in those social democratic or corporativist Western democracies where employers do play a bigger role than the one accepted in liberal market economies. It was more a consequence of centrally distorted prices and wages and a far from clear-cut distinction between company and state.

The state also operated an all-encompassing system of *price subsidies* that led to very low prices for some goods (e.g. basic foodstuffs, drugs) and services (rented accommodation, heating, gas, electricity, public transport), created bottlenecks and shortages, and made rationing inevitable. The state was also the sole provider of some *merit goods*. Merit goods were usually provided as in-kind benefits, either for free or for a nominal charge. In such a system, the state and the company could effectively together control their subjects or employees and maintain discipline by providing or denying access to vitally important goods and services. As far as cash benefits are concerned, the communist welfare system was based primarily on work-related cash benefits. Under the conditions of labour shortage benefits tied to employment in the state-owned sector functioned also as instruments to achieve a high activity ratio. The coverage rate of transfer programmes has been gradually extended by including employees of the cooperative sector and liberalising eligibility conditions. Thus we can depict a trend towards (quasi-)universal benefits in the 1970s and 1980s. This development could also be considered as a partial compensation for the limited political freedom and the lost economic prospects constituting an important part of the implicit deal[3] between the population and the party state. Social expenditures relative to GDP doubled between 1960 and 1981 and Hungary together with Czechoslovakia and East Germany, formed a group of Eastern bloc countries with a relatively high 'welfare effort' (Gács, 1987; Kornai 1992). It should be noted, however, that in the early 1980s total welfare spending was well below the average of the developed market economies and it did not reach the level of OECD countries at a similar degree of economic development.

2.2 Redefinition of state responsibilities and the challenge of economic transition

It is quite evident that transition to a market economy brought about a strong decline in the importance of subsidies and the free provision of merit goods, and gave a more prominent role to cash benefits that at least do not impose limitations on consumers' choices. There has also been an inevitable shift from universal benefits towards means-testing. It was also generally accepted that the inherited system, with its strange mix of conflicting roles and functions within the enterprise sector, had to be demolished during the transition as it was incompatible with the requirements of an open and democratic market economy, where enterprises should in the first place aim at profits and efficiency, while the state should explicitly take on some social functions or responsibilities (not denying the important role of self-help, voluntary organisations and charities). It was also more or less understood that such a change in the social policy paradigm would inevitably lead to an increase in the share of government welfare spending to GDP, though (especially at the beginning of the transition) there were some illusions that budgetary savings due to the cut in price subsidies might compensate the expenditure effects of introducing new elements to the social safety net. However, as we shall see later, this was not the case and welfare expenditures kept growing as compared to a steadily decreasing GDP.

The emerging welfare system and the associated social expenditures were influenced by (1) economic performance, (2) need and (3) policies. Hungary, similarly to other post-communist economies, experienced a transitory recession. It was perhaps somewhat less severe than in countries usually associated with shock therapy, however, it took the economy somewhat longer to recover from it. Real GDP had fallen to 80 per cent of its 1988 level by 1993, while industrial output fell even more dramatically, reaching its deepest point (at 74 per cent of its 1988 level) in 1991. An important reason behind this was that exports fell drastically (from a 39.2 per cent average level of GDP between 1979 and 1989 to 26.5 per cent of a much smaller real GDP) due to mainly external factors: the collapse of the COMECON market and a lasting recession in Western Europe. In addition, the transition and privatisation process itself also contributed to a certain extent to the transitory recession. While some countries have chosen a transitory path with moderate or gradual structural adjustment and they managed to escape or postpone high unemployment rates, Hungary has chosen a more radical approach. Loss making production was no longer tolerated, and the hardening of the budget constraint in the enterprise sector was indeed impressive.[4]

However, this welcome process had some grave employment consequences: high open unemployment and an increasing number of
discouraged workers. The government's response to intensifying labour
market tensions was to pursue policies that allowed an increase in the
economically inactive population depending on social transfers. Between
1989 and 1995 the share of the employed population dropped from 46.2
to 35.5 per cent while more than 1.4 million jobs were lost (Andorka,
1996).

The increased need for welfare could also be indicated through the extent
of poverty – a largely hidden phenomenon and a political taboo in the
communist past – which became visible and explicit. From 1989 to 1993,
the incidence of poverty increased substantially for each poverty line used
in the World Bank's report on poverty (World Bank, 1996). The share of
households with income below the minimum pension (on a per adult
equivalent basis) increased from 1.6 per cent in 1989 to 8.6 per cent in
1993, while the proportion of households with income at half of mean
household income increased from 4.3 per cent in 1989 to 34.6 per cent in
1993 (see World Bank, 1996, p. 3). However, a narrow (15–20 per cent)
poverty gap[5] clearly indicates that poverty in Hungary has remained
'shallow'. This fact could be attributed to the intensifying 'welfare
efforts' of the government to contain the social costs of transition.

2.3   Social expenditures

While the share of total public expenditures remained relatively stable
during the transitory period (representing approximately 57 per cent of
GDP) there were significant changes in the composition of governmental
outlays. The role of 'economic redistribution' and public investment was
steadily diminishing, to be replaced by an increasing share of social
expenditures (Manchin and Szelényi, 1987). Consequently expenditures
on social welfare occupied an increasing proportion of the national
product in the early 1990s.

As table 10.1 indicates, in the peak year the share of social spending to
GDP was 17 per cent higher than in 1989. However, the various spending
programmes did not change in the same direction. Subsidies on consumer
goods, services and housing played a decreasing role[6] (see table 10.2)
while spending on unemployment, social assistance and retirement
pensions increased remarkably: the structure of social spending became
more similar to that of the developed market economies. This changing
composition of public welfare activities also contributes to the fact that
Hungary realised a share in social expenditures which is comparable with
the highest spending countries within the OECD. Using the OECD

Table 10.1. Social expenditures (share of GDP), by programmes, 1989–93

	1989	1990	1991	1992	1993
Pensions	9.1	9.7	11.3	11.6	11.3
Family support	4.0	4.8	5.4	4.8	4.6
Unemployment[a]	0.2	0.3	1.3	2.9	3.2
Sick pay	1.2	1.2	1.3	1.0	0.9
Health care	4.6	5.2	6.0	6.1	6.3
Education	5.2	5.5	6.2	6.9	6.9
Housing	5.2	4.5	3.9	2.8	2.5
Price subsidies[b]	3.7	3.1	3.5	2.2	2.1
Total	33.2	34.3	38.9	38.3	37.8
Real growth (1989=100)	100	99.6	99.5	94.5	92.6

Notes:
[a] Including unemployment benefits and expenditures on social assistance.
[b] Subsidies on consumer goods and public services excluding subsidies on medicine.
Sources: Andorka *et al.* (1994); unemployment: UNICEF (1995); education: Halász and Lannert (1996).

Table 10.2. Structure of price subsidies, 1991–5 (expenditure on main types of price subsidies as percentage of total price subsidies)[a]

	1991	1992	1993	1994	1995
Milk and dairy products	8.7				
Household energy	48.8				
Local transport	15.0	37.9	36.3	38.1	38.8
Railways	10.4	33.1	31.3	27.6	25.1
Bus transport (excl. local)	8.7	28.4	32.2	33.9	35.7
Other	0.1	0.6	0.2	0.5	0.4
Water and sewage	8.4				
Total price subsidies (mn HUF, current price)	40,400	16,900	22,850	26,332	32,720

Note: [a] Subsidies to drug prices are not included.
Source: MoF.

classification of welfare programmes Hungary reached a share which is 5–6 per cent above the average of the most developed market economies while having much lower *per capita* GDP (see table 10.3).

The relative growth of social spending took place in a period of economic recession: in other words the denominator was reduced to a considerable degree. This implies that the income elasticity of welfare

Table 10.3. Social expenditures in an international context, 1993 (share of GDP)

	Public health	Aged	Non-aged	Total
Hungary (1993)	6.3	9.9	11.5	27.7
EU average	5.4	8.5	7.7	21.8
OECD average	5.7	9.2	7.7	22.3

Note: OECD data refer to 1991.
Source: World Bank (1995).

spending was below one. When studying expenditure figures it also should be taken into account that the marketisation of the economy involved the expansion of the black market partly due to the limited tax collecting ability of the state: thus the actual share of public welfare might be considerably over-estimated. The 'true' GDP may be 30 per cent higher than the officially published one, which is only partially taken into account when measuring the share of public programmes (Árvay and Vértes, 1994, see also chapter 5 in this volume). Even using the official figures the picture is somewhat different if we study social expenditures in real terms: despite the increasing relative share the absolute size of welfare programmes was decreasing in the same period. From the point of view of the welfare burden imposed on the economy, however, those are the relative expenditures that matter. Moreover, with the presence of a wide 'black' economy this burden is shared unevenly. In 1994 in the 'official' economy the total wedge due to social security contributions and income tax constituted 54 per cent of total employer costs and 117 per cent of net wages, which also implies a considerable wedge between the taxed and the untaxed sectors of the economy (World Bank, 1995). This can have adverse effects not only from the equity point of view. Taking into account the considerable wage rigidity the high contribution rates might have an impact on unemployment. In addition, the increased attractiveness of the 'black' economy is also likely to generate misallocation problems.

The relative growth of redistributive programmes could also be seen as the government's effort to compensate individuals for the losses in their market income. Paradoxically, at household level the transition to the market economy resulted in a reduced role of market revenue as a share of total household income. Although transfer policies could not completely fill the gap the fall in household incomes was below the drop in the GDP. Table 10.4 illustrates the growth in the share of transfer incomes during the transitory years.

Table 10.4. Share of income categories in total household incomes, 1991–5

Year Income categories	1991/2	1992/3	1993/4	1994/5
Market incomes	62.8	55.8	54.3	59.8
Social insurance	30.0	34.2	34.8	32.6
Public social transfers	5.6	6.2	6.0	5.2
Inter-household transfers	0.5	0.4	0.7	0.5
Other income	1.1	3.4	4.2	1.9
Total	100.0	100.0	100.0	100.0

Note: The data in this table refer to 12-month periods starting from April of the first year (before the slash) and ending in March, next year (after the slash).
Source: Tóth (1996).

There are no comprehensive data (at least not in a breakdown comparable with the one used in table 10.1) yet on welfare spending for the period following 1993. However, all available evidence suggests that the relative size of the social budget has been shrinking in subsequent years. The mid-1990s represent a marked policy turn as far as welfare policies are concerned. In the early transitory period social policy was used as an instrument of managing the social problems caused by economic recession. The extensive system of public transfers was able to contain poverty in a considerable degree, but it also offered a non-negligible source of income for middle classes with a declining economic position. In this respect, some analysts argue that welfare policies have contributed to the legitimisation of the rather dramatic economic and social changes and to the stability of the new democratic system. However, this strategy had its own costs. Although the economic recovery started in 1994 it was accompanied with increasing macroeconomic and fiscal imbalances. From the policy makers' point of view these imbalances reached an intolerable level. Moreover, the budgetary burdens associated with the welfare system were perceived as a key factor behind the emerging situation. This led to austerity measures (named 'Bokros-package' after the finance minister of the time) introduced by the new socialist–liberal government in early 1995. The consolidation package included measures that aimed to curb social spending by explicitly tightening eligibility rules and the quality of welfare programmes. At the same time ambitious plans were announced to push the boundaries of the state back and to tackle the perceived inefficiencies of social services. (These measures and reform proposals are illustrated below for the case of public pensions and health care.) Apart from explicit policy changes, that received strong and often effective public resistance, the inflationary erosion of benefits has also contributed to the lessening of the welfare burden. A similar effect is likely to be associated with restrained public spending in the period when the economy, though rather slowly, started to grow.

2.4   Institutional developments

The process of institutional reforms aimed at the welfare sector had already started at the end of the 1980s. The reform agenda was certainly influenced by the main trends of Western welfare policies and public finance. There were some general principles and methods prevailing in the reshaping of welfare institutions. However, these principles influenced the actual course of the institutional development to a very different extent in the various sectors. Perhaps the four most important elements of this reform process are:

- the *strengthening of the insurance principle*
- a *shift from universal benefits towards means-testing*
- *decentralisation*
- a *gradually increasing role of private provision and privatisation* of welfare services.

2.5   The strengthening of the insurance principle

There has been a shift from non-contributory benefits to benefits based on previous contribution. This trend does not necessarily mean greater reliance on private insurance markets, though that also can be observed; however, it clearly shows that greater emphasis has been given to risk sharing techniques in welfare policy. Hungarian social policy makers seem to understand that in many cases where private insurance is doomed to fail due to some problems of insurance markets, social insurance can offer a viable alternative. This trend can be observed in the creation of an unemployment insurance system, and also notably in public pension policy and health care. Universal entitlements were gradually converted into insurance coverage based on premium payments (e.g. health care reform). Similarly, some non-contribution-based elements of pension entitlements have been (or are being) reconsidered. This trend actually requires that some entity – the central budget or some extra-budgetary funds – pay the contributions for all entitlement-earning periods. Some other endeavours of pension policy also can be interpreted in the spirit of this principle.

2.6   The increased role of means-tested benefits

The old welfare system contained many universal or quasi-universal entitlements, the latter associated with the high activity ratio and the corresponding high coverage rate of employment-related benefits. The dramatic rise of unemployment, together with the strengthened contributory principle, has led to an increased role being played by means-tested benefits. In the early 1990s the existing social insurance and universal transfers were supplemented by public assistance programmes, in particular for those with a lengthy unemployment spell. The increasing fiscal tensions and widening income inequality subsequently turned the attention of policy makers towards better targeting of scarce resources. The nature of compensatory policies pursued in the first period of economic transition are well characterised by the fact that in 1993 more than 90 per cent of all households were recipients of one or more cash benefits (World Bank, 1996). The policy shift aiming at improving this pattern and containing public expenditures meant not only an increased emphasis on targeting, but also the identification of targeting with means-testing. The fiscal consolidation package of 1995 which turned maternity benefits and family allowances into means-tested benefits, represents an important milestone in this policy change. However, it should be noted that these reshaped programmes resemble rather the Australian means-tested arrangements as opposed to narrowly targeted poor relief benefits: the statistics indicate that only about 7 per cent of all children were excluded from family allowances as a consequence of the income ceiling introduced (Tóth, 1997).

2.7   Decentralisation

Decentralisation of welfare services meant in Hungary that many former government responsibilities were formally redefined as local public services. The new law on governments (enacted in 1990) redefined the roles and responsibilities of municipalities; it made democratically elected local governments obliged to provide some basic services to their inhabitants. The elements of this system bear a strong resemblance to the distribution of powers and responsibilities between local and central governments in many West-European countries. The system as a whole, however, can be viewed as a rather unique and unhappy combination of two models: one[7] is based on a wide scope of welfare responsibilities assigned to a relatively small number of localities with relatively high population numbers, the other[8] is based on relatively few and less significant welfare responsibilities assigned to a great number of local authorities, having much smaller average populations than in the previous case. In Hungary, the number of municipalities exceeds 3,000 and the average population of local municipalities is only 3,300. Yet municipalities were assigned a wide array of responsibilities (Illés, 1996). This is also reflected in the fact that the share of local government expenditures in general government expenditures is about twice the usual size of those in countries with comparably small average population numbers in municipalities. Local authorities receive non-categorical formula grants from central government as well as being able to retain some part of Personal Income Tax (PIT) revenues collected from their inhabitants, and they can also levy certain taxes. However, their wealth and financial possibilities are diverse and only vaguely related to need (this is especially the case in the sphere of local social services and public assistance). The most important examples of local public welfare services are education for the 3–18 age group and some personal social services. Local municipalities can also play a significant role in the provision of rented accommodation or social housing. Hungarian municipalities, due to a relatively over-sized rented housing sector in the cities and the transfer of the ownership rights of rented housing stock from central to local (municipal) level at the start of the transition, seemed to be predestined to play such a role. However, they decided to follow a different path (see further details below).

2.8   Increasing role of private provision and privatisation

Given the extensive role played by the state in the welfare sector it is not surprising that the emergence of private welfare is rather limited as compared to the privatisation taking place in the other parts of the economy. Nevertheless, in some areas such as education or primary health care private providers became a viable alternative to the public sector. There is a growing non-profit economy offering welfare services to the population and in some cases for-profit providers have also appeared on the market. Privatisation (or denationalisation) became especially important in two sectors: one is education where it mostly means the transfer of schools back to their previous church owners; however, the role of foundation-run schools is also likely to increase in education.[9] The other is housing, actually the rented accommodation within the housing sector. The privatisation of state-owned housing stock started with the transfer of the ownership rights of the rented housing stock from the state to the newly formed municipalities. Between 1990 and 1994 51 per cent of the rented housing stock was sold to tenants at a nominal price and with subsidised long-term credits from the local government (Dániel, 1996). The expectation is that 80 per cent of the former rented housing stock will soon be privatised. Although this way of privatisation implies that a great deal of 'national gift' is given to the average new owner-occupier, there are groups of former tenants unhappy with the result as their current housing costs move up to a high level relative to their income. It is fair to point out that rented housing could have been sold to private landlords instead of tenants (perhaps at a higher price). However, the actual privatisation led to an almost total elimination of rented housing: there is hardly any big city in the world where the rented accommodation sector is so small as in Budapest.

2.9 Other developments

Some other important general institutional developments are represented by greater reliance on *user charges* in the case of public services; *cooperation with* the emerging *NGO sector* in the form of *contracting out* public services (especially in education and in social welfare services) and the emergence of *quasi-market* type arrangements. The health sector provides an example for the latter development (see later); it can also be traced in some other sectors, though to a much lesser extent (Bara, 1996; Semjén, 1995a). Nevertheless, as the Hungarian way of socialism after 1968 was characteristically based on simulating market forces, it is somewhat surprising that the problem of X-inefficiency in the public sector and quasi-markets has not been given greater emphasis as a suitable technique to reduce this problem.

3 Public pensions[10]

3.1 Institutional developments

The present pay-as-you-go (PAYG) public pension system is the successor of the 1946 PAYG pension scheme that was introduced in the place of the funded system that had collapsed previously.[11] By creating the PAYG system the government was able to preserve benefit entitlements while cutting the direct connection between individual contributions and benefits: in the early phase, benefit payments could be financed by a relatively low contribution rate (originally set at 3 per cent of wages and salaries). As the number of elderly increased and entitlements were extended – in particular as a consequence of the 1975 Social Security Act – contribution rates were raised. Nevertheless, the balance of the pension system was difficult to assess in the post-war period owing to the lack of any formal separation between the central and the social insurance budget:[12] if in any given year revenues from contributions exceeded expenditures[13] the resulting surpluses were not used to accumulate pension fund reserves but were simply spent by the central budget.

Hungary arrived at the threshold of transition with a defined benefit PAYG pension scheme that had reached a high degree of maturity. In 1990, the separate Social Security Fund (SSF) was formed. This was a major step in the gradual process of strengthening the insurance features of the Hungarian public pension system at the expense of diminishing its redistributive functions. Pension insurance contribution rates were set at a high level: 23 per cent (after 1997 24 per cent) of gross wage was to be paid by the employer and 6 per cent by the employee. In 1992 the SSF was actually divided into two independent funds to allow the separate financing of public health care and pensions. Task-shedding started in both funds: for the Pension Insurance Fund (PIF) it meant that some pension payments were taken over by other entities – early retirement pensions are covered by employers and the Employment Fund, while disability pensions are financed by the Health Insurance Fund.

In parallel with the institutional diversification within the SSF the foundations of a multi-pillar pension system were laid down by the creation of a legal framework for voluntary mutual pension schemes. Personal saving in these pension funds was encouraged by strong tax incentives as compared to other forms of voluntary old age security (buying pension insurance or life insurance from private insurance companies or investing personally in the securities market). Given these conditions this new form might be attractive for anyone wanting to increase his or her personal replacement rate and having some money to save. It seems to have had a particular appeal for two groups: the first consists of well paid employees, company executives and other similar categories with uncovered earnings (earnings above the ceiling on employee's contribution); the other is a group avoiding payroll tax payments[14] (inter alia, by keeping those forms of income that involve contribution liabilities down to a minimum and transferring the main part of their income into tax exempted forms). Creating a legal framework for private pension funds must be considered a most welcome measure which might have had beneficial effects on savings. However, it might have also contributed to a further erosion of the contribution base of the mandatory pension scheme.

The history of the public pension system in the 1990s could be characterised as a series of adjustments to tackle emerging pressures and improve the financial viability of the scheme. These adjustments were primarily directed to the pension formula. Thus the *earnings replacement formula* was adjusted twice in the 1990s: while the 1991 changes strengthened the existing redistribution in the formula towards those with lower earnings the 1993 modifications benefited higher earners.[15] At the same time, the accrual factors that allocated greater value to the earlier years of employment, diminishing the incentives to stay on, were left unchanged. The modifications affected the length of *assessed wage history* as well, which was extended. Originally only the best three of the last five years of earnings were used in the pension formula to determine the average wage on which pensions were based. In 1992 the fourth best year was also included, and since 1993 earnings for all years since 1988 are used when calculating average earnings. This measure was taken partly to prevent the manipulation of pay rises during the last years of employment; it also helped to reduce the replacement rate. Indexation of earning history was not a concern when inflation was low and the earnings assessment period short; however, with the lengthening of this period and the arrival of two-digit inflation rates it became a crucial issue. The presently used method of revaluing earnings history indexation is far from adequate, as the last two years are excluded from the revaluation. With yearly inflation rates around 20–25 per cent this practice reduces the average earnings in the pension formula nearly by half. This is a major factor behind the decreasing real value and replacement rate of new pensions.

Prior to 1993 there was no *automatic indexation of benefits*: ad hoc adjustments were made from time to time. As pension increases always had to exceed a certain absolute minimum and were capped by a maximum, the inner proportions between pensioners with low and high initial awards within the same pension cohort changed considerably. This led to a situation where the lowest pensions became 'over-compensated', while average and higher pensions lost their value as compared to prices or to wages (see Antal *et al.*, 1995a, 1995b). The automatic indexation of pensions introduced in 1993 was based on the growth rate of net average wages. This practice did not prevent further losses in the real value of pensions, but it ensured that real pensions followed the trend of net real wages. During a period of declining real wages this method was less costly than indexing to prices. However, when real wages grow (as had already happened in 1994 due to political motives[16] and as is bound to happen eventually) this method will over-compensate pensioners for price inflation, increasing pension expenditures further.

The effect of the adjustments discussed above could be depicted by studying the trend in the value of average pensions. The modified rules resulted in the relative reduction of pensions for the newly retired. While

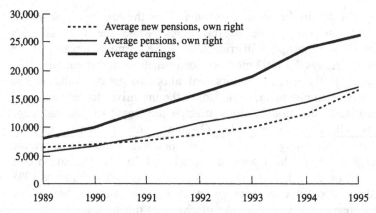

Figure 10.1 Average pensions, new pensions and average earnings, 1989–95
Sources: Pensions: ONYF data; earnings: CSO *Statistical Yearbooks* data.

until 1990 the cumulated effect of inflow to and outflow from the stock of pensioners was clearly contributing to the increase of the average value of pensions, this trend was later reversed (see Antal *et al.*, 1995a). In 1989, the average new pension exceeded the pension average by 10 per cent (own-right pensions only in both cases); by 1992–3 new pensions already lagged behind the pension average by 20 per cent (see Tóth, 1994). Figure 10.1 also clearly shows this as well as the decline of the replacement ratio.

3.2   Problems of the present pension system

The recent performance of the public pension insurance provoked many criticisms from all sides: employers, employees, pensioners, ministries, foreign investors, international organisations, and others. Although these criticisms do not always point in the same direction, we can speak about a common core. Let us briefly sum up here the typical views concerning the performance of the current pension system.

3.2.1 An excessively high share of GDP spent on public pensions
This is often claimed in studies prepared by the government or international organisations. While public spending on old-age, disability and survivor pensions in 1980 totalled a manageable 7.8 per cent of GDP, in the 1990s these expenditures went up to around 11 per cent. An OECD study claims that 'the annual share of Hungarian resources allocated to public pensions rivals that of the most generous systems in

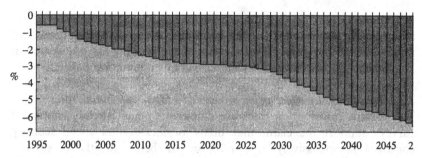

Figure 10.2 PAYG deficits in the absence of reforms, 1995–2050
Source: Rocha and Palacios (1996, p. 15).

OECD countries' (OECD, 1995, p. 97). It is certainly true that this share is more than twice as high as in Japan, the USA, Australia or Canada. However, if we compare it to that of other European countries it does not seem so much out of line: Finland, France, Germany, Italy, the Netherlands, Sweden and Greece all had higher shares than the Hungarian one in 1990 (cf. table 4.1 in OECD, 1995). Nevertheless, the relatively high share of pension expenditures might somewhat reduce the propensity to invest in the economy, and this might be a serious problem in the transition period with tremendous structural adjustment tasks.

3.2.2 Long-term financial viability of the PAYG system at risk

All long-term simulations – despite some differences in their assumptions concerning demographic trends or GDP growth rates – corroborate the finding that in the next century the Hungarian public pension system might become unmanageable if serious changes are not made in due time (see, for example, Augusztinovics, 1995; World Bank, 1995; or different calculations made by the Ministry of Finance and the self-government and the PIF). This is documented in figure 10.2, showing that in the absence of reforms,[17] by 2050 (keeping the current contribution rates fixed) the current PAYG deficit would amount to more than 6 per cent of GDP (Rocha and Palacios, 1996). The 'no reform' scenario would also result by 2050 in a system dependency ratio exceeding 120 per cent with an implicit contribution rate – the rate required to cover pension expenditures – more than 60 per cent.

One word of caution is probably needed here: the demographic forecasts (indicating the drastic drop in population to 8.5 million and the parallel rise of the age-dependency ratio) on which the long-term unsustainability even of a *reformed PAYG* can be predicted might be overly pessimistic, not least because they ignore the possibility of migration. Given the fact that there are significant Hungarian ethnic minorities living in neighbouring countries, where living standards fall well below the Hungarian level, the size of the working-age population in Hungary might be considerably influenced by immigration policies.

3.2.3 Tax avoidance and evasion produced by high contribution rates

The present contribution rates are dangerously high already: empirical surveys support the claim that many businesses find social security contributions excessively high and many of them – mostly the smaller ones – try to diminish payroll tax payments by taking advantage of the different loopholes[18] (Semjén, 1995b; Semjén and Tóth, 1996). Not only did payroll tax avoidance become an increasingly common practice in all spheres of the economy, including the public sector, but tax evasion due to unreported employment and income also became a significant problem (see chapter 5 in this volume).

3.2.4 Inequitable pension system

Most of those who criticise the current pension scheme on equity grounds point to the loose or arbitrary relationship between individual efforts – contributions – and the size of individual entitlements. From this point of view 'equity' is often interpreted in terms of the contributory principle as opposed to vertical equity and thus inequities are attributed to the non-linearity of accrual factors and the regressiveness of the pension formula which promises a higher replacement rate at lower income. At the same time, the continuous tinkering with eligibility rules and the often ad hoc inflation adjustments would be difficult to justify from any equity point of view. These practices not only eroded the value of pensions in absolute terms or relative to wages but they also altered the relative value of pensions within cohorts (see Antal et al., 1995a, 1995b). While the equity concerns discussed above present higher-income individuals as losers, the picture may be different when taking into account the life expectancy and the age–earnings profiles of different groups (World Bank, 1995). Given the fact that lower income groups typically have a lower life expectancy and their age–earnings profile is flatter compared to higher income and skilled workers, they may end up realising a lower return on their contributions despite the degressive formula.

3.2.5 The pension system does not provide sufficient old-age security

That pensions are inadequate is also a commonly held view. However, even if benefits are regarded as low it cannot be due to low replacement rates or the benefit formula but should be related to the low level of earnings. The effectiveness of the pension system in providing old-age security could be evaluated considering the incidence of poverty according to age. Analyses based on micro data indicate that the age profile of poverty is U-shaped, but this age–poverty line is rather asymmetric: when using different measures the incidence of poverty is typically the highest amongst the youngest while the age group between 50 and 69 years faces the lowest risk of poverty which increases again above 70 (Andorka and Spéder, 1997). Therefore it could be argued that the pension system provides a relatively good protection against poverty especially for the 60–69 age group. At the same time the majority of pensioners belongs to lower-income households (in 1994 62.3 per cent of old age pensioners belonged to the first two income quintiles) and amongst the retired there are some groups facing relatively high poverty risk such as invalidity pensioners and widows living alone (Tóth, 1994).

3.3 Determinants of the pension system

We now try to analyse the underlying factors determining the performance of the pension system before we get down to the discussion of the possible courses of treatment. In particular, three groups of determinants deserve attention:

(1) demographic trends combined with the maturation of the PAYG system
(2) factors related to transition
(3) specific rules of the Hungarian pension system.

When discussing the role of these factors we make use of a well known identity of PAYG pension systems between the implicit contribution rate[19] (p), the system dependency ratio (SDR) and the replacement rate (RR):

$$p = SDR \cdot RR$$

where SDR shows the rate of pension recipients to contributors (active population)[20] and RR is the ratio of average pension benefits to average earnings. Table 10.5 presents the changes in these variables for the time period 1960–94, where implicit contribution rates are expressed relative to the net average wages.

3.3.1 Demographic trends combined with the maturation of the PAYG system

The system dependency rate has been increasing steadily with the maturation of the pension scheme: between 1960 and 1990 it has more

Table 10.5. Long-term changes in the characteristics of the public pension system during its maturation process, 1960–94

Year	1960	1965	1970	1975	1980	1985	1990	1994
System dependency ratio (%)	13.4	23.7	27.7	34.4	35.8	40.8	46.1	71.8
Replacement rate (% of net wages)	32.4	32.3	34.4	42.2	55.5	56.2	66.1	60.8
Implicit contribution rate (% of net wages)	4.3	7.6	9.5	14.5	19.8	22.9	30.4	43.6

Source: Based on Bod (1995) and CSO, *Hungarian Statistical Yearbook* data.

than tripled. This development, however, is closely associated with extended eligibility rather than the accelerated aging of the population (OECD, 1995). It is quite common to relate the problems of the Hungarian pension system to demographic factors, yet it is not quite justified. Population aging in Hungary is neither more extensive nor faster than in most OECD countries. In fact, the demographic situation has been temporarily improving: the old-age dependency ratio (the ratio of 60+ population to 20–59 population) was 0.36 in 1994 as compared to 0.38 in 1990. (Ironically, this improvement is not due to steadily increasing birth rates but is an unhappy consequence of earlier demographic fluctuations and the poor health status of the population.) However, eventually it will rise to 0.42 by 2015.

3.3.2 Factors related to transition

The largest increase in the system dependency ratio was realised between 1990 and 1994. The system dependency ratio not only became excessive in international comparison, but also extraordinarily high as compared to the old-age dependency ratio. If we measure the old-age dependency ratio on the horizontal and system dependency ratio on the vertical axis, the point representing present-day Hungary is one of the furthest upwards from the 45 degree line when compared to other countries (cf. figure 3.2 in World Bank, 1995). The emerging situation cannot be attributed to the maturation of the pension system, but it mirrors the consequences of the transition in the labour market. In the period analysed the rate of unemployment rose from 0.4 to 13 per cent. In addition, the economically active population dropped by more than 900,000 and members of the active-age population leaving the ranks of the economically active were responsible for about about 69.5 per cent of total exits to inactivity. This has also resulted in an increasing numerator of the system dependency ratio as the number of retired active age individuals increased by about 160,000, totalling 14 per cent of all pensioners in 1994. The most important source of this development is the number of newly awarded disability pensions for younger workers resulting in one of the highest ratios (15 per cent) of disability pensioners to contributing workers (Rocha and Palacios, 1996). It might be suspected that lenient control of disability pensions offered an easy exit for workers facing unemployment and also for those who could become better off by combining pensions with income derived from the black market. This point raises the possibility that governmental policies – increasing the room for exit into inactivity and retirement – also contributed to the worsening situation of the pension system.

3.3.3 Specific rules of the Hungarian system

The rules built into the pension scheme affect the system's performance both directly and indirectly. The direct effects are represented by the actual regulations stipulating the age of retirement and the methods used for calculating the amount of pensions, while the indirect effects are related to the incentives provided by these rules. The very low in international comparison statutory age of retirement (55 and 60 years for women and men, respectively, left unchanged for decades before the 1996 enactment of its gradual increase) is also responsible for the high system dependency ratio. At the same time the replacement rate relative to net wages offered by the public pension system is far from being exceptionally high in the international scene: the average replacement rate peaked at 66 per cent in 1990 and it has declined since then, primarily as a consequence of modifications in the pension formula and the inflationary erosion of benefits discussed above. Although these measures helped to ease financial pressures they could not prevent the increase of the implicit contribution rate, which rose to more than 43 per cent relative to net wages and to around 35 per cent compared to the gross wage bill. The pension system thus offers decreasing benefits and rates of return on contributions at increasing expense, providing a strong incentive to evade. The incentives to pay contributions are also weak due to the fact that the calculation of pensions is based only on earnings of the final years. At the same time, the accrual factors give diminishing incentives to stay in employment: this circumstance is also associated with the fact that the system-wide effective retirement age decreased well below the statutory one: it was 53.3 years in 1993 (World Bank, 1995). These features point towards the need for a reform which increases the effective retirement age and increases the link between contributions and benefits. However it should also be taken into account that the performance of the pension system is fundamentally dependent on the general economic situation. Measures that aim to increase the age of retirement through changing the rules of the pension system might have a positive effect on the level of (official) economic activity but it is primarily determined by the ability of the economy to absorb labour. The problem of a high system dependency ratio cannot be very easily overcome. One might be able to get around it by reducing pension eligibility for those below retirement age or with short contribution periods. However, unless labour demand increases and there is a growth in economic activity the burden of low economic activity will not be reduced but it will only be passed over to some other transfer programmes or will result in a changed pattern of redistribution.[21]

3.4   Reform options

As has been already mentioned, there is a general consensus about the unsustainability of the present system; the need for reform is also generally accepted. The problems associated with low retirement age and inappropriate incentives have also gained widespread recognition. The first major step towards a long-term solution was the implementation of the gradual increase of the statutory retirement age, enacted in 1996 after a lengthy political struggle. The new statutory retirement age, 62 years, unified for both sexes, is planned to be reached by 2009. Other measures strengthened the relationship between contributions and benefits and aimed to broaden the tax base of social security contributions. At the same time there is a strong disagreement about the future of the PAYG system in itself. The conflicting views are manifested by two prominent reform proposals – one prepared by the government the other one proposed by the Pension Insurance Fund (PIF). At the time of writing it is not known which one is going to gain acceptance.[22] In the remaining part of this section we thus discuss both reform proposals.

3.4.1 The reform package supported by the government
This proposes a multi-pillar scheme where the compulsory elements are represented by a consolidated PAYG scheme and privately-run fully funded schemes. The latter pillar will be financed from a proportion of mandatory contributions by the new entrants to the labour market and by those older workers who decide to opt out from the PAYG system. Those who stay in but retire after 2009 will get a new reformed PAYG pension: in this scheme, credits for non-contributory years[23] will be eliminated and the pension formula will become linear (with a yearly accrual rate of 1.5 per cent) allowing 60 per cent replacement after 40 years of service. Earnings up to 200 per cent of average earnings will be

covered: above this level no employee contributions will be levied on earnings (employer contributions will not be capped). At the same time, indexation of all PAYG pensions will be based on the average of price and wage index (i.e. 'the Swiss formula'). This reformed PAYG system will also become the basis of the first pillar of the new multi-pillar system. In this first pillar, however, the yearly accrual rate would be reduced to 1 per cent, and there would be a parallel reduction in benefit levels to the two-thirds of benefits available under the one-pillar PAYG option. In both cases there will be some room for flexibility in individual choices concerning the retirement age using discount factors or bonuses in the case of earlier or delayed retirement.

In the new system employers would contribute to the PAYG pillar only, while roughly one-third of total pension contributions would be paid into individualised pension accounts held in private pension funds: a 10 per cent employee contribution would be set out and paid into the mandatory funded pillar. The main part of the contributions diverted to the funds would then be invested on capital markets and the returns on investments would be credited to the individual accounts. Administrative costs and provisions for a mutual Guarantee Fund financed by the pension funds themselves would also be covered by the contributions. The government offers strict regulation, strong supervision and monitoring, but it does not intend to guarantee directly the accounts held in pension funds.

Pension fund accounts can be inherited under the new system in case of death before retirement. Accounts will be converted into annuities upon retirement, and annuities will reflect actuarial principles. This would mean that women would get lower yearly benefits than men with the same amount of money accumulated on their accounts, due to their longer life expectancy. To increase the security of contributors asset management in a typical case would be trusted to big specialised firms fulfilling strict capital adequacy requirements. Accounts will be fully 'transportable': the individual choices regarding pension funds might be altered once a year. Funds with rate of returns falling well below the average rate of return for two consecutive years will probably be liquidated. Investment policies would also probably be strictly regulated to keep risks at a tolerable level. The actual regulations might have crucial consequences on macroeconomic effects of the reform; however, these are not very clear at the time of writing.

Those opting out to the new system would not be given recognition bonds as a compensation for the lost part of their previous contributions (as happened in Chile), but would get compensatory pensions instead. However, the benefit entitlements earned by these years will be reduced by one-third or more (consequently the yearly accrual rates would be reduced to 1 per cent or less). The difference is the price one has to pay for choosing the option of diverting some part of the contributions to a funded tier. This reduction of benefits can be considered an important element of the reform: it can reduce PAYG expenditures and make the transition smoother, but it must also be well calibrated to enable the government to keep the number of employees switching to the new system under control. The voluntary third pillar will supplement the system, allowing employees to achieve higher individual replacement rates at an additional cost. However, as in this new system there is no minimum pension (not even in the reformed PAYG system) there will be a need to finance some redistribution towards the lifetime poor from the central budget. A means-tested social assistance for the elderly as a zero-pillar of the system has been proposed.

If the reform follows the lines of the government proposal, Hungary will become the first Central European country to implement a three-pillar system with a fully funded second tier. This will mean that a significant part of the public pension system will be privatised to a degree which, although not unique in Europe, would place the country in the *avant-garde* of European nations facing the challenges of pension reform.

3.4.2 The PIF's proposal for pension reform

This proposal (see Réti, 1996 for details) contains some measures to consolidate the PAYG system that also constitute an integral part of the government policies presently being implemented, such as the gradual increase of retirement age and broadening of the payroll tax base (Nyugdíjbiztosítási Önkormányzat, 1995). At the same time the PIF proposal is more concerned with the pension system itself than with its macroeconomic impacts or its impacts on the Hungarian capital market. The reform package outlines a system consisting of three tiers. Once the system reached its full maturity the desired proportions between the tiers would be 30:60:10. The first tier would be a universal flat-rate basic pension, financed from general taxation. It would be automatically awarded to everyone above 62, and its level would probably be tied to a minimum wage (it should be somewhere between two-thirds and three-quarters of that). This would make any minimum pension provision in the contribution-based PAYG second tier called 'work pension' unnecessary, so that the redistributive elements in this tier could be kept at a minimum: the non-linearity in the pension formula and in accrual factors could be abolished. The work pension scheme would be based on pension points, resembling the German model. Each year of contribution history with contributions paid on the average wage in the given year

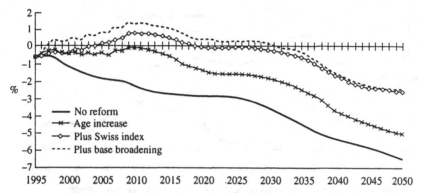

Figure 10.3 Impact of reforms on the PAYG balance, 1995–2050
Source: Rocha and Palacios (1996, p. 28).

would result in one pension point: higher or lower covered wages would result in proportionately higher or lower points. The contribution payment would be equally distributed between employers and employees with wages grossed up accordingly. Wages up to 250–300 per cent of the average wage would be covered and liable for contribution payments. The above two tiers would roughly produce a 60 per cent replacement rate.[24] To these two tiers voluntary pension savings, managed by the already existing mutual pension insurance funds (or some other institutions), would be added as a third tier.

3.5 Assessment

One way to compare the reform proposals discussed above is to study their long-term financial performance. Both reform proposals contained simulation results: unfortunately these are not fully comparable due to differences in time horizon and the underlying macroeconomic assumptions, and in some cases also some vagueness concerning details.[25] For this reason, we rely here mostly on simulations by Rocha and Palacios, allowing us to present separately the hypothetical impact of the consecutive introduction of different reform elements in the government package (Rocha and Palacios, 1996). As some of these elements are also integral parts of the PIF reform package, these results would allow us to draw some conclusions concerning that as well.

  Figure 10.3 incorporates the predicted effects of two measures already legislated: the gradual increase of the retirement age up to a unified 62 years and the broadening of the payroll tax base covering wider income categories. In addition, the simulation assumes the use of the 'Swiss

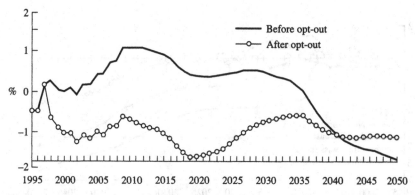

Figure 10.4 Reformed PAYG balance, before and after opt-out, 1995–2050
Source: Rocha and Palacios (1996, p. 31).

indexation' which is a part of the government's package but opposed by the PIF. As shown, the age increase itself can keep PAYG deficits at a manageable level until 2010–15. If it is combined with Swiss indexation the balance will turn into surpluses around 2005 and with the help of base-broadening surpluses can be achieved much sooner. However, the beneficial effect of the latter is diminishing as the broadened base eventually translates into higher pension benefits. The fact that surpluses can be realised through consolidating the PAYG scheme is due to favourable short-term demographics. If the simulation is correct, it indicates advantageous conditions to switch to a multi-pillar pension system by providing the financial sources to cover the deficits in the PAYG scheme resulting from the transition. Similarly, the improvements in the PAYG scheme would create some room to reduce the contribution rate as well. However the potential surpluses to be realised at a reformed PAYG eventually melt away: under the different scenarios the consolidated system stays close to equilibrium until around 2030, but after that increasing deficits appear. The 'before opt-out' line on figure 10.4 shows the cumulated effects of consolidation measures (age increase, base-broadening, Swiss indexation, tightened eligibility rules and a tightened link between contributions and benefits[26] from 2009 onwards) on the PAYG balance, also taking into account the potential positive labour market effects of a 2.5 per cent decrease in the contribution rate. Although the underlying assumptions of this scenario certainly differ from that of the PIF proposal, it certainly shows how far one can get with reasonable measures within the PAYG system alone and in this sense it can be used as a rough approximation of the possible results of the PIF/PAYG reform package.

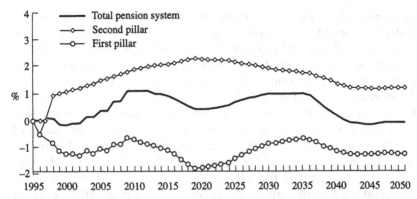

Figure 10.5 Multi-pillar pension system, impact on national savings, 1995–2050
Source: Rocha and Palacios (1996, p. 32).

The main element of the government's reform proposal is, of course, not the reform of the PAYG pillar but the introduction of the mandatory funded pillar for new entrants to the labour market, with an option for older employees to opt out. As was mentioned earlier, those choosing to switch voluntarily to the new pillar would face a certain reduction in their accrued pension rights. In spite of this 'loss' opting out can be 'profitable' for younger workers, due to the expected positive difference between real rate of return of the second pillar and real wage growth. This difference is assumed to be 1 percentage point in the simulations. It is assumed that under these circumstances male employees under 40 and female employees under 35 would opt out to the new system. This would lead to considerable PAYG deficits immediately, as shown in figure 10.4. However, due to the reduced PAYG replacement ratio in the new system and a loss in accrued rights for those opting out, after 2023 the deficit starts to diminish gradually and eventually becomes smaller than in the absence of the opt-out.

The case for this option is presented in figure 10.5: the deficits due to the opt-out would probably be soon offset by an increase in private savings due to the introduction of the second pillar. The simulation shows the multi-pillar system to be clearly superior to the reformed PAYG option in the longer run. The reformed PAYG starts to produce deficits earlier than the multi-pillar system accumulating an increasing debt in the last decade of the simulation period, while the multi-pillar system is projected to have only negligible deficits by the end of the same period.

The simulations discussed above lend support to the government's proposal. Nevertheless, there are several issues that may raise doubts concerning the attractiveness of this reform option. During the lengthy and often heated public debate on the future of the pension system many pros and cons of both proposals were listed. Sometimes the multi-pillar system was presented as the only means to achieve higher national savings, higher investments and economic growth, and sometimes it was depicted as a system with mandatory contributions to a private lottery. On one side of the barricade the risk of pension fund frauds and dangerously increasing administrative costs due to the mushrooming of private funds was (over-)emphasised, indicating that the total return of investing the surpluses could be higher if this task was given to the PIF, while on the other side the low efficiency of public sector investments was contrasted to the expected positive effects of competition between pension funds on investment returns. The possible extent of the expected positive effects on capital markets and growth performance might have been over-estimated by some proponents of the partial switch to fully funded schemes. Even analysts generally sympathetic towards this option note that if the reform was primarily debt-financed (involving the replacement of explicit for implicit debt), its potential growth effects would be very limited. However, if the government is willing to cover PAYG deficits in excess of 1 per cent of GDP from the central budget (as was indicated), this mixed tax and debt financing would allow a gradual increase in national savings at the expense of greater costs borne by current generations. Nevertheless, this line of reasoning clearly shows that the outcome of such a multi-pillar reform will be strongly influenced by the actual regulation with regard to pension fund investment policies and portfolios, which is not yet fully clear.

The extent to which the funded system is immune to demographic shock is also debated. The point has been raised that a demographic shock eventually would lead to 'disinvestment' even in a funded system, and the overall effect of this on the aggregate savings ratio is not much different from that of a deficit in a PAYG system due to the same demographic factors (Augusztinovics, 1995). Once the system matures there arises another risk: if the demographic shock is strong enough to cause considerable disinvestment and at the same time the capital market is relatively small, a considerable disinvestment by the funds might adversely affect stock prices, and consequently realised returns. This example again emphasises the crucial importance of concrete regulations: if capital investment was liberalised, allowing pension funds to invest in foreign securities at will, this would no longer pose a serious problem. However, if foreign investments are fully liberalised for pension funds, or if pension funds are required to invest mainly in gilt-edged securities, the beneficial effect of the proposed pension reform on domestic economic growth becomes less obvious.

Since there is no minimum pension in the new PAYG pillar envisaged by the government, redistribution towards the lifetime poor will be financed by the central budget. The tightened link between contributions and pensions is expenditure neutral within the PAYG system. However, expenditure neutrality must be observed at the level of overall public expenditures if the increase in national savings is to be achieved. Shifting the responsibility for poverty alleviation of the aged into another part of the general governmental budget (social assistance) will not solve anything if aggregate spending increases. However, neither this, nor the other problems indicated above mean that the multi-pillar reform is doomed to fail: these arguments rather emphasise the importance of details and the need for carefully designed reform measures.

4 Health care

4.1 The health system in the communist period

The OECD has distinguished seven models of health care organisation related to the sources of financing and ways of paying providers (OECD, 1992, 1994).[27] Using this categorisation the development of the Hungarian health system could be summarised as a shift from the *public integrated model* towards a version of the *public contract model*, which is based on social insurance financing and involves centrally determined prices as a major method of reimbursing providers. In addition, as we will see below, the health system in both periods incorporated a *voluntary out-of-pocket element* of a specific nature. The main characteristics of the old and the emerging new health systems are summarised in table 10.6.

As in the case of most of the Eastern European countries many features of the pre-1990 Hungarian national health service are captured well by the ideal–typical public integrated model: health facilities were both owned and financed by the state while medical doctors and other clinical staff were state employees; health care was a state monopoly and within the public system no role was intended to be given to competition or patient choice. Similarly, microeconomic efficiency or the quality aspects of health care received little attention. Nevertheless, this organisational arrangement proved to be suitable to run a health system with universal coverage of the population at a rather low expenditure level and to organise major public health programmes (Orosz, 1992).

The resource allocation followed the logic of central planning. Individual units were given fixed annual budgets the determination of which

Table 10.6. Summary of institutional changes in the Hungarian health system

	Pre-1990 health system	The new health system
Systemic description	Public 'integrated' model with a 'shadow' out-of-pocket element	Evolution towards the public contract model with a 'shadow' out-of-pocket element
Sources of finance	General taxation (96%), private expenditures (4%), and 'gratuities'	Social insurance contributions (79%), general taxation (14.5%), private expenditures (6.5%), and 'gratuities'
Ownership	Hospitals and other health facilities owned by the central government	Teaching hospitals: central government Acute and long-term care hospitals and outpatient clinics: local governments Primary health care facilities: local governments and private practices
Reimbursement of providers	Hospitals and outpatient clinics: global budgeting Hospital and primary care physicians: centrally set salaries	Hospitals: DRG-based prospective payment Outpatient clinics: fee-for-service reimbursement Capital expenses: 'line-item' budgeting financed by central and local governments Hospital physicians: centrally set salaries Primary care: capitation
Investment decisions	Central planning and resource allocation based on the principle of 'progressive care' and bureaucratic competition for resources	Considerable local autonomy which is counteracted by intensifying efforts to regulate capacities: new facilities are reimbursed on a contractual basis and regional quotas to be introduced to limit the number of beds
Patient choice	Patients attached to local primary care physicians; strict 'progressive' referral system which is eroded by informal arrangements	Free choice of primary care physicians; the role of referrals is reduced resulting in increased proportion of patient initiated contacts
Entitlement	Health care provided as a citizenship right; the principle of need distorted by informal rationing impacted by gratuity payments and other transactions	Health care provided as a social insurance entitlement or on the basis of means testing; incremental introduction of user charges; persistence of informal rules in affecting the access to publicly financed health care

was influenced by preexisting patterns and by the principle of 'progressive care'. According to this principle, at the bottom of the pyramid patients were assigned to local primary care physicians who could refer their patients to local polyclinics. These outpatient clinics were the main entry points to local hospitals where transfer decisions could be made to specialty centres (mainly in the capital city) or teaching hospitals. These 'traffic rules' were intended to be enforced by a strict referral system. While in theory the principle of progressive treatment and the regulation of access could serve as an instrument to ensure the efficient utilisation and allocation of medical capacities, in practice the resulting structure of health care was over-specialised and inadequate to meet patients' needs. The system inherited from the socialist period was hospital- and Budapest-centred with arbitrary differences across specialties.[28] As a consequence, a considerable proportion of patients shuttled amongst different tiers of health care without receiving adequate care. Moreover, the funding rules made it possible for providers to minimise effort without penalty by referring their patients further rather than treating them themselves. The distorted structure of the Hungarian health system cannot be simply attributed to arbitrary decisions and to the obvious under-valuation of primary care by policy makers. The mechanism of central planning was far from being a top-to-bottom engineering exercise: the important role played by bargaining and by competition amongst rival interest groups should also be recognised (Kornai, 1992). In contrast with representative democracies where the legislature is also an important arena of such influences, under state socialism these interactions took place mainly through bureaucratic and party-political channels (Becker, 1983). The health service as a whole was in a disadvantageous position in this bureaucratic competition for resources as compared, for instance, to heavy industries (Szalai, 1986). However, different groups interested in the health sector had different 'power resources' to influence allocative decisions: while patient groups could not play any significant role in this process, professional interest groups representing large acute and teaching hospitals were particularly well equipped to incur their influence. This circumstance may help to explain why services such as primary care, preventative medicine, long-term care for the elderly and the mentally and chronically ill were neglected.[29]

4.2 The gratuity system

The discrepancy between declared principles and actual practice was an everyday experience of citizens living under communist regimes. In the case of health care, this dichotomy was prevalent not only in the case of resource allocation. While the referral system tended to restrict the choice of providers in the shadows the official 'traffic rules' were often broken through informal arrangements. There is some empirical evidence that patients following 'unofficial' ways had a greater likelihood of receiving proper care (Antal, 1987). One possibility to cut corners and to secure preferential access to better health facilities was to rely on the protection and connections of friends and relatives working in the health sector. Patients could also pay a 'toll' to be driven on 'private roads' in the form of gratuities: the strict referral rules provided medical doctors with an opportunity to sell the access to quality treatment. The role of gratuity money was not simply to avoid restrictions imposed by the referral system. Although it was declared that health care was free of charge for every Hungarian citizen it was a common perception amongst patients that without paying their doctors they risked receiving health care of a poor quality. In the Hungarian economic literature there are several explanations for the emergence of the gratuity system, such as cultural factors, lack of patient choice and the associated monopolistic position of providers, global budgeting of providers, the under-funding of health care and the resulting deterioration of relative salary level of medical professionals coupled with the absence of private medicine (Balázs, 1991; Bondár, 1991; Csekő, 1991). All these factors probably contributed to a certain extent to the erosion of the principle of free health care at the point of need. Nevertheless, it is remarkable that the practice of gratuity payments still persists in the reformed health system despite the increased freedom gained by patients to exercise choice, the considerable changes introduced in the field of reimbursement methods and the existence of the legal opportunity to run private health care. This seems to support the hypothesis that the gratuity system represents a 'semi-legal' market which infiltrated into a public health service: thus the Hungarian health system is characterised in both periods by the coexistence of a 'shadow' voluntary out-of-pocket payment component (Antal, 1991). Little is known about the extent of this 'shadow' market. Studies based on questionnaires suggest that the amount of gratuity payments varies considerably, and is likely to be positively correlated with the severity of illness and the invasive nature of the medical intervention undertaken: it is not unusual to pay gratuity to specialists, physicians and surgeons higher than 50 per cent of average monthly personal earnings (Ötlet, 1984; Galasi and Kertesi, 1991). Different estimates suggest that the total sum of out-of-pocket payments associated with these transactions represent between 9 and 20 per cent of total official health expenditures (Andorka et al., 1994; World Bank, 1995). However, the importance of the gratuity system in affecting provider behaviour may be greater than its share in total health spending. The welfare effect of gratuities is also uncertain. By paying their physicians patients can get extra services that may result in increased total supply of health care: this may lead to a Pareto-improvement.[30] At the same time the semi-legal nature of these payments often means that an undefined amount of money is paid for undefined services which is likely to be a source of monopoly rents appropriated by clinicians working in well paying specialties. Moreover, gratuities affect the allocation of publicly financed resources as well: doctors use public facilities and services of hospital staff without contributing to their costs when being paid by their patients. Thus if the gratuity payment affects the allocation of relatively fixed capacities then it may lead to a Prisoner's Dilemma-type situation: patients pay in the hope of receiving extra services, but because most of them do so they may end up worse off similar to those who are unable or reluctant to pay (Galasi and Kertesi, 1991).

4.3   The Health Insurance Fund

While the gratuity system remained intact significant institutional changes were introduced within the public health system after the collapse of communism. The influence of the *Bismarckian–continental* arrangements on these reforms, which was the characteristic feature of the welfare system in Hungary before the Second World War, is apparent (Ferge, 1992; see also n. 1 below on the Bismarckian model). The general budget has been replaced by social insurance as a main source of financing health care.[31] In 1992 a separate *Health Insurance Fund* was created which is also responsible for paying sickness benefits and invalidity pensions financed out of 19.5 per cent employer and 4 per cent employee contributions. At the same time, in contrast with the German model and the reforms introduced in the Czech republic, health insurance has not been fragmented across employee groups (Massaro *et al.*, 1994). There was a generally shared view that the *earmarked financing* of health care ensured the security of resources available for health care as compared to the situation when the health sector had to compete with other spending programmes. It was also believed that by turning health care into a social insurance entitlement the tax compliance of income earners involved in the black economy in increasing proportions could be enforced, as health insurance coverage could be refused in the case of non-payment of contributions. While the former expectation might have been fulfilled, the effect of insurance financing on the Hungarian tax system and the 'black' economy is rather controversial. The creation of the Health Insurance Fund has been parallel with an increase of payroll taxes paid by employees and employers into the newly established extra-budgetary funds, contributing to labour market distortions and to a widening 'black' economy. In 1997, to mitigate the problem of tax avoidance, a lump-sum health insurance contribution was levied on employers while the employer contribution rate towards health insurance was reduced to 15 per cent.

It also represents a Bismarckian influence that the Health Insurance Fund is governed by a general assembly made up of the representatives of employer organisations and trade unions, the latter elected through general ballots. The self-governance of social insurance can serve as a political safeguard protecting social insurance entitlements and it may also enhance democratic control over the publicly financed health care. However, as some critics pointed out, this arrangement could also involve adverse effects as far as equity and economic efficiency were concerned. It should be noted that different social groups do not have an equal representation in the elected assembly as the level of unionisation and organisation varies considerably between industrial sectors and different social strata. As the public sector employees are typically highly unionised there is a danger of biased decisions favouring the interests of provider groups and thus continuing the traditional pattern in resource allocation. For similar reasons, the effectiveness of social protection may be weakening. Although individuals without an appropriate contribution record can get public funding on a means-tested basis and thus the coverage rate is theoretically complete some particularly vulnerable groups such as the homeless may be left without health care.[32] A further complication arises from the specific division of responsibilities between Parliament and the Health Insurance Fund: while the former sets taxes and contribution rates the self-governing body proposes the expenditure budget, which creates an asymmetry between the goals of cost containment and securing adequate resources for health care. Recent developments suggest that the central government aims to limit the role of self-governance: it was a response to the worsening economic and fiscal balance occurring in the mid-1990s that increased the influence of the Ministry of Finance at the expense of spending departments.

As compared to the health sector under communism which was a *unitary* organisation the emerging new system is characterised by *multiple players* and *complex financial channels*. Social insurance expenditure accounts for about 84 per cent of the total public health expenditure which covers the operating costs of health facilities and the insurance component of pharmaceutical expenditures. A fraction of operating costs and all the capital expenses are covered by general taxation. A considerable proportion of primary care and most of the capital expenses, the latter in the form of general grants, is passed to local councils who, apart from being responsible for the operation of primary care became the main owners of hospitals and outpatient clinics. So far, the roles of the Health Insurance Fund, the central government and the local authorities in financing, operating and regulating health care are not clearly defined, which can produce difficulties in coordinating decisions. This problem has already manifested itself in the field of capacity allocation and investment decisions that are often influenced by prestige motives without considering the real needs of the population on a regional or national basis. The emerging solution to tackle the fragmentation of the provider market and to regulate capacities relies on contracts between the Health Insurance Fund and providers or local governments running their facilities: providers are financed on a contractual basis. Attempts have been made to undertake the long-awaited restructuring of the health system by stipulating staff size and the number of beds at provider level in these contracts; not surprisingly, this triggered a massive opposition from local governments and professional groups.

4.4 Privatisation of provision and finance

The privatisation that has taken place in the health sector has been rather modest. On the *provider* side the most significant developments happened at the level of primary care, where physicians could opt to run their practices on a private basis. In 1996, about 75 per cent of primary care physicians worked on a self-employed basis or as a member of a private partnership[33] (TÁRKI, 1996). Most dental care practices are also run privately and local pharmacies have been sold to private owners. At the same time, apart from some newly opened private polyclinics, outpatient clinics and hospitals remained predominantly publicly-owned. The complete transfer of providers into for-profit proprietary status may not be desirable as non-profit organisations are less likely to exploit the informational asymmetry between providers and patients (cf. Laffont and Tirole, 1991). However, the available evidence suggests that the extent of *microeconomic inefficiency* is considerable at provider level, which may be associated with inappropriate management: the financial directors of hospitals function as administrators rather than managers, the opportunities to retain savings are limited, and little effort has been made to replace the centrally set salaries with performance-related pay. At the time of writing the government is considering a partial privatisation of outpatient facilities and the transformation of hospitals into non-profit organisations that resemble the NHS Trust hospitals in the UK. As far as the *financial* side is concerned, a legal framework for private and mutual health insurance has been laid down: so far, the proportion of the population covered by these organisations is negligible. Apart from the declining income of the middle classes the main obstacle for the expansion of private insurance is the existence of the gratuity system.[34]

4.5   Financing providers

The most far-reaching reforms were introduced in the methods of provider financing. Hospitals that were given *global budgets* previously are paid for inpatient care according to the number and complexity of cases measured using the *diagnostic-related groups* (DRG) classification. Outpatient activity is partially financed on a *fee-for-service* basis while primary care 'family' doctors receive a *capitation* payment reflecting the number of patients registered with their practice. At the same time, patients were allowed to choose their primary care physicians and the 'official' referral system, which had in any case been eroded, was considerably liberalised, opening a greater window for patient-initiated contacts. These measures sum up to the creation of a provider market where the 'money follows the patient'. In contrast with competitive arrangements introduced in the UK or represented by American Health Maintenance Organisations (HMOs), price competition does not play a role in this market, but providers can engage in quality competition to attract more patients (Enthoven, 1990). However, this quality competition may not be effective enough given the idiosyncratic preferences of patients and the serious informational problems associated with the special commodity we are dealing with (i.e. health care). Apart from physician referrals, geographic proximity, personal contacts and sporadic information are all likely to determine the providers' patient flow. The efficiency-improving capacity of competitive forces depends crucially on the gate-keeping and orientating function of primary care doctors which is not yet sufficient: according to a recent survey about half of the contacts with specialist doctors is patient-initiated (TÁRKI, 1996).

The shift to activity- and output-related payment has altered the *incentives* faced by providers. It is often claimed that global budgeting provides weak incentives as far as hospital workloads are concerned, though it is a sufficient instrument to constrain health expenditures. However, the health economics literature and the experience with global budgeting in other countries suggests that from the point of view of provider behaviour the crucial question is how those budgets are determined (Barnum *et al.*, 1995). In the Hungarian case, global budgets were adjusted on the basis of previous occupancy rates: this arrangement is likely to provide incentives to keep the turnover rate low and to fill capacities with the use of excessive length of stay. These perverse effects were at least partially offset by the incentives generated by the gratuity system. It is fair to point out that the low activity level in itself was not a problem in the old health system partly due to the high ratios of medical doctors and hospital beds compared to population size. While the impact of capitation payment on activity level is ambiguous both the fee-for-service and the DRG-based financing are likely to result in case-load expansion (Hodgkin and McGuire, 1994). This is not necessarily efficiency-improving given the possibility of supplier induced demand (Evans, 1974; Cromwell and Mitchell, 1986). The resulting aggregate effect on cost inflation is counteracted in the case of the DRG-based prospective reimbursement which makes hospitals interested in reducing cost per case as well. The policy makers have recognised the potential dangers involved in activity-related payment. However, the solution invented does not seem to be sufficient. Aggregate spending caps were introduced that could be characterised as a 'Cournot-type' price regulation: the price paid after each case is decreasing as the total activity level of all the providers increases. This arrangement, as in the case of the Cournot-type quantity setting models, creates a negative externality amongst providers as the price reduction due to an unnecessary low-cost admission affects all the hospitals while the potential benefits are realised at the level of an individual provider: the end result is likely to be an excessive overall activity level (Tirole, 1989, pp. 212–18). An empirical study analysing the activity statistics in acute hospitals indicates that providers have learnt quite quickly how to cope with the new payment methods (Belicza and Boján, 1995). Within an 18-month period following the introduction of the DRG financing the average length of stay has been cut by 9 per cent. At the same time, the number of admissions increased by 8 per cent and the proportion of multiple episodes (the transfer of the same patient amongst specialties) and the average case-mix index went up by about 10 per cent. The latter figure may reveal the effect of 'DRG-creep', the artificial inflation of case-mix. In summary, the changes introduced in provider reimbursement do not have an unambiguous effect on efficiency and they seem to contradict the declared policy of shifting the emphasis from hospital care. The most recent plans to fine tune the incentives faced by providers are directed towards the introduction of a two-part tariff system in hospital financing where a part of the case-related revenue would be replaced by block payments.

4.6   Expenditures, efficiency and effectiveness

There is a clear difference between the 1990s and previous decades when comparing expenditures on health care (see table 10.7). Under socialism, similar to most of the public integrated health systems the level of total and public expenditures was low in international comparison and relative to *per capita* GDP as well.[35] The expansion of health expenditures relative to GDP started in the second half of the 1980s, but the largest increase was realised during the transition period: the share of health expenditures in national product in 1994 was more than 30 per cent higher than in 1989 and about 60 per cent greater than in 1980. This change is only partly explained by the approximately 20 per cent drop in national output. The data suggest that the health budget has increased in real terms as well during the recession; the real growth took place between 1989 and 1991, which coincides with the establishment of the Health Insurance Fund, followed by a declining trend in subsequent years. One explanation for this development lies in the institutional changes discussed above that strengthened the political position of the health sector. In addition, as a result of the collapse of COMECON trade relations the price inflation of medical inputs was above the general price index, therefore the figures are likely to over-estimate the actual size of the health budget. Nevertheless, the share of health expenditures in domestic product reached a level (exceeding 7 per cent of GDP, with the amount of gratuity payments estimated between 0.6 and 1.3 per cent) which is comparable with the OECD average and higher compared to lower-income OECD countries and the average in Eastern Europe.[36] The *per capita* health expenditures are about $250, that is much lower than in the developed industrial nations, but not relative to *per capita* GDP. In the mid-1990s the reduction of public expenditures became a top priority in economic policy and the containment of public health expenditures was put on the agenda. One option faced by the government was to shift costs onto patients: the average co-payment rate on prescribed medicine was cut and user charges introduced in the case of some residual services (e.g. dental care).[37] However, the government backed away from the plan to introduce user charges across the board. This measure would have hurt the gratuity income of medical doctors and posed formidable administrative difficulties. The government's efforts were thus concentrated on improving the efficiency of the health service.

As was mentioned above, the Hungarian health system inherited a structure characterised by the coexistence of waste and shortages and arbitrary asymmetries between service levels and regions. In this respect, little improvement was achieved up to the mid-1990s. In the communist

Table 10.7. Health expenditures, 1980–94

	1980	1989	1990	1991	1992	1993	1994[a]	OECD[b]	Former Warsaw Pact countries[c]
Total exp.[d] (as % of GDP)	4.0	4.8	5.5	6.3	6.5	6.6	6.4	8.1	....
In real terms (1989=100)	82	100	108	109	107	107	106	....	....
Total public (as % of GDP)	3.8	4.6	5.2	6.0	6.1	6.3	6.1	6.1	4.6
In real terms (1989=100)	82	100	108	109	106	107	106	....	....
$ equivalent *per capita*[e]	122	149	187	205	236	244	243	1,429	....

Notes:
[a] Estimates.
[b] The OECD figures are arithmetic averages of the corresponding figures in 1991 excluding Turkey, the Czech republic, Poland and Hungary.
[c] 1991; the former Warsaw Pact countries include Bulgaria, the Czech and Slovak republics, Hungary, Poland, Romania and the Russian Federation.
[d] Figures do not include 'gratuity' payments.
[e] The $ equivalents were calculated on the basis of official exchange rates and are expressed in 1992 currency terms (OECD, 1992).
Sources: CSO (1993, 1994, 1995); Ministry of Welfare (1995); OECD (1993, 1994); UNICEF (1995); World Bank (1995).

period, the development of the health system was concentrated on the quantitative aspects of service capacities, which is reflected in the dynamic expansion in the number of medical doctors and hospital beds (see table 10.8, p. 334). While Hungary and other Eastern European countries have leading figures in the supply of medical doctors and hospital beds, they lag behind in the adaptation of medical technologies including those that increase the possibilities for health care out of hospitals and shortened inpatient stay. Although technological progress typically increases the resource intensity of health care, the present structure shows clear signs of allocative and technical inefficiency. The most striking example of this is the *excessive supply of hospital beds*. Despite the high hospitalisation rate and the comparatively long average length of stay, which suggests the effect of Roemer's Law, hospitals operate at inefficiently low occupancy rates.[38] The bias towards hospital care is also illustrated by the fact that the number of hospital doctors between 1980 and 1990 increased more than twice compared to the number of primary care doctors. Although this tendency has been reversed in recent years the evidence suggests that the over-staffing with regard to the number of medical doctors is still a symptom of the health system: this results in a low salary level of doctors compared to professionals employed in other sectors and consequently a strong hunger for gratuity money. At the same time, the health service suffers from a chronic shortage of nursing staff. The recent efforts to streamline the Hungarian health structure are based on the combination of financial incentives and direct regulation. Regional inequalities and differences amongst hospitals are being reduced through the gradual equalisation of prices paid for providers per diagnostic or activity category. The activity-related payment method also provides some incentives to reshape supply and shorten the length of inpatient stay. However, the government has realised that the reimbursement method in itself is not sufficient to tackle the underlying structural problems as providers are able to impact their caseload. The direct regulation of capacities is therefore playing an increasing role. The intake of medical universities has been limited. Instead of establishing regional health funds financed on a capitation basis, *regional quotas* were introduced to cut hospital beds that were calculated rather mechanically: the policy objective is to reduce the number of beds from the current level to 85 per 10,000 residents. At the same time home care services and the practice of one-day surgery have been promoted and these are intended to absorb redundant physicians through increasing the number of primary care practices (Ministry of Welfare, 1995). It is too early to evaluate the effect of these measures. The first emerging statistics indicate about a 10 per cent reduction in hospital beds without a major hospital closure. However, the government has realised that the reimbursement method is in itself not sufficient to tackle the underlying structural problem as providers are able to manipulate their caseload. At the same time, recent developments seem to justify the assumption that in the new pluralistic health system influential interest groups in favour of the status quo are able to exercise an effective opposition and to mobilise the public concern with health care to hinder the government's ambitious plans. This is a well known phenomenon in modern welfare states where attempts have been made to reshape welfare policies.

Another aspect of evaluating the efficiency and the effectiveness of a health system is to study outcome rather than activity levels or resource utilisation. The final product of health care is the health status of the population. However, health depends on multiple factors and to identify the contribution made by health care is an extremely difficult task. One possibility is to examine life expectancy statistics although these data could also be regarded as indicators of need faced by the health service. The average life expectancy data reveal a rather gloomy picture: the life expectancy at birth of both men and women is much worse than the OECD average and it is even below the similar figures in Eastern Europe (see table 10.8). Moreover, in the case of men the data suggest a deteriorating situation similar to most of the countries in the region. The life expectancy of men increased until the late 1960s parallel with the major reduction of mortality rates associated with infectious diseases (Orosz, 1992). The age gap between the OECD countries and Hungary was less than a year at the peak point, since then it has widened to more than eight years. There are several factors that may explain this worsening tendency such as environmental pollution, the high rate of alcohol and tobacco consumption, unhealthy nutrition and obesity, and stress (Andorka et al., 1988). In addition, there are some indications (but no hard evidence) that the inadequacies of the health service also contributed to the deteriorating health statistics. This suggestion is supported by the fact that Hungary is also performing below the regional average on the scale of the WHO-defined avoidable mortality index as well (Ministry of Welfare, 1995). At the same time in the case of the infant mortality rate, which is often regarded as a more direct performance indicator of a health system, Hungary could be credited with a considerable improvement although it still lags far behind the more advanced countries.

To sum up, the Hungarian health reforms introduced during the 1990s did not go so far in the marketisation of health care as the Czech health system, but they represent a more radical break with the previous

Table 10.8. Vital statistics, activity and inputs, 1980–94

	1980	1989	1990	1991	1992	1993	1994	OECD[a]	Former Warsaw Pact countries[b]
Life expectancy: men	65.5	65.4	65.1	65.0	64.6	64.5	64.8	73.1	66.3
Life expectancy: women	72.7	73.8	73.2	73.8	73.7	73.8	74.2	79.6	74.6
Infant mortality (per 1000 births)	23.2	15.7	14.8	15.6	14.1	12.5	11.5	7.4	15.9
Admission rate[c] (as % of pop.)	18.7	.....	21.4	21.7	22.1	22.2	23.3	16	.....
Average length of inpatient stay (LOS)[d]	14.2	.....	12.7	12.4	12.0	11.8	11.3	8.5	.....
Hospital beds (per 10,000 pop.)	90.6	.....	101.5	.....	98.7	97.7	97.8	75.7	119.0
Active doctors (per 1,000 pop.)	2.5	.....	3.2	3.3	3.4	3.3	3.2	2.1	.....

Notes:
[a] As in table 10.2, admission rate and average stay for 1989. Number of beds for 1990. Number of doctors for 1988.
[b] As in table 10.2, number of beds for 1990.
[c] Inpatient admissions relative to total population in percentages.
[d] For Hungary, the LOS figures include mental health and acute care; for OECD countries the values are for acute care only and without Italy, Japan and New Zealand.
Sources: CSO (1993, 1994, 1995); Ministry of Welfare (1995); OECD (1993, 1994); UNICEF (1995); World Bank (1995).

arrangements compared to the Polish case (Massaro *et al.*, 1994; Perker, 1995). The new health system is based on social insurance financing and a provider market with activity-related payment methods and predominantly public ownership of health facilities. The health expenditures increased their share in GDP to a considerable degree, which includes some real growth as well. The containment of health care costs became a priority of health policy, which proved to be a difficult task given the pluralistic nature of the emerging health system and the deteriorating health status of the population. Efforts were made to tackle the inherited inefficiencies of the health care structure, relying on financial incentives and regulation of capacities, so far with varying success. Hungarian governments remained committed to preserve the universal coverage of the population and the predominantly public funding of health care. However, the equity of the health system is distorted as a result of the gratuity system and the wide regional inequalities in resource allocation.

5   Conclusions

The general trends and institutional changes within the welfare sector reflect a gradual policy shift concerning the role of the safety net and social welfare measures. At the beginning of the transition the welfare system was generally considered as an important remedy helping the government to smooth the social and political tensions due to transition. Later on, it was more often seen as a major source of budgetary problems, incorporating costly and wasteful subsystems that impose a heavy burden on the economy and constrain its growth potential. The first phase was characterised by the removal of the bulk of social responsibilities from the economy itself and by the introduction of specialised welfare subsystems covering new and increased risks due to the transition. The welfare efforts of the government could not prevent the increase of poverty and inequality, but they certainly mitigated their extent. In this respect, Hungary has patterns similar to the 'Visegrád countries' and the former East Germany. However, after a while the government's willingness to meet the cost requirements of an expanding safety net diminished, while structural reforms within general government and in particular within the welfare system, emerged as top priority issues. At the same time targeting of welfare spending became a major concern. Important steps were taken to contain the growth of welfare spending and to limit its share within the general government budget. These reforms, however, have until now been more successful at the macro level, in reversing some dangerous public expenditures trends, than at micro level, in achieving greater efficiency (more value for the public money spent) at the level of institutions within the welfare sector. There are some promising signs in health care and the pension system. Still it will take some time and a fair amount of fine tuning before these reforms can be fully successful at the micro level as well, and the transition will come to an end in the welfare sector.

NOTES

The present study is based on a research project sponsored by the National Scientific Research Fund (OTKA T– 1365).The authors are grateful to Roberto Rocha and Robert Palacios from the World Bank for their permission to use some of their figures in this chapter. András Simonovits gave usefulcomments on an earlier version, and Barbara Docherty helped us in making the message of the chapter clearer.

 1 The Bismarckian social insurance model strongly emphasises the contributory principle, and in particular the labour market position and merit, and often involves corporativist elements in the governance of insurance funds. (See, for example, Esping-Andersen, 1990.)
 2 This model of the distribution of social functions between the state and the enterprise is not unique or exclusive to communist states. In some market economies (e.g. in Japan) there are marked similarities to these practices.
 3 Without referring to this implicit deal it is hard to understand how and why the relatively 'soft' Kádár regime could survive uninterrupted well over 30 years while in other communist countries (usually relying on more dictatorial methods) the turnover of political leaders was much greater and political turmoil more evident.
 4 Unfortunately this did not apply to most of the financial sector, where the accumulation of bad loans could go on for years during the transition period (see chapter 8 in this volume). The consolidation of the banking sector took place in such a way that it involved high moral hazard and high costs borne by the taxpayers.
 5 The poverty gap means here the (percentage) difference between the poverty line and average equivalent income.
 6 Housing subsidies started to grow dramatically at the beginning of the transition due to the effect of growing inflation on interest rate support on subsidised (fixed interest) housing loans. However, there has been a significant decline in these subsidies (in real terms or as a percentage of GDP) as the contracts were modified and/or terminated as many repaid half of their outstanding debts (the other half of the debt was forgiven). Nevertheless, after a while, due to some ill-designed new housing subsidies, the total amount of subsidies spent on housing started to grow again.
 7 This model prevails in Scandinavian countries.
 8 This model can be associated with a number of countries in Southern Europe.
 9 In 1994 out of about 3,800 primary schools there were altogether 143 private schools, out of which 110 were church-run. Of the 886 secondary schools about 48 are denominational and 25 are run by foundations or private persons; however, within the group of secondary schools with an academic

profile ('gimnázium') the likelihood of being in private hands is much higher, 55 out of 278 (OKI, 1996).

10 Due to space limitations and the scope of the related problems we cannot aim at an extensive treatment of the topic. A far more detailed account of the issues covered here can be found in English in Institute of World Economics, HAS – International Center for Economic Growth, 1995; OECD, 1995; World Bank, 1995. An excellent briefing of the reform options is given by Rocha and Palacios, 1996.

11 Contribution-based mandatory public pensions were introduced in Hungary by Act XL/1928 for industrial and commercial employees; the system did not cover farmers or agricultural workers. (Public servants already gained eligibility for public pensions in 1912; however, the pensions they received were budgetary income transfers as no contribution was needed to build up eligibility.) Contribution rates were fixed at 4–5 per cent of gross earnings. During the first few years all contribution payments went into a capital reserve fund. The system was based on sound actuarial calculations; benefits were defined as a linear function of total (individual) contribution paid. The new scheme started to pay relatively low old age pensions in 1937. Capital reserves and reasonable asset management provided a relatively sound financial basis for this partially funded pension scheme. Although the sound financial management of the system was somewhat eroded by inflation due to war preparations and a reduction of retirement age in 1944 without a parallel increase in reserves, the big blow came well before these developments could lead to financial problems: in 1944–5 the physical capital stock (houses, etc.) of the reserve fund was nearly completely destroyed, and the remaining financial investments lost their value in the subsequent hyperinflation. By 1946 the scheme had practically collapsed. Parallel to stabilisation and currency reform the government introduced a PAYG pension scheme in 1946.

12 Payroll taxes are used throughout the text as a synonym for social security contributions.

13 The PAYG system was already experiencing deficits from the 1970s; however, there were some years with a surplus (in 1989 it reached 1 per cent of GDP). Due to a politically motivated gradual extension of eligibility without previous contributions, the interpretation of the balance is rather vague, anyway. Eligibility was granted without contribution for imputed years for child care of children born before paid child care leave (*GYES–GYED*) was introduced, for mandatory military service, for years spent in higher education, etc.

14 It also increased the options for buying old-age security for tax evaders; however, those simply under-reporting their income (instead of restructuring them into payroll tax-exempted forms or disguising them as costs in the booming small enterprise sector) are less likely to be attracted by the tax incentives attached to these pension savings, as they evade PIT payments anyway.

15 Cf. table 4.10 in OECD (1995).

16 1994 was an election year, and the government found it too difficult to resist the temptation of trying to attract voters by heating up the economy.

17 This 'no reform' scenario (Rocha and Palacios, 1996) is based on the following assumptions: formal labour force participation rate is held constant at 1995 level; unemployment falls to 7 per cent after 2000; contribution rate is

34.5 per cent throughout; existing pension benefits are indexed (backward) to net wages; inflation rates are reduced gradually to around 3 per cent by 2005; real GDP growth rate is 3 per cent per annum, and productivity growth determines the growth of real wages. Some caution is needed as the drop in inflation rates has a very strong effect on simulated deficits in the first 8 years due to the indexation rule and the 'no inflation adjustment for the last two years in employment' principle in the benefit formula. If the present system was maintained the government might not want to diminish inflation as much as assumed here, so the size of the deficits would be lower (under the present inflation rate the difference in 2005 amounts to 1 per cent of GDP), however, as under such circumstances a 3 per cent GDP growth would probably seem too optimistic, the final result is somewhat uncertain.

18 With an intelligent design of the benefit package payroll tax liabilities can be reduced significantly (see Semjén, 1995b). Tough economic conditions and high tax rates forced many employees to found their own small businesses so that labour compensation could easily be disguised as costs or dividends.

19 This theoretical contribution rate would ensure that pension payments were fully financed by the contributions received (provided that there was full compliance in contribution payments and there were no administrative costs to be covered).

20 As no data were available for the actual numbers of contributors, these had to be replaced by the size of the active population. (Active population can serve as a proxy for the number of contributors, though there were some population groups earning pension entitlement without contribution payments.)

21 If pension benefits in these cases ('fake' disability pensions, early retirements, etc.) were replaced by social assistance benefits there might be *some* savings, provided that the replacement rate in social assistance was below the replacement that could be previously achieved in the pension system. A similar effect might be achieved by simply an actuarially fair reduction of pension entitlements for these groups, as proposed in OECD (1995).

22 The government proposal, with slight modifications, was finally accepted in mid-1997 (some months after this chapter was finalised); it will take effect in January 1998.

23 Sick pay periods and military service would, however, be counted as normal contributory years, and mothers would be credited one contributory year (up to a maximum of three years) after each child they bring up. Extra contribution payments could also buy service years for the time spent in higher education and on child care leave.

24 Since the PIF proposal refers to 'individualised' replacement rates showing the ratio of pensions to previous covered earnings (instead of comparing average pensions to average wages at the time of the pension payment), these data cannot be easily translated into conventional replacement rates.

25 While the MoF simulations extend to 2050, the PIF simulation ends in 2030. GDP growth and inflation assumptions behind the PIF results are somewhat unclear, and the exact accrual factors and pension formula are not given in the PIF proposal.

26 The impact of the tightened link between contributions and benefits on the PAYG balance is neutral unless long-term effects (improving tax compliance) are taken into consideration.

27 The seven configurations are the following: (1) the voluntary out-of-pocket model; (2) the voluntary reimbursement-of-patients model; (3) the public reimbursement model; (4) the voluntary contract model; (5) the public contract model; (6) the voluntary integrated model; (7) the public integrated model.

28 At the end of the 1980s the ratio of active medical doctors to the resident population in the capital city, Budapest, was twice as high as the similar figure in the rest of the country. Similarly, about 30 per cent of hospital beds were in Budapest with a resident population of 20 per cent as compared to the national total (Andorka *et al.*, 1994).

29 The experience of public health care systems in democratic welfare states suggests that these services are usually vulnerable to receive little priority similar to the Hungarian situation. This may suggest that the relative power of interest groups is not considerably different under the conditions of representative democracies. However, as the history of resource allocation in the UK demonstrates the transparent and normative nature of resource allocation could limit in a certain extent the role played by well organised professional groups. Obviously, transparency in resource allocation could not be a feasible option under state socialism.

30 There is some anecdotal evidence that gratuities generate adverse effects similarly to fee-for-service regimes. For instance, doctors can undertake unnecessary and costly medical interventions (e.g. operations) to increase the patients' readiness to pay a gratuity.

31 Parallel with the establishment of the Health Insurance Fund the financing of child benefits, which was previously a social insurance entitlement, became the responsibility of the state budget.

32 The policies of the Health Insurance Fund that aim to 'separate health care from social policy' and thus reduce some financial obligations have an effect in a similar direction.

33 In the typical case, however, the facilities of the practice are owned by local governments.

34 Insurance for gratuity payments is not feasible because of their semi-legal character. Moreover gratuities are tax-free and neither the patients nor the medical doctors have to cover the full costs of treatment.

35 Table 10.7 does not include gratuity payments. It could be argued that the government turned a blind eye to the gratuity system because it represented an opportunity to contain public expenditures with the use of a hidden cost-shifting.

36 In the region only the Czech republic realised a higher spending level, 8.3 per cent of GDP in 1994 (UNICEF, 1995).

37 Hungary operates a complex price-subsidy system in the case of medication. Medicines are divided into groups according to the subsidy rates that could be 100, 90, 70, 50 and 0 per cent. In addition the co-payment rate depends also on the illness of the patient, on the specialty of the prescribing doctor and the patient's income. Low-income individuals could be made exempt from prescription charges in the case of a defined list of medicaments. Drug prices are negotiated between the government, the Health Insurance Fund and pharmaceutical companies, using cost formulas and European yardstick prices.

38 The average occupancy rate is currently about 70 per cent.

340   Iván Csaba and András Semjén

REFERENCES

Amsden, A.H., J. Kochanowicz and L. Taylor (1994) *The Market Meets Its Match. Restructuring the Economies of Eastern Europe*, Cambridge, MA and London: Harvard University Press

Andorka, R. (1996) 'A társadalmi jelzőszámok tükrében' (In the mirror of social indicators), in R. Andorka, T. Kolosi and G. Vukovich (eds.), *Társadalmi riport*, Budapest: TÁRKI, 16–43

Andorka, R. and Z. Spéder (1997) 'Szegénység' (Poverty), in E. Sík and I.G. Tóth (eds.), *Az ajtók záródnak*, Budapest: TÁRKI, 55–68

Andorka, R., Z.L. Antal, J. Hegedűs, D.T. Horváth, I. Tosics and I.G. Tóth (1994) *The Hungarian Welfare State in Transition: Structure, Developments and Options for Reform*, Budapest: Blue Ribbon Commission

Andorka, R., Z.L. Antal, B. Buda, Z. Elekes, Z. Forgács, I. Forgács, J. Gerevich, P. Józan, Á. Losonczi and K. Ozsváth (1988) 'A társadalmi környezet, életmód, interperszonális kapcsolatok hatása a lakosság egészségi állapotára' (The effects of social environment, life style and interpersonal relations on the health status of the population), Budapest University of Economics, Department of Sociology, mimeo

Antal, K., J. Réti and M. Toldi (1995a) 'Értékvesztés és aránytorzulás a magyar nyugdíjrendszerben' (Loss of value and distortions in the Hungarian pension system), Budapest: Institute of World Economics of the Hungarian Academy of Sciences, mimeo

(1995b) 'Loss of value and distortions in the Hungarian pension system', in Institute of World Economics of the Hungarian Academy of Sciences, *Human Resources and Social Stability during Transition in Hungary*, San Francisco: International Center for Economic Growth

Antal, K., J. Réti, A. Rézmovits and M. Toldi (1995) 'Pension outlays and changes in the pension system in the nineties', in Institute of World Economics of the Hungarian Academy of Sciences, *Human Resources and Social Stability during Transition in Hungary*, San Francisco: International Center for Economic Growth

Antal, Z.L. (1987) 'Betegutak' (Patient paths), *Medvetánc*, **1986/4–1987/1** (double issue), 101–23

(1991) 'Piaci mechanizmusok szerepe az állami egészségügyben' (The role of market mechanism in the health system), in K. Hanák (ed.), *Terhesség – Szülés – Születés II*, Budapest: Research Institute of Sociology of the Hungarian Academy of Sciences, 114–30

Árvay, J. and A. Vértes (1994) 'A magánszektor és a rejtett gazdaság súlya Magyarországon (1980–1992)' (The weight of the private sector and the hidden economy in Hungary (1980–1992)), Budapest: GKI Gazdaságkutató Rt

Augusztinovics, M. (1995) 'The long-term financial balance of the pension system macrosimulations', in Institute of World Economics of the Hungarian Academy of Sciences, *Human Resources and Social Stability during Transition in Hungary*, San Francisco: International Center for Economic Growth

Balázs, P. (1991) 'Hálapénz-paradigma' (The paradigm of gratuities), *Valóság*, **35**, 72–80

Bara, Z. (1996) 'Quasi-markets for higher education', *Society and Economy*, 168–90

Barnum, H., J. Kutzin and H. Saxeman (1995) 'Incentives and provider payment methods', *International Journal of Health Planning and Management*, **10**, 23–45

Becker, G. (1983) 'A theory of competition among pressure groups for political influence', *Quarterly Journal of Economics*, **98**, 371–400

Belicza, É. and F. Boján (1995) 'A teljesítményfinanszírozás bevezetésének első tapasztalatai' (The first evidence on the effects of the activity-related reimbursement in health care), DOTE, Department of Public Health, mimeo

Bod, P. (1995) 'Formation of the Hungarian social insurance based pension system', in Institute of World Economics of the Hungarian Academy of Sciences, *Human Resources and Social Stability during Transition in Hungary*, San Francisco: International Center for Economic Growth

Bondár, E. (1991) 'Három cikk ürügyén a hálapénz közgazdaságtani – természetéről' (The economic nature of gratuities – A comment), *Replika*, **3**, 65–80.

Central Statistical Office (1993) *Magyar statisztikai évkönyv 1992* (*Hungarian Statistical Yearbook*, 1992), Budapest: Central Statistical Office (Központi Statisztikai Hivatal)

(1994) *Magyar statisztikai évkönyv 1993* (*Hungarian Statistical Yearbook*, 1993), Budapest: Central Statistical Office (Központi Statisztikai Hivatal)

(1995) *Magyar statisztikai évkönyv 1994* (*Hungarian Statistical Yearbook*, 1994), Budapest: Central Statistical Office (Központi Statisztikai Hivatal)

Chang, H.J. and P. Nolan (eds.) (1995) *The Transformation of the Communist Economies. Against the Mainstream*, New York: St Martin's Press

Cromwell, J. and J.B. Mitchell (1986) 'Physician induced demand for surgery', *Journal of Health Economics*, **5**, 293–313

Csekő, I. (1991) 'Korrupció és hatékonyság – Megjegyzések Galasi Péter és Kertesi Gábor dolgozataihoz' (Corruption and efficiency – comments on papers by Péter Galasi and Gábor Kertesi), *Közgazdasági Szemle*, **38**, 616–43

Dániel, Z. (1996) 'A bérlakás pivatizáció paradoxona. Nemzeti ajándék vagy ráfizetés?' (The paradox of privatization of rented housing. Gift to the nation or loss?), *Közgazdasági Szemle*, **43**, 204–30

Enthoven, A.C. (1990) 'What can Europeans learn from Americans?', in *Health Care Systems in Transition*, Paris: OECD

Esping-Andersen, G. (1990) *The Three Worlds of Welfare Capitalism*, Cambridge: Cambridge University Press

Evans, R. (1974) 'Supplier-induced demand: some empirical evidence and implications', in M. Perlman (ed.), *The Economics of Health Care and Medical Care*, New York: Wiley

Ferge, Z. (1992) 'Social policy regimes and social structure – hypotheses for the prospects of social policy in Central and Eastern Europe', in Z. Ferge and J. E. Kolberg (eds.), *Social Policy in a Changing Europe*, Frankfurt: Campus Verlag

Gács, E. (1987) 'Szociális kiadásaink nemzetközi összehasonlításban' (Hungarian social expenditures in international comparison), *Szociálpolitikai Értestő*, **1987/3**, 117–37

Galasi, P. and G. Kertesi (1991) 'A hálapénz ökonómiája' (The economics of gratuities), *Közgazdasági Szemle*, **38**, 147–81

Halász, G. and J. Lannert (eds.) (1996) *Jelentés a magyar közoktatásról, 1995* (Report on Hungarian primary and secondary education, 1995), Budapest,

Országos Közoktatási Intézet (National Institute for Primary and Secondary Education)

Hodgkin, D. and T.G. McGuire (1994) 'Payment levels and hospital response to prospective payment', *Journal of Health Economics*, **13**, 1–29.

Illés, I. (1996) 'A területi közigazgatás korszerűsítése és az államháztartás reformja' (Modernisation of regional public administration and public finance reform), Regional Research Centre of the Hungarian Academy of Sciences, mimeo

Institute of World Economics of the Hungarian Academy of Science (1995) *Human Resources and Social Stability during Transition in Hungary*, San Francisco: International Center for Economic Growth

Kornai, J. (1992) *The Socialist System*, Oxford: Oxford University Press

Laffont, J.-J. and J. Tirole (1991) 'Provision of quality and power of incentive schemes in regulated industries', in W. Barnet, B. Cornet, C. d'Aspremont, J. Gabszewicz and A. Mas-Colell (eds.), *Equilibrium Theory and Applications*, Cambridge: Cambridge University Press

Manchin, R. and I. Szelényi (1987) 'Social policy under state socialism: market redistribution and social inequalities in East European socialist societies', in G. Esping-Andersen and M. Rein (eds.), *Stagnation and Renewal in Social Policy*, New York: M. E. Sharpe

Massaro, T.A., J. Nemec and I. Kalman (1994) 'Health reform in the Czech Republic', *Journal of the American Medical Association*, **271**, 1870–4

McLure Jr., C.E., A. Semjén, G. Baczko-Fiszer and R. Venyö (1995) *Tax Policy in Central Europe*, San Francisco: International Center for Economic Growth

Ministry of Welfare (1995) 'Az egészségügy korszerűsítésének programja' (The modernisation programme of health care), Budapest: Népjóléti Minisztérium (Ministry of Welfare), mimeo

Organisation for Economic Cooperation and Development (OECD) (1992) *The Reform of Health Care: A Comparative Analysis of Seven OECD Countries*, Paris: OECD

    (1993) *OECD Health Care Systems: Facts and Trends, 1960–1991*, Paris: OECD

    (1994) *The Reform of Health Care: A Comparative Analysis of Fourteen OECD Countries*, Paris: OECD

    (1995) *Social and Labour Market Policies in Hungary*, Paris: OECD

Orosz, É. (1992) 'Egészségügyi rendszerek és reformtörekvések' (Health systems and reform policies), Budapest, Politikai Tudományok Intézete (Institute of Political Science)

Ötlet (1984) 'Mennyit fizetnek a betegek?' (How much is paid by patients?), *Ötlet* (October)

Perker, A. (1995) 'A new public/private mix in the health sector of the emerging market economies', Washington, DC: World Bank, mimeo

Réti, J. (1996) 'The calculations underlying the pension reform: the latitude of reform', Budapest, Nyugdíjbiztosítási Önkormányzat (Self-Government of the Pension Insurance Fund), mimeo

Rocha, R. and R. Palacios (1996) 'The Hungarian pension system in transition', Washington, DC: World Bank, mimeo (preliminary version)

Semjén, A. (1995a) 'Miért jobb? Normatív iskolafinanszírozási modell a Józsefvárosban' (Why is it better? Formula funding for schools in József-

város), in *Korszerű iskolavezetés, Közoktatási kézikönyv*, **13**, Budapest, RAABE Könyvkiadó
(1995b) 'Tax policies in Hungary during economic transition', in C.E. McLure Jr., A. Semjén, G. Baczko-Fiszer and R. Venyő, *Tax Policy in Central Europe*, San Francisco: International Center for Economic Growth
(1996) 'A szociális ellátórendszer átalakításának koncepciója. Alternatív munkaanyag' (A concept for reforming social welfare provisions. An alternative proposal), Budapest: Népjóléti Minisztérium (Ministry of Welfare), mimeo
Semjén, A. and I.J. Tóth (1996) 'Vállalkozások fiskális környezete és annak hatásai: Társaságok adózással kapcsolatos magatartása' (Fiscal environment of enterprises and its effects: tax behaviour of corporations), Budapest, Institute of Economics of the Hungarian Academy of Sciences, mimeo
Szalai, J. (1986) *Az egészségügy betegségei* (The illnesses of health care), Budapest: Közgazdasági és Jogi Könyvkiadó
TÁRKI (1996) 'Az Európai Únió HU9302 sz. Phare Egészségügyi reformprogramja keretében végzett kutatás dokumentációja és alapsorai' (The EU Phare HU3902 Programme health care reform project research data and documentation), Budapest: TÁRKI
Tirole, J. (1989) *The Theory of Industrial Organisation*, Cambridge, MA: MIT Press
Tóth, I.G. (1994) 'Változások a szociálpolitikai rendszerben: biztosítás, állampolgári jog vagy segélyezés?' (Changes in the social welfare system: insurance, citizen right or means tested assistance?), in R. Andorka, T. Kolosi and E. Vukovich (eds.), *Társadalmi Riport*, Budapest: TÁRKI, 270–92
(1996) 'Hungarian income inequalities in comparative perspective', Budapest: TÁRKI, mimeo
(1997) 'A háztartások jövedelmi szerkezete: a munkaerőpiac és a szociálpolitika szerepei' (The income structure of households: the role of the labour market and social policy), in E. Sík and I. G. Tóth (eds.), *Az ajtók záródnak*, Budapest: TÁRKI, 55–68
Tóth I.J. and A. Semjén (1996) 'Tax behaviour of small and medium-size enterprises', *Review of Sociology (Szociológiai Szemle), Special Issue*, 67–87
UNICEF (1995) *Poverty, Children and Policy: Responses for a Brighter Future*, Florence: UNICEF
World Bank (1995) *Hungary – Structural Reforms for Sustainable Growth*, Washington, DC: World Bank
(1996) *Hungary – Poverty and the Social Safety Net*, Washington, DC: World Bank

Discussion

CHRISTINE H. ALLISON

1   Rethinking the role of the state – the world over

In their chapter 10, Iván Csaba and András Semjén address one of the most interesting questions facing Central and Eastern Europe (CEE) and the Former Soviet Union (FSU) as well as much of the world today – what should be the role of the state, and how should that role be carried out by governments? With the collapse of command-and-control systems, and the general failure of pervasive government, state-led development is clearly an era of the past, and CEE and FSU countries are redefining the role of the state. In common with western market economies, direct state intervention is generally being withdrawn from the *productive* sectors, but the role of the state in the financing and provision of welfare and other social services still predominates. Here, the appropriate role for the state is more complex, in part due to market failure and redistributive concerns, and guidance from the West is varied. Until recent times, Hungary could look to Scandinavia and other West European welfare states to find reaffirmation of the pervasive role of the state, both as a financier and provider. But today rich countries around the world, such as the USA and the UK, are revisiting some aspects of their welfare programmes. Even Sweden, where citizens remain firmly committed to the welfare state, has embarked on wide-reaching reforms to find a better balance between social benefits and heavy – often invisible – economic costs. Yet governments of CEE and FSU countries remain reluctant to fundamentally reposition welfare programmes: mutual social support, often equated with universal or near-universal programmes that fail to respond to increasing income inequalities and changing incentives, remains the preferred approach.

2   Refocusing on the effectiveness of welfare programmes and social spending

Driving the quest for a redefinition of the role of the state is the fiscal crisis of welfare states throughout much of the world, which is calling into question the wisdom of such heavy public spending on welfare programmes: spending that provides consumption for the present generation of recipients but at the expense of investment that will generate future growth. Also of grave concern are the labour market consequences of high welfare spending, the cost it imposes on employers, and the incentive effects for both employers and workers. Countries are exploring ways to reduce public spending, to improve the efficiency of spending through increased competition, contracting out of services to private providers and to subnational institutions, and to reduce dependence on social transfers and welfare programmes. However, as more and more countries attempt to focus public resources more efficiently on the provision of collective goods and services, and to reallocate expenditures, the importance of stable political systems and capable institutions is emerging. This is a particularly tough challenge for the CEE countries and the FSU, where democracies are still in a fledgling state, the roles of various levels of government are still evolving, and institutions are struggling to drop the shackles of the 'command' economy.

3   How well has Hungary done in recasting the role of the state?

Csaba and Semjén set out in their chapter to document the evolution of Hungary's welfare programmes in the transition years. They choose pensions and health care to document in detail the changing role of the state, and the search for efficiency gains in welfare spending. They also touch on the equity implications of the various reforms. They conclude that welfare reforms thus far implemented have had a greater impact at the macro level, reversing some dangerous expenditure trends, than at the micro level of the institutions within the welfare sector. How well does Hungary stand up in international comparison as it tries to roll back the state from the pervasiveness of the communist years, to redefine the role of government, and to improve the efficiency of public spending? The current *World Development Report* (World Bank, 1997) comments that 'the job of reorienting the state toward the task of "steering, not rowing" is far from complete in eastern Europe. But most countries, including Hungary, have made progress in refocusing the state's role and are also on the way to improving capacity and accountability'. Let us explore this a little further.

3.1   The paternal state

In Eastern Europe and the FSU the state traditionally *financed* and *provided* a wide range of social services and welfare benefits. These were tightly intertwined with the rest of the economy and in the main were

predicated around the notion of dependence on the state during child-
hood and old age, punctuated by a working life with a relatively low cash
wage. The welfare system differed from that of a fully developed market
economy in five important respects. First, because the system was based
on the premise of full employment guaranteed by the state (and social
services and welfare benefits were provided through the workplace), there
was no unemployment insurance. Second, social protection (the social
safety net) focused on individuals who could not work (disability). Third,
most benefits and services were uniform, and there was little relationship
between contribution (or effort) and benefit. Fourth, in-kind subsidies
played an important role. And fifth, there was no place for private
enterprise and/or voluntary initiatives, although a strong private (family-
based) safety net was evident (World Bank, 1996b).

3.2   Hungary: an extreme welfare state

More than many other countries in the region, Hungary spent heavily on
welfare programmes. Despite concerns for the high level of welfare
expenditure in the second half of the 1980s, at the time of the collapse of
the Berlin Wall approximately 20 per cent of GDP was spent on welfare
programmes (including health care); by 1993, the figure had risen to 26
per cent of GDP, surpassing averages for both the European Union and
OECD, and approximating the spending levels of Scandinavia, France
and the Netherlands, countries with higher income levels (World Bank,
1995). In part, this was the result of a contracting GDP, but expenditures
also rose: pensions increased by 2 per cent of GDP as early retirements
and disability pensions were given in place of unemployment benefit;
rapidly growing unemployment pushed expenditure on unemployment
benefit above 3 per cent of GDP; health care expenditures rose with the
introduction of health insurance; and spending on social assistance rose
as wage incomes declined and entitlements to other social transfers
expired. At this time, around 90 per cent of the population benefited
from one type of cash transfer programme or another, and although
private consumption was generally protected by the generous welfare
programmes, it failed to prevent more people from falling into poverty
through the lack of targeting and weak correlation between 'need' and
benefit level (World Bank, 1996a).

3.3   Reform efforts

1994 saw some cutting of welfare programmes as the fiscal deficit grew,
but little was done to address fundamental entitlements; in the main, real

benefit levels were reduced across the board through inflation. It was left to Finance Minister Bokros in his austerity package of early 1995 to withdraw certain benefits for the first time, and to tighten eligibility rules. Bokros and his team were determined to begin the process of reducing the role of the state and tackling fundamental public sector inefficiencies. Although the measures were harsh, in reality welfare payments were withdrawn from a modest 7 per cent of the population (Tóth, 1997). This illustrates the robustness of welfare programme entitlements. However, an important corner had been turned, and some fundamental (new) principles were established.

Subsequent to the Bokros austerity programme, there have been some other major developments. In the area of pensions, legislation is currently with the Hungarian Parliament which, if successful will introduce a multi-pillar scheme where the compulsory elements are represented by a consolidated PAYG scheme and privately-run fully funded scheme. This follows an increase in the statutory retirement age, approved by Parliament in 1996, changes in the contributions–benefits relationship, and a broadening in the tax base for social security contributions. In the area of health care, there has been some rationalisation of hospital beds.

3.4   Significant achievements

Although characteristically gradual, the reform measures of the post-1989 period add up to a significant recasting of the policy framework governing welfare programmes in Hungary. Of note are the following changes:

- there was a rapid decline in price subsidies and the free provision of merit goods, and a move toward cash benefits that enhanced consumer choice
- the state quickly assumed responsibility for social services and welfare programmes, removing them from state-owned enterprises, but necessarily requiring enterprises to help meet the cost of provision through increased taxation
- the role of social insurance was increased (in pensions, health care, maternity, and unemployment), and the relationship between (private) contributions and (private) benefits was enhanced
- targeting on the basis of means testing as well as categorical targeting was introduced (family allowance and social assistance)
- financing and provision of some services were delegated to sub-national levels of government (e.g. hospitals, social assistance)

- private provision, both for profit and not for profit, emerged, both spontaneously and as a result of contracting out
- some privatisation, albeit limited, of public services (e.g. health) occurred
- quasi-market arrangements were developed (e.g. in the health sector).

3.5 Measuring up

How do these developments measure up against the West, and other countries in the region? Hungary has embraced many of the principles underlying welfare programmes in the developed market economies. It has adopted *insurance-based* programmes which protect people against risks such as unemployment and ill-health; *income smoothing* programmes which allow people to protect their living standards in old age by redistributing income from their working years to retirement years (and provision by the private sector of savings schemes for retirement is emerging); and *poverty relief*, ensuring a minimum standard of living for the population at large. These principles guide a number of legitimate functions of the state which western countries continue to adhere to: redistribute income, maintain political stability, promote efficient labour markets and insure against important risks where private markets cannot. However, like the West, Hungary is still struggling to disentangle legitimate *public financing of public (or mixed) goods* from less legitimate *public provision* or *government production of public (or mixed) goods*, and opening the way for greater competition and efficiency gains through private providers. Hungary is also struggling to reduce welfare entitlements, and to promote greater self-reliance and less state dependence.

Relative to other CEE countries, Hungary's current standing is generally good, but it could be argued that Hungary had a head-start. The command-and-control approach was never as fundamental in Hungary as elsewhere in the region, and attempts to reform the welfare system had already begun in the 1980s. The years 1986–96, however, were not wasted: the success of recent reforms, especially of deeply entrenched entitlement programmes and the pension system, bear witness to the careful consensus-building that necessarily preceded legislation. With the 1996 increase in the statutory retirement age and the legislation currently before Parliament which will provide a partial privatisation of the pension scheme, Hungary is well ahead of neighbouring countries in pension reform (and, for that matter, ahead of Germany and France) (World Bank, 1996d). In other areas, such as reforming the health system, Hungary is in the leading pack, but the Czech and Slovak Republics, Croatia and FYR Macedonia have pioneered a number of more ambitious reforms (World Bank, 1996c). In the area of cash transfers, no other country in the region had Hungary's vast array of programmes, so any comparison is of modest value. Nonetheless, it should be said that Hungary still resembles a welfare state in this regard.

3.6 Strengthening institutions for an effective public sector

Hungary has clearly made significant strides in adopting the principles underlying welfare programmes akin to western market economies, and has introduced a number of promising reforms, especially in the area of pensions. As Csaba and Semjén conclude, these reforms have been quite effective at the macro level in containing public expenditure. But like many countries in the region, Hungary still faces the daunting challenge of building and refining the institutional capacity, both within and outside the public sector, to respond effectively to the many demands of transition and the evolving market economy. Whether it be the ministries of the central government, local government, Parliament, the semi-autonomous governing bodies, research institutes and universities, or the front-line delivery institutions, all face similar problems in terms of playing their appropriate roles. Some still want to 'row' when they should 'steer', others 'steer' (often with their hands off the rudder) when they should be rowing, and yet others who should be charting the course are ill-prepared to do so. Effective implementation of well-crafted welfare policies and programmes and the microefficiency gains that the government is seeking will continue to centre on the further strengthening of key institutions.

As for equity concerns, these are gradually being abandoned by inappropriate macro and labour market interventions. Social insurance programmes are increasingly being run with greater attention to the contributions–benefit relationship and their importance *vis-à-vis* incentives, and with less immediate concern for equity. However, it remains an open question whether the more appropriate taxation instruments and transfer programmes are doing an adequate job with redistribution and poverty reduction.

REFERENCES

Tóth, I.G. (1997) 'A háztartások jövedelmi szerkezete: a munkaerőpiac és a szociálpolitika szerepei' (The income structure of households: the role of the labour market and social policy), in E. Sik and I.G. Tóth (eds.), *Az ajtók záródnak*, Budapest: TÁRKI

350   **Discussion by Christine H. Allison**

World Bank (1995) *Hungary – Structural Reforms for Sustainable Growth*,
Washington: DC, World Bank
(1996a) *Hungary – Poverty and Social Transfers*, Washington, DC: World
Bank
(1996b) *From Plan to Market: World Development Report 1996*, New York:
Oxford University Press
(1996c) 'Trends in health status, services, and finance', *World Bank Technical
Paper, 341*, Washington, DC: World Bank
(1996d) 'The financing of pensions systems in Central and Eastern Europe',
World Bank Technical Paper, 339, Washington, DC: World Bank
(1997)*The State in a Changing World: World Development Report 1997*,
Washington, DC: World Bank

11 Regional unemployment rate differentials in Hungary, 1990–1995: the changing role of race and human capital

ÁRPÁD ÁBRAHÁM AND GÁBOR KERTESI

This chapter[1] is a comparative study of the role and the changing relative importance of schooling and discrimination against the Gypsy minority in shaping regional unemployment rate differentials in the course of the evolution of unemployment in Hungary in the period between 1990 and 1995. As is well known, with the change of political structure and the collapse of the socialist economic system, unemployment started to rise rapidly in 1990. The emergence of unemployment was accompanied by widening regional differences: regional inequalities received a new dimension with unemployment.

Empirical research on regional inequalities has some history in Hungary. Fazekas' (1993) analysis was able to show how unemployment rate differentials in *cross–section* can mainly be traced back to two key factors: differences in regional entrepreneurial and industrial capacity, entrepreneurship being the more important factor. We follow a different approach, analysing the *time path* of the determinants of regional unemployment rate differentials. In extending the analysis in time, we faced severe data problems and methodological difficulties:

(1) The standard methodology – separate analysis of inflow and outflow processes (Hall, 1972; Svejnar, Terrell and Münich, 1995) – could not be used here. Inflow and outflow data on the unemployed are not available at an appropriately disaggregated level – only at a national and county level (20 observations). Lacking appropriate flow data, we had to be satisfied with stock data which already reflect the results of heterogeneous inflow and outflow processes.

(2) Another difficulty arises from the fact that we have very few explanatory variables with a time dimension. This creates measurement problems and makes interpretation more difficult.

(3) Perhaps the most severe problem is that we could not rely on some widely used and accepted theoretical model. Hungary is not an

351

established market economy with a steady-state value of unemployment rate or natural rate of unemployment and fluctuations around that rate. Instead, during the transition unemployment emerged from nowhere, and is moving towards an as yet unknown steady rate. Lacking a theoretical model, a statistical model is created here in order to reveal the main factors which determine regional unemployment rate differentials. Since data problems allowed us to use only a highly simplified methodology, only very robust results are presented and interpreted in this chapter.

In section 1 the time pattern of regional unemployment rate differentials is examined. Then time paths of the main determinants of these inequalities are identified from a statistical model. Finally the role of the Gypsy population – the largest ethnic minority in Hungary – is examined as a factor shaping regional unemployment rate differences. A glance at the regional distribution of unemployment rates and the Gypsy population of the country is enough to persuade us that the density of the Gypsy population in an area has something to do with its level of unemployment. It is also known (Kertesi, 1994) that the unemployment rate of Gypsies is significantly – at least three times – higher than the Hungarian average. All these facts suggest that the size of the Gypsy population has an important role in forming regional differentials. How much is this due to discrimination or is it related purely to low education? Using some micro data, section 3 tries to estimate the magnitude of employment discrimination. Section 4 draws some conclusions.

1   The time pattern of regional unemployment rate differentials

The basis of observation throughout this study is districts of regional labour centres – institutions which are responsible for registering unemployed people in the area of the district, and paying unemployment benefit to them. The number of districts was changing in the period; it amounted to a number between 170 and 182. Therefore in order to be able to set up district level time series we aggregated our data to the smallest number of districts, 170. We have altogether 20 quarterly observations for each district from December 1990 until September 1995. Data cover the stock of people on the unemployment register in the given month. We calculated unemployment rates by using the standard procedure: dividing the number of unemployed by the sum of unemployed and employed people. A difficulty arises from this. Since district level time series are not available for the number of employed – only national level quarterly data exist in the Central Statistical Office's

Table 11.1. Content and source of variables used

Variable name	Content of variable		Mean	Std dev.
UNEMP	Seasonally adjusted quarterly unemployment rates,[a] quarters: t =1–20, 1=1990 December, 20=1995 September		12.15	6.01
EDUC	Average number of completed classes *per capita* for population older than 7 years in 1990[b]		8.13	0.46
GYPSY	Ratio of Gypsy pupils to the total number of children attending primary schools in the 1992/3 school year[c]		8.65	6.78
GYPPCT	Ratio of Gypsy population of working age to the total adult population of the same age (estimated)		4.52	3.76
ENTR	Number of private entrepreneurs having no employees per 1000 *capita* of population in the area[b]	1992 1993 1994		23.96 25.34 28.01
INDEMP	Ratio of industrial workers in industrial plants with more than 50 employees to the total number of employed (1990)[b]		24.16	12.02
LANDQ	Average agricultural land quality as measured by the average gold crown value of plot-lands in the area (1990)[b]		19.50	5.91

Notes:
[a] Unemployment register of the National Labour Centre.
[b] CSO, community level data base.
[c] Ministry of Education.

labour force survey – we had to be satisfied with a proxy measure of regional employment level: the 1990 census data.[2] Since the observed district level unemployment rates fluctuate seasonally, and our independent variables have no time dimension, instead of observed unemployment rates seasonally adjusted rates are used.[3] As we focus on the trend of unemployment, and not on the short-run variations, we do not lose too much important information as a result.

Table 11.1 shows the variables used throughout the chapter. Educational level of districts is measured by the average number of completed classes *per capita* for population older than 7 years in census year 1990 (*EDUC*). Regional ethnic composition is measured by a proxy variable: by the ratio of Gypsy children to the total number of primary school pupils in the 1992/3 school year (*GYPSY*). No better information is available on a *district* level. Later on we use another variable: the ratio of the Gypsy population of working age[4] to the total adult population of the same age (*GYPPCT*). *GYPPCT* is estimated from regional educational data by using national level adult:child ratios from two different surveys (the national representative *Gypsy Survey* of 1993/4 and the regular *Labour Force Survey* of the Central Statistical Office, Fall 1993). District level numbers of Gypsy and non-Gypsy children are multiplied by uniform[5] 'adult:pupil' ratios for both the Gypsy and the non-Gypsy population respectively, then percentages of Gypsy adults (of working age) are calculated from the estimated data.

Control variables comprise variables on entrepreneurship, industrial employment and agricultural land quality. *ENTR* represents the number of private small entrepreneurs (mostly self-employed people[6]) divided by 1000 *capita* of population living in the district. *ENTR* measures how much entrepreneurship took place in the given district after the change in political and economic system. This is our only time dependent explanatory variable (three yearly observations – December 1992, 1993 and 1994 – are available). *INDEMP* – the number of industrial workers who had jobs in industrial plants with more than 50 employees in 1990 divided by the total number of employed people in the same year – measures the extent of state-owned industry in the given district at the start of the economic transition. *LANDQ* represents average agricultural land quality as measured by the average gold crown value of plot-lands in the area. Finally a series of dummy variables stands for the geographical regions of Hungary.[7]

First the change in distribution of regional unemployment rates is followed over time. In figure 11.1 densities of unemployment rates are shown for 6 dates. It is clear from the figure that the biggest leap in the spread of unemployment occurred in 1991: while at the end of 1990 the range of local unemployment rates was between 0 and 10 per cent, and only a small number of districts (less than 15 per cent) had a higher than 5 per cent unemployment rate, by the end of 1991 the situation had deteriorated considerably: the maximum reached 25 per cent, and half of the regions had a more than 10 per cent unemployment rate. Although the rate of deterioration slowed down a little in 1992 compared to 1991, the increase in range and average continued. By the end of 1992 half of the regions already exceeded the 15 per cent, one-fifth of the regions the 20 per cent unemployment rate. The increase of unemployment stopped in 1993, and in 1994 some improvement began to take place; by 1995 the distribution and range was much the same as in 1994.

The decrease in unemployment in 1994 did not mean any improvement in the position of the unemployed. It meant rather that many people exhausted their eligibility for unemployment benefit, gave up searching for jobs, and exited the labour force. The higher the regional unemploy-

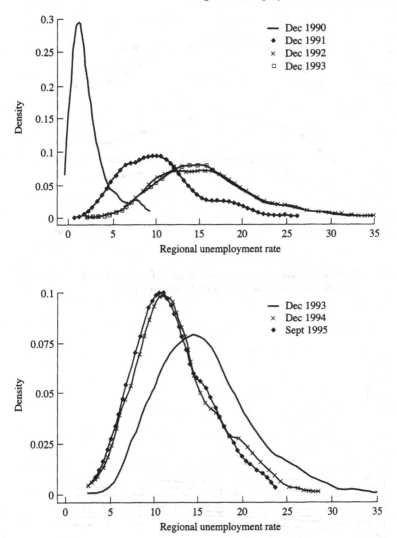

Figure 11.1 Densities of unemployment rates, December 1990–September 1995

ment rate, the larger the increase in the number of people exiting the labour force – especially after 1992, when unemployment rates reached their peak (Fazekas, 1996).

Figure 11.2 shows the evolution of the average unemployment rate of the top and the bottom decile and that of the median districts. The time paths are very similar: an increasing section until March 1993 (which is a

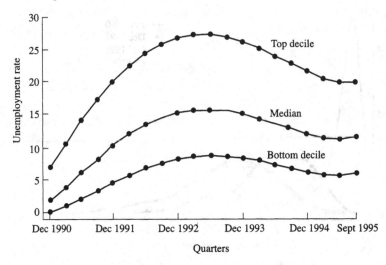

Figure 11.2   Evolution of average unemployment rate of top and bottom decile and median districts, December 1990–September 1995

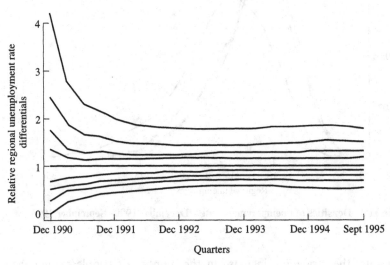

Figure 11.3   Time path of relative unemployment differentials, December 1990–September 1995

common maximum), then a uniform slow decrease. The rates were stabilising by 1995.

The relative differences are more interesting. Expressing mean unemployment rates of the different (10th, 9th, 8th, 7th, 4th, 3rd, 2nd, 1st) deciles in percentages of the median (50th centile) at each period of time, we get a picture of the *time path of the relative unemployment rate differentials* (figure 11.3). This measure of relative differential is – by definition – independent of the prevailing levels. It can be seen from figure 11.3 that when unemployment appeared in Hungary, relative differences in regional unemployment rates were extremely large, but shortly afterwards started to shrink rapidly (the period of most significant decrease is 1991), then the relative position of the different deciles began to stabilise, relative unemployment rate differentials being almost constant over time. The 90th centile has the largest gap relative to the median. At our starting period (in December 1990) the average unemployment rate of the 10th ('the worst') decile was four times higher than the median then, after a very sharp decrease in 1991, the ratio stabilised around 1.7–1.8. The same is true of the 8th and to a lesser extent the 1st deciles. Interestingly enough, the very large relative inequalities across regions in the early phase of unemployment are almost entirely due to the *extremely high relative[8] unemployment rates of the districts having the starting period's highest unemployment rates.* The very existence of these extraordinarily high relative unemployment rates in the most backward areas in 1990, their rapid reduction in 1991, and their stabilisation thereafter seems to relate to a certain type of causality. To our intuition, certain factors which at the start might have had a temporarily decisive influence on relative regional differences began to lose their importance, and were being replaced gradually by some more basic factors that in the long run shape regional inequalities.

However, there may be considerable changes in the relative position of *individual* districts with respect to their actual unemployment rates over time. As different factors may determine relative differentials in the early phase of unemployment, and later on when relative positions are gradually stabilising, it seems reasonable to compare relative positions at the start and at the end of the 1990–5 period. This is done in table 11.2.

Table 11.2 shows a significant stability of the relative positions. Most of the cases are found in or in the neighbourhood of the main diagonal. Only 15 districts (9 per cent) changed position by more than one quartile. The stability of the relative positions of individual districts seems to reaffirm the appropriateness of the use of time invariant independent variables in the statistical model. If relative positions are stable enough

Table 11.2. Interquartile unemployment rate transitions, December 1990–September 1995

Unemployment rate (December 1990)	Unemployment rate (September 1995) (quartiles)				Number of districts
	Lowest	Second	Third	Highest	
Lowest quartile	25	13	4	1	43
Second quartile	16	12	11	3	42
Third quartile	2	12	18	10	42
Highest quartile	0	5	9	29	43
Number of districts	43	42	42	43	170

over time, then time invariant explanatory variables can account for cross-sectional variability of the unemployment rates fairly well.

Finally the country's characteristic geographical regions may have some independent role in shaping unemployment rate differentials. In table 11.3 values of mean educational level, Gypsy ratio and average unemployment rate for 6 dates are presented by geographic regions. It can be seen that there are fairly big differences across these regions with respect to all these variables.

The unemployment rate is highest in the North-Eastern part of Hungary. This region has the lowest educational level and the highest Gypsy population. This region was also the centre of the obsolete state-owned heavy industry which collapsed immediately after the transition. The other parts of the region are mainly agricultural areas with poor infrastructure. This region is the most backward part of the country. The South-Eastern region is also of mainly an agricultural character; however, it differs from the North-Eastern region by its higher share of private enterprises and private farms. The ratio of Gypsy population is relatively small here. The low educational level in both of these regions is closely related to the relatively large weight of agriculture. The Central and North-Western regions are the two most developed parts of Hungary. Historically these regions are more industrialised than the rest of the country, mainly due to their geographical location: the Central region is very close to the capital, the economic centre of Hungary, the North-Western region is close to Austria, the western border of Hungary. The proximity of Budapest and Austria means more invest-ment and more employment opportunities in these regions. The average educational level is relatively high, and the percentage of the Gypsy population is the smallest here. Finally, the South-Western region is a mixture of backward agricultural areas and industrialised districts. The

Table 11.3. Unemployment rate, average schooling and Gypsy ratio, by geographical regions, unweighted regional means with standard deviations in parentheses

Variable	Budapest	Central	North-Western	South-Western	South-Eastern	North-Eastern	Hungary
UNEMP (Dec. 1990)	0.07	0.94	0.81	2.14	1.92	3.84	2.18
	–	(0.89)	(0.56)	(0.93)	(1.37)	(2.38)	(1.99)
UNEMP (Dec. 1991)	3.08	7.36	6.95	9.64	11.19	14.19	10.52
	–	(2.37)	(2.93)	(2.53)	(3.16)	(4.69)	(4.49)
UNEMP (Dec. 1992)	6.31	12.35	10.94	14.22	16.45	20.24	15.68
	–	(3.22)	(2.75)	(3.40)	(3.42)	(5.29)	(5.29)
UNEMP (Dec. 1993)	6.82	12.33	11.09	14.12	16.24	20.05	15.58
	–	(3.22)	(2.74)	(3.23)	(3.26)	(4.93)	(5.15)
UNEMP (Dec. 1994)	5.43	9.33	8.90	11.53	12.99	16.29	12.48
	–	(2.83)	(2.39)	(2.75)	(3.27)	(4.18)	(4.46)
UNEMP (Sept. 1995)	5.62	9.45	8.35	11.47	12.19	15.23	11.90
	–	(2.66)	(2.28)	(3.08)	(3.07)	(3.72)	(4.06)
EDUC	9.64	8.37	8.45	8.17	7.98	7.88	8.13
	–	(0.36)	(0.38)	(0.36)	(0.38)	(0.43)	(0.46)
GYPSY	4.05	3.82	3.87	10.94	6.92	14.30	8.65
	–	(1.73)	(2.33)	(4.53)	(5.06)	(7.42)	(6.78)

size of the Gypsy community is fairly large, and the average educational level is low.

2   An intertemporal statistical model

In this section a statistical model will be presented. Changing unemployment rate differentials are explained by Gypsy ratio, average schooling, control variables (private entrepreneurship, pretransitional industrial employment, agricultural land quality), and five regional dummies. As a method of analysis cross-sectional multivariate regressions on standardised variables are applied and repeated 20 times (as 20 subsequent observations of quarterly unemployment rates are available). We want to determine the time paths of regression coefficients on standardised independent variables.

The model rests on the following equation:

$$u_j^t = \beta^t g_j + \gamma^t m_j + \sum_{i=1}^{3} \delta_i^t c_{ij} + \sum_{k=1}^{5} \eta_k^t r_{kj} + \varepsilon_j^t \qquad (1)$$

$$(j = 1, 2, \ldots, 170; \quad t = 1, 2, \ldots, 20)$$

u_j^t being the standardised, seasonally adjusted unemployment rate in the jth district at the tth quarter (from December 1990 to September 1995); g_j the standardised Gypsy ratio (measured by percentage of Gypsy primary school pupils) in the jth district; m_j the standardised average schooling level in the jth district; c_{ij} the standardised values of control variables (entrepreneurship, pretransitional industrial employment, land quality) in the jth district; and finally r_{kj} are standardised region-type dummies.[9] We are interested in the time paths of the standardised regression parameters. Standardisation eliminates differences in magnitude of variables, thus the strength of the effects is directly comparable.

The average number of completed classes (*EDUC*) measures the quality of the labour force, which can affect the unemployment rate in two ways. First, better educated employees usually have more firm-specific skills, which makes their dismissal highly expensive. Secondly, new investments are concentrated in areas with a fairly high schooling level – modern technology usually requires skilled labour (educated labour and new capital assets based on modern technology are complementary factors).

The Gypsy ratio (*GYPSY*) stands for two effects in the equation. First: if it is true that Gypsy persons are disproportionately more exposed to *employment discrimination*[10] than any other group, then their high proportion in the labour force will raise the local unemployment rate, simply because of the properties of arithmetic means. Secondly: a relatively high Gypsy population can also itself be an *indirect indicator of economic backwardness* of a given district. In this case causality is more complicated. The Gypsy ratio does not cause a high unemployment rate but both high unemployment and a high Gypsy percentage are results of one and the same cause: economic backwardness. This sort of backwardness (economic decline, poor infrastructure and poor earnings opportunities) was characteristic of some parts of the country many years before the appearance of unemployment. A clear sign of this was (and is) the high migration rate from these regions. The fact that the regions whose migration balance[11] is negative – *both* in the 1980s and in the early 1990s – are precisely those which are most densely populated by Gypsies, proves that Gypsies can improve themselves by changing their residence much less than the average Hungarian family. This was true well before the transition, under the regime of almost full employment. The 1980–90 model in Appendix 11.2 (p. 375) clearly proves that the Gypsy ratio and negative migration balance were strongly related to each other in the 1980s. This has not changed after 1989 – see again Appendix 11.2, but now the 1990–3 model – however the mechanism is modified somewhat. After 1990, the decline of employment opportunities – measured by the mean educational level – is what results in high values of outmigration. As Gypsies are highly over-represented in low-educated areas, they again get stuck disproportionately in regions which are hardest hit by economic crises. Moreover, high, and especially persistently high, unemployment rates may cause significant depreciation in the market price of real estates which makes outmigration very difficult. However, this obstacle to migration is highly selective: as education raises the chances of employment elsewhere, and young age and lack of marriage reduce the costs of leaving, we can expect more *educated* young, unmarried people to leave. Since non-Gypsies are strongly over-represented among educated people, this will reduce the proportion of non-Gypsies in the economically declining areas. On the other hand, the employment chances of low-educated Gypsies are often no better in prosperous areas. For them decreasing housing prices in declining regions – and sometimes abandoned houses – can be attractive enough to cause migration into high-unemployment districts. Both processes raise the proportions of Gypsies in backward regions.

Entrepreneurship (*ENTR*) measures two things: the extent of self-employment and the economic prosperity of the given region. Both reduce the risk of unemployment. The number of employees in larger industrial companies (*INDEMP*) in 1990 is applied to measure the weight of medium-sized and big state-owned industrial companies on the eve of the economic transition. As these firms were among the first

Table 11.4. The determinants of the regional unemployment rate, December 1990 – September 1995, OLS regressions

Independent variables[a]	Dec. 1990	Mar. 1991	June 1991	Sept. 1991	Dec. 1991	Mar. 1992	June 1992	Sept. 1992	Dec. 1992	Mar. 1993	June 1993	Sept. 1993	Dec. 1993	Mar. 1994	June 1994	Sept. 1994	Dec. 1994	Mar. 1995	June 1995	Sept. 1995
Standardised regression parameters																				
GYPSY	0.36*	0.31*	0.29*	0.27*	0.27*	0.28*	0.27*	0.27*	0.27*	0.26*	0.26*	0.25*	0.24*	0.23*	0.21*	0.20*	0.19*	0.19*	0.20*	0.22*	0.26*
EDUC	−0.23+	−0.33+	−0.35*	−0.37*	−0.36*	−0.35*	−0.35*	−0.35*	−0.36*	−0.37*	−0.39*	−0.41*	−0.43*	−0.45*	−0.47*	−0.49*	−0.50*	−0.49*	−0.46*	−0.39*
ENTR	0.08	0.04	0.01	−0.01	−0.04	−0.06	−0.08	−0.09	−0.10	−0.11+	−0.10+	−0.09+	−0.09+	−0.08	−0.07	−0.07	−0.06	−0.07	−0.09	−0.14+
INDEMP	0.02	0.00	−0.02	−0.02	−0.03	−0.06	−0.03	−0.03	−0.03	−0.02	−0.00	0.01	0.02	0.04	0.05	0.07	0.08	0.09	0.09	0.08
LANDQ	−0.02	−0.05	−0.07	−0.08	−0.08	−0.09	−0.09	−0.09	−0.09+	−0.09	−0.08	−0.08	−0.07	−0.06	−0.05	−0.05	−0.04	−0.04	−0.04	−0.05
CENTRAL	−0.02	−0.07	−0.07	−0.06	−0.04	−0.02	−0.00	0.01	0.01	−0.00	−0.03	−0.05	−0.08	−0.12	−0.16+	−0.20+	−0.22*	−0.23*	−0.20+	−0.12
NORTH-WEST	−0.04	−0.04	−0.05	−0.05	−0.05	−0.05	−0.05	−0.06	−0.07	−0.08	−0.10	−0.12	−0.14+	−0.16+	−0.19*	−0.20*	−0.21*	−0.22*	−0.21*	−0.18+
SOUTH-WEST	0.01	−0.00	−0.01	−0.01	−0.00	0.00	0.00	0.00	−0.01	−0.01	−0.03	−0.05	−0.07	−0.09	−0.12	−0.13+	−0.14+	−0.13+	−0.10	−0.04
SOUTH-EAST	0.04	0.09	0.11	0.12	0.14	0.15	0.15	0.15	0.14	0.12	0.10	0.07	0.03	−0.00	−0.05	−0.08	−0.10	−0.11	−0.09	−0.04
NORTH-EAST	0.30+	0.26+	0.24+	0.23+	0.24+	0.25+	0.26+	0.26+	0.25+	0.24+	0.22+	0.20+	0.17	0.14	0.10	0.07	0.04	0.03	0.04	0.08
Regression diagnostics[b]																				
No. of observations	167	169	169	170	170	170	170	170	170	170	170	170	170	170	170	170	170	170	170	170
R^2	0.52	0.60	0.62	0.63	0.66	0.67	0.69	0.70	0.70	0.71	0.71	0.71	0.72	0.72	0.71	0.71	0.71	0.70	0.69	0.67
F-statistics[c]	16.7*	23.3*	25.4*	27.6*	30.4*	33.0*	35.1*	36.7*	37.9*	38.8*	39.3*	39.8*	40.0*	39.9*	39.4*	38.5*	36.4*	36.7*	35.8*	32.6*
Unrestricted model[d]	3.71*	5.11*	5.35*	5.47*	5.85*	6.40*	7.05*	7.72*	8.32*	8.82*	9.23*	9.45*	9.49*	9.34*	8.84*	8.50*	8.11*	7.49*	6.34*	5.01*
Heteroscedasticity[e]	59.8*	44.4*	35.5*	29.5*	25.2*	22.2*	20.1*	18.8*	18.3*	18.5*	18.9*	20.4*	22.1*	23.5*	23.6*	22.3*	19.6*	16.5*	14.4*	14.3*
Normality[f]	3.29*	3.66*	3.23*	2.69*	2.32+	2.16+	2.01+	2.02+	2.23+	2.54+	2.71+	2.81+	2.81+	2.62+	2.19+	1.67+	0.15	−0.72	−1.27	0.32
RESET-test[g]	2.01	2.32	1.81	1.58	1.44	1.39	1.38	1.39	1.40	1.41	1.27	1.26	1.28	1.31	1.45	1.43	1.36	1.24	1.03	0.63

Notes:

* Significant at 1 per cent level. ⁺Significant at 5 per cent level.

[a] Reference is Budapest among region-type dummies.

[b] Multicollinearity was tested by computing variance inflation factors (*VIF*). See Kennedy (1992, p. 183). Test values were never larger than 3.82, which means that no harmful collinearity was present.

[c] *F*-statistics measuring the power of explanatory variables.

[d] *F*-statistics measuring the joint significance of regional variables. See Greene (1993, p. 204).

[e] Cook–Weisberg test for heteroscedasticity. See Cook and Weisberg (1982). Chi² -statistics are presented in the table.

[f] Shapiro–Wilk test for normality of residuals. See Shapiro and Wilk (1965). Values of the standard–normal distribution are presented in the table.

[g] Ramsey's *RESET*-test for omitted variables in linear regression model. See Ramsey (1969). *F*-statistics are presented in the table.

companies that went bankrupt and laid off their employees, this measure of industrial employment in 1990 is expected to raise future unemployment. The use of land quality (*LANDQ*) is an attempt to measure the employment capacity of agriculture in the given district; better land quality is expected to reduce unemployment. Regional dummies are used to control for the individual characteristics of geographical regions. The proximity of Budapest in the case of the Central region and the proximity of Austria in the case of the North-Western region can mitigate the unemployment, whereas geographical location in the South-Western and North-Eastern regions – which lost their natural cultural and business centres with the Peace Treaties in 1920 and are still poorly integrated with any other business centres – may amplify the employment crisis.

Table 11.4 presents our regression results. The *F*-statistics and adjusted R^2 prove that the models fit well and have strong explanatory power. *F*-statistics measuring the appropriateness of use of regional dummies support the use of the unrestricted model. Residuals proved to be heteroscedastic, thus *t*-tests were computed by using White's heteroscedasticity consistent estimator (White, 1980). Heteroscedasticity is possibly due to the fact that our independent variables have no time dimension. The detected non-normality of residuals (16 cases out of 20) is most likely due to the heteroscedasticity of the residuals. *RESET*-tests do not indicate omission of important explanatory variables. Tests of multicollinearity (*VIF*) proved that no harmful collinearity was present.

The results clearly support our expectations concerning the importance of the Gypsy ratio and schooling. There is no doubt that they are the key factors (their parameters are significant in each quarter). Even after controlling for the effect of entrepreneurship, industrial employment, land quality and regional dummies, differences in the Gypsy ratio and educational level are the strongest forces which determine regional unemployment rate differentials. Standardised regression parameters move between 0.19 and 0.36 (*GYPSY*) and 0.23 and 0.50 (*EDUC*[12]), only the weakest parameters being close to the strongest regional parameters. The control variables (*ENTR*, *INDEMP* and *LANDQ*) play no role in forming unemployment rate inequalities. With five exceptions, their parameters are not significant, although their signs meet our expectations. Regional dummies are important, but surprisingly in a complementary form: dummies with significant parameters replace each other in time. *NORTHEAST* had significant and *positive* parameters until September 1993 (when the national unemployment rate reached its peak), while the parameters of *CENTRAL* and *NORTHWEST* became significant and *negative* after 1993.

Figure 11.4 shows the paths of parameters of average schooling and the

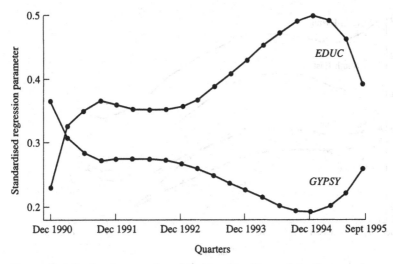

Figure 11.4 Paths of parameters of average schooling and the Gypsy ratio, December 1990–September 1995

Gypsy ratio. A strong inverse relationship shows up between the time patterns of these parameters. In the early phase of unemployment, in the transitional period (mostly 1991) racial differentials play the major role in shaping regional unemployment rate differentials. In the first period the impact of the Gypsy ratio is more than 50 per cent bigger than the impact of schooling differentials. By the end of 1994 this relation was completely reversed: the importance of schooling is more than twice as big as the importance of ethnic composition in regional unemployment rate differentials. The transition from the predominantly race dependent regional unemployment rate differentials to the predominantly human capital dependent unemployment rate differentials is very smooth. (The reverse movement in 1995 will be discussed at the end of this section.)

To our intuition, the large importance of the Gypsy ratio and the moderate effect of schooling differentials right after the beginning of unemployment, when local unemployment rates were relatively low, cannot be interpreted as if inter-regional human capital differentials were not so important. Similarly, the fact that the impact of the Gypsy variable is weakening over time does not mean that the employment chances of Gypsy workers are getting better. A different interpretation is suggested: at the very start – when levels of local unemployment rates were mostly below 5 per cent[13] – employment opportunities of low-educated people had already collapsed. Even at the start of unemploy-

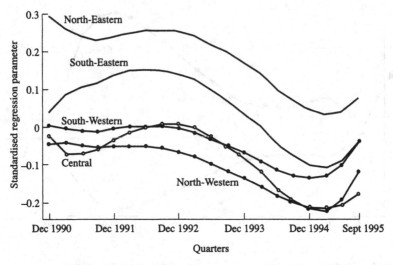

Figure 11.5   Time paths of regional parameters, December 1990–September 1995

ment low-educated people were strongly over-represented in the pool of unemployed people. However, Gypsies were similarly over-represented among low-educated unemployed people, as well. At the start the burden of the employment crisis fell on Gypsy workers to a disproportionately large extent: they were the first to be laid off and the last to be hired. As the spread of unemployment reached its full extent – which required considerable time – non-Gypsy workers were also increasingly hit by the shrinking of employment opportunities. And in the pool of these new entrants again low-educated people were over-represented. The lower is the average schooling the more severe is the employment crisis as it reaches its peak. This fundamental relationship is, however, distorted by the fact that discrimination against Gypsy workers in those regions where the proportion of Gypsy employees was high was an appropriate means to spare many low-educated non-Gypsy workers the burden of unemployment – at least for a while: until unemployment rates reached such an extent that no group of uneducated workers could any longer be spared.

In figure 11.5 the time paths of the regional parameters are shown. Again an interesting inverse relationship can be captured. Until September 1993 the North-Eastern region had an important role in increasing the unemployment rate. After 1993 this region lost its significance and the Central and North-Western regions gained the key role in reducing the unemployment rate. (At the end of the observed period these tendencies again reversed.) The major role of the North-Eastern region in the first period's high unemployment was due to the crisis of heavy industry in the area and the collapse of the Soviet Union which had been the main customer of the region's agriculture. These processes had practically ended by the last quarter of 1993, probably explaining why that parameter lost its significance by that time.

On the other hand, the Central and North-Western regions gained significance precisely from that date. This phenomenon was accompanied by the 1994 boom of investment activity in the Hungarian economy. These (mostly Western) investments were mainly concentrated in these two regions. Even though the Central and North-Western regions are highly educated areas and thus the favoured centres of new investment activities, the fact that as geographical areas they have an independent role in reducing unemployment shows the autonomous role of the physical proximity of Budapest and the western border in job creation and new investments. We may refer to the big investment of 1994 in the automobile industry in order to illustrate the important and independent role of the geographical location of these regions. In the automobile industry four Western companies carried out big investments after 1994 in these two regions: Opel in Szentgotthárd, Ford in Székesfehérvár, Audi in Győr (all in the North-Western region), and Suzuki in Esztergom (Central region). These facts clearly indicate the prosperity of these regions.

Finally, it is striking that in 1995, and especially in the last quarter of the observed period, all the parameters switched to an opposite direction. This is most likely due to some sort of registration problem. Until the end of 1994 two labour market programmes were at work on a large scale: a retraining programme for all unemployed and a wage subsidy programme for the long-term unemployed. As the participants in these programmes – simply because they were in these programmes – could not accept job offers in a short period of time, they were not registered as unemployed by the local labour centres. This meant that several thousand practically unemployed people were not registered as unemployed. There are two reasons why this affects our regression results. First, as funds of these programmes were used up, fewer and fewer people got onto these programmes, and more and more were registered as unemployed. This is what happened in 1995.[14] Second, these programmes were working mainly in big urban centres with a well educated labour force. The big urban centres are more capable of maintaining retraining institutions, and people with a relatively high educational level are more capable of participating in these programmes. As these programmes are reduced by budget cuts unemployment increases in precisely those districts where these programmes used to be large. That is why unemployment is increasing in regions with a relatively high schooling level. For this reason the parameters of *all* the independent variables changed. At this moment the future path of our parameters seems to be uncertain, but if the former explanation is correct, we can expect them to stabilise again.

3   On the employment discrimination against the Gypsy minority

In this section we try to present some independent evidence to support the claim that high positive and significant regression coefficients on the Gypsy ratio can be traced back to heterogeneous causes: to the employment discrimination against the Gypsy minority and to the economic backwardness of – mainly rural – regions densely populated by Gypsies. Using a simple statistical model based on stylised facts, we try to give an interpretation of the strong inverse relationship between the time pattern of the parameters on the Gypsy ratio and the schooling level, as well.

Imagine two identical districts which differ only in two respects: in the size of their Gypsy population and their average schooling level. District A has a small Gypsy population, and the percentage of Gypsies in district B is high. As Gypsies are usually low-educated people, this is reflected in the difference of the average schooling level. However, the average educational level of district B – which has a larger Gypsy population – is *disproportionately* lower than that of district A. This is because in districts where the Gypsy population is large, the mean schooling level of non-Gypsies is also lower than the national average. As a result of particular kinds of long-run migration patterns,[15] a high Gypsy ratio is also an indirect indicator of the economic and infrastructural backwardness of a region itself.

Figure 11.6 shows the idealised model of the evolution of unemployment in these two kinds of districts. Since in our idealised model a high Gypsy percentage implies a disproportionately low schooling level, it is no wonder that the unemployment rate will be significantly higher – even without any discrimination – in districts where the Gypsy population is large. However if discrimination is present, not only is the unemployment rate higher in areas with a large Gypsy population but at the same time unemployed Gypsies are over-represented among similarly uneducated unemployed people. We will show empirically that this is precisely the case – particularly in the early stages of evolution of unemployment in Hungary. With perfect discrimination – this case is modelled in figure 11.6 – the burden of unemployment falls only on Gypsy people as long as the absolute size of unemployment and the absolute size of the Gypsy

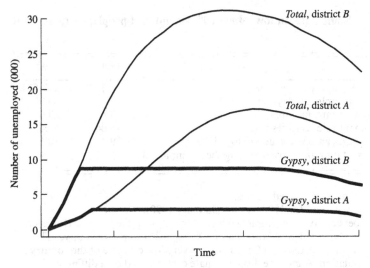

Figure 11.6 **Idealised model of evolution of unemployment in district *A* and district *B*, December 1990–September 1995**

labour force permit this. As long as there are some Gypsies still among the employed, they will provide the only source of the inflow into the pool of unemployed. This is the reason why in this early phase the Gypsy ratio comoves so strongly with the regional unemployment rate – even after controlling for educational differentials across regions. The situation changes as the employment crisis deepens and the majority of Gypsy people have already been driven out of the labour market. As more and more non-Gypsy workers become unemployed, the importance of regional differentials in educational attainments increases since in the pool of new entrants low-educated non-Gypsies gain more weight. On the other hand, the importance of regional ethnic differentials decreases as the weight of Gypsy unemployed among low-educated unemployed people gradually decreases. That is why the regression parameters of Gypsy ratio and schooling level follow inverse paths.

Table 11.5 provides direct evidence of all that has been said about the employment discrimination against the Gypsy minority – especially in the early phase of evolution of unemployment in Hungary. It does not matter that the statistical model had uncertain implications as to the interpretation of significant positive parameters on the Gypsy ratio; if it is true that in the early stage of unemployment Gypsies were significantly over-represented among similarly educated unemployed people, this directly proves that they were discriminated against in hirings and

370   Árpád Ábrahám and Gábor Kertesi

Table 11.5. Some data on low-educated^a unemployed people, by race, 1990 and 1993

	1990^b	1993
Number of unemployed, national	68,544	247,534^e
Number of unemployed, Gypsies	20,139^c	45,997^f
Unemployment rate, national (%)	3.80	20.08
Unemployment rate, Gypsies (%)	18.04	52.66
Ratio of Gypsies among the unemployed (%)	29.38	18.58
Over-representation of Gypsies among the unemployed^d	5.51	3.49

Notes:
^{a} Not more than 8 completed classes.
^{b} Figures are based on the 1990 Census (January 1990).
^{c} Raw numbers of Gypsy unemployed were derived from the Census. However, the Census' Gypsy subpopulation cannot be regarded as representative. The self-identification used by the Census gave a very low estimate of the country's Gypsy population. A more realistic estimate can be based on a different – sociological – criterion which relies on the identification of Gypsies by the non-Gypsy environment. This criterion was used by the *National Representative Gypsy Survey* of 1993/4. Census' data were reweighted by the *Gypsy Survey* with respect to the regional distribution and the absolute numbers were gained by the use of inverses of the *Survey*'s regional sampling rates.
^{d} The ratio of low-educated Gypsies in the age group of 15–74 years (regular students excluded) was 5.33 per cent in 1993. This is the denominator in the ratio which quantifies the over-representation. The source of the national data was the *Labour Force Survey* (Fall 1993) of the Central Statistical Office, the source of the Gypsy data was the *Gypsy Survey*. The numerators are taken from the fifth row of this table (ratio of Gypsies among the unemployed).
^{e} *Source*: *Labour Force Survey* (Fall 1993) of the Central Statistical Office.
^{f} *Source*: *National Representative Gypsy Survey* (1993/4).

layoffs. In the language of the idealised model of figure 11.6 the time path of Gypsy unemployment in its early period coincides with the time path of total unemployment. The share of Gypsies among the unemployed is thus 100 per cent. Naturally, this relationship is stochastic in reality. As table 11.5 shows, at the very start of the economic transition[16] – when the national unemployment rate of low-educated people was below 4 per cent – the unemployment rate of the similarly defined Gypsy population was 18 per cent, and in the pool of low-educated unemployed the share of Gypsy workers was almost 30 per cent. This means a *550 per cent over-representation* relative to their share in the similarly defined low-educated adult population. However, as unemployment expanded – and reached its peak in the second half of 1993 – the share dropped significantly: from 30 per cent to below 20 per cent. Thus the over-representation of Gypsies in the pool of low-educated unemployed relative to their proportion in the

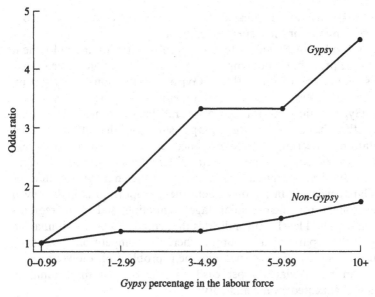

Figure 11.7 Odds ratios: probabilities of unemployment relative to probabilities of employment

adult population also dropped: from 550 per cent to 350 per cent. This is the reason why the value of the parameter on the Gypsy ratio decreases over time. These figures provide strong evidence of the existence of employment discrimination with respect to race.

We cannot say, however, that discrimination is the only meaning of the positive parameters of the Gypsy ratio in the regional unemployment rate equations. As indicated earlier, a high proportion of the Gypsy population is also an indirect indicator of the economic and infrastructural backwardness of geographical areas. This is why Gypsy parameters do not lose their statistical significance – and remain strong, even after educational differentials seem to replace them as basic determinants of regional unemployment differentials. This proposition can again be supported by some direct evidence.

Individual chances of unemployment were predicted[17] on separate samples of Gypsy and non-Gypsy persons in the labour force by a series of personal characteristics (gender, age, number of dependent children, schooling dummies) and two sorts of district level contextual variables (mean schooling level, *EDUC*; and a series of dummy variables created from the ratio of the Gypsy population of working age to the adult population of the same age). Detailed results are to be found in Appendix

11.1 (p. 374). We are interested here in the parameters of Gypsy percentage dummies or the respective odds ratios.

Figure 11.7 shows these odds ratios – the probabilities of unemployment relative to the probabilities of employment – in the function of the Gypsy ratio in separate graphs for both the Gypsy and the non-Gypsy group. On the one hand, the non-Gypsy graph seems to support the claim that the high Gypsy ratio is also a sign of overall backwardness of an area. On the other hand, the Gypsy graph supports the other sort of interpretation concerning the significance of the Gypsy ratio in explaining regional unemployment rate differentials. The employment chances of Gypsies are significantly worse than the employment chances of non-Gypsy workers in regions where their proportion is high – even after controlling for their gender, age, schooling and their region's average educational level. This indicates that employment discrimination is strong in those parts of the country where the competition is tight for low-skill jobs, and where the unemployment problem of a low-educated majority can be alleviated most easily at the cost of discriminating against a low-educated ethnic minority.

4   Conclusion

We have examined the role and the changing relative importance of schooling and discrimination against the Gypsy minority in shaping regional unemployment rate differentials in the course of the evolution of unemployment in Hungary in the period between 1990 and 1995. These differentials in relative terms proved to evolve in a very peculiar manner. In the early phase of economic transition relative differences were extremely large but shortly afterwards they started to shrink rapidly and by 1992 they had stabilised. Since then relative unemployment rate differentials have been almost constant over time. The very large relative inequalities across regions in the early stage of unemployment were almost entirely due to the extremely high unemployment rates of regions in the top decile. The very existence of these extraordinarily high relative unemployment rates in the most backward areas in 1990, their rapid reduction in 1991, and their stabilisation afterwards seem to relate to a certain type of causality. In searching for the causes of this changing pattern of relative regional inequalities, an intertemporal statistical model was set up.

The intertemporal model came to the following conclusions. The proportion of the Gypsy population and average schooling level proved to be the key determinants of regional unemployment differentials throughout the period. However we found a strong inverse relationship between the importance of these two factors. In the early phase of the economic transition, regional differences in the size of the Gypsy population dominated the unemployment differentials across regions. By the end of 1994 this relationship had been completely reversed. The transition from predominantly race dependent regional unemployment rate differentials to predominantly human capital dependent inequalities proved to be very smooth.

The positive parameter of the Gypsy ratio was considered to be the result of two different factors. On the one hand Gypsies are discriminated against in the labour market, and for this reason the size of their population simply raises the stock of the unemployed. This factor was the key element in the total impact of the Gypsy ratio at the start of the transition. On the other hand the size of the Gypsy population indirectly measures the economic prosperity and decline of a region as well – the proportion of Gypsies tends to be higher in areas where the economy and infrastructure is poor. Long-run migration patterns are responsible for this. After 1993 the significance of the Gypsy parameter is most likely due to this sort of externality. Independent evidence was presented to support the existence of employment discrimination against Gypsies and the existence of these external effects. As to the interpretation of predominantly human capital dependent unemployment rate differentials, we stressed that the role of schooling was starting to increase rapidly just as the transitory opportunities of alleviating the consequences of unemployment for the non-Gypsy majority by discriminating against the Gypsy minority had already been exhausted. As the majority of Gypsy people has already been driven out of the labour market, it is education – the decisive factor of growth – which comes to be effective, with great power, in the labour market.

Interestingly, the economic control variables (entrepreneurship, industrial employment, land quality) did not play a significant role in shaping regional unemployment differentials. However the use of region-type dummies revealed that geographical characteristics play an important role in determining inequalities independently of the differences in educational attainment and ethnic composition. In the early stages it was location in the most backward North-Eastern region which seriously aggravated the employment situation of a district; since 1994 the proximity of Budapest and the western border was the factor that has helped to hold local unemployment rates down.

Appendix 11.1: the determinants of individual chances of unemployment (logit estimation)

Indep. var.	Dependent variable: Unemployed? yes=1, no=0 if in the labour force					
	Non-Gypsy sample			Gypsy sample		
	Odds ratio	Std err.	$P>\|z\|$	Odds ratio	Std err.	$P>\|z\|$
Male	0.772	0.032	0.000	0.912	0.088	0.342
Age	0.996	0.012	0.756	1.104	0.034	0.001
Age^2	1.000	0.000	0.051	0.998	0.000	0.000
Children^a	0.927	0.023	0.002	1.197	0.040	0.000
0 class	5.843	4.236	0.015	4.522	1.331	0.000
1–7 classes	1.828	0.232	0.000	1.629	0.188	0.000
Vocational	0.661	0.034	0.000	0.702	0.089	0.000
Secondary	0.499	0.027	0.000	0.535	0.162	0.039
Higher	0.153	0.017	0.000	0.213	0.231	0.155
$EDUC^b$	0.777	0.029	0.000	0.774	0.074	0.000
$GYP1–3\%$	1.195	0.082	0.009	1.937	0.647	0.008
$GYP3–5\%$	1.194	0.103	0.040	3.319	1.151	0.048
$GYP5–10\%$	1.398	0.111	0.000	3.314	1.105	0.000
$GYP10\%+$	1.693	0.180	0.000	4.510	1.589	0.000
No. of obs	23,216			No. of obs	2,199	
$\chi^2(14)$	1002.95			$\chi^2(14)$	238.18	
prob > χ^2	0.00001			prob > χ^2	0.00001	
pseudo R^2	0.0564			pseudo R^2	0.0781	

Notes:
^{a} No. of dependent children in the observed person's household.
^{b} Average number of completed classes *per capita* for population being older than
   7 years in 1990 in the observed person's district (see table 11.1).
GYP-1%–GPY10%+ are dummy variables created from the ratio of the Gypsy
population of working age to the adult population of the same age ($GYPPCT$) in
the observed person's district, the reference being districts whose Gypsy
population is below 1 per cent (GYP-1%). The category of reference among
individual schooling dummies is the variable of 8 classes.
Sources:
Gypsy equation: *National Representative Gypsy Survey* (1993/4).
Non-Gypsy equation: *Labour Force Survey* of the CSO (Fall 1993).

Appendix 11.2: relationship between the Gypsy ratio (*GYPSY*) and the migration balance (*MIGBAL*), standardised regression parameters

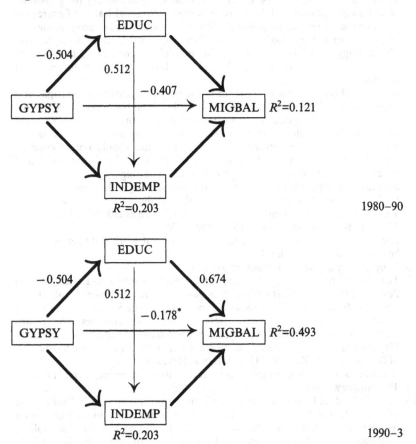

1980–90

1990–3

Notes:
* $p \leq 0.01$, all other marked parameters are significant at $p \leq 0.0001$ level. Insignificant parameters are not marked ($N = 170$ districts).
The equation of *MIGBAL* in the 1980–90 period was estimated by White's heteroscedasticity consistent estimator.

NOTES

1 Thanks are due to György Lázár (National Labour Centre) for providing regional unemployment data, to Judit Székely (National Labour Centre) for providing data on participation in different labour market programmes, to Michael Burda, Péter Galasi, László Halpern, János Köllő, Gábor Kőrösi, Gyula Nagy, and Charles Wyplosz for helpful criticism and advice and to Barnabás Ferenczi, Gábor Kézdi and the late Éva Juhász for research assistance.

2 Naturally this is a source of some bias: first because some of those people who became unemployed between 1990 and 1995 had been employed in the Census year, they are counted twice in the denominator, second because some of the former employed may have lost their propensity to work in the meantime. As they are exiting the labour force they should not be counted again in the denominator. Both of these effects raise the denominator and reduce the estimated unemployment rate. The higher the number of unemployed or people exiting the labour force, the larger the bias.

3 In the adjustment, fourth-degree polynomials of the time variable were used. The fit of the equations was extremely good: R^2 were usually 95–97 per cent.

4 Men: 15–60 years old, women: 15–55 years old.

5 Because of the relatively low sample sizes different adult:child ratios cannot be computed in district level.

6 They usually do not have other employees.

7 The Central region contains 31 districts of Fejér, Komárom–Esztergom and Pest counties. The North-Western region contains 28 districts of Győr–Sopron–Moson, Vas, Veszprém and Zala counties. The South-Western region contains 20 districts of Baranya, Somogy and Tolna counties. The South-Eastern region contains 36 districts of Bács–Kiskun, Csongrád and Jász–Nagykun–Szolnok counties. The North-Eastern region contains 54 districts of Borsod–Abaúj–Zemplén, Hajdú–Bihar, Heves and Nógrád counties.

8 Relative to the prevailing median (or national average) unemployment rate.

9 The category of reference is the district of Budapest.

10 In an individual level logit equation which tried to predict the individual risk of unemployment, we found that average differences in characteristics (gender, age, marital status, number of dependent children, schooling, residence, local unemployment rate) do not explain more than half of the predicted unemployment rate differential of the Gypsy and non-Gypsy group. It is hard to avoid the conclusion that at least part of the remaining large residual is caused by some kind of employment discrimination (see Kertesi, 1994).

11 The migration balance (*MIGBAL*) is defined as the sum of movings in (+) and movings out (–) in a given time period divided by the total population of the base date.

12 For graphical convenience, the variable was multiplied by −1.

13 See the density function of December 1990 in figure 11.1.

14 According to the data of the National Labour Centre between September 1994 and September 1995, the number of participants in retraining programmes decreased by 36 per cent and the number of participants in the wage subsidy programme for long-term unemployed decreased by 53 per cent.

15 See the arguments on pp. 360–1.

16 In the first month of 1990.
17 Logit estimation was used.

REFERENCES

Cook, R.D. and S. Weisberg (1982) *Residuals and Influence in Regression*, New York: Chapman & Hall
Fazekas, K. (1993) 'A munkanélküliség regionális különbségeinek okairól' (On the causes of regional unemployment rate differentials), *Közgazdasági Szemle*, 7–8
—— (1996) 'Regional problems', in P. Galasi and G. Kertesi (eds.), *Economic Transition and Labour Markets, 1989–1995*, Budapest: ILO Study Mission
Greene, W.H. (1993) *Econometric Analysis*, New York: Macmillan
Hall, R.E. (1972) 'Turnover in the labor force', *Brookings Papers on Economic Activity*, 3
Kennedy, P. (1992) *A Guide to Econometrics*, Cambridge, MA: MIT Press
Kertesi, G. (1994) 'The labour market situation of the Gypsy minority in Hungary', *ILO Working Paper*, 35, ILO–Japan Project, Employment Policies for Transition in Hungary
Ramsey, J.B. (1969) 'Test for specification errors in classical linear least squares regression analysis', *Journal of the Royal Statistical Society*, Series B, **31**, 350–71
Shapiro, S.S. and M.B. Wilk (1965) 'An analysis for variance test for normality (complete samples)', *Biometrika*, 591–611
Svejnar, J., K. Terrell and D. Münich (1995) 'Unemployment in the Czech and Slovak republics', in J. Svejnar (ed.), *The Czech Republic and Economic Transition in Eastern Europe*, New York: Academic Press
White, H. (1980) 'A heteroscedasticity-consistent covariance matrix estimator and a direct test for heteroscedasticity', *Econometrica*, 817–30

Discussion

MICHAEL BURDA

Chapter 11 investigates the determinants of regional unemployment variation in Hungary using a data set of quarterly observations on 170 county units from 1990 to 1995. The authors find that while the variation of regional unemployment has declined, the role of explanatory variables in explaining this variability has changed over the course of the transformation. In a series of standardised cross-sectional equations, they show how the coefficients on various factors have changed over time; in particular, the coefficient on the Gypsy population has declined steadily, while the influence of education – a human capital variable presumably standing for productivity, and therefore employability – has steadily risen over time. They interpret these results as a changing ability over time to discriminate against the Sinti and Roma population; in times of high unemployment, poorly educated non-Gypsies can no longer be shielded from unemployment risk.

The authors should be commended for seeking out the characteristics which can explain an important fact in Hungary as well as the rest of Central and Eastern Europe (CEE): the plague of unemployment has not hit all regions equally, and large regional imbalances emerged early on in the transition (Burda, 1993; Boeri and Scarpetta, 1995). In a world with perfect geographic mobility, this could not occur, since the unemployed would simply move to those regions where employment prospects are higher (unemployment rates are lower). The emergence of durable differences in regional unemployment rates recalls the discussion in the USA in the late 1960s and early 1970s, when strikingly high unemployment rates were observed in some regions and demographic groups despite a low national aggregate rate. In his pioneering work, Hall (1970, 1972) showed that persistent differences in turnover rates and especially the rates of unemployment incidence could lead to different equilibrium rates of unemployment among different racial, gender and other groupings; similar findings have been confirmed for European countries by Layard, Nickell and Jackman (1991).

Following the insights of these papers, any empirical analysis of regional differences in equilibrium unemployment should include factors which determine incidence and duration of unemployment as covariates.[1] Limited data availability hampers the authors' ability to control for all factors; yet the authors are able to link regional unemployment to a number of stock and level variables in a way which can be rationalised by a Hall-type analysis. For example, the inclusion of the Gypsy population is a proxy for discrimination, which takes the form of both higher turnover (confining Gypsies to 'dead-end' jobs) or higher duration (preferential hiring of other groups over Gypsies). Similarly, human capital is negatively correlated with both incidence and duration, so it should be negatively correlated with unemployment rates in the regions.

As long as the most important determinants are included in the regression analysis, the authors have a story about the relative importance of these factors in determining the structure of unemployment in Hungarian counties. The regressions reported in this chapter control for a number of variables, including entrepreneurship, concentration of large enterprises, land quality, as well as dummies for the broad regions. One general comment is that a number of other important variables were not included, such as posted vacancies, proximity to the Austrian border, population density, concentration of agricultural activity, and the intensity of active labour market programmes, all of which may affect average unemployment incidence and duration at the regional level. To the extent that variables are omitted which are correlated with the included regressors, estimated coefficients will be biased and will vitiate the confidence we can place in the authors' conclusions.

With this overall caveat in mind, I have three brief comments on the authors' work. First, the authors employ 'standardised' regressions (which I take to mean that all variables are normalised with respect to their empirical means and standard deviations in the period). While this approach has the advantage of allowing comparability of coefficients over time and therefore gauging structural change, it may be less valid if the data generating process is also changing over time, as is certainly plausible. (One example would be that the Sinti and Roma population has become more concentrated since mobility is less difficult.) Some of the estimated results may simply be an artefact of changing variation in the independent variables; it would be useful to see a plot of their coefficients of variation over time to see if this is a significant effect.

Second, while the time variation of the estimated Gypsy and education coefficients displayed in figure 11.4 is smooth and almost monotone, it remains unclear whether it is 'significant' in some statistical sense. Here it would have been useful to pool the 20 cross-sections and test the hypothesis explicitly; with roughly 1,400 observations, simple tests for subsample stability would easily establish whether parameter values in the regression model were changing over time. Since time variation of the variables $GYPSY$ and $EDUC$ is likely to be rather small, the gain in precision in a pooled regression may be modest and it may be difficult to reject the null hypothesis of constant coefficients over time.

Finally, consistent with my earlier remarks about omitted variables, Ábrahám and Kertesi surmise that an underlying third cause – economic backwardness – could be responsible for their results. They argue that because counties with large Sinti–Roma populations tend to be economically backward, the Gypsy variable will proxy for the unobservable backwardness. It might have been interesting to use the Oaxaca–Blinder approach – developed by Oaxaca (1973) and Blinder (1973) in the discrimination literature – to assess this hypothesis further. Let u_{Ai} and u_{Bi} be the unemployment rate in the ith region, where A and B denote two exhaustive groupings of the counties, denoting 'highly and poorly developed regions' where some other (possibly subjective) classification scheme is used. Let X be the set of explanatory variables. We then have the regression models

$$u_{Ai} = X_{Ai}'\beta_A + \varepsilon_{Ai}$$
$$u_{Bi} = X_{Bi}'\beta_B + \varepsilon_{Bi}$$

where the εs are the respective error terms fulfilling the usual requirements. After obtaining OLS estimates b_A and b_B of β_A and β_B, it is possible to write the difference in *average* unemployment rates in the groups A and B in each year $\bar{u}_A - \bar{u}_{B'}$ as

$$\bar{u}_A - \bar{u}_B = \bar{X}_A'b_A - \bar{X}_B'b_B$$
$$= (\bar{X}_A' - \bar{X}_B')b_B + \bar{X}_A'(b_A - b_B)$$

where upper bars denote averages. In doing so, one decomposes the observed average difference in the Hungarian county unemployment rates into two components. The first component is that part due to differences in average observable covariates; the second component is 'discrimination' or, more broadly, the additional effect of being economically backward. In this manner, the authors could bring more subjective information at their disposal to bear on the interesting question they pose in this chapter.

NOTE

1 With a constant labour force with homogeneous workers, the equilibrium unemployment rate is equal to the rate of incidence divided by the total turnover rate (the sum of the incidence rate and the inverse of the expected unemployment duration).

REFERENCES

Blinder, A.S. (1973) 'Wage discrimination: reduced form and structural variables', *Journal of Human Resources*, 8, 430–55
Boeri, T. and S. Scarpetta (1995) 'Emerging regional labour market dynamics in Central and Eastern Europe', in S. Scarpetta and A. Wörgötter (eds.), *The Regional Dimension of Unemployment in Transition Countries*, Paris: OECD/CCET
Burda, M. (1993) 'Unemployment, labor markets and structural change in Eastern Europe', *Economic Policy*, 16, 101–37
Hall, R. (1970) 'Why is the unemployment rate so high at full employment', *Brookings Papers on Economic Activity*, 3, 369–402
(1972) 'Turnover in the labor force', *Brookings Papers on Economic Activity*, 3, 709–64
Layard, R., S. Nickell and R. Jackman (1991) *Unemployment*, Oxford: Oxford University Press
Oaxaca, R.L. (1973) 'Male–female wage differentials in urban labour markets', *International Economic Reivew*, 14, 693–709

Index

Note: 'n.' after a page reference indicates the number of a note on that page